A GRAMMAR OF JORDANIAN ARABIC

Cambridge Semitic Languages and Cultures

General Editor: Geoffrey Khan

This is the first Open Access book series in the field; it combines the high peer-review and editorial standards with the fair Open Access model offered by OBP. The series includes philological and linguistic studies of Semitic languages, editions of Semitic texts, and studies of Semitic cultures. Titles cover all periods, traditions and methodological approaches to the field. The editorial board comprises Geoffrey Khan, Aaron Hornkohl, Esther-Miriam Wagner, Anne Burberry, and Benjamin Kantor.

You can access the full series catalogue here: https://www.openbookpublishers.com/series/2632-6914

If you would like to join our community and interact with authors of the books, sign up to be contacted about events relating to the series and receive publication updates and news here: https://forms.gle/RWymsw3hdsUjZTXv5

A Grammar of Jordanian Arabic

Bruno Herin and Enam Al-Wer

UNIVERSITY OF CAMBRIDGE
Faculty of Asian and Middle Eastern Studies

OpenBook Publishers

https://www.openbookpublishers.com

Any digital material and resources associated with this volume will be available at https://doi.org/10.11647/OBP.0410#resources

Semitic Languages and Cultures 39

ISSN (print): 2632-6906

ISSN (digital): 2632-6914

ISBN Paperback: 978-1-80511-334-8

ISBN Hardback: 978-1-80511-335-5

ISBN Digital (PDF): 978-1-80511-336-2

DOI: 10.11647/OBP.0410

Cover image: *The City of Al-Salt* by Mohammed Bilbeisi, all rights reserved by the artist.
Cover design: Jeevanjot Kaur Nagpal

The fonts used in this volume are Charis SIL and Scheherazade New.

TABLE OF CONTENTS

Acknowledgments.. ix

List of Figures xi

List of Tables xiii

Abbreviations xxiii

1. Introduction 1

   1.1. The Present Work 1

   1.2. Previous Literature.. 4

   1.3. A Social Dialectology of Jordan.................... 9

2. Phonology 17

   2.1. Consonants... 17

   2.2. Vowels 28

   2.3. Phonotactics... 33

3. Morphology... 45

   3.1. Words, Clitics and Affixes 45

   3.2. Nouns.. 48

   3.3. Adjectives 89

3.4. Verbs 93
3.5. Pronouns 165
3.6. Demonstratives 179
3.7. Interrogative Proforms 182
3.8. Other Proforms 189
3.9. Prepositions 190
3.10. Numerals 207
3.11. Adverbs 211
3.12. Other Minor Parts of Speech 234

4. Syntax 253
4.1. The Noun Phrase 253
4.2. The Verb Phrase 298
4.3. Agreement 332
4.4. Simple Clauses 341
4.5. Pragmatically Marked Structures 372
4.6. Complex Predicates and Complex Clauses 418

5. Texts 461

5.1. Text 1: *il-ʔamīr il-mihdāwi* 'Prince Il-Mihdāwi' 463

5.2. Text 2: *il-bagara* 'the cow' 467

5.3. Text 3: *riḥlit ṣēd* 'a hunting trip' 471

References 475

Index of Authors 491

General Index 493

ACKNOWLEDGMENTS

The preparation of this book benefitted from the generosity of a great many people over the years, and we wish to express our heartfelt gratitude to them.

We begin by acknowledging the generosity of the speakers who participated in our research, some of whom are sadly no longer with us and we will always remember them with fondness and gratitude. The participants in this research received us warmly into their homes, introduced us to their families and shared memorable stories with us. Most of all, we would like to thank them for entrusting us with precious data that will guide generations of scholars. We hope that the publication of a book-length monograph that brings their dialects to the attention of academics around the world repays some of the debt that we owe them.

We would like to acknowledge the help of certain individuals and families who were pivotal in introducing us to local communities and hence facilitated access to speakers. They are:

Dr Khawla Hadidi, Professor Hani Al-Amad, Ayid Tadros and the Tadros family, Ehab Hiasat and the Hiasat family, Nour El-Mneyzel, the late Atif Farah and the Farah family, Ashraf Al-Awamleh, the Arabiyat family, the Atiyat family, the Aranki family, Khaldoun Gharaibeh, Miss Radwa Gharaibeh, Miss Myassar Abasi, Dr Safa Khasawneh and the Khasawneh family, Ahamad Shaman Obeidat and the Obeidat family, Noora Al-Wer, Randa Naffa and the Naffa family, Rana Al-Wer, Nadia Naffa, the Oweis family, the Rabadi family.

We thank our friend and colleague Uri Horesh for his constant support and willingness to help.

We are extremely grateful to Michael Jones for reading several drafts of the manuscript and for making numerous insightful comments on the analysis and presentation of the material.

Specific parts of the analysis presented in the book are based on research that was supported through two grants: a British Academy Small Research Grant (SG160689) and a Leverhulme Trust Senior Research Fellowship (MRF-2016-075), awarded to Enam Al-Wer. We thank these organisations for their support.

We thank the General Editor of the Cambridge Semitic Languages and Cultures series, Geoffrey Khan, for his support of this volume and his prompt responses to our queries. We are grateful to the Associate Editor of the series, Anne Burberry, for her advice, comments and patience throughout the process of publication.

Moh'd Bilbeisi has once again generously contributed one of his many magnificent paintings to adorn the cover of this book. We are humbled by his generosity and thank him warmly.

We would like to thank our families for their support and love: Anca, Lina and Sonia; Mike and Petra.

Finally, on a personal note, we remember our late mothers, Béatrice Theunissen and Nahil Oweis, for their continuous and unstinting support throughout our education and research endeavours. May they rest in peace.

LIST OF FIGURES

Figure 1: Spectrogram of *ṭarābīš*, plural of *ṭarbūš* 'fez'

Figure 2: Pitch (blue) and intensity (green) in *b-tanaka* 'in a tank'

Figure 3: Pitch (blue) and intensity (green) in *bandōra* 'tomato'

Figure 4: Prosody of *mā bidd-i* 'I don't want' (pitch in blue and intensity in green)

Figure 5: Prosody of *mā ʕind-hū-š* 'he doesn't have' (pitch in blue and intensity in green)

Figure 6: Prosody of *ygūlin a-bihimm-əš* 'it doesn't matter' (pitch in blue and intensity in green)

Figure 7: Prosody of *mā bitwassix* 'it doesn't stain' (pitch in blue and intensity in green)

Figure 8: Prosody of *bitwassx-əš* 'it doesn't stain' (pitch in blue and intensity in green)

Figure 9: Rising pitch (blue) and intenstity (green) on focused constituents

Figure 10: The prosody of the proclitic *ma* vs the negator *mā*

Figure 11: Intonation contour in polar questions

Figure 12: Rising contour in tag questions

LIST OF TABLES

Table 1: Consonant inventory
Table 2: Affrication of /k/ in the Levant
Table 3: Secondary velarisation
Table 4: Short vowels
Table 5: /a/ vs /i/ and /u/
Table 6: /i/ vs /u/
Table 7: Long vowels
Table 8: Oppositions between long vowels
Table 9: Syllable types
Table 10: Epenthesis
Table 11: Vowel harmony and epenthesis
Table 12: Word stress
Table 13: Elision of /a/
Table 14: Assimilations
Table 15: Assimilation of /h/ at morpheme boundaries
Table 16: Phonetics of *-a*
Table 17: Raising differences in Amman and Salt
Table 18: Allomorph *-at* in the construct state
Table 19: Pseudo-dual and bound pronouns
Table 20: Morphological layout of the imperfective
Table 21: Inflection of the imperfective
Table 22: Morphological layout of the perfective
Table 23: Inflection of the perfective
Table 24: Morphological layout of the imperative
Table 25: Inflection of the imperative
Table 26: Derivational templates for three-consonant roots

Table 27: Perfective of *ḏabaḥ–yiḏbaḥ* 'slaughter'
Table 28: Perfective of *ričib–yirčab* 'ride'
Table 29: Imperfective of *ričib–yirčab* 'ride'
Table 30: Imperfective of *nizil–yinzil* 'go down'
Table 31: Imperfective of *marag–yumrug* 'pass by'
Table 32: Imperative of *ričib–yirčab* 'ride', *nizil–yinzil* 'descend' and *marag–yumrug* 'pass by'
Table 33: Active participle and passive participle of *ričib–yirčab* 'ride'
Table 34: Imperfective of *akal–yōkil* 'eat' and *axaḏ–yōxuḏ* 'take'
Table 35: Active participle of *akal–yōkil* 'eat' and *axaḏ–yōxuḏ* 'take'
Table 36: Imperative of *akal–yōkil* 'eat' and *axaḏ–yōxuḏ* 'take'
Table 37: Suppletive imperative of *axaḏ–yōxuḏ* 'take'
Table 38: Traditional imperfective of *wiṣil–yaṣal* 'arrive'
Table 39: Innovative I imperfective of *wiṣil–yiṣal* 'arrive'
Table 40: Innovative II imperfective of *wiṣil–yūṣal* 'arrive'
Table 41: Traditional imperfective of *yibis–yabas* 'get dry'
Table 42: Innovative I imperfective of *yibis–yibas* 'get dry'
Table 43: Innovative II imperfective of *yibis–yības* 'get dry'
Table 44: Imperative of *wigif–yagaf* 'stand', *wirid–yarid* 'fetch water', *yibis–yabas* 'get dry'
Table 45: Perfective of *rāḥ–yrūḥ* 'go', *xāf–yxāf* 'be scared', *ṭāḥ–yṭīḥ* 'go (descend)'
Table 46: Imperfective of *rāḥ–yrūḥ* 'go'
Table 47: Imperfective of *xāf–yxāf* 'be scared'
Table 48: Imperfective of *ṭāḥ–yṭīḥ* 'go (descend)'

Table 49: Imperative of *rāḥ–yrūḥ* 'go', *xāf–yxāf* 'be scared', *ṭāḥ–yṭīḥ* 'go (descend)'
Table 50: Active participle of *ṭāḥ–yṭīḥ* 'go', *xāf–yxāf* 'be scared', *ṭāḥ–yṭīḥ* 'go (descend)'
Table 51: Passive participle of *bāʕ–ybīʕ* 'sell'
Table 52: Perfective of *gara–yigra* 'study' and *nisi–yinsa* 'forget'
Table 53: Imperfective of *diri–yidri* 'know', *nisi–yinsa* 'forget'
Table 54: Imperative of *bana–yibni* 'build' and *nisi–yinsa* 'forget'
Table 55: Active and passive participle of *nisi–yinsa* 'forget'
Table 56: Perfective of *ladd–ylidd* 'look'
Table 57: Imperfective of *ladd–ylidd* 'look'
Table 58: Active and passive participle of *ḥaṭṭ–yḥuṭṭ* 'put'
Table 59: Imperative of *ladd–ylidd* 'look'
Table 60: Perfective of *ağa–yīği* 'come'
Table 61: Imperfective of *ağa–yīği* 'come'
Table 62: Active participle of *ağa–yīği* 'come'
Table 63: Imperative of *ağa–yīği* 'come'
Table 64: Perfective of *čammal–yčammil* 'complete, continue'
Table 65: Imperfective of *čammal–yčammil* 'complete, continue'
Table 66: Imperative of *čammal–yčammil* 'complete, continue'
Table 67: Active and passive participle of *ḥammal–yḥammil* 'load'
Table 68: Perfective of *sawwa–ysawwi* 'do, make'
Table 69: Imperfective of *sawwa–ysawwi* 'do, make'
Table 70: Imperative of *sawwa–ysawwi* 'do, make'
Table 71: Imperative of *nagga–ynaggi* 'choose'
Table 72: Perfective of *sāʕad–ysāʕid* 'help'
Table 73: Imperfective of *sāʕad–ysāʕid* 'help'

Table 74: Active participle of *sāʕad–ysāʕid* 'help'
Table 75: Imperative of *sāʕad–ysāʕid* 'help'
Table 76: Perfective of *nāda–ynādi* 'call'
Table 77: Imperfective of *nāda–ynādi* 'call'
Table 78: Active participle of *nāda–ynādi* 'call'
Table 79: Imperative of *nāda–ynādi* 'call'
Table 80: Form IV
Table 81: Perfective of *(a)ṭlaʕ–yiṭliʕ* 'take out'
Table 82: Imperfective of *(a)ṭlaʕ–yiṭliʕ* 'take out'
Table 83: Active participle of *(a)ṭlaʕ–yiṭliʕ* 'take out'
Table 84: Imperative of *(a)ṭlaʕ–yiṭliʕ* 'take out'
Table 85: Perfective of *ōǧaʕ–yōǧiʕ* 'hurt'
Table 86: Imperfective of *ōǧaʕ–yōǧiʕ* 'it hurts'
Table 87: Active participle of *ōǧaʕ–yōǧiʕ* 'hurt'
Table 88: Imperative of *ōgad–yōgid* 'kindle'
Table 89: Perfective of *(a)nṭa–yinṭi* 'give'
Table 90: Imperfective of *(a)nṭa–yinṭi* 'give'
Table 91: Active participle of *(a)nṭa–yinṭi* 'give'
Table 92: Imperative of *(a)nṭa–yinṭi* 'give'
Table 93: Perfective of *ōḏa–yōḏi* 'light'
Table 94: Imperfective of *ōḏa–yōḏi* 'light'
Table 95: Active participle of *ōḏa–yōḏi* 'light'
Table 96: Imperative of *ōḏa–yōḏi* 'light'
Table 97: Perfective of *tḥammal–yitḥammal* 'endure'
Table 98: Imperfective of *tḥammal–yitḥammal* 'endure'
Table 99: Active participle of *tḥammal–yitḥammal* 'endure'
Table 100: Imperative of *tḥammal– yitḥammal* 'endure'
Table 101: Perfective of *txabba–yitxabba* 'hide'

Table 102: Imperfective of *txabba–yitxabba* 'hide'
Table 103: Active participle of *txabba–yitxabba* 'hide'
Table 104: Imperative of *txabba–yitxabba* 'hide'
Table 105: Perfective of *thāwaš–yithāwaš* 'quarrel'
Table 106: Imperfective of *thāwaš–yithāwaš* 'quarrel'
Table 107: Active participle of *thāwaš–yithāwaš* 'quarrel'
Table 108: Imperative of *thāwaš–yithāwaš* 'quarrel'
Table 109: Perfective of *tlāga–yitlāga* 'meet'
Table 110: Imperfective of *tlāga–yitlāga* 'meet'
Table 111: Active participle of *tlāga–yitlāga* 'meet'
Table 112: Imperative of *tlāga–yitlāga* 'meet'
Table 113: Perfective of *nkatal–yinkatal* 'be killed, beaten up'
Table 114: Imperfective of *nkatal–yinkatal* 'be killed, beaten up'
Table 115: Imperative of *nʕazam–yinʕazim* 'be invited'
Table 116: Perfective of *nṭaxx–yinṭaxx* 'be shot'
Table 117: Imperfective of *nṭaxx–yinṭaxx* 'be shot'
Table 118: Active participle of *nṭaxx–yinṭaxx* 'be shot'
Table 119: Imperative of *nṭaxx–yinṭaxx* 'be shot'
Table 120: Perfective of *nbāʕ–yinbāʕ* 'be sold'
Table 121: Imperfective of *nbāʕ–yinbāʕ* 'be sold'
Table 122: Active participle of *nbāʕ–yinbāʕ* 'be sold'
Table 123: Imperative of *nbāʕ–yinbāʕ* 'be sold'
Table 124: Perfective of *nʕama–yiʕami* 'be blind'
Table 125: Imperfective of *nʕama–yiʕami* 'be blind' and *ngara–yingara* 'be read'
Table 126: Active participle of *nʕama–yiʕami* 'be blind'
Table 127: Imperative of *nʕama–yiʕami* 'be blind'
Table 128: Perfective of *štaġal–yištaġil* 'work'

Table 129: Imperfective of *štaġal–yištaġil* 'work'
Table 130: Active participle of *ltazam–yiltazim* 'be committed'
Table 131: Imperative of *štaġal–yištaġil* 'work'
Table 132: Active participle of *ttākal–yittākal* 'be eaten', *ttāxaḏ–yittāxaḏ* 'be taken', *ttāgad–yittāgad* 'be ignited' and *ttāǧaʕ–yittāǧaʕ* 'be in pain'
Table 133: Perfective of *xtār–yixtār* 'choose'
Table 134: Imperfective of *xtār–yixtār* 'choose'
Table 135: Active and passive participles of *xtār–yixtār* 'choose'
Table 136: Imperative of *xtār–yixtār* 'choose'
Table 137: Perfective of *štara–yištari* 'buy'
Table 138: Imperfective of *štara–yištari* 'buy'
Table 139: Active participle of *ltaga–yiltagi* 'meet'
Table 140: Active participle of *štara–yištari* 'buy'
Table 141: Perfective of *ḥmarr–yiḥmarr* 'become red'
Table 142: Imperfective of *ḥmarr–yiḥmarr* 'become red'
Table 143: Active participle of *ḥmarr–yiḥmarr* 'become red'
Table 144: Imperative of *ḥmarr–yiḥmarr* 'become red'
Table 145: Perfective of *staʕmal–yistaʕmil* 'utilise'
Table 146: Imperfective of *staʕmal–yistaʕmil* 'utilise'
Table 147: Active and passive participles of *staʕmal–yistaʕmil* 'utilise'
Table 148: Imperative of *staʕmal–yistaʕmil* 'utilise'
Table 149: Perfective of *staġall–yistaġill* 'exploit'
Table 150: Imperfective of *staġall–yistaġill* 'exploit'
Table 151: Active and passive participles of *staġall* 'exploit'
Table 152: Imperative of *staġall* 'exploit'
Table 153: Perfective of *starāḥ–yistarīḥ* 'rest'

Table 154: Imperfective of *starāḥ–yistarīḥ* 'rest'
Table 155: Active participle of *starāḥ–yistarīḥ* 'rest'
Table 156: Imperative of *starāḥ–yistarīḥ* 'rest'
Table 157: Perfective of *starğa–yistarği* 'dare'
Table 158: Imperfective of *starğa–yistarği* 'dare'
Table 159: Active participle of *starğa–yistarği* 'dare'
Table 160: Perfective of *stanna–yistanna* 'wait'
Table 161: Imperfective of *stanna–yistanna* 'wait'
Table 162: Active participle of *stanna–yistanna* 'wait'
Table 163: Imperative of *stanna–yistanna* 'wait'
Table 164: Perfective of *falfal–yfalfil* 'cook rice'
Table 165: Imperfective of *falfal–yfalfil* 'cook rice'
Table 166: Active and passive participles of *falfal–yfalfil* 'cook rice'
Table 167: Imperative of *falfal–yfalfil* 'cook rice'
Table 168: Perfective of *sōlaf–ysōlif* 'narrate'
Table 169: Imperfective of *sōlaf–ysōlif* 'narrate'
Table 170: Active participle of *sōlaf–ysōlif* 'narrate'
Table 171: Imperative of *sōlaf–ysōlif* 'narrate'
Table 172: Perfective of *warğa–ywarği* 'show'
Table 173: Perfective of *warğa–ywarği* 'show'
Table 174: Active participle of *warğa–ywarği* 'show'
Table 175: Imperative of *warğa–ywarği* 'show'
Table 176: Perfective of *tḥarkaš–yitḥarkaš* 'provoke'
Table 177: Imperfective of *tḥarkaš–yitḥarkaš* 'provoke'
Table 178: Active participle of *tḥarkaš–yitḥarkaš* 'provoke'
Table 179: Imperative of *tḥarkaš–yitḥarkaš* 'provoke'
Table 180: Masdars of hollow verbs

Table 181: Morphology of the verb
Table 182: Free pronouns
Table 183: Frequency of short and long forms
Table 184: Bound pronouns
Table 185: Dative pronouns
Table 186: Inflections of *iyyā-*
Table 187: Demonstratives
Table 188: Pronominal and post-nominal demonstratives
Table 189: Inflections of *hāy*
Table 190: Inflections of *hari*
Table 191: Interrogatives
Table 192: Inflections of *bi* ~ *fi*
Table 193: Inflections of *min*
Table 194: Inflections of *ʕan*
Table 195: Inflections of *la*
Table 196: Inflections of *maʕ*
Table 197: Inflections of *ʕala*
Table 198: Inflections of *ʕind*
Table 199: Inflections of *baʕd*
Table 200: Inflections of *tiḥt*
Table 201: Inflections of *fōg*
Table 202: Inflections of *gabl*
Table 203: Inflections of *giddām*
Table 204: Inflections of *wara*
Table 205: Inflections of *wāḥad* and *ṯnēn*
Table 206: Numerals 1–10
Table 207: Numerals 11–19
Table 208: Tens

Table 209: Hundreds
Table 210: Thousands
Table 211: Ordinals
Table 212: Functional views on word classes (Croft 2001, 89)
Table 213: *aṯārī* ~ *aṯrīt* and bound pronouns
Table 214: *tabaʕ* and *tāʕ* in Amman
Table 215: *tabaʕ* in Salt and Ḥōrāni
Table 216: The linker *giyy*
Table 217: *Šiyy* in Salt
Table 218: Inflections of *badd-* 'want'
Table 219: *ḏ̣all* and bound pronouns
Table 220: Inflections of *xalli*
Table 221: Agreement patterns in the plural
Table 222: The verbal properties of prepositional predicates
Table 223: Ditransitive constructions
Table 224: Distribution of *mā…*, *mā… -š*, *a-… -š*, *…-š*
Table 225: The status of *mā a- and -š*
Table 226: The negative copula
Table 227: *ma* + free pronouns
Table 228: Inflections of *inn-*
Table 229: Inflections of *lawinn-*
Table 230: Summary of conditional markers

ABBREVIATIONS

1SG	first person singular
1PL	first person plural
2MS	second person masculine singular
2FS	second person feminine singular
2MP	second person masculine plural
2FP	second person feminine plural
3MS	third person masculine singular
3FS	third person feminine singular
3MP	third person masculine plural
3FP	third person feminine plural
AP	active participle
ADJ	adjective
ASSER	asseverative
COMP	complementiser
COP	copula
CSTR	construct
DAT	dative
DEF	definite
DEM	demonstrative
DM	discourse marker
DU	dual
EXCLAM	exclamative
EXIST	existential
F	feminine
FOC	focus
FP	feminine plural

FS	feminine singular
HORT	hortative
IMP	imperative
INDEF	indefinite
IPFV	imperfective
MOD	modifier
M	masculine
MP	masculine plural
MS	masculine singular
N	noun
NEG	negation
NOM	nominative
NP	noun phrase
OBJ	object
OBL	oblique
OPT	optative
PFV	perfective
PL	plural
PP	passive participle
PRED	predicate
RECP	reciprocal
REFL	reflexive
REL	relativiser
SG	singular
SING	singulative
SBJV	subjunctive
SUB	subordinator
St.	Standard Arabic

SUBJ	subject
TAG	tag question
TOP	topic
VOC	vocative
*	reconstructed
**	unattested or impossible

1. INTRODUCTION

1.1. The Present Work

The goal of the present monograph is to describe the main structures of the traditional sedentary dialects of central and northern Jordan. It is in many respects a follow-up to Herin (2010), which provided the first full-length grammatical description of a sedentary Jordanian dialect, that of the town of Salt in central Jordan. The pool of data on which the present work draws has been significantly expanded, encompassing both central and northern Jordan. Most discussions have been extensively revised and many others have been added.

The need for such a grammar is multifaceted. Primarily, it stems from the observation that no full-length grammar of any sedentary dialect of Jordan has ever been published, which in itself is a huge gap that needs to be filled. In addition to this, the traditional dialects of Jordan are threatened by the emergence of new urban dialects, most notably that of the capital Amman. Moreover, Jordanian dialects may rightly be considered the poor sibling of Levantine Arabic. Although a handful of scholars (see below) have devoted a sizeable part of their scholarship to Jordanian dialects, many recent and earlier discussions only mention Jordan in passing, if at all. Jordan is pervasively described as a fringe *terra nullius* and a land of various resettlement situations, because its indigenous population is either non-existent, or nomadic. These claims are of course profoundly inaccurate and either stem from ignorance or are driven by ideology. On the

 https://doi.org/10.11647/OBP.0410.01

contrary, Jordan is a land of ancient civilisations that go back to the twelfth century BC and has been inhabited without interruption since time immemorial. Jordanian dialects are likely, in the light of the most recent analysis of the Safaitic inscriptions in the Ḥarrah region in northern Jordan (Al-Jallad 2015), to be descendants of the oldest Arabic varieties. For these reasons, we hope that the present work will help researchers to do justice to Jordanian Arabic and include it in wider discussions on Arabic dialectology.

The methodology followed in this book is that of descriptive linguistics, defined as the "scientific endeavour to systematically describe the languages of the world in their diversity, based on the empirical observation of regular patterns in natural speech" (François and Ponçonnet 2013, 184). The approach is bottom-up, aposterioristic and primarily inductive. From a limited set of data (a corpus), hypotheses are formulated to account for the observed facts. These hypotheses are subsequently put to the test by confronting them with more data, which allows us to turn these hypotheses into rules. Lesser-studied languages lack large corpora, which raises the question of the representativity of the sample. To overcome this problem, one can either wait until larger corpora become available, or resort to elicitation and grammaticality judgements. One of the most frequent quotations in descriptive linguistics, attributed to the Boasian tradition, is that every language 'should be described in its own terms', thus moving away from the aprioristic apparatus posited by formal theories. A "framework-free grammatical theory" is often advocated in recent grammatical descriptions (Haspelmath 2010b), but in practice, much of the linguistic meta-language comes from the ever-growing body of literature in linguistic typology. The present description of Jordanian Arabic is no exception to this trend, which may at times conflict with the habits and customs of Arabic linguistics. General works that have inspired the present description are Creissels (2006a), Croft (2001; 2002), Shopen (2007) and more generally the World Atlas of Language Structures (Dryer and Haspelmath 2013).

There are broadly two approaches to grammaticography: form-to-function or function-to-form. Both are used here, in an attempt to cater for our intended readership: Arabic dialectologists and general linguists. Arabic dialectologists will probably want to know how a certain morpheme is realised in the present variety, and go through the Table of Contents accordingly, hence the need for a form-to-function approach. General linguists may want to know how a certain function is instantiated in the present dialect, hence the function-to-form approach. Although the present grammar follows the usual division between phonology, morphology and syntax, the main focus is to delve somewhat deeper into morphosyntactic discussions. The reason for this is that the main concern of traditional Arabic dialectology is to provide an inventory of forms, with limited attention paid to constructions. The present work is therefore an attempt to give constructions their due attention. The phonology section tackles relevant questions from a cross-dialectal perspective, such as the realisation of certain phonemes, contrast between short vowels and certain suprasegmental features. The morphology section starts with the open classes of nouns, adjectives and verbs, followed by closed classes such as proforms, prepositions, quantifiers, adverbs and other 'minor' parts of speech such as interjections, discourse markers and focus-sensitive particles. The section on syntax starts with phrases, nominal and verbal, and agreement, then ventures into clauses, from simple to complex. In the last section, texts taken from broad speakers that represent the traditional register of the dialect are presented.

1.2. Previous Literature

The first source to document dialectal data from central Jordan is Bergsträsser's (1915) *Sprachatlas von Syrien und Palästina.* The first comprehensive coverage of northern Jordan and southern Syria is found in Cantineau (1940; 1946). More recently, Heikki Palva devoted much of his scholarship to Jordanian dialects, both sedentary and Bedouin, and amongst them those of central Jordan. Palva's first publications were collections of texts from central Jordan (Palva 1969a; 1969b; 1970). His first monographical work was Palva (1976), which describes the essentials of the grammar of the Bedouin dialect of the *ʕağārma* confederation, complemented with texts in Palva (1978). Another collection of texts is found in Palva (1992a), which also includes valuable grammatical observations. The first fully descriptive paper on Central Jordanian is Palva (2003), which describes the negation strategies in the dialect of Salt. Texts in the dialect of Salt can be found in Palva (2007). Other works with a descriptive scope are Palva (1980) on the dialect of the Bani Ṣaxar tribe, Palva (1984a; 2004) on the dialect of the Ḥwēṭāt in southern Jordan, Bani-Yasin and Owens (1984) on the dialect of the Bdūl, Palva (1989) on the dialect of Kerak, Bani-Yasin and Owens (1987) on the phonology of Northern Jordanian, Owens and Bani-Yasin (1987) on the lexical conditioning of agreement in Northern Jordanian and Al-Wer (2011) on the dialect of Amman. Another description of Ammani can be found in Mion (2012).

Works dealing with the classification of Jordanian dialects are Cleveland (1963), Palva (1984b; 1992b; 1994; 2008) and Herin (2013; 2019).

Another very productive field that has made significant contributions to research on linguistic variation and change in Jordan is sociolinguistics. Work in this field started in the 1980s with Abdel-Jawad's (1981) study on Amman, followed by Al-Khatib (1988) and Al-Tamimi (2001) on Irbid, and Al-Wer (1991) on Salt, Ajloun and Kerak. More recently, two further doctoral theses were completed by Al-Hawamdeh (2016) on Sūf and Abu Ain (2016) on Saḥam, both in north Jordan. Additionally, a large-scale research project on the formation of the Amman dialect was completed in 2020; a monograph based on this research is forthcoming. On Amman, see also Al-Wer (1999; 2002; 2007; 2014; 2020), Al-Wer et al. (2015) and Al-Wer and Herin (2011).[1]

The data on which the present description draws were collected by the authors over a period of time that spans more than three decades, from the early 1980s up to the present. The first piece of data is a recording of Essa Al-Wer, carried out in 1982. It consists of a family conversation recorded by family members.

[1] Enam Al-Wer's research on Amman was funded by a Leverhulme Trust Major Research Fellowship (MRF-2016-075).

Essa Al-Wer, the father of one of the present authors, was born in 1902 in Salt. He was a prominent landowner and food producer in Jordan. According to the apparent-time hypothesis, the speech of Essa Al-Wer in the 1980s was the closest approximation one could obtain to the speech patterns that existed in the city of Salt in the early twentieth century. In 1987, Enam Al-Wer collected further material from three speech communities (Salt, Ajloun and Kerak) for her doctoral thesis (Al-Wer 1991). This material was not initially collected for descriptive purposes, but the kind of sampling and data collection methods used in sociolinguistics are consonant with the descriptive agenda, especially since the data obtained through such methods resemble the vernacular and represent the community as a whole as closely as possible. The Kerak corpus was not included in the present study because the local Keraki dialect belongs to a different sub-group within southern Levantine Arabic. In Salt, more recordings were made in 2005 with members of the Tādrus and ʕArabiyyāt clans. The data collected in 2005 reflected a koineised register, where local features were levelled out in favour of supralocal ones. In 2006, we solicited the help of Professor Hani al-ʕAmad, a respected academic and a pillar of the community, who facilitated data collection among the Dabābse clan. In 2007, we decided to investigate whether claims that religious affiliation played a role in dialect variation were substantiated (Palva 2008, 57). We therefore turned our focus to the small town of Fḥēṣ, originally a settlement founded by Christian clans from Salt. This social makeup of the town is confirmed by both oral history and travel narratives. For instance, according to one of our informants:

sukkān lə-fḥēṣ kull-hum ḏallu sāknīn is-salṭ 'all the inhabitants of Fḥēṣ used to live in Salt'. In a travel narrative from the early nineteenth century, we read: "In the time of the harvest the Szaltese transport their families thither, where they live for several months under tents, like true Bedouins. The principal encampment is at a place called Feheis, about one hour and a half to the S. E. of Szalt" (Burckhardt 1822, 350–51).

Fḥēṣ is a quintessential tight-knit community, and to a large extent a microcosm of Salt before the latter diversified and expanded. The vast majority of Fḥēṣ's original inhabitants live on land passed down among the clan's extended families for generations. Land ownership is largely organised by clan, such that each clan owns and inhabits a certain plot. A straightforward corollary of this social and spatial organisation of the town is that its neighbourhoods are referred to by the name of the clan who originally owned and inhabited it. Importantly, this type of structure is conducive to linguistic conservatism, in the form of maintenance of local norms of speech (see Milroy 1987).

In order to establish a local network of contacts in Fḥēṣ, we solicited the help of ʕĀṭif Faraḥ, a local contractor, very well versed in the history and geography of Fḥēṣ. His help was invaluable in securing a good number of speakers as well as good-quality samples of casual speech. This material was the basis for a doctoral thesis which aimed at providing a descriptive account of the most salient features of the phonology and morphosyntax of the dialect of Salt (Herin 2010).

We carried out further research both in Salt/Fḥēṣ and in parts of northern Jordan to further consolidate the generalisations put forward in Herin (2010) by significantly expanding the corpus and also providing the basis for a description that would include the dialects of both central and northern Jordan. One of the conclusions in Herin (2010) was that Central Jordanian, as represented by the dialect of Salt, is essentially Ḥōrāni. All the deviations from Ḥōrāni that Central Jordanian exhibits can be accounted for in terms of adstrate, mostly from Palestinian varieties (Herin 2013), and also from the dialects of the Bedouin of the Jordan Valley and the Balga region, such as the ʕAdwān.

In 2012, we collected more data from Fḥēṣ to further investigate a potential sectarian division and also because we had noticed that the traditional dialect was well preserved in some segments of the population, most notably by an elderly individual from the ʕAranki clan. In this second round of fieldwork in Fḥēṣ, we interviewed older members of the ʕAranki and Sweis clans. Additionally, we were supplied with recordings of family conversations from the Faraḥ and Mnēzil clans. The analysis pertaining to the effect of religious affiliation on linguistic variation appears in Al-Wer et al. (2015).

We resumed data collection in 2017. In this round, we expanded our research to the northern locations of Jerash and Ajloun, where we conducted interviews with elderly speakers in the towns themselves and surrounding villages. Our colleague Areej Al-Hawamdeh, a native of the town of Sūf on the outskirts of Jarash, was our primary local contact who facilitated access to potential speakers (see also Al-Hawamdeh 2016). Our final fieldwork was in 2019 in three Jordanian Ḥōrāni villages, namely Kufur Yūba, Ḥuwwāra and Ḥuṣun. Simultaneously, we conducted further interviews in Salt with elderly speakers from the Ḥyāṣāt clan. In the same year, we took exploratory trips and established contacts for future research with the ʕbēdāt clan in Kufur Sūm.

In total, over forty hours of recorded material were collected from the locations mentioned above, which formed the basis of the analysis presented in the present book. With respect to the transcription protocol, the earlier recordings were transcribed using mainstream word-processing software. Although simple to use, these techniques became cumbersome at later stages when we wanted to check transcriptions or extract samples for phonetic analysis. Therefore, for all of the recordings from 2017 onwards, we used the time-aligned transcriber ELAN, which greatly facilitated checks, searches and extractions. The phonetic analyser PRAAT, now commonly used in linguistic analysis, was used sporadically in the present work, mostly to exemplify the acoustic correlates of phenomena such as lexical stress, negation and focus-marking. The corpus that resulted from the transcriptions and on which much of the present analysis draws amounts to approximately 100,000 words.

1.3. A Social Dialectology of Jordan

The linguistic border of what is perceived as 'Jordanian' among the Southern Levantine Arabic group extends beyond Jordan's current political borders. This situation is a natural outcome of the redrawing of the map of the region after World War I. In the north, the political border between Syria and Jordan cuts across the Ḥōrān plateau, which stretches from the Ghouta, just south of Damascus, to central Jordan. Ḥōrān was home to hundreds of agrarian communities, organised in clans and extended families. After 1920, those clans whose land and villages happened to be located close to the new border found themselves split between two different political entities, Syria and Jordan. The dialects of Ḥōrān in general show stronger linguistic affinity with Jordanian dialects than with the dialects of Damascus or central and coastal Syria. For instance, in phonology, traditional Jordanian and Ḥōrāni dialects have the same reflexes of: /q/, /k/, /ṯ/, /ḏ/, /ḏ̣/, /ḍ/, /ǧ/, /l/; and they share the same phonology and phonetics of the feminine ending. In morphology, they share nominal endings and derivations, and both maintain gender distinctions in the second- and third-person pronouns and pronominal and verbal endings. In syntax, they share the same negation system, involving the enclitic *-š* in addition to the negative particle *mā*. Additionally, they share the bulk of the lexicon. This sub-group of Southern Levantine can be placed on a linguistic continuum that extends southwards to Wadi il-Mujib and includes the central (Balga) dialects in the heart of Jordan. The capital city Amman is located in this region, as are the largest and most densely-populated cities in the country (Irbid, Salt and Zarga). From a sociolinguistic perspective, Ḥōrāni dialects enjoy a firmer position and higher status in Jordan than in Syria, precisely because of their close linguistic similarity to the traditional as well as the koineised modern Jordanian dialects.

The Mujib, a steep river canyon, marks the beginning of a second dialect continuum, which we shall call Muʔābi, also classified as Southern Levantine. Muʔābi is represented by the dialects of the southern cities of Kerak, Tafila, Shawbak and Ma'an and the surrounding villages. This group has several distinctive features, e.g., the feminine suffix *-ki* instead of Ḥōrāni *-ik*, as in *ʔamm-ki* 'your (f) mother'. At the same time, the Muʔābi group shares numerous features with the central and northern Ḥōrāni continuum of dialects.

This classification of the southern dialects does not include the southernmost coastal city of Aqaba, Jordan's only port on the Red Sea. There is so far no research on the dialect of Aqaba. The Aqaba region as a whole falls within the tribal zone of the Ḥwēṭāt tribe. Typically for a port city, Aqaba has always attracted migrant workers and investors from all over Jordan as well as from neighbouring countries—particularly from Gaza and Egypt. One of the distinctive linguistic features used in the city relates to the treatment of the feminine ending *-at* in pause, which is invariably realised as [a], unlike in all other Jordanian dialects of the Levantine type, in which the feminine ending is raised under certain conditions (see Al-Wer 2007). Diversity in the city's population has increased further over the past two decades. In 2001, Aqaba was made a 'special economic zone', with the aim of turning it into a regional hub for trade and tourism. Since then, the city has been going through extensive expansion in all domains, including provision of private schools and institutions of higher education. These developments and the new types of employment in the tourism industry, financial sector and civil service have attracted a new class of permanent residents: highly educated professionals, such as university lecturers, doctors, high-ranking civil servants, etc. This transformation in the make-up of Aqaba's population seems to have led to a diffuse linguistic situation, where a plethora of dialects can be heard in the city but as yet no distinctive local dialect.

In addition to dialects of the Southern Levantine type, Jordan is home to dialects that are traditionally classified as 'Bedouin' and are spoken in all regions of the country by settled communities. Representatives of this type are the dialects of the tribes of Ḥwēṭāt, Bdūl, Zawāyda (south); ʕAǧārma, ʕAdwān, ʕAbābīd, Bani Ṣaxr (central); Bani Ḥasan, ʔĀl ʕĪsa, Masāʕīd, Sirḥān (north and north east). This group too shows variation at various levels, e.g., the presence or absence of final *-n* in the imperfective, *ygūlu* vs *ygūlūn* 'they say' (see Herin 2019). Together, the two types of dialects, Southern Levantine and Bedouin, constitute Jordanian Arabic.

Until relatively recently, Jordan did not have a linguistic centre, nor did the conventional dichotomy of urban versus rural, found in neighbouring countries, have sociolinguistic significance. The emergence of linguistic metropolises and stratification along the lines of urban–rural and socioeconomic class divides developed as a result of the unusual increase in the population and expansion of new urban conurbations. Until the 1920s, Amman was a village compared with Salt, for instance, which had historically served as the major urban centre in Jordan. This transition, with its focus on the development of Amman, has transformed the sociolinguistic profile of the country altogether. The dialect of Amman, called 'Ammani' by its native speakers, was formed over three generations by migrants, originally speakers of various Jordanian and Palestinian dialects. This dialect now serves as a *de facto* standard Jordanian dialect and enjoys considerable prestige. Importantly, Amman has become a focal area from which linguistic innovations radiate, influencing other cities and suburbs all over the country. Most notably, Ammani features have spread to the heartlands of the traditional Jordanian dialects: nearby Salt, Irbid in the north and Kerak in the south. Unlike Amman, these cities had their own distinctive traditional dialects, which are now undergoing dedialectalisation;[2] localised central, northern and southern features are being levelled out in favour of supralocal koineised features, whereas the former traditional dialects are increasingly relegated to surrounding rural areas. Dedialectalisation in the major cities is therefore simultaneously a process of linguistic divergence from the traditional dialects as spoken in the villages surrounding the cities, leading to a new dimension of stratification in the context of the traditional dialects, namely 'city talk' (*madani*) versus 'village talk' (*garawi*). A further important sociolinguistic development in Jordanian dialects is the emergence of gender as a major social factor in structuring linguistic variation and in directing change in the traditional dialects. As pointed out in Al-Wer and Herin (2011), differences between women and men in the frequency of usage of certain linguistic features became particularly visible during the

[2] The term 'dedialectalisation' was coined by Peter Trudgill (1996) in relation to the death of traditional English dialects.

1970s and 1980s. Jordanian women increasingly adopted features associated with the *madani* 'urban' varieties while men maintained localised features more consistently. In successive generations, frequency of usage led to the emergence of social values that associated urban features with 'softness' and traditional features with 'toughness'. Since modernisation and social development were concentrated in Amman, to the detriment of the rest of the country, urban linguistic features eventually also became associated with progress and a cultured lifestyle (*taḥaḍḍur*). The linguistic market[3] of urban speech inevitably expanded to include employees in the new business sectors: large shopping malls, finance, the hospitality industry, international schools, etc. On the other hand, the linguistic market of the traditional features tends to be favoured among employees in public services which represent the authority of the state: police, army and civil service. Therefore, in addition to gender, type of occupation has also become a salient social variable.

The extraordinary rate of population increase over the past five decades, as a direct result of the arrival of millions of refugees, has additionally altered the Muslim–Christian ratio, since the vast majority of the newcomers are Muslims. Until the 1920s, Jordan's Christian population formed about 20% of the total population, which has since fallen to 4%–6%. This drastic decrease is due to an increase in the number of Muslims in the country, while the size of the Christian community increased naturally—from 75,000 in 1921 to 220,000 in 2008, according to church

[3] See Bourdieu (1977). For further applications of the notion of 'the linguistic market' in sociolinguistics, see Eckert (1989; 2000).

sources. Since marriage between Muslims and Christians is prohibited by local customs, Muslim Jordanians have over the years become increasingly multiethnic. Al-Wer et al. (2015) found that, in areas affected by the mixture in population, the Christians demonstrated a more conservative linguistic behaviour vis-à-vis the traditional dialects. Linguistic differentiation according to religious affiliation is likely to intensify in Jordan due to the prevalent political instability in the region, in particular the influx of huge numbers of refugees within a relatively short period of time (for details, see Al-Wer et al. 2015).

2. PHONOLOGY

2.1. Consonants

The consonant inventory is presented in Table 1.

Table 1: Consonant inventory

	Bilabial	Labio-dental	Dental	Alveolar	Post-alveolar	Palatal	Velar	Pharyngeal	Glottal
Nasal	m								
Stop	b			t d			k g		ʔ
Fricative		f	ṯ ḏ	s z	š	y	x ġ	ḥ ʕ	h
Velarised			ḏ̣	ṭ ṣ					
Affricate				č ǧ					
Approximant	w			l					
Trill				r					

Cross-dialectally, the most interesting characteristics of this inventory are the presence of the interdentals /ḏ/ (I.P.A. [ð]), /ṯ/ (I.P.A. [θ]) and /ḏ̣/ (I.P.A. [ðˤ]); the affricate /ǧ/ (I.P.A. [ʤ]) as a reflex of etymological /ǧ/; the voiced realisation /g/ of etymological /q/, and /č/ (I.P.A. [tʃ]) as a reflex of etymological /k/. Only these features and the glottal /ʔ/ will be discussed in this grammar, because they have some interest both synchronically and diachronically and from a comparative perspective. Note that gemination, as in all varieties of Arabic, is distinctive and can affect any consonant: *šarad* 'he ran away' vs *šarrad* 'he caused to run away'.

 https://doi.org/10.11647/OBP.0410.02

2.1.1. The Glottal /ʔ/

Glottal /ʔ/ surfaces most often as a phonotactic feature in vowel-initial items: /umm/ [ʔʊmm] 'mother', /int/ [ʔɪnt] 'you (M)', /ēš/ [ʔeːʃ] 'what'. Medially, /ʔ/ is usually maintained in derived and inflected forms of glottal-initial roots such as *tʔaxxar* 'he was late', *staʔǧar* 'he rented'. Glottal /ʔ/ is also maintained in all the inflections and derivations of the root *s-ʔ-l* 'ask': *sāʔil* 'having asked', *masʔūl* 'responsible'. The glottal is also preserved in the causative derivation of the root *ʔ-k-l* 'eat': *ʔakkal–yʔakkil* 'feed', as opposed to other varieties, which usually exhibit /w/ (*wakkal–ywakkil*). For other /ʔ/-initial roots, the normal dialectal realisation of the causative derivation is /w/-initial: *wadda* 'bring' (< *ʔaddā*), *wakkad* ~ *waččad* 'recall' (< *ʔakkada*), *wa*d̲d̲*an* 'call for prayer' (< *ʔa*d̲d̲*ana*).

Otherwise, and as in most varieties, the dialectal reflex of medial etymological /vʔ/ is /v̄/, as in *kās* 'glass', *rās* 'head' (St. *kaʔs* and *raʔs*). Etymological /vʔv̄/ sequences are normally realised /v̄/: *kūs* 'glasses', *rūs* 'heads' (St. *kuʔūs* and *ruʔūs*). Intervocally, historical /ʔ/ surfaces as /y/: *grāye* 'study' (St. *qirāʔa*), *malyān* 'full' (St. *malʔān*, although *malān* was recorded once), *miyaddab* 'well-behaved' (St. *muʔaddab*). Another interesting case is the elative derivation of the adjective *ʔaṣīl* 'authentic', which surfaces as *ʔēṣal*, from **ʔaʔṣal* > **ʔayṣal* > *ʔēṣal* 'more authentic'. Apparent instances of shifts to /w/ are observed in *mwakkat* 'temporary' (St. *muʔaqqat*) and *mwakkad* 'ensured', but these roots are /w/-initial in Salt: *w-k-t* and *w-k-d* (St. respectively *w-q-t* and *ʔ-k-d*).

Etymological final /ˈv̄ʔ/ is either realised as a short vowel with stress shift, as in *sáma* 'sky' (St. *samā́ʔ*) and *ʕarǧa* 'limping (F)' (St. *ʕarǧā́ʔ*), or vowel length and stress are preserved but /ʔ/ drops: *štā́* 'rain' (St. *šitā́ʔ*), *ašyā́* 'things' (St. *ʔašyā́ʔ*), *aṣdigā́* 'friends' (St. *ʔaṣdiqā́ʔ*). Final /ʔ/ is otherwise maintained in loans from the standard variety: *sūʔ* 'evil', *ǧuzəʔ* 'part', *xaṭaʔ* 'error'.

Despite the fact that etymological /ʔ/ is often reduced in its dialectal reflexes, its phonemic status, as indicated by pairs such as *asʔal* 'I ask' vs *ashal* 'easier' and *hayy* (presentative) vs *ʔayy* 'which', is undisputed.

2.1.2. The Interdentals

All the indigenous dialects of Jordan, whether sedentary or Bedouin, preserve the interdentals /ḏ/, /ṯ/ and /ḏ̣/. In all these varieties, etymological /ḍ/ and /ḏ̣/ merged into /ḏ̣/ (Al-Wer 2003). Examples are *ṯgīl* 'heavy', *ḏāg* 'he tasted', *gaḏ̣ab* 'he grasped'. In current practice, these are subject to variation with the corresponding alveolar stops and fricatives in the speech of innovative speakers: *čaḏḏāb* (or *kaḏḏāb*) ~ *kazzāb* 'liar', *ṯāni* ~ *tāni* 'second, other', *ḏ̣ayyaf* ~ *ḍayyaf* 'he welcomed'. Probably due to Standard Arabic borrowings from Ottoman Turkish, some etymological interdentals surface as fricatives, as in *ʕuṣmalliyyāt* 'jewellery' (< *ʕuṯmān* 'Osman') and, most saliently, in the root *ẓ-b-ṭ* (< *ḍ-b-ṭ*): *maẓbūṭ* 'correct', *minẓabbiṭ* 'we put in order'.

Minimal pairs between the interdentals and the corresponding alveolar stops and fricatives are not numerous, which may partially account for their overall instability in Arabic. Nevertheless, the following pairs could be identified: *marat-o* 'his wife' vs *maraṯ-o* 'his heritage', *ḥāriṯ* 'having ploughed' vs *ḥāris* 'guard', *hāḏi* 'this (F)' vs *hādi* 'calm', *aḏka* 'cleverer' vs *azka* 'more tasteful'.

2.1.3. The Affricate /ǧ/

As noted above, the dialectal reflex of etymological /ǧ/ is the affricate /ǧ/ (I.P.A [ʤ]). In this regard, sedentary Jordanian is conservative, because most urban dialects exhibit [ʒ]: *ṯalǧ* 'ice', *ǧōz* 'husband'. In the traditional dialect, deaffrication occurs when /ǧ/ is followed by an apical: *tiǧla* [tɪʒla] 'you flee', *ǧdūd* [ʒdu:d] 'forefathers', *ḥiǧǧto* [ħɪʒʒto] 'his needs'. In the speech of innovative speakers, /ǧ/ may be realised [ʒ]: [aʒa] 'he came', [ʒe:ʃ] 'army', [ʃaʒara] 'tree'. Consequently, the fricative [ʒ] has two different statuses in contemporary sedentary Jordanian, as it is both a combinatory allophone and a 'free' variant of /ǧ/.

2.1.4. The Voiced Velar /g/

The normal reflex of etymological /q/ in sedentary Jordanian is the voiced velar /g/. Although this is often considered a Bedouin realisation from a cross-dialectal point of view, there is no other realisation in traditional sedentary Jordanian. The glottal reflex [ʔ], found in Amman and typical of urban Levantine, is reported to be a post-1948 phenomenon; this period saw the forced migration of huge numbers of Palestinians into Transjordan. The glottal stop never surfaces in the corpus, suggesting that /q/ is not a sociolinguistic variable in Salt and rural Ḥōrāni. Examples of /g/ are *gēḍ* 'hot summer', *baga* 'he was', *marag* 'he passed'. Contrary to what occurs in neighbouring Bedouin dialects, /g/ is never affricated in the vicinity of front vowels: *giddām* 'in front of', *gidər* 'pot'. Devoicing of /g/ occurs in the vicinity of voiceless consonants: *kṭēšāt* (clan in Salt, < *gṭēšāt*), *mikṯā* 'cucumber field' (< *migṯā*, PL *magāṯi*). Interestingly, in the two roots *g-t-l* 'kill' and *w-g-t* 'time', devoicing was generalised to all the derivations and inflections and the normal reflexes are now respectively *k-t-l* and *w-k-t*:

> *w-k-t*: *wakt* 'time', *mwakkat* 'temporary'
> *k-t-l*: *katal* 'he beat (up), killed', *nkatal* 'he got beaten (up), killed', *maktūl* 'beaten (up), dead', *katle* 'beating'

The uvular /q/ of Standard Arabic is seemingly not part of the inventory of the traditional dialect, because it never surfaces in the speech of those who received little or no formal education. For these speakers, even loans from the standard variety are realised with /g/: *fundug* 'hotel', *mugābil* 'in front of', *fagaṭ lā ġēr* 'only this and nothing more'. This is further suggested by the approximation found in the speech of some speakers who have failed to acquire the uvular realisation and realise it as [k^ʕ]: [k^{ʕ}ali:l] 'little' (St. *qalīl*, dialectal *galīl*), [tak^{ʕ}a:li:d] 'customs' (< St. *taqālīd*). Some speakers fail to acquire the uvular realisation precisely because it involves a late acquisition. For speakers who have successfully acquired /q/, contrast can be found between /q/ and /g/ in the following pairs: *ṭāga* 'window' vs *ṭāqa* 'energy', *ygīm* 'he takes off' vs *yqīm* 'he dwells'.

2.1.5. The Affricate /č/

The affricate /č/ (I.P.A. [ʧ]) most often surfaces in the second-person feminine singular suffix *-(i)č*, in contrast to the second-person masculine singular suffix *-(a)k*: *wlād-ič* 'your (F) children' vs *wlād-ak* 'your (M) children'. The affricate also occurs root-internally as a reflex of etymological /k/. On the surface, the presence of /č/ seems to be triggered by the vicinity of a front vowel, as suggested by the following tokens:

/i/:	*čin* (discourse marker), *čifər* (toponym, *čifər hūda*), *ʕičər* 'lees', *ričib* 'he rode', *čibəd* (toponym), *čilme* 'word', *čibər* 'garment', *čitəf* 'shoulder', *bičər* 'first-born', *činne* 'daughter-in-law'
/ī/:	*bičīd* 'it arms', *bičīl* 'he measures', *hadīč* 'that (F)'
/e/:	*birče* 'pond'
/ē/:	*čēf* 'how', *hēč* 'so', *čēl* 'weight unit', *čfēlān* (clan name)
/a/:	*(a)čam(m)* 'how many', *čaʕčabān* 'cake', *čalb* 'dog', *ḥača* 'he spoke', *azča* 'tastier', *ḥarrač* 'move', *čammal* 'finish', *čadbe* 'lie', *čaff* 'palm'
/ā/:	*mačān* 'place', *čānūn* 'stove', *čtāf* 'shoulders', *člāb* 'dogs'

The situation depicted so far closely resembles what is found in surrounding Bedouin varieties, in which /k/ does indeed have two allomorphs: [ʧ] in the vicinity of front vowels and [k] in other contexts. On closer scrutiny, however, the dialects of Central and Northern Jordan also permit the affricate /č/ in a back context, albeit marginally: *dyūč* 'rosters', *člūb* (clan name), *čfūf* 'palms'. In Bedouin dialects, these items are all realised with /k/. There are, however, traces of conditioned affrication in certain items, such as the verbal nouns of certain roots including *ḥ-r-k* 'move' and *r-k-b* 'ride'. The verbal derivation of *ḥ-r-k* is affricated:

ḥarrač 'he moved', but not the verbal noun: *ḥaraka* 'movement'. The root *r-k-b* is normally affricated in the verb *ričib* 'he rode' and its verbal noun *rčāb* 'riding', but not in the other nominal derivation *rkūb* 'riding'. Moreover, affrication is not consistent across the lexicon, as many items that should be affricated if affrication were conditioned are not: *kṯīr* 'a lot', *kbīr* 'big', *kīs* 'bag', *akīd* 'sure', *sikkīn* 'knife'. Neighbouring Bedouin dialects usually exhibit affricated reflexes of these items: *čiṯīr*, *čibīr*, *čīs*, *siččīn*. The overall picture that emerges is one of inconsistency. This inconsistency was already noted by Cantineau (1946, 122) in his study of the dialects of Ḥōrān.

Another well-documented case of affrication in the region is found in rural Palestine. These dialects are known for the unconditioned affrication of /k/. It appears, therefore, that there are three types of affrication in the region, as summarised in Table 2.

Table 2: Affrication of /k/ in the Levant

	Rural Palestinian	Sedentary Jordanian	Bedouin
'he was'–'he is'	*čān–yčūn*	*kān–ykūn*	*čān–ykūn*
'palm'–'palms'	*čaff–čfūf*	*čaff–čfūf*	*čaff–kfūf*
'roster'–'rosters'	*dīč–dyūč*	*dīč–dyūč*	*dīč–dyūk*

Both the rural Palestinian and the Bedouin affrications are straightforward to account for: unconditioned and conditioned. It seems that sedentary Jordanian lies somewhere in the middle. But is the sedentary Jordanian affrication really phonetically conditioned? Since the neo-grammarians, it is now well-established that sound changes tend to be regular, unless mitigated by social constraints. It therefore seems reasonable to suppose that the sedentary Jordanian distribution of /č/ is not phonetically conditioned, but rather the outcome of specific social constraints such as contact. The most probable scenario is that sedentary Jordanian acquired affrication through the transfer of affricated lexical items from neighbouring Bedouin dialects. This affrication was subsequently applied to most derivations and inflections of these roots, albeit not consistently. What we have is therefore a root-based lexical distribution whose apparent phonetic conditioning is only reminiscent of the source distribution. This explains why sedentary Jordanian has *čaff–čfūf* and *dīč–dyūč* on the one hand but *kān–ykūn* on the other, instead of Bedouin *čaff–kfūf*, *dīč–dyūk* and *čān–ykūn*.

Synchronically, the distinction between /k/ and /č/ is further confirmed by the presence of a series of minimal pairs. Consider the following tokens, some of them already noted by Palva (1992a, 56): *sakan* 'housing' vs *sačan* 'cinder', *kibir* 'he grew' vs *čibər* 'garment', *rākib* 'passenger' vs *rāčib* 'having ridden', *čān* 'if' vs *kān* 'he was', *kēf* 'pleasure' vs *čēf* 'how'.

As with /ǧ/, deaffrication of /č/ into [ʃ] occurs when it is followed by an apical: *hadičt il-lēle* [hadi:ʃt ɪlle:lɛ] 'that night'.

2.1.6. Secondary Velarisation and Emphasis Spread

Velarisation, called 'emphasis' in Arabic studies, is a common feature of most dialects of Arabic. It combines a primary articulation and a secondary articulation involving "some sort of pharyngeal constriction" (Bellem 2008, 22). Emphatics are usually divided into primary emphatics and secondary emphatics. Primary emphatics are well-established phonemes: /ṣ/, /ṭ/ and /ḍ/. Minimal pairs contrasting these with their non-emphatic counterparts are well documented: *ṣalla* 'he prayed' vs *salla* 'he entertained', *tiḥt* 'under' vs *ṭiḥt* 'I went down', *ḏāg* 'he tasted' vs *ḍāg* 'it got narrow'. An on-going debate is whether other phonemes should be added to the list of primary emphatics. These are principally /ṛ/, /ḷ/ and also /ḅ/, /ṃ/ and /f̣/. In the dialects of Central and Northern Jordan, contrast seems available only for /ṛ/ and /ḷ/: *dāri* 'knowing' vs *dāṛ-i* 'my house' and *walla* 'he entrusted' vs *waḷḷa* 'by God'. Besides /ḅ/, /ṃ/ and /f̣/, emphatic allophones are available for /k/, /g/, /x/, /ġ/ and /w/. This is referred to as secondary emphasis, i.e., non-phonemic. Secondary emphasis may be triggered by emphasis spread, understood as the propagation of velarisation to surrounding segments from a primary emphatic, or may be lexically conditioned. Summarising existing literature, Hellmuth (2013, 55) notes that, cross-dialectally, (1) leftward spreading is less restricted than rightward spreading, (2) emphasis is more likely to spread from emphatic coronals than gutturals and (3) palatal vowels and consonants tend to block emphasis spread in one or both directions. Huneety and Mashaqba (2016) found that, in Ḥōrāni dialects, emphasis spreads bidirectionally. They state that leftward spread is unbounded whereas rightward spread is inhibited by /i/, /ī/, /š/ and /y/. The bidirectionality of emphasis spread in the dialects of Northern Jordan was already noted by Cantineau (1946), but he states that emphasis is blocked by palatals in both directions. It has long been noted that "The most salient effect is backing (F2 lowering) of immediately adjacent vowels” (Hellmuth 2013, 53). Our data confirm Cantineau’s account, as evidenced both perceptually and by the different second formant mean values of /a/ in items such as *šarīṭa* [ʃariːtˁɑ]. The mean value of F2 of the first [a] was measured at around 1600 and the second [ɑ] at around 1200, showing that emphasis does not spread leftward as far as the first /a/ and is blocked by adjacent /ī/.

Examples of emphasis spread from primary emphatics are: *haḍāḳa* [hɑðˁɑːkɑ] ‘that (M)’, *gaḍaḅ* [gɑðˁɑƀ] ‘he grasped’, *x̣ūṣa* [x̴usˁɑ] ‘knife’, *ġṭēṭa* [ɣtˁeːtˁɑ] ‘fog’, *ṭfāḷ* [tˁf̴ɑːɫ] ‘children’. In other cases, secondary emphasis is lexically conditioned, in the absence of any primary emphatic. Consider the following items:

Table 3: Secondary velarisation

gaḷḅ	[gɑ̴ɫƀ]	‘heart’
ʕuḅi	[ʕʊƀi]	‘over-garments’
ʕuguḅ	[ʕʊgʊƀ]	‘after’
x̣āḷa	[x̴ɑːɫɑ]	‘maternal aunt’
šaġḷa	[ʃɑɣ̴ɫɑ]	‘thing’
aṛṃaḷa	[ɑr̴m̴ɑ̴ɫɑ]	‘widow’
wḳāḷa	[ukɑːɫɑ]	‘old venue in the center of Salt’
ʕuggāḷ	[ʕʊggɑːɫ]	‘wise men’
mx̣aḷx̣aḷ	[m̴x̴ɑ̴ɫx̴ɑ̴ɫ]	‘vinegary’
ngūḷa	[n̴guːɫɑ]	‘Nicolas’
x̣aḷāyle	[x̴ɑ̴ɫɑːylɛ]	‘inhabitants of Il-Xalīl (city in Palestine)’
il-ʕagaḅa	[ɪlʕɑgɑƀɑ]	‘Aqaba’
ṃayy(e)	[m̴ɑjjɛ]	‘water’
ḅḅahāt	[ƀƀahɑːt]	‘fathers’
x̣aṃṃāṛa	[x̴ɑm̴m̴ɑːr̴ɑ]	‘tavern’
gaṛāḅa	[gɑr̴ɐ̴ːƀɑ]	‘closeness’
fṛān	[f̴r̴ɑːn]	‘ovens’

It appears from this list that secondary velarisation is not purely a lexical phenomenon and that the surrounding vowels clearly play a role in triggering emphasis, as it often involves the adjacency of a back vowel or consonant. Minimally, the presence of only an adjacent /ā/ is enough to trigger the velarisation of /r/, as in *nāṛ*. The proximity of /ī/ is enough to develarise /r/ in the speech of some speakers, as in *ǧīrān* [ʤiːraːn] 'neighbours', although more often [ʤiːɍɑːn]. The liquid /l/ requires minimally two surrounding instances of /a/ or /ā/, or one /a/ and a back consonant. Compare *xāl* [xaːl] 'uncle' and the feminine *x̣āḷa* [χɑːɫa] 'aunt'. The same phenomenon occurs with /b/ in the pair *ġāb* 'he was absent', realised without velarisation [ɣaːb], and *ġāḅa* 'wood', realised with velarisation [ɣɑːƀɑ]. Often, though, it is impossible to determine what the trigger of velarisation is. For instance, the item *ʕuḅi* [ʕʊƀɪ] 'cloaks' is realised with a strongly velarised /b/. Is it triggered by the presence of /u/, or is the rounding of an underlying /i/ an assimilatory consequence of the labiality and emphasis of /b/? Some speakers realise this item as [ʕɪbɪ], with [ɪ] and no velarisation. To avoid the 'chicken or the egg' dilemma, one has to consider that these features are to a certain extent lexically distributed. Other items that show variation are *wḳāḷa* 'venue in the old city of Salt', which may equally surface as *wakāle*, and *šaġḷa* 'thing', realised by some speakers as *šaġle*. There is also no inherent phonetic reason for /m/ in *ṃayy(e)* 'water' to be velarised. In this case, lexical distribution is the only explanation. There is of course always the possibility to consider that these apparent instances of secondary velarisation are in fact primary emphasis, i.e., they are not allophones but plain phonemes. This cannot be ruled out as a future development, but in pure synchrony, this stance is not justified, because no minimal pairs can yet be identified.

Secondary velarisation is particularly prominent in Northern Jordan. The proximity of /ā/, for instance, is enough to trigger the velarisation of /l/: *xāḷ* (Central Jordan *xāl*), *gāḷ* 'he said' (Central Jordan *gāl*), although one instance of *gāḷ* was recorded in Salt, which suggests that the velarisation of /l/ may have been the same in both Central and Northern Jordan at some point.

2.2. Vowels

2.2.1. Short Vowels

Like most varieties of the southern Levant, the dialect of Salt has three phonemic short vowels:

Table 4: Short vowels

/i/	/u/
/a/	

Minimal pairs involving short /a/ are easy to find, with both /i/ and /u/:

Table 5: /a/ vs /i/ and /u/

šaʕr	'hair'	*šiʕr*	'poetry'
fall	'he ran away'	*fill*	'run away!'
sakkar	'he closed'	*sukkar*	'sugar'
xašš	'he entered'	*xušš*	'Enter!'

Pairs contrasting /i/ and /u/ are rarer, but still available, as shown in Table 6. These are admittedly not numerous and there might not be much to add to the list presented below.

Table 6: /i/ vs /u/

ʕigib	'children'	*ʕugub*	'after'
bugʕud	'he sits down'	*bigʕid*	'he wakes (someone) up'
gimt	'I took away'	*gumt*	'I stood up'
fill	'Run away!'	*full*	'jasmine'
fitt	'Crumble!'	*futt*	'I entered'
ṭibb	'medicine'	*ṭubb*	'Arrive unannounced!'
ḥibb	'Kiss!'	*ḥubb*	'love'
kibir	'he grew'	*kub(u)r*	'size'
midin	'urban'	*mudun*	'towns'

The limited number of pairs contrasting /i/ and /u/ implies that their phonemic status is not firmly established in the language. This fact is inherited from older stages of the language. Other dialects are known to have merged /i/ and /u/ into /ə/. In sedentary Jordanian, /i/ and /u/ are sociolinguistic variables, as they are socially distributed (Abu Ain 2016). Recorded items in our data are *giṣṣa* ~ *guṣṣa* 'story', *miš* ~ *muš* 'it's not', *yiktib* ~ *yuktub* 'he writes', *yisrig* ~ *yusrug* 'he steals', *yirkiḍ* ~ *yurkuḍ* 'he runs', *hiğra* ~ *huğra* 'exodus', *yḥibb* ~ *yḥubb* 'he loves, kisses', *midde* ~ *mudde* 'period of time', *mismār* ~ *musmār* 'nail', *giṭʕa* ~ *guṭʕa* 'piece', *ğimʕa* ~ *ğumʕa* 'Friday', *simʕ* ~ *sumʕ* 'listening', *ʕinwān* ~ *ʕunwān* 'address'.

The phonetics of /a/ can be described as follows. In neutral contexts, it lies between [æ] and [a]: *balad* [bælæd] 'downtown'. Gutturals (laryngeals, pharyngeals and velars) were not found to modify significantly the place of articulation of /a/. The only environment that clearly modifies the place of articulation is emphasis. As noted above, it has a backing effect on /a/ and situates it in the region of [ɐ] and [ɑ]: *ṭarīg* [tˤɑɾɪːg] 'way'. The vowel /a/

is raised towards [ɛ] in the vicinity of /y/: *bnayye* [bnɛjjɛ] 'little girl'.

The vowel /i/ is realised in neutral contexts in the region of [ɪ]: *binət* [bɪnɪt]. The adjacency of guttural consonants does not significantly modify the place of articulation. In velarised contexts, centralisation towards [ɨ] occurs: *ṭill* [tˤɨɫɫ] 'look!'.

The vowel /u/ is realised [ʊ] in neutral contexts: *gult* [gʊlt] 'I said'. The proximity of post-velar consonants has a lowering effect towards [o]: *ʕurs* [ʕors] 'wedding', *ḥurr* [ħorr] 'free', *nġuzz* [nɣozz] 'we plant'. As with /i/, velarisation centralises the vowel towards [ʉ]: *ṣubḥ* [sˤʉbħ] 'morning'.

The third-person masculine singular bound pronoun *-o* is realised between [o] and [ɔ], although closer to the latter: *šāf-o* [ʃaːfɔ] 'he saw him', *ktāb-o* [ktaːbɔ] 'his book'. This vowel is also found in the third-person masculine plural free pronoun *hummu* [hʊmmɔ] 'them'. It is possible to find opposition of /o/ and /u/ word-finally in pairs such as *šāf-o* 'he saw him' vs *šāfu* 'they saw', which would imply that /o/ is a phoneme, albeit marginal, in sedentary Jordanian.

2.2.2. Long Vowels

As in many eastern varieties, the inherited three-way system /ā/, /ī/, /ū/ was supplemented with /ē/ and /ō/ as a result of the monophthongisation of etymological /ay/ and /aw/. Examples are *gēḏ̣* 'hot summer' (< **qayḍ*) and *ġōr* 'Jordan Valley' (< **ġawr* 'depression'). The diphthong /aw/ is preserved is certain items such as *mawǧūd* 'present', *mawgaʕ* 'place' and *ṭawlān* 'which has become tall'. The term 'Systemzwang' has been put forward to account for the maintenance of the diphthong in these positions as the response "to the need apparently felt by speakers to avoid forms that are not morphologically transparent" (de Jong 2003, 154), as a form such as *mōǧūd* could no longer be assigned to the maCCūC pattern of the root *w-ǧ-d*.

Table 7: Long vowels

/ī/				/ū/
	/ē/		/ō/	
		/ā/		

A five-way contrast is found in items such as those presented in Table 8.

Table 8: Oppositions between long vowels

dār	'house'	*māt*	'he died'
dūr	'houses'	*mūt*	'Die!'
dōr	'turn'	*mōt*	'death'
dēr	'convent'	*mēt*	'When?'
dīr	'Manage!'	*mīt*	'hundred'

Phonetically, /ā/ is realised slightly lower than /a/, getting closer to [aː], as in *kān* [kaːn] 'he was'. The proximity of an emphatic has a backing effect and locates the vowel in the region of [ɑ] and [ɐ]: *ṣāḥib* [sˤɑːħɪb] 'friend, owner'.

The vowel /ī/ in neutral contexts is higher than /i/ and is closer to [iː]: *gīm* [giːm] 'take away'. Post-velar consonants have no lowering effect on /ī/. Velarisation pushes /ī/ towards [ɪː]: *gaṣīr* [gɑsˤɪːr] 'short'.

The main reflex of the vowel /ū/ in neutral contexts is [uː]: *mūne* [muːnɛ] 'provisions'. Post-velar and velarised consonants lower /ū/ towards [ʊː]: *ʕūd* [ʕʊːd] 'stick', *ṭūl* [tˤʊːl] 'length'.

The vowel /ē/ is realised closer to [e] than [ɛ] in neutral contexts: *mēt* [meːt] 'when'. Post-velar consonants do not significantly change the place of articulation: *ʕēb* [ʕeːb] 'shame'. In the vicinity of a velarised consonant, /ē/ is lowered towards [ɛ]: *ḥaṭṭēt* [ħɑtˤtˤɛːt] 'I put'.

The main reflex of /ō/ in neutral contexts is closer to [oː] than [ɔː]: *šōf* [ʃoːf] 'sight'. Neither velarised nor post-velar consonants have a significant effect on the place of articulation: *ṭōše* [tˤoːʃɛ] 'quarrel', *haḏ̣ōl* [hɑðˤoːl] 'these'.

Unlike in other Levantine dialects, unstressed long vowels tend to remain perceptually long. This is evidenced by the spectrogram of *ṭarābīš* [tˤɑrˤɑːˈbiːʃ], plural of *ṭarbūš* 'fez', in which /ā/ of /rā/ is still realised as long [aː] despite being unstressed, as shown in Figure 1. It clearly shows that unstressed /ā/ in /rā/ is significantly longer than /a/ in /ṭa/ (approximate measures are 0.06 seconds for /a/ and 0.1 seconds for /ā/).

Figure 1: Spectrogram of *ṭarābīš*, plural of *ṭarbūš* 'fez'

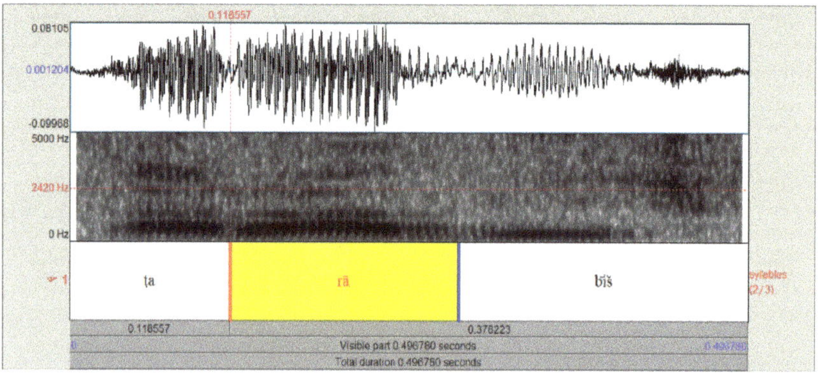

2.3. Phonotactics

2.3.1. Syllable Structure

Maximally, the syllable structure can have this shape: (C)(C)V(C)(C). All the possibilities are broken down below (Table 9):

Table 9: Syllable types

V	*a.gūm* 'I stand up', *i.fill* 'he runs away'
VC	*ug.ʕud* 'sit down', *iʕ.mil* 'Do!'
CV	*sa.ne* 'year', *la.ban* 'curdled milk'
CV:	*šā.fū* 'they saw him', *ḥā.kū.ṛa* 'front yard'
CVC	*miḥ.kama* 'tribunal', *min.saf* 'mansaf (dish)'
CV:C	*gūl* 'Say!', *na.d̲īr* (surname)
CCV	*ġra.bat* 'it got dark', *nha.zam* 'he withdrew'
CCV:	*hnā.ka* 'there', *fḥē.ṣi* 'from Fḥēṣ'
CCVC	*rǧaʕ* 'he gave back', *ṭlaʕ* 'he took out'
CCV:C	*tgūl* 'you say', *nxāf* 'we fear'
CVCC	*šift* 'I saw', *ruḥt* 'I went'
CV:CC	*zāmm* 'having carried', *šābb* 'young'
CCVCC	*ʕmilt* 'I did', *ḥbilt* 'I got pregnant'

The structure CV:CC is limited to active participles of $C_2 = C_3$ roots: *zāmm* (< *z-m-m*) 'having carried', *šādd* (< *š-d-d*) 'having tightened'. The type CCV:CC is not attested. Because of epenthesis and the tendency to avoid zero onsets through the prosthesis of a glottal stop in vowel-initial syllables, the most encountered structure is CV(C). In accordance with this, a sequence such as *nzilt* 'I went down' will often be resyllabified into [ʔɪn.zɪ.lɪt]

2.3.2. Epenthesis

As noted above, initial and final CC clusters and medial CCC(C) clusters will tend to be resolved through epenthesis.

Table 10: Epenthesis

ø → ʔə / #_CC	*mbāriḥ* → *əmbāriḥ* [ʔɪmbaːrɪħ] 'yesterday'
ø → ə / C_C#	*ʕinb* → *ʕinəb* [ʕɪnɪb] 'grape'
ø → ə / (C)C_CC	*xidmtak* → *xidəmtak* [xɪdɪmtak] 'your service'
	mart slēmān → *mart əslēmān* [martɪsleːmaːn] 'Suleiman's wife'

As shown in Table 10, the default value of the epenthetic vowel is [ɪ]. The adjacency of a velarised segment centralises the vowel towards [ɨ]: *ṣaʕəb* [sˤɑʕɨb] 'hard', *saṭəl* [sˤɑtˤɨl] 'bucket'. Vowel harmony occurs in the presence of /u/ and velar and labial consonants, the value of the epenthetic vowel becoming [ʊ]. In this context too, velarisation has a centralising effect, bringing the vowel into the region of [ʉ]. Technically, the first example below *ruzg-it-hum* 'their food' is not an example of epenthesis, because the main allomorph of the feminine morpheme is *-it*. Vowel harmony still normally occurs.

Table 11: Vowel harmony and epenthesis

ruzgit-hum	[rʊzgʊttʊm]	'their food'
rukəbto	[rʊkʊbtɔ]	'his knee'
a-maʕ-hum-əš	[ʔamaħħʊmmʊʃ]	'they don't have'
ḥuḏ̣ən	[ħoðˤʉn]	'arms'

2.3.3. Stress

At the lexical level, stress in not distinctive. Word stress assignment rules are mostly shared across the Levant. Three types of syllables are usually identified: light, heavy and super-heavy (Watson 2011). Light means CV, heavy means CV: and CVC, and super-heavy means anything from CV:C to CCVCC. The general rule can be formulated in two ways, (a) or (b):

(a) The rightmost super-heavy syllable from the right bears stress, or the rightmost non-final heavy syllable.

Or

(b) The first vowel after the first CC cluster or the first long vowel from the right receives stress.

In the absence of such segments, the first syllable attracts stress. This can be illustrated by the following examples (Table 12). The last example *miḥrámati* 'my tissue' illustrates the fact that only the three last syllables are part of the domain of stress, otherwise it would surface as ***míḥramati*. Another example from the corpus is *rassábat-o* 'she made him fail'.

Table 12: Word stress

mafātī́ḥ [mafaːˈtiːħ]	'keys'	First long vowel from the right
míltazim [ˈmɪltazɪm]	'engaged'	First CC cluster from the right
zálame [ˈzalamɛ]	'man'	First syllable
míḥrama [ˈmɪħrama]	'tissue'	first CC cluster from the right
miḥrámati [mɪħˈramatɪ]	'my tissue'	First syllable of the three last

Epenthetic vowels in Central Jordan are normally not stressed: *laḥagət-hum* [laˈħagɪttʊm] 'I knew them', *šifət-ha* [ˈʃifɪtta] 'I saw her'. Northern (Ḥōrāni) dialects behave differently in that epenthetic vowels in these positions are stressed: *darrasət-hum* [darraˈsɪthʊm] 'I taught them'.

In the speech of some speakers, there is occasionally one exception to these rules in verbs of type CCaCaC–yiCCaCiC (measure VII *nfaʕal* and VIII *ftaʕal*). The perfective CCaCaC is normally stressed on the first syllable: *nbána* [ˈnbana] 'it was built', *nḥábas* [ˈnħabas] 'he was jailed'. In derivations and inflections involving the prefixation of consonantal morphemes, stress should move to the first syllable, but it actually remains on the second syllable: *yinḥábis* [jɪnˈħabɪs] 'he is jailed' instead of the expected form *yínḥabis* [ˈjɪnħabɪs] or *muḥtáram* [mʊħˈtaram] instead of *múḥtaram* [ˈmʊħtaram].

Material added to the left of the phonological word, such as monosyllabic prepositions, the apocopated demonstrative *ha-* and the article, does not change the place of stress: *bálad* 'country' [ˈbalad] vs *b-ha-l-balad* [bhalˈbalad] 'in this country' (in-DEM-DEF-country).

Inversely, material added to the right modifies the structure of the phonological word and therefore stress assignment. This is illustrated by morphemes such as the bound pronouns, the feminine ending and the negation marker *-š*:

bġánnu 'they sing' + *-hin* → *bġannū́hin* [bɣanˈnuːhɪn] 'they sing them (F)'
míltazim 'committed' + *-e* → *miltázme* [mɪlˈtazmɛ] 'committed (F)'
bínsarig 'it is stolen' + *-š* → *binsárgəš* [bɪnˈsargɪʃ] 'it's not stolen'

Consequently, material that attaches to the left should be considered clitics, since it is not part of the phonological word, whereas material added to the right is part of the phonological word and therefore affixal (see §3.1 for more on wordhood). For notational convenience, we decided to maintain the use of the dash, instead of {=}, even with material added to the left.

Acoustically, stress correlates with an increase in pitch and intensity but not length, as shown in Figure 2, where the first syllable [bta] in *b-tanaka* [ˈbtanaka] 'in a tank' displays a higher pitch and intensity than the last segment [naka].

Figure 2: Pitch (blue) and intensity (green) in *b-tanaka* 'in a tank'

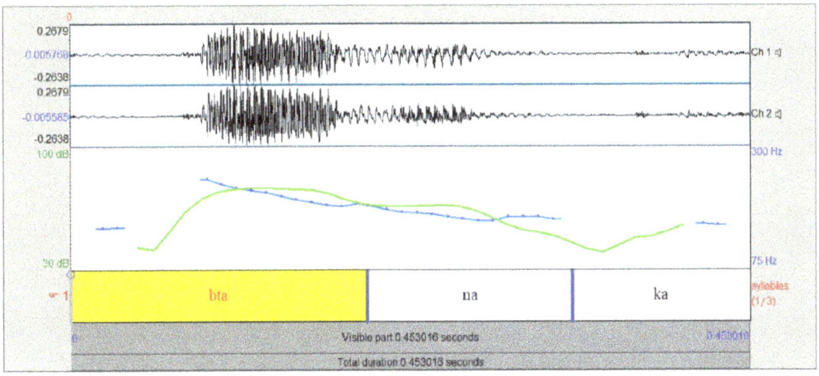

This is further exemplified in Figure 3, which displays an increase in pitch and intensity on the second syllable [doː] in *bandōra* 'tomato'.

Figure 3: Pitch (blue) and intensity (green) in *bandōra* 'tomato'

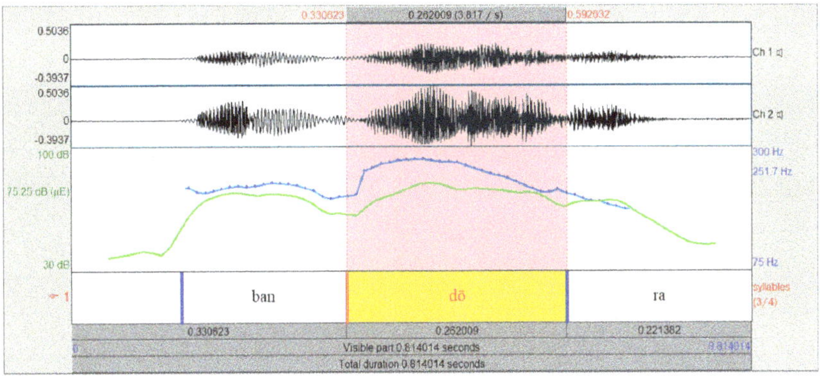

2.3.4. Vowel Deletion

As in all Levantine dialects, high vowels are elided in unstressed open syllables. This usually yields consonant clusters that need to be resolved through epenthesis according to the rules presented in Table 10. This mostly happens with the feminine morpheme *-it*, medial high vowels in verb stems and also the imperfective third-person subject agreement marker /i/. In terms of rule ordering, stress assignment must occur before epenthesis, because epenthetic vowels are not stressed.

samne + *-o* → *samn-it-o* → *samnto* → *samənto* [ˈsamɪnto] 'his fat'
burguṣ + *-in* → *burguṣin* → *burgṣin* → *burəgṣin* [ˈbʊɾʊgsˤɪn] 'they dance'
biṣīr → *bṣīr* [psˤiːr] 'he becomes'

High vowel elision also happens in sandhi (across word boundaries), as shown in (1).

(1)	Underlying	*haḏ̣āka*	*yfarriġ*	*il-xams*	*fašakāt*
	Surface	*haḏ̣āka*	*yfarrġ*	*il-xaməs*	*fašakāt*
		DEM	empty.IPFV.3MS	DEF-five	bullets
		'The other empties the five bullets'			

Elision of high vowels in unstressed positions is blocked in ...$C_aC_avC_b$... sequences when C_a and C_b are homorganic, as shown in the following examples:

makattitēn [ma.kat.tɪ.ˈteːn] 'two ashtrays'
ǧidditi [ˈʤɪd.dɪ.tɪ] 'my grandmother'
ykallilu [ɪˈkal.lɪ.lʊ] 'they marry'

The vowel /a/ is normally stable in unstressed positions. An exception is in CaCaCaC segments, in which case medial /a/ drops, yielding CaCCaC. This rule is phonological because it occurs everywhere, irrespective of morphology or word class (Table 13). Deletion can also occur in the imperfective paradigms of *stāhal–yistāhal* 'deserve' and *wiṣil–yaṣal* 'arrive' when the negator *-š* or another morpheme attaches to the right: *bastāhal* 'I deserve' + *-š* → *bastāhl-əš* [basˈtaːhlɪʃ] 'I don't deserve', *mā yaṣal* 'he would not arrive' + *-š* → *mā yaṣl-əš* [maː ˈjasˤlɪʃ]. The suffixation of *-š* is expected to attract stress on the last syllable, after which epenthesis should occur. Optional deletion also happens with the augments *-i*, *-u* and *-in*: *taṣal-i* ~ *taṣl-i* 'you (F) (would) arrive'. It may be tempting to posit a rule of the type /a/ → Ø / ...ˈVC_C... where V stands for /ā/ and /a/, but this seems only to occur with these two verbs, as shown by the maintenance of /a/ in *mā ḥaṣal-əš* [maː ħaˈsˤalɪʃ] 'it didn't occur' (not **[maː ˈħasˤlɪʃ]).

Table 13: Elision of /a/

	Underlying	Surface
zalame 'man' + *-ku*	*zalamat-ku*	*zalmat-ku* [zalˈmatkʊ] 'your man'
ragaba 'neck' + *-i*	*ragabat-i*	*ragbati* [ˈragbatɪ] 'my neck'
tanaka 'tank' + *zēt* 'oil'	*tanakat zēt*	*tankat zēt* [ˈtankat ˈzeːt] 'oil tank'
marag 'he passed' + *-at*	*maragat*	*margat* [ˈmargat] 'she passed'
stalam 'he received' + *-at*	*stalamat*	*stalmat* [ˈstalmat] 'she received'

2.3.4.1. Vowel Deletion in ...V#V...

In connected speech and in the absence of pause, vowel deletion often occurs when a word ending in a vowel is immediately followed by a vowel-initial item. If two short vowels are involved, the second vowel is deleted. The rule can be formulated in this way:

V → Ø / ...V#_C...

bištari minno (a)xū [bɪʃtarɪ mɪnno xʊː] 'His brother buys from him'
min il-midrase (a)xaḏū-ni [mn ɪlmɪdrasɛ xaðʊːnɪ] 'They took me from school'
ilha (a)wwal [ɪlha wwal] 'It has a beginning'
ʕala (i)dē [ʕala deː] 'On his hands'
twaddi la (u)mm̥-ha [twaddɪ la mm̥ha] 'She brings to her mother'
miṯəl-ma (i)nt šāyif [mɪθɪlma nt ʃaːjɪf] 'As you can see'

If the first vowel is short and the second is long, the first, short vowel undergoes elision:

V → Ø / ..._#V̄...

burudd yiǧ(i) ēš [bʊrʊdd jiːʤ eːʃ] 'And then comes what?'
ʕal(a) ēš bithāwašu [ʕal eːʃ bɪthaːwaʃʊ] 'What are they quarrelling about?'
m(ā) ōxḏ-əš minno [m oːxðɪʃ mɪnno] 'I don't take from him'

2.3.5. Consonant Deletion

2.3.5.1. Deletion of /f/ before a Labial

The labio-dental /f/ optionally drops when followed by a labial in high-frequency sequences. This occurs mostly with the interrogative *čēf* ~ *kēf* 'how' followed by the pseudo-verb *badd-* ~ *bidd-* 'want' or a verb in the *b*-imperfective. Example (2) also features the vowel deletion presented above: [keː badd iʕiːʃ] 'how should (one) live'.

(2) *ma-hu kē(f) badd-(o) yʕīš il-wāḥad*

TOP-3SG how want-3MS live.SBJV.3MS DEF-one

‘Well, how should one live?’

Deletion of /f/ was also recorded before /m/, as illustrated in (3), but this is seemingly marginal:

(3) *mā baʕri(f) manu ṯ-ṯāni*

NEG know.IPFV.1SG who DEF-other

‘I don’t know who the other one is’

2.3.5.2. Deletion of /ḥ/ before /ʕ/ and /ġ/

Unlike /f/ before a labial, /ḥ/ systematically drops before /ʕ/, as shown below in (4), realised as [ntˤiː ʕa daːr ʕammɪ]:

(4) *nṭī(ḥ) ʕa dār ʕamm-i*

descend.SBJV.1PL to house uncle-1SG

‘We used to go to my uncle’s house’

Elision of /ḥ/ was also recorded sporadically before /ġ/, but much less consistently than before /ʕ/, as shown in (5), realised as [wala bartaː ɣeːr ʕaleː]:

(5) *wala bartā(ḥ) ġēr ʕalē*

NEG rest.IPFV.1SG except on.3SG

‘I can only rest (when I sit) on it’

2.3.6. Assimilations

As in most Arabic varieties, the article *il-* assimilates to the following consonants: /ṯ/, /ḏ/, /ḏ̣/, /t/, /ṭ/, /d/, /s/, /ṣ/, /n/, /l/, /r/ and also /ǧ/ and /č/: *iǧ-ǧabal* ‘the mountain’, *ič-čal(ə)b* ‘the dog’. The most common assimilations recorded in the corpus are the following.

Table 14: Assimilations

Partial regressive assimilation			
/b/ + /n/ → mn	*bniḥči*	[mnɪħtʃɪ]	'we speak'
Total regressive assimilation			
/t/ + /s/ → ss	*bitsaǧǧil*	[bɪssadʒdʒɪl]	'you record'
/t/ + /z/ → zz	*bitzimm*	[bɪzzɪmm]	'you carry'
/t/ + /ḏ̣/ → ḏ̣ḏ̣	*bitḏ̣all*	[bɪðˤðˤall]	'you stay'
/t/ + /ḏ/ → ḏḏ	*batḏakkar*	[baððakkar]	'I remember'
/t/ + /š/ → šš	*bitšuxx*	[bɪʃʃʊxx]	'you pee'
/t/ + /d/ → dd	*bitdaxxin*	[bɪddaxxɪn]	'you smoke'
/t/ + /ṭ/ → ṭṭ	*bitṭīḥ*	[bitˤtˤiːħ]	'you go down'
/ṯ/ + /t/ → tt	*ṯ(a)laṯ tālāf*	[θalattaːlaːf]	'three thousand'
/d/ + /t/ → tt	*gaʕadt*	[gaʕatt]	'I stayed'
/ḏ/ + /t/ → tt	*axaḏt*	[axatt]	'I took'
/n/ + /r/ → rr	*minrūḥ*	[mɪrruːħ]	'we go'
/n/ + /l/ → ll	*bigūlin-li*	[bɪgʊllɪllɪ]	'they tell me'
/b/ + /m/ → mm	*ʕugub-mā*	[ʕʊgʊmma]	'after'
/l/ + /n/ → nn	*gulna*	[gʊnna]	'we said'
/l/ + /r/ → rr	*ḏ̣all raḥmit*	[ðˤarr raħmɪt]	'late X was…'
/l/ + /t/ → tt	*gultlo*	[gʊttlo]	'I told him'
/nd/ + /d/ → nn	*ʕindna*	[ʕɪnna]	'at us'
/dd/ + /n/ → nn	*baddna*	[banna]	'we want'
Progressive assimilation			
/ḥ/ + /h/ → ḥḥ	*gamǝḥ-hum*	[gamɪħħʊm]	'their wheat'
Reciprocal assimilation			
/ʕ/ + /h/ → ḥḥ	*maʕ-hum*	[maħħʊm]	'with them'

Although commonly found in Northern Jordan as a whole (Bani-Yasin and Owens 1987, 300) and some Sinai dialects (de Jong 2000, 136–37), the assimilation of /h/ to preceding unvoiced consonants across morpheme boundaries is a recessive feature peculiar to the traditional dialect.

Table 15: Assimilation of /h/ at morpheme boundaries

/t/ + /h/ → tt	*tirbāyit-ha*	[tɪrba:jɪtta]	'her education'
/ṭ/ + /h/ → ṭṭ	*turbuṭ-hum*	[tʊrbʊtˤtˤʊm]	'you tie them'
/f/ + /h/ → ff	*sōlaf-ha*	[so:laffa]	'he told it'
/s/ + /h/ → ss	*yidʕas-hin*	[yɪdʕassɪn]	'he tramples them'
/ṣ/ + /h/ → ṣṣ	*yunguṣ-hum*	[yʊngʊsˤsˤʊm]	'they miss'
/k/ + /h/ → kk	*stamlak-ha*	[stamlakka]	'he took possession of it'
/x/ + /h/ → xx	*tārīx-ha*	[ta:ri:xxa]	'her history'

This kind of assimilation also occurs in sandhi:

tiḥət ha-l-milʕab [tɪħɪttalmɪlʕab] 'under the stadium'

In addition to this, /d/ followed by /h/ at morpheme boundaries undergoes devoicing and assimilation occurs, both at bound-morpheme and word boundaries:

badd-hum	[battʊm]	'they want'
blād-hum	[bla:ttʊm]	'their country'
lə-blād hāye	[lɪbla:tta:ye]	'this country'

2.3.7. Compensatory Gemination in *gāl* 'he said'

One of the most salient features in the dialect is the compensatory gemination of /l/ in both the imperfective and perfective inflections of *gāl* 'he said' as a result of the shortening of the medial vowel when dative suffixes are added:

gālū-li	[gallu:li]	'They told me'
gāl-ilhum	[gallɪlhʊm]	'He told them'
bigūlū-lo	[bgʊllu:lo]	'They tell him ~ they call it'
ngūl-ilha	[ngʊll-ɪlha]	'We tell her ~ we (used to) call it'
bigūlin-li	[bɪgʊllɪl-li]	'They (F) tell me'

3. MORPHOLOGY

This chapter describes the morphology of the dialect. It starts with open word classes such as nouns, adjectives and verbs and then continues with closed word classes such as pronouns, demonstratives, adverbs, prepositions and numerals. Morphology is the study of the internal structure of words. What counts as a word is notoriously different across languages, so it can only be defined using language-specific properties. In the following section, we make explicit how we identify words, as opposed to other units such as clitics or affixes. This partially overlaps with arguments presented in §2.3.3 about stress and §3.5.3 about dative pronouns.

3.1. Words, Clitics and Affixes

In the present description, a word is understood as phonological. The way we identify a phonological word is primarily by stress assignment (§2.3.3). A word is a phonological sequence characterised by the presence of one primary stress. Affixes create new phonological words, which potentially modifies primary stress according to the new syllabic structure. In practice, this is a property of suffixes such as bound pronouns. The phonological word *ṣṣawwir* [ɪsˤˈsˤawwɪr] 'she (wants to) film' (film.SBJV.3FS) is stressed on the penultimate syllable [sˤaw]. When the 2MP bound pronoun *-ku* attaches to the right, a new phonological word is created and stress shifts to [wir]: *ṣṣawwir-ku* [əsˤsˤawˈwɪrkʊ] 'she (wants to) film you' (film.SBJV.3FS-2MP).

 https://doi.org/10.11647/OBP.0410.03

If the diagnosis for establishing affixhood is clear, this is not the case with clitics. In practice, a clitic is any bound form that cannot be clearly classified as an affix, i.e., any bound form that does not create a new phonological word and therefore has no impact on stress assignment. Such forms usually reflect an ongoing process of grammaticalisation. This can be exemplified by dative pronouns (§3.5.3), especially in the speech of broad speakers. Dative pronouns arose from the grammaticalisation of the preposition *la* 'to, for' augmented with bound prounouns (§3.9.1.4). In the speech of most speakers, dative pronouns are unmistakably affixal, because they consistently create a new phonological word with their host, as shown in the following example:

ṣalla [ˈsˤaɫɫa]	+	*il-ha* [ˈʔɪlha]	→	*ṣallā-lha* [sˤaɫˈɫaːlha]
'he prayed'		'for her'		'he prayed for her'

Some elderly speakers, however, exhibit a different pattern, exemplified below:

ḥalagu [ˈħalagʊ]	+	*il-o* [ˈʔɪlɔ]	→	*ḥalagū-lo* [ˈħalaguːlɔ]
'they shaved'		'for him'		'they shaved for him'

In this case, stress remains on the first syllable. Most speakers would have realised this sequence as [ħalaˈguːlɔ], stressing the penultimate, as expected according to the rules of stress assignment. The realisation [ˈħalaguːlɔ] reflects an earlier phase of coalescence between the bound morpheme and its host, which can be summarised as follows:

Stage I	Stage II	Stage III
[ˈħalagʊ (ˈʔɪ)lo]	[ˈħalaguː=lɔ]	[ħalaˈguː-lɔ]

Stage I is only attested in the case of informational processes such as focalisation. In Stage II, the morpheme is bound to its host, as shown by the lengthening of the contact vowel [uː], but not fully integrated, because stress remains unchanged. This is when it could be classified as a clitic, i.e., a bound form that is not fully affixal. In Stage III, the bound morpheme is fully coalesced to its host, and is therefore affixal.

One problem arises with bound morphemes that attach to the left, because they almost uniformly do not modify stress assignment. Such morphemes are the article *il-*, the apocopated demonstrative *ha-* and prepositions such as the locative-instrumental *b(i)* 'in, with'. Consider the word *ḥağar* 'stone', realised as [ˈħaʤar]. Stress rules state that bisyllabic words are stressed on the first syllable. In the sequence *b-ha-l-ḥağar* 'with this stone', stress remains on [ħa], irrespective of the material that occurs to the left: [bhalˈħaʤar]. If *b-ha-l-ḥağar* were a phonological word, then the syllable [bhal] should be stressed: **[ˈbhalħaʤar], as in the phonological word *milḥafe* [ˈmɪlħafɛ] 'sheet', in which stress falls as expected on the first syllable [mɪl]. Consequently, the morphemes that attach to the left in *b-ha-l-ḥağar* are not affixes, but rather clitics. Interestingly, things are different with monosyllabic words of the type CCā. These are not numerous; the group includes the lexeme *štā* 'rain, winter' and plurals such as *dlā* 'buckets' (plural of *dalu* 'bucket') and *ğdā* 'goats' (plural of *ğidi* 'goat'). When the article attaches to the left, stress remains unchanged, as expected: *štā* [ˈʃtaː] 'winter', *iš-štā* [ɪʃˈʃtaː] 'the winter'. With the preposition *bi*, however, stress shifts to the first syllable: *bi-š-štā* (or *b-iš-štā*) [ˈbɪʃʃtaː] 'in the winter'. This would imply that, in this case, the preposition and probably the article show affix-like behaviour. If we were to opt for a strict notational distinction between affixes and clitics, we should then transcribe *b=ha=l=ḥağar* 'with this stone' and *bi-š-štā* 'in the winter'.

It appears from the discussion above that a strict distinction between affixes and clitics is not fully sustainable. What we can say, however, is that bound morphemes that attach to the right tend to be affixal, whereas bound material that occurs leftward tends to show clitic-like behaviour. We decided to use the same notational device (the dash) for all bound forms, whether they exhibit clitic-like behaviour or are fully affixal, because, as shown above, the degree of coalescence of certain morphemes to their host either is not consistent across speakers or depends, albeit marginally, on the syllabic structure of the host.

3.2. Nouns

3.2.1. Non-concatenative Morphology

Arabic and Semitic languages in general are widely known for their templatic non-concatenative morphology, which involves a root and a template or pattern. All spoken varieties of Arabic inherited this system. The lexicon is mostly structured around triconsonantal roots and to a lesser extent quadriconsonantal roots, leaving biconsonantality extremely marginal. In the dialect under study, for example, standard Arabic biconsonantals have been reinterpreted as triconsonantals, through either second-consonant doubling or adding a third root letter /w/: *ʔaxu* 'brother' (St. *ʔax*), *ʔabu* 'father' (St. *ʔab*), *damm* 'blood' (St. *dam*), *ṯumm* ~ *ṯimm* 'mouth' (St. *fam*). The standard word *luġa* 'language', although well-attested, is realised as *laġwa* in the vernacular. The only truly biliteral words are *mara* 'woman' and *sane* 'year'. Below is an inventory of the nominal templates that have been identified. Most of these are shared with other dialects. The following patterns, although carefully collected, do not pretend to be comprehensive. The number of items in each category gives a rough idea of the productivity of each template.

3.2.1.1. CāC

Masculine	*bāb* 'door', *dār* 'house (F)', *ḥāl* 'situation', *nār* 'fire', *ʕām* 'year', *gāʕ* 'floor', *xāl* 'maternal uncle', *ǧār* 'neighbour', *zād* 'provisions', *ṣāʕ* 'weight unit', *ṣāǧ* 'heating plate for local bread', *fās* 'axe', *rās* 'head', *kās* 'glass', *bāṣ* 'bus', *šāy* 'tea', *ʔāb* 'August', *kāz* 'kerosene', *ġāz* 'stove', *wād* 'valley' (St. *wādi*), *nās* 'people', *šām* 'Damascus, Syria'
+ -*a*	*ḥāra* 'neighbourhood', *sāʕa* 'hour', *ṭāga* 'little window', *sāḥa* 'square', *ġāba* 'wood', *rāḥa* 'rest'
Miscellaneous	*ḅāḅa* 'dad', *ṃāṃa* 'mum', *bāša* 'Pasha', *sāda* 'black coffee', *sāba* 'farming instrument'

3.2.1.2. CūC

Masculine	*ṭūl* 'length', *ṣūf* 'wool', *sūg* 'market', *ʕūd* 'stick', *sūr* 'wall', *ǧūʕ* 'hunger', *sūʔ* 'evil', *nūr* 'light', *ǧūd* 'generosity', *kūz* 'goblet'
Plural	*dūr* 'houses' (SG *dār*), *kūs* 'glasses' (SG *kās*), *rūs* 'heads' (SG *rās*)

+ -*a*	*ġūla* 'female ogre', *ǧūra* 'slot', *ṣūra* 'image', *mūne* 'provision', *šūne* (place name)

3.2.1.3. CīC

Masculine	*ṭīn* 'heart', *kīs* 'bag', *tīn* 'fig', *ǧīl* 'generation', *rīḥ* 'wind', *ḏīb* 'wolf', *bīr* 'well', *ʕīd* 'feast', *ṭīb* 'good-heartedness', *ḥīn* 'moment', *dīn* 'religion', *hīš* 'wood'
Feminine	*ʔīd* 'hand'
Plural	*bīḍ* 'white'
+ -*a*	*ʕīše* 'life' (singulative of *ʕīš*), *ḥīle* 'interest', *sīre* 'story', *ǧīre* 'neighbourhood', *ǧīze* 'union'

3.2.1.4. CēC

Masculine	*xēr* 'good', *zēn* 'good', *kēf* 'pleasure', *bēt* 'house', *ǧēš* 'army', *ʕēn* 'eye', *zēt* 'oil', *ṣēf* 'summer', *gēḏ* 'intense heat', *lēl* 'night', *xēṭ* 'thread', *xēl* 'horse', *sēf* 'sword', *šēx* 'sheikh', *ḥēṭ* 'wall', *ḏēf* 'guest', *ġēṯ* 'rain', *ʕēb* 'shame', *dēr* 'monastery', *ṭēr* 'bird', *hēl* 'cardamom', *mēs* 'type of tree, of the myrtle family', *sēr* 'traffic', *ṣēd* 'hunting'
+ -*a*	*ʕēle* 'family', *xēme* 'tent', *lēṛa* 'dinar', *ǧēbe* 'pocket', *ṣēḥa* 'cry', *lēle* 'night'

3.2.1.5. CōC

Masculine	*yōm* 'day', *gōm* 'group of men', *fōg* 'above', *ġōr* 'Jordan Valley', *šōb* 'heat', *nōʕ* 'type', *lōn* 'colour', *dōr* 'queue, turn', *ṣōt* 'voice', *kōm* 'pile', *gōs* 'arc',

	gōl 'saying', *ǧōz* 'husband', *šōk* 'fork, prickle', *bōg* 'betrayal', *ṯōb* 'garment', *ḥōš* 'court', *šōf* 'vision', *nōm* 'sleep', *xōf* 'fear'
+ *-a*	*rōḥa* 'one way', *ʕōne* 'help', *gōse* 'arc', *hōše* 'quarrel', *ṭōše* 'quarrel', *dōle* 'state'

3.2.1.6. CaCC

Masculine	*ʔaxx* 'brother', *ṣalṭ* 'Salt', *sabt* 'Saturday', *farg* 'difference', *šarr* 'evil', *nafs* 'spirit', *hamm* 'worry', *galb* 'heart', *waḏ̣ʕ* 'situation', *wakt* 'time', *ʔarḏ̣* 'earth', *šarg* 'East', *ʔahl* 'people', *faṣl* 'part', *ǧaww* 'air', *ṭags* 'climate', *sagf* 'roof', *lagn* 'basin', *damm* 'blood', *šakl* 'style', *ṣaḥn* 'plate', *ṭaʕm* 'taste', *barg* 'lightning', *kahf* 'cave', *kaff* ~ *čaff* 'palm', *ʕabd* 'slave', *waǧh* 'face', *šarṭ* 'condition', *rabb* 'lord', *gaṣr* 'castle', *ʔaṣl* 'origin', *ṣaff* 'class', *ǧahl* 'ignorance', *šaʕb* 'people', *baṭn* 'belly', *ġaṣb* 'constraint', *ḥagg* 'price, right', *ʕamm* 'paternal uncle', *bard* 'cold', *fann* 'art', *ḥaǧǧ* 'pilgrimage', *bank* 'bank', *saṭl* 'bucket', *wafd* 'delegation', *ʕaṣr* 'period', *ġarb* 'west', *ḏ̣ahr* 'back', *šahr* 'month', *ḥamm* 'heat', *karm* 'vineyard', *ʕarḏ̣* 'honour', *taxt* 'bed', *ʕagl* 'intelligence', *ʕagd* 'contract', *ʔaǧl* 'term', *ḏanb* 'fault', *faḏ̣l* 'virtue', *ṯalǧ* 'ice', *xaṭṭ* 'line', *baġl* 'mule', *tall* 'hill', *faǧr* 'dawn', *gabr* 'grave', *kalb/čalb* 'dog', *xass* 'lettuce', *ḥarf* 'letter', *barr* 'land', *nasl* 'descendants', *ʔamn* 'safety', *raṭl* 'pound', *ʕahd* 'treaty', *nahr* 'river', *baḥr* 'sea', *marǧ* 'meadow', *ḥalg* 'throat', *samn* 'fat', *laḥm*

	'meat', *šaʕr* 'hair', *gamḥ* 'wheat', *ṣaxr* 'rock', *ʕanz* 'goat', *tamr* 'date', *ḥabb* 'seed', *wašm* 'tattoo', *farš* 'mat', *ṭarš* 'camel', *gaml* 'lice', *ʕatm* 'darkness', *faḥm* 'charcoal', *nabʕ* 'source', *naḥl* 'bee', *waṣf* 'description', *ḥamd* 'praise', *ʔakl* 'food', *ḥağz* 'holdback', *dafn* 'burial', *ḥabl* 'pregnancy', *zarʕ* 'seeding', *ḏabḥ* 'slaughtering', *rasm* 'drawing', *salx* 'skin', *harğ* 'speech', *ʕağz* 'weakness'
Feminine	*ḥarb* 'war', *ṃayy* 'water' (contracted form of *ṃayye*), *šams* 'sun'
Adjectives	*ğadd* 'serious', *ṣaḥḥ* 'correct', *sahl* 'easy', *faxm* 'superb'
+ -*a*	*fatra* 'period', *maṛṛa* 'time', *laḥḏ̣a* 'moment', *gahwa* 'coffee', *naxwa* 'dignity', *galʕa* 'castle', *sarwa* 'early', *xaṭṛa* 'time', *ğarra* 'jar', *ṃayye* 'water', *ṣaḥğe* 'clapping', *bahğe* 'splendour', *lahğe* 'dialect', *garye* 'village', *maḥle* 'drought', *fatte* 'crumbled bread', *ḥafle* 'ceremony', *ğanne* 'paradise', *wağbe* 'meal', *nabte* 'plant', *šadde* 'cards', *naḏ̣ra* 'look', *fatḥa* 'entry', *nafxa* 'swelling', *ṣaxṛa* 'rock', *ṭalʕa* 'climb', *kasra* 'defeat', *sahra* 'evening', *rabṭa* 'knot', *ġalṭa* 'error', *šaġḷa* 'thing', *basṭa* 'support', *ʕağwa* 'pressed date', *farwa* 'fur', *ğamṛa* 'firebrand', *farḥa* 'joy', *ṭabxa* 'dish', *rağʕa* 'return', *dafʕa* 'push', *gaḏ̣wa* 'case', *ğalse* 'session', *farše* 'mat', *šamle* 'cloak', *ʔakle* 'food', *ʕatme* 'darkness', *nabḏe* 'fragment', *laḥme* 'meat', *rasme* 'drawing', *laffe* 'turning', *katle* 'beating', *ġasle* 'cleaning', *gadde* 'quantity', *nahğe* 'way'

3.2.1.7. CiCC

Masculine	*gism* 'part', *gird* 'monkey', *ʕičr* 'sediment', *ʔibr* 'needle', *ṣidr* 'pot', *ʔism* 'name', *ʔibn* 'sun', *sitt* 'grandmother', *ʕinb* 'grape', *gidr* 'pot', *ḏ̣ill* 'shade', *dibs* 'molasses', *bizr* 'seed', *ǧidd* 'grandfather', *nimr* (name), *wiǧh* 'face', *zift* 'asphalt', *šiʕr* 'poetry', *tilṯ* 'third', *sirǧ* 'saddle', *sinn* 'age', *ǧizʔ* 'part', *ṣinf* 'type', *giṭf* 'bunch', *ḥifḏ̣* 'conservation', *girš* 'piaster', *siǧn* 'prison', *šikl* 'way', *sirr* 'secret', *ḥizb* 'party', *firʕ* 'branch', *biss* 'cat', *mitr* 'metre', *ǧism* 'body', *ṭifl* 'kid', *hind* (name), *silf* 'brother-in-law', *litr* 'litre', *ǧiḏr* 'root', *ṣiʕn* 'gourd', *ǧisr* 'bridge', *milk* 'property', *čibr* 'coat', *tibn* 'straw', *milḥ* 'salt', *ʕiǧl* 'calf', *ḥiml* 'load', *gišr* 'skin', *ǧild* 'skin', *ʕilm* 'science', *simʕ* 'hearing', *fikr* 'idea', *ʕirf* 'knowing'
Feminine	*bint* 'girl', *riǧl* 'foot'
Plural	*ʕigb* 'kids'
+ *-a*	*giṭʕa* 'piece', *ǧimʕa* 'Friday', *giṣṣa* 'story', *ṣiḥḥa* 'health', *silʕa* 'commodity', *hiǧra* 'exodus', *zibde* 'butter', *ʕilbe* 'box', *čilme* 'word', *šille* 'gang', *wiḥde* 'unity', *sidde* 'first floor of a traditional house', *ḏ̣iffe* '(West) bank', *nisbe* 'relation', *girbe* 'gourd', *wihbe* (name), *niʕme* 'blessing', *hirre* 'cat', *mihne* 'occupation', *ǧibne* 'cheese', *birke* 'pond', *liǧne* 'committee', *fikra* 'idea', *milḥa* 'piece of salt', *ǧilde* 'piece of skin', *ḥimle* 'load', *liḥme* 'meat', *girde* 'female monkey', *ḥible* 'pregnant', *xiṣbe* 'fertile', *xilfe* 'progeny'
Adjectives	*bišʕ* 'ugly', *xišn* 'rough', *ḥilw* 'sweet'

3.2.1.8. CiCCa (< CiCCā)

Feminine *dinya* 'world', *miʕza* 'goat', *ḥinna* 'henna' (< *ḥinnāʔ*)

3.2.1.9. CuCC

Masculine *ʕumr* 'age', *kull* 'all', *nuṣṣ* 'half', *šuġl* 'work', *bunn* 'coffee beans', *furn* 'oven', *luġz* 'enigma', *ʕurs* 'wedding', *ruzz* 'rice', *ṣubḥ* 'morning', *rubʕ* 'quarter', *kubr* 'size', *muxx* 'brain', *rumḥ* 'spear', *ḥuḏn* 'lap', *xubz* 'bread', *šurb* 'drinking', *ṣulḥ* 'peace', *ḥukm* 'rule', *šukr* 'gratitude'

Feminine *umm* 'mother'

Plural *šugr* 'blondes', *luḥf* 'cover', *busṭ* 'carpet'

+ -*a* *xuḏra* 'vegetables', *ḥurma* 'woman', *guwwa* 'force', *surʕa* 'speed', *xuṭba* 'engagement', *guṣṣa* 'story', *ġurfa* 'room', *ʕukka* 'sack made of the skin of a sheep for keeping fat in', *ǧumʕa* 'Friday', *šurṭa* 'police', *guṭʕa* 'piece', *ḏura* 'corn', *ʕumra* 'small pilgrimage to Mecca', *ġurba* 'expatriation, to live in a foreign land', *ṣurra* 'navel', *ḥuṣba* 'measles', *ʕuṭla* 'holiday', *huǧra* 'exodus', *mudde* 'period', *kutle* 'block, mass', *nukte* 'joke', *sukne* 'residence', *ṣulḥa* 'reconciliation', *kuṯra* 'abundance'

Adjectives *murr* 'bitter', *ḥurr* 'free'

3.2.1.10. CuCCa (<CuCCā)

Miscellaneous *yusra* (name), *bukra* 'tomorrow', *ḥumra* (place name), *ʕulya* 'high' (from Standard Arabic), *ʔuxra* 'also'

3.2.1.11. CaCaC

Masculine	*walad* 'boy', *nasab* 'lineage', *ṣafaṭ* 'box, bundle', *ḥağar* 'stone', *ʕadas* 'lentil', *faras* 'horse', *laban* 'yoghurt', *šabaḥ* 'ghost', *ḥaras* 'guard', *maṯal* 'proverb', *ṯaman* 'price', *sabab* 'cause', *karam* 'generosity', *darağ* 'stairs', *gaṣal* 'stalks', *maṭar* 'rain', *ğabal* 'hill', *ṭalab* 'request', *zaman* 'time', *ʕarag* 'arak', *maraḏ̣* 'illness', *ʕalam* 'flag', *kabar* 'old age', *darak* 'police', *maraṯ* 'inheritance', *ṭaraf* 'edge', *ğazar* 'carrot', *ğamal* 'camel', *ḏakar* 'male', *šağar* 'tree', *samak* 'fish', *waṣax* 'dirt', *ʕadad* 'number', *ḥakam* 'judge', *xaṭar* 'danger', *gamar* 'moon', *gabal* 'go forward', *falak* 'orbit', *taʕab* 'fatigue', *ganaṣ* 'hunt', *warag* 'leaf', *bagar* 'cow', *xašab* 'wood', *ḥaṭab* 'firewood', *ġanam* 'sheep', *baṣal* 'onion', *ġalaṭ* 'error', *ṭabag* 'a tray made of straw'
Feminine	*balad* 'land'
Plural	*ʕarab* 'Arabs'
+ *-a*	*tanaka* 'can', *baraka* 'blessing', *ḥaraka* 'motion', *ʕagaba* 'Aqaba', *šabaka* 'net', *šafaga* 'sympathy', *waḥade* 'one', *nasame* 'individual', *šağara* 'tree', *bagara* 'cow', *waraga* 'leaf', *baṣala* 'onion', *ṭabaga* 'plate'
+ *-a* (masculine)	*zalame* 'man'

3.2.1.12. CaCiC

In the dialect under consideration here, etymological CaCiC forms are realised as CaCC, since unstressed medial /i/ undergoes elision: *il-malk* 'the king'. When /i/ is maintained, whether in the masculine *malik* or the feminine *malika* 'queen', it is best considered a borrowing from Standard Arabic. Standard *šaris* [ʃarɪs] 'fierce' also surfaces as [ʃarɪs] in the colloquial, but the underlying form is *šars* with anaptyctic insertion: *šarəs*, yielding the surface form [ʃarɪs].

3.2.1.13. CuCaC

Plural	*ṣuwar* 'images', *duwal* 'states', *rukab* 'knees', *ġuraf* 'rooms', *ḥuṣaṣ* 'shares', *buʔar* 'epicentres' (borrowed from Standard Arabic), *nukat* 'jokes', *guṭaʕ* 'pieces'

3.2.1.14. CuCaCa

Plural	*fugara* 'poor (PL)'

3.2.1.15. CiCaC

Plural	*šigag* 'flats', *giṣaṣ* 'stories', *giṭaʕ* 'pieces'

3.2.1.16. CaCa (< CaCāʔ, CiCāʔ, CvC(v)ʔ)

Masculine	*sama* 'sky', *masa* 'evening', *ġala* 'high prices', *ġada* 'lunch', *ʕaša* 'dinner', *waṭa* 'shoes', *ḏaka* 'intelligence', *ġaṭa* 'cover', *dafa* 'heat', *ʕaza* 'wake (funeral)', *bala* 'misfortune'
CaCā (+ *-a*)	*waṭā* 'land', *ḥayā* 'life', *ʕabā* 'mantle', *ʕaṣā* 'stick' (also *ʕaṣāye* and *ʕáṣa*), *ṣaḷā* 'prayer'

3.2.1.17. CaCi (< $C_1aC_2C_3$ C_3 = /y/, $C_1aC_2īC_3$ C_3 = /ʔ/ or /y/)

Masculine	*nabi* 'prophet', *ḥači* 'talk', *maši* 'walking', *waʕi* 'awareness', *šawi* 'roasting'
Adjectives	*gawi* 'strong', *ṭari* 'tender', *radi* 'bad', *ḏaki* 'intelligent'
CaCy-a	*garye* 'village'
CaCīC-a	*galiyye* 'roasted wheat', *gawiyye* 'strong', *faḏ̣iyye* (name), *hawiyye* 'identity'

3.2.1.18. CiCi

Masculine	*ǧidi* 'kid (baby goat)', *gili* 'alkaline (cleaning agent)'
Plural	*ʕibi* ~ *ʕuḅi* 'gowns'

3.2.1.19. CiCa

Masculine	*šita* 'winter, rain', *ġina* 'singing'

3.2.1.20. CāCaC

Masculine	*ʕālam* 'world', *wāḥad* 'one', *ʕāzar* (name)

3.2.1.21. CāCiC

Masculine	*ṭābig* 'floor, storey', *ǧānib* 'side', *šāriʕ* 'street', *ṣāḥib* 'owner', *rākib* 'passenger', *lāǧiʔ* 'refugee', *ṭālib* 'student', *šāʕir* 'poet', *fāris* 'horse rider', *ḏ̣ābiṭ* 'officer', *ḥādiṯ* 'incident', *nāʔib* 'deputy', *ǧāmiʕ* 'mosque', *ʕāmir* (name), *rāyib* 'yoghurt', *rātib* 'salary', *ḥāǧiz* 'obstacle', *kātib* 'writer'

Adjectives and active participles	*šāyif* ‘seeing’, *lābis* ‘wearing’, *rāyiḥ* ‘going’, *gāʕid* ‘sitting’, *ʕārif* ‘knowing’, *ṭāliʕ* ‘ascending, leaving’, *sākin* ‘dwelling’, *nāšif* ‘dry’, *xāyif* ‘fearing’, *nāzil* ‘going down’, *gādir* ‘able’, *kāmil* ‘complete’, *rāǧiʕ* ‘returning’, *wāsiʕ* ‘wide’, *ʔāxir* ‘last’, *nāʕim* ‘soft’, *ḥāfiḏ̣* ‘keeping’, *kāsir* ‘breaking’, *ḏābiḥ* ‘slaughtering’, *rāḥil* ‘quitting’, *ḥāmil* ‘carrying’, *dāris* ‘studying’, *šāṭir* ‘gifted’, *sāmiʕ* ‘hearing’, *ʕāyiš* ‘living’, *wārid* ‘possible’, *ḥākim* ‘ruling’, *ʕāmil* ‘doing’, *dāyir* ‘turning’, *ḏāyib* ‘melting’, *fātiḥ* ‘opening’, *xābir* ‘knowing’, *sāʔil* ‘asking’, *sātir* ‘protecting’, *ʕāgil* ‘rational’, *gāyim* ‘standing’, *fāyit* ‘entering’, *ṭāyiḥ* ‘descending, going down’, *wāṣil* ‘arriving’, *rāčib* ‘riding’, *gāḏ̣ib* ‘gripping’, *sākit* ‘mute’, *ḥādir* ‘going down’, *nāyim* ‘sleeping’, *xārib* ‘destroyed’, *ḥāḏ̣ir* ‘present’, *māniʕ* ‘preventing’, *xāliṣ* ‘finished’, *yābis* ‘dry’, *māsik* ‘holding’, *nādir* ‘rare’, *ṣāyir* ‘becoming’, *xāṭib* ‘engaged’, *bārid* ‘cold’, *gāṭiʕ* ‘cutting’
C_3= /y/	*rāʕi* ‘owner, shepherd’, *nāwi* ‘intending’, *ʕādi* ‘normal’, *zāki* ‘tasty’, *māši* ‘walking’, *ʕāli* ‘high’, *fāḏ̣i* ‘empty’, *gāsi* ‘hard’, *dāri* ‘knowing’, *tāli* ‘last’, *sāri* ‘waking up early’, *ṣāfi* ‘pure’, *šāri* ‘buying’, *bāgi* ‘rest’, *gāḏ̣i* ‘judge’, *ṣāḥi* ‘awake’, *ġāli* ‘expensive’, *ḥāši* ‘female dancer at wedding ceremonies’
C_3 = /y/ + *-a*	*bādye* ‘steppe’, *zāwye* ‘corner’, *nāḥye* ‘district’

3.2.1.22. CēCaC

Masculine	*bēdar* 'threshing floor'
+ *-a*	*hēzaʕa* 'excited movement, commotion'

3.2.1.23. CaCāC

Masculine	*ḥamām* 'pigeons', *zamān* 'time', *salām* 'peace', *ġazāl* 'antelope', *ḏ̣alām* 'obscurity', *ḏ̣abāb* 'fog', *ḥarām* 'forbidden', *ṭalāg* 'divorce', *gazāz* 'glass', *šamāl* 'north', *tamām* 'good, complete', *balāṭ* 'slab', *xarāb* 'wreck', *naǧāḥ* 'success', *ǧawāz* 'marriage', *ḏ̣amān* 'insurance'
Plural	*banāt* 'girls', *šabāb* 'youth'
+ *-a*	*baṭāṭa* 'potato', *rabāba* 'rebab (stringed musical instrument)', *baṣāṭa* 'simplicity', *ǧamāʕa* 'group', *šaǧāʕa* 'courage', *ḥaḏ̣āra* 'civilisation', *ʕalāqa* 'relation', *ṯaqāfa* 'culture', *maḏ̣āfa* 'reception room', *ṣadāqa* 'friendship', *masāḥa* 'surface', *naḏ̣āra* 'police station, detention centre', *garāba* 'relatives', *karāma* 'dignity', *ṣarāḥa* 'sincerity, frankness', *ʔamāra* 'emirate'

3.2.1.24. CaCāCa (< CaCāCā)

Plural	*garāya* 'villages', *ḥayāya* 'snakes', *ʔawāla* 'first (ones)'
Loan	*sarāya* 'serail'

3.2.1.25. CaCīC

Masculine *ǧamīd* ‘strained and dried buttermilk (a staple in the local cuisine)’, *ḥadīd* ‘iron (metal)’, *ḥalīb* ‘milk’, *baṭīn* ‘prairie’, *wazīr* ‘minister’, *ʔamīr* ‘prince’, *ʕarīs* ‘bridegroom’, *ʔasīr* ‘captive’, *dalīl* ‘proof’, *ṭarīg* ‘way’, *zabīb* ‘raisin’, *ḥadīṯ* ‘speech’, *xamīs* ‘Thursday’, *ṭaḥīn* ‘flour’, *ʔamīn* ‘secretary general’, *raʔīs* ‘president’, *xabīr* ‘expert’, *masīḥ* ‘Christ’, *ʕamīd* ‘dean’, *rabīʕ* ‘spring’, *yamīn* ‘right’, *kafīl* ‘guarantor’, *wakīl* ‘representative’, *xaṭīb* ‘fiancé’, *safīr* ‘ambassador’, *ṣadīg* ‘friend’, *nazīf* ‘bleeding’, *ṭabīb* ‘doctor’, *zaʕīm* ‘leader’, *gaṭīʕ* ‘herd’, *bahīm* ‘beasts of burden’, *farīg* ‘team’, *ṣalīb* ‘crucifix’, *ṭabīx* ‘cooked food’, *xazīn* ‘storing’, *ganīṣ* ‘hunting’, *gaṣīd* ‘poem’, *marīs* ‘rehydrated strained buttermilk (local cuisine)’

Feminine *ṭarīg* ‘road’

Plural *ḥamīr* ‘donkeys’, *ḥarīm* ‘women’, *ʕabīd* ‘slaves’, *latīn* ‘Roman Catholic’

Adjectives *karīm* ‘generous’, *ṣaḥīḥ* ‘correct’, *gadīm* ‘old’, *ʕazīz* ‘dear’, *ṭawīl* ‘long’, *saʕīd* ‘happy’, *waḥīd* ‘unique’, *naḏ̣īf* ‘clean’, *xabīṯ* ‘cunning’, *rahīb* ‘terrific’, *wasīʕ* ‘large’, *ʕarīḏ̣* ‘wide’, *galīl* ‘few, little’, *garīb* ‘close’, *ʕanīd* ‘stubborn’, *ḥabīb* ‘beloved’, *gaṣīr* ‘short’, *fagīr* ‘poor’, *faḏ̣īʕ* ‘marvellous’, *xafīf* ‘light’, *marīḏ̣* ‘sick’, *gadīr* ‘almighty’, *ʔaxīr* ‘last’, *šadīd* ‘strong’, *salīm* ‘fit, hale’, *ġarīb* ‘strange’, *daxīl* ‘foreign, alien’

+ *-a*	*šarīṭa* 'rag, cloth', *xabīṣa* 'grape paste (confectionery)', *šarīʕa* 'the Jordan river', *gabīle* 'tribe', *ʕašīre* 'clan', *ḥaṣīde* 'harvest', *natīğe* 'result', *waḏ̣īfe* 'task', *katībe* 'brigade', *kanīse* 'church', *ġazīre* 'abundant', *ğarīde* 'newspaper', *madīne* 'city', *ğazīre* 'island', *ḥaṣīre* 'mat', *hazīme* 'defeat', *ṭalībe* 'fiancée', *marīse* 'buttermilk sauce', *ḏabīḥa* 'slaughtered animal', *gaṣīde* 'poem', *basīṭa* 'simple', *sarīʕa* 'fast', *gadīme* 'old', *ṭawīle* 'long', *gaṣīre* 'short', *ġarībe* 'strange', *ḥadīṯe* 'modern', *ʔaṣīle* 'authentic', *xaṭībe* 'fiancée', *waḥīde* 'unique', *garībe* 'close'

3.2.1.26. CaCūC

Masculine	*ğanūb* 'south', *ʕarūs* 'bride', *rašūf* 'a type of soup (local cuisine)', *faṭūr* 'breakfast', *ʕağūz* 'old woman'
+ *-a*	*ḥamūle* 'family, clan'

3.2.1.27. CCā

Masculine	*štā* 'rain'
Plural	*ğdā* 'goats' (< *ğidi*), *dlā* 'buckets' (< *dalu*)
Clan name	*gḏ̣ā*

3.2.1.28. CCāC

Masculine	*ʕgāḷ* 'headband', *trāb* 'soil', *ḥmār* 'donkey', *šrāk* 'round flat bread', *gmāš* 'fabric', *nḥās* 'copper', *ḥṣān* 'horse', *lsān* 'tongue', *zgāg* 'alley', *flān* 'someone', *nhār* 'daytime', *ktāb* 'book', *lbās* 'underwear', *ḏrāʕ* 'arm', *slāḥ* 'weapon', *xyār* 'cucumber', *ḥsāb*

	'calculation, account, expense', *ḥzām* 'belt', *šwāl* 'sack, bag', *ḥrāṯ* 'ploughing'
Plural	*blād* 'countries, country', *ʕyāl* 'kids', *xwān* 'brothers', *ṣfāṭ* 'boxes, bundles', *xbār* 'news', *bzāz* 'bosom', *zġār* 'small', *zlām* 'men', *ǧdād* 'new', *frān* 'ovens', *ḥǧār* 'stones', *rǧāl* 'men', *ʕrās* 'weddings', *kbār* 'big', *ǧmāl* 'camels', *frāš* 'mat', *gṣār* 'short', *ṭwāl* 'tall', *bwāb* 'doors', *ṣḥāb* 'friends', *ǧyāb* 'pockets', *ṣwāt* 'voices', *ḏbāʕ* 'hyenas', *mlāḥ* 'good', *klāb* 'dogs', *wlād* 'children', *kṯār* 'numerous', *bʕād* 'far', *ʕḏām* 'bones', *bsās* 'cats', *ǧbāl* 'hills', *ʕmām* 'paternal uncles', *xwāl* 'maternal uncles', *ḥrāš* 'forests', *ǧyāl* 'generations', *ṯmām* 'mouths'
+ *-a*	*syāḥa* 'tourism', *flāḥa* 'farming', *kwāra* 'granary', *gḏāma* 'roasted chickpeas', *mġāra* 'cave', *zyāra* 'visit', *bḏāʕa* 'goods', *gḏāḏa* 'white veil', *nxāḷa* 'bran', *grāye* 'study', *ḥrāṯe* 'ploughing'

3.2.1.29. CCīC

Masculine	*šʕīr* 'barley', *ṭḥīn* 'flour', *kdīš* 'cart horse', *zbīb* 'raisin', *bʕīr* 'camel', *rġīf* 'loaf', *šrīṭ* 'tape', *šbīn* 'godfather'
Adjectives	*mlīḥ* 'good', *bʕīd* 'far', *kbīr* 'big', *ṯgīl* 'heavy', *zġīr* 'small', *rfīʕ* 'thick', *ǧdīd* 'new', *kṯīr* 'numerous', *gṣīr* 'small', *ḏʕīf* 'weak', *nḏīf* 'clean', *rxīṣ* 'cheap'
+ *-a*	*knīse* 'church', *frīke* 'cooked green wheat'

3.2.1.30. CCūC

Masculine	*sbūʕ* 'week'

Plural	*grūš* 'piasters', *krūm* 'vineyards', *ʕyūn* 'eyes', *byūt* 'houses', *ḏ̣yūf* 'hosts', *šyūx* 'sheikhs', *sṭūl* 'buckets', *ḥmūl* 'loads', *ṣḥūn* 'plates', *ḏ̣hūr* 'backs', *gbūr* 'graves', *txūt* 'beds', *dmūʕ* 'tears', *ḏ̣rūf* 'conditions', *flūs* 'money', *sgūf* 'roofs', *ǧnūd* 'soldiers', *rfūf* 'shelves', *ǧyūš* 'armies', *gṣūr* 'traditional summer stone dwellings'

3.2.1.31. CCēC and CCayyiC (Diminutive Pattern)

Our corpus only contains three adjectives with the pattern CCayyiC, only two of which are true diminutives: *glayyil* from *galīl* 'few' and *zġayyir* ~ *ṣġayyir* from *zġīr* 'small'. Diminutive derivations from nouns with the pattern CCēC are equally lexically restricted, with only a handful of nouns, mostly kinship terms and endearment terms. Consequently, it is safe to state that the diminutive derivation is largely non-productive in the dialect.

CCēC (surnames and clans)	*ḥsēn, ʕwēd, šʕēb, ʕbēd, hnēš, ʕwēs, ḥlēm*
CCēC (diminutive)	*wlēd* 'little kid', *glēb* 'little heart', *wlēf* (< *walf* 'beloved'), *xayy* 'little brother' (< *axu*), *bnayy* 'little son' (< *ibn*)
CCēCa	*ġṭēṭa* 'fog', *xmēʕa* 'lentils mixed with bread', *mēme* 'little mum', *xayye* 'little sister', *bnayye* 'little daughter'
CCayyiC (adjectives)	*kwayyis* 'good', *glayyil* 'few', *zġayyir* 'small'

3.2.1.32. CāCūC

Masculine	*šāʕūb* 'garden fork', *čānūn* 'December–January', *bārūd* 'rifle', *tābūt* 'coffin', *qānūn* 'law', *ṣābūn* 'soap', *šākūš* 'hammer', *xārūf* 'sheep'
+ -*a*	*fārūʕa* 'axe', *xāšūga* 'spoon', *ḥākūṛa* 'yard', *ṭāḥūne* 'mill'

3.2.1.33. CēCūC

Masculine	*zētūn* 'olive'

3.2.1.34. CīCāC

Masculine	*mīdān* 'square', *dīwān* 'guest reception room, diwan'
Plural	*ǧīrān* 'neighbours', *fīrān* 'mice', *xīṭān* 'threads', *ḥīṭān* 'walls', *šīšān* 'Chechens'

3.2.1.35. CōCāC

Masculine	*gōšān* ~ *gūšān* 'property deed', *kōbān* 'traitor, liar'

3.2.1.36. CaCCāC

Masculine	*fallāḥ* 'peasant', *saxxān* 'boiler', *faddān* 'ploughing ox or oxen', *rassām* 'painter', *ḥaǧǧār* 'stone mason', *šaġġāl* 'working', *ḥallāg* 'barber', *xayyāṭ* 'tailor', *farrān* 'baker', *naǧǧār* 'carpenter', *kayyāz* 'kerosene seller', *faǧǧār* 'liar', *kaḏḏāb* ~ *čaḏḏāb* 'liar', *laḥḥām* 'butcher', *ṣawwān* 'flint', *xayyāl* 'horseman', *mayyāl* 'following', *dawwār* 'changeable'

+ -*a*	*xammāra* 'bar, tavern', *sayyāra* 'car', *bawwāba* 'gate', *gaššāṭa* 'mop', *sammāʕa* 'earphone', *saḥḥāra* 'a wooden box', *maḥḥāye* 'eraser', *laḥḥāme* 'butcher's shop', *baggāle* 'grocery shop'
+ -*a* (plural)	*xayyāle* 'horsemen'

3.2.1.37. CaCCīC

Masculine	*maṣṣīṣ* 'string (cotton)', *baṭṭīx* 'watermelon', *daggīg* (*əḥǧār*) 'carver', *fallīn* 'cork', *šannīr* 'chukar partridge'
+ -*a*	*baṭṭīxa* 'watermelon'
+ -*a* (plural)	*šaġġīle* 'workers'

3.2.1.38. CaCCūC

Masculine	*faggūs* 'cucamelon, American cucumber', *ballūṭ* 'oak', *kabbūt* 'mantle'
Diminutive	*šaṭṭūr* (< *šāṭir*) 'gifted', *ḥammūde* (< *mḥammad*) (name)

3.2.1.39. CuCCēC

Masculine	*guṣṣēb* 'bamboo'

3.2.1.40. CuCCāC

Masculine	*duxxān* 'smoke', *ʕummād* 'baptism', *rummān* 'pomegranate', *tuffāḥ* 'apple'

Plural	*ṭullāb* 'students', *fuxxār* 'pottery', *ḥukkām* 'leaders', *rukkāb* 'passengers', *ḏubbāṭ* 'officers', *nuwwāb* 'deputies', *ḏullām* 'oppressors', *tuǧǧār* 'traders', *sukkān* 'inhabitants'
+ *-a*	*tukkāne* ~ *dukkāne* 'shop', *guṣṣāde* 'short poem' (apparently diminutive of *gaṣīde*)

3.2.1.41. CiCCīC

Masculine	*xirrīǧ* 'graduate', *širrīb* 'heavy smoker'
+ *-a*	*sikkīne* 'knife'

3.2.1.42. CiCCāC

Masculine	*šibbāk* 'window', *ǧinnāz* 'burial'

3.2.1.43. aCCaC

Adjectives	*awwal* 'first', *aḥsan* 'better', *aḥmar* 'red', *aġlab* 'most', *asraʕ* 'faster', *akbar* 'bigger', *akṯar* 'more', *ashal* 'easier', *ašṭar* 'more gifted', *agdam* 'older', *ašhar* 'more famous', *aṭwal* 'taller', *abkar* 'sooner', *aʕlam* 'wiser', *aṯgal* 'heavier', *aṭlag* 'more agile', *azrag* 'blue', *azġar* 'smaller', *absaṭ* 'simpler', *axḏar* 'green', *aswad* 'black', *aṣfar* 'yellow', *aḥdaṯ* 'more modern'
C_3 = /y/	*aḥla* 'more beautiful', *agwa* 'stronger', *aʕla* 'higher', *aġla* 'more expensive', *azča* 'tastier'

3.2.1.44. aCiCCā

Plural	*aṭibbā* 'doctors', *aṣdigā* 'friends'

3.2.1.45. CaCCiC

Masculine *sayyid* 'sir'

Adjectives *ṭayyib* 'good', *mayyit* 'dead', *sayyiʔ* 'bad', *ǧayyid* 'good'

3.2.1.46. CuCCaC

Masculine *sukkar* 'sugar', *ḥummar* (toponym)

3.2.1.47. CuCCuC

Masculine *ḥummuṣ* 'chickpea'

3.2.1.48. maCCiC

Masculine *mawʕid* 'appointment', *mawsim* 'season', *mawgiʕ* 'place', *manṣib* 'position', *maġrib* 'sunset' (also realised *muġrib*, *miġrib* or *miġrab*)

+ *-a* *manṭiga* 'area', *maškile* 'problem' (also *miškile* and *muškile*)

3.2.1.49. miCCaC ~ maCCaC

Masculine *mansaf* (traditional dish), *maxzan* 'store room', *maḥmaṣ* 'a shop that sells roasted coffee and nuts', *mafrag* (toponym), *matban* 'straw-stack', *madxal* 'entrance', *maṭʕam* 'restaurant', *manǧal* 'sickle', *marǧaʕ* 'source', *markaz* 'centre', *maktab* 'office', *maṭbax* 'kitchen', *magsam* 'telephone exchange', *maṣnaʕ* 'factory', *mākal* 'trough' (< *maʔkal*), *maḥall* 'place, shop'

miCCaC	*minsaf* (traditional dish), *minğal* 'sickle', *milʕab* 'stadium', *miṣnaʕ* 'factory', *migʕad* 'bench', *miṭraḥ* 'place'
C_3 = /y/	*maṭwa* 'mattress storage shelf', *marʕa* 'pasture', *maʕna* 'meaning'
+ -*a*	*magbaṛa* 'cemetery', *maḥkama* 'court', *maʕraka* 'battle', *maṣṭaba* 'stone or concrete seat', *mazraʕa* 'farm', *maṣlaḥa* 'interest', *maʕlaga* 'spoon', *mamlaka* 'kingdom', *makrama* 'grant (fund)', *madrase* 'school', *maktabe* 'library', *maṭḥane* 'mill', *masalle* 'a large needle'
miCCaC + -*a*	*miʕlaga* 'spoon', *migbara* 'graveyard', *miṣṭaba* 'raised terrace', *mizraʕa* 'farm', *miḥkama* 'court', *midraga* 'traditional women's dress', *mimlaka* 'kingdom', *mikrama* 'grant (fund)', *midrase* 'school'

3.2.1.50. maCāC

Masculine	*madār* 'orbit', *mağāl* 'domain', *mačān* 'place', *magām* 'tomb'
+ -*a*	*maḍāfa* 'a traditional reception room', *masāḥa* 'area, surface'

3.2.1.51. miCCāC

Masculine	*mihbāš* 'pestle', *mišwār* 'outing', *mismār* 'nail', *miftāḥ* 'key'
+ -*a*	*misṭāḥ* 'flattening'

3.2.1.52. maCCūC

This pattern is used for passive participles. Some of these are lexicalised:

Masculine	*mas?ūl* 'person in charge', *mašrūʕ* 'project'
+ *-a*	*mağmūʕa* 'group', *maʕlūma* '(a piece of) information'

3.2.1.53. taCCīC

This pattern is the verbal noun of CaCCaC verbs. Verbs whose third consonant is weak form verbal nouns with tiCCāCe.

Masculine	*tanšīf* 'drying', *taksīr* 'breaking', *taḥmīṣ* 'roasting', *tadxīn* 'smoking', *tamyīz* 'distinguishing', *tartīb* 'arranging', *ta?līf* 'composing', *tašʕīl* 'igniting', *tasğīl* 'recording', *taʕlīm* 'educating', *taṣnīʕ* 'fabrication', *tağdīd* 'renewing', *tadrīb* 'training', *taṣrīḥ* 'authorisation', *talbīs* 'clothing', *ta?mīn* 'insurance', *tagdīr* 'estimation', *tafkīr* 'thinking', *tağhīz* 'preparation', *ta?sīs* 'establishment', *taʕrīb* 'arabisation', *taglīd* 'custom'
taCCiC + *-a*	*tadfi?a* 'heating'
tiCCāye	*tirbāye* 'upbringing', *tislāye* 'entertainment', *tingāye* 'selecting'

3.2.1.54. CaCCān

Nouns	*fannān* 'artist'
Adjectives	*malyān* 'full', *zaʕlān* 'angry', *xalgān* 'born', *fahmān* 'a connoisseur', *kabrān* 'aged', *xarbān* 'broken',

	farḥān 'happy', *ʕadmān* 'bereft (of something)', *šabʕān* 'replete, sated'

3.2.1.55. CiCCān

Masculine	*nisyān* 'forgetting'
Plural	*niswān* 'women', *xirsān* 'mutes', *billān* 'thorny burnet', *ṣibyān* 'boys'

3.2.1.56. CuCCān

Masculine	*sulṭān* 'sultan'
Plural	*ʕurbān* 'Bedouins', *ġuzlān* 'gazelles', *furgān* 'teams'

3.2.1.57. Quadriliteral Patterns

3.2.1.57.1. CaCCaC

Masculine	*daftar* 'notebook'
Collective	*ʔarman* 'Armenians', *šarkas* 'Circassians', *ʕaskar* 'soldiers'
+ *-a*	*kahraba* 'electricity', *ṭanǧara* (~ *ṭunǧara*) 'cooking pot', *ʔarmala* 'widow', *nagnaga* 'nibbling', *ḏabḏabe* 'hypocrisy'
Weak roots	*hōdaǧ* 'camel-mounted bride's palanquin', *bēdar* 'threshing floor'

3.2.1.57.2. CiCCiC

Masculine	*filfil* 'pepper', *thillil* 'singing lullabies' (masdar of Form V *thallal*)

3.2.1.57.3. CuCCuC

Masculine *burġul* 'bulgur', *ʕurmuṭ* (name), *fundug* 'hotel', *burṭum* 'lip' (collective, singulative is *burəṭma*, PL *barāṭim*)

3.2.1.57.4. CuCCi

Masculine *kursi* 'chair'

3.2.1.57.5. CaCCāC

Family name *gaʕwār*

3.2.1.58.6. CiCCāC

Masculine *dišdāš* 'kaftan, a long, loose dress', *bistān* 'garden', *libnān* 'Lebanon', *finǧān* 'cup'

3.2.1.57.7. CuCCāC

Masculine *gumbāz* 'traditional men's garment', *muṭrān* 'bishop'

3.2.1.57.8. CaCCīC

Masculine *kafkīr* 'serving-spoon', *barmīl* 'barrel'
\+ *-a* *nargīle* ~ *ʔargīle* 'shisha'

3.2.1.57.9. CaCCūC

Masculine *ṭarbūš* 'fez', *sandūg* 'box', *ġalyūn* 'pipe', *ṭašṭūš* 'serving dish', *ʔaylūl* 'September'

3.2.1.58. Quadriliteral Plurals

3.2.1.58.1. CaCāCiC

Plural *ḥamāyil* 'clans', *madāris* 'schools', *waḏāyif* 'job, positions', *ʕašāyir* 'clans', *gabāyil* 'tribes', *salālim* (toponym), *malābis* 'garments', *sakāyir* 'cigarettes', *mazāriʕ* 'farms', *gaṭāyif* 'kataif', *šawārib* 'moustache', *manāsif* (plural of *mansaf*, a traditional dish), *maṣāniʕ* 'factories', *šawāriʕ* 'streets', *ṭawābig* 'floors', *manāṭig* 'areas', *maxāzin* 'shops', *maṭāḥin* 'mills', *gaṣāyid* 'poems', *mağālis* 'meeting places', *ṭanāğir* 'cooking pots', *marāğiʕ* 'references, sources', *maṣādir* 'sources', *maḥāğir* 'stone quarries', *barāmiğ* 'programmes', *xarāyiṭ* 'maps', *maʕālig* 'spoons', *ğamārik* 'customs authority', *maḥākim* 'courts', *sarāyir* 'beds', *maʕārif* 'state schools', *ṭawābiʕ* 'stamps', *šarāyiṭ* 'rags, cloths', *magāʕid* 'seats', *waṣāyif* 'qualities', *badāyil* 'exchange (of brides)',[1] *malāyik* 'angels', *ʕağāyiz* 'old women', *mašākil* 'problems', *habāyil* 'idiots', *čanāyin* 'daughters-in-law', *garāyib* 'relatives', *bayādir* 'threshing floor', *kanāyis* 'churches', *marāḥil* 'levels', *fawāke* 'fruits', *marākiz* 'centres', *kawākib* 'stars', *bahāyim* 'beasts of burden', *ganābil* 'grenades', *ʕarāyis* 'brides', *ḏabāyiḥ* 'slaughtered animals', *ganāṭir* 'arches'

[1] This term refers to a local tradition whereby a man marries another man's sister and in return gives his sister in marriage to that man.

+ *-a*	*dakātre* 'doctors', *maṣārwa* 'Egyptians'
Clans	*ʕawāmle, raḥāḥle, ḥamāyde, xaḷāyle, ʕamāyre, ḥadāyde, dabābse, hawāyše, hazāyme, ramāmne, ġasāsne, ḥanāḥne, ṣalāyṭa, ḏarāyba, naʕānʕa, darādka*
CawāCiCCe	*tawādirse* (plural of the family name *tādrus*), *nawābilse* (plural of *nābilsi* 'from the town of Nablus')

3.2.1.58.2. CaCāCīC

Plural	*tagālīd* 'customs', *ṣarāṣīr* 'cockroaches', *ṭawāḥīn* 'mills', *sawālīf* 'stories', *ṭašāṭīš* 'serving dishes', *takākīn* ~ *dakākīn* 'shops', *basātīn* 'gardens', *ṭarābīš* 'fezzes', *mawāʕīd* 'appointments', *zaġārīd* 'ululations', *faṣāṭīn* 'dress', *tahālīl* 'cheers', *manāšīr* 'flyers', *sakākīn* 'knives', *salāṭīn* 'sultans', *dawāwīr* 'roundabouts', *mawālīd* 'those who were born in (date), generation', *ʕabābīd* 'from the ʕAbbādi tribe', *bawārīd* 'rifles', *malāyīn* 'millions'
Clan	*maḏāʕīn* (PL of *miḏʕān*)

3.2.1.58.3. CaCāCi

Plural	*marāʕi* 'pastures', *ʔahāli* 'families, local', *fanādi* 'carcasses', *maṭāwi* 'mattress storage shelves', *ġanāni* 'songs', *maḥāči* 'style of speaking', *ʔarāḏi* 'lands', *ʔasāmi* 'names', *maṣāri* 'money', *ṭawāri* 'emergencies', *balāwi* 'great quantities', *mawāši* 'livestock', *magāṯi* 'cucurbit fields'

3.2.2. Concatenative Morphology

3.2.2.1. Gender

All varieties of Arabic have two grammatical genders: masculine and feminine. Masculine nouns are usually zero-marked, whereas feminine nouns are marked with the feminine suffix *-a*: *manṭig-a* (F) 'area', *rumḥ-Ø* (M) 'spear'. There is some variation across Arabic dialects with respect to the number of zero-marked feminine nouns (Procházka 2003). In the dialect under discussion here, some zero-marked feminine nouns are: *riǧəl* ~ *iǧər* 'leg', *ʕēn* 'eye, spring', *rūḥ* 'spirit', *arḏ̣* 'earth', *m̩ayy* 'water', *dinya* 'world', *trāb* 'soil', *balad* 'country', *dār* 'house', *ṭarīg* 'path', *ḥarb* 'war', *šams* 'sun'. Although *balad* is feminine in the traditional dialect, some speakers oscillate between feminine and masculine, sometimes in the same utterance, as shown in (6). The word *balad* triggers feminine agreement on the demonstrative *hāye* and the third-person feminine singular pronoun *hiyye*, but masculine agreement on the adjective *mistarīḥ* and the third-person masculine bound pronoun *-hū*. The word *balad* is masculine in most Northern Levantine dialects, so this gender assignment indeterminacy is in all likelihood contact-induced.

(6) *il-balad hāye hiyye aḥsan balad*
DEF-country DEM.F 3FS best country
mistarīḥ fī-hū-š mašākil
relaxed in-3SG-NEG problems
'This country is the best, it's relaxed. There is no problem in it'

With the exception of the word *zalame* 'man', nouns marked with the feminine suffix *-a* are feminine: *ḥurm-a* 'woman', *mimlak-a* 'kingdom', *ḥaṣīr-e* 'mat'.

3.2.2.1.1. The Phonetics of *-a*

As hinted by the examples above, the morpheme *-a* has two main realisations: *-e* (I.P.A. [ɛ]) and *-a* (I.P.A. [a], or [ɑ] if adjacent to a velarised segment). With the exception of rural Palestinian dialects, which never raise *-a*, raising of *-a* is a salient feature of most Levantine dialects. Consequently, the dialects of central and northern Jordan seem to agree with the general Levantine pattern. A closer look, however, reveals that raising of *-a* differs both phonetically and distributionally. Phonetically, it raises to [ɛ], rather than [e] as in most Levantine dialects; and the distribution of the two allophones is different. In the rest of the Levant, raising appears everywhere except in the vicinity of post-velar and velarised consonants. In central and northern Jordan, the distribution is more complex. This topic has already been discussed in Al-Wer (2002), where the main argument is that, in Palestinian Arabic, the default value is [e], and lowering occurs in guttural (post-velar) and emphatic environments, whereas in Central and Northern Jordan (Balga and Ḥōrān), the default value is [a], and raising occurs after coronals.

Table 16: Phonetics of -*a*

Place	Environment	-*e*	-*a*
Coronals	/y/	*šibriyye* 'dagger'	
		wgiyye 'uqiyya'	
	/ǧ/	*lahǧe* 'dialect'	
		ḥāǧe 'need'	
	/č/	*birče* 'pond'	
		frīče 'cooked green wheat'	
	/š/	*ṭōše* 'quarrel'	
		ʕīše 'life'	
	/n/	*tukkāne* 'shop'	
		sane 'year'	
	/ḏ/	*mʔāxaḏe* 'offence'	
		nabḏe 'overview'	
	/ṯ/	*ṯalaṯe* 'three'	
		ḥadīṯe 'new'	
	/s/	*midrase* 'school'	
		knīse 'church'	
	/z/	*ǧīze* 'union'	
		barīze 'five-piaster coin'	
	/t/	*makatte* 'ashtray'	
		sitte 'six'	
	/d/	*waḥade* 'one (F)'	
		mudde 'period'	
Labials	/m/	*ḥamāme* 'pigeon'	*ḥukūma* 'government'
		xēme 'tent'	*miḥkama* 'court'
		laḥme 'meat'	*raḥma* 'mercy'
	/b/	*ǧēbe* 'pocket'	*bawwāba* 'gate'
		girbe 'waterskin'	*ġurba* 'expatriation'
	/f/	*xilfe* 'progeny'	*ġurfa* 'room'
		laffe 'tour'	*miġrāfa* 'ladle'
Liquids	/l/	*ḥamūle* 'family'	*baṣaḷa* 'onion'
		gabīle 'tribe'	*ʕuṭḷa* 'holyday'
	/r/	*ṣāyre* 'becoming'	*šaǧaṛa* 'tree'
		ǧīre 'neighbourhood'	*bagaṛa* 'cow'

Velarised	/ṭ/	*ġalṭa* 'error'
		xārṭa 'map'
	/ṣ/	*xabīṣa* 'grape paste'
		guṣṣa 'story'
	/ḏ̣/	*laḥḏ̣a* 'instant'
		mḥāfḏ̣a 'conservative'
Velars	/k/	*baraka* 'blessing'
		mimlaka 'kingdom'
	/g/	*šafaga* 'pity'
		maraga 'sauce'
Gutturals	/ḥ/	*ḏabīḥa* 'slaughtered animal'
		ṣulḥa 'reconciliation'
	/ʕ/	*sāʕa* 'hour'
		fārūʕa 'axe'
	/h/	*ǧiha* 'side'
		mōǧha 'next (F)'
	/w/	*sarwa* 'early morning'
		gahwa 'coffee'

It appears from the table presented above that raising occurs after the coronals /y/, /ǧ/, č/, /š/, /n/, /ḏ/, /ṯ/, /s/, /z/, /d/ and /t/. After labials, there is a kind of vowel harmony whereby proximity of a front vowel will trigger raising (*xēme*) and a back vowel will inhibit raising *(ḥukūma)*. As far as [a] is concerned, raising will depend on the adjacent allophone: back [a] inhibits raising (*miḥkama*) and front [a] triggers it (*ḥamāme*). An interesting pair is found between *laḥme* 'meat' and *raḥma* 'mercy', which clearly shows the backing effect /a/ has on /r/ in *raḥma*. This feature propagates rightward, crosses /ḥ/ and inhibits raising after /m/.

After liquids, raising occurs with the non-velarised reflex of /r/ and /l/, whereas emphatic /r/ and /l/ will inhibit raising.

After velars, gutturals and emphatics, raising is inhibited. Note also that raising is inhibited after /w/. This is not surprising given the velar articulation of /w/.

Compared to other Levantine varieties, the dialects of central and northern Jordan differ in raising after labials, /k/, /l/ and /w/. Compare in this respect the realisations of the following items in Amman and Salt:

Table 17: Raising differences in Amman and Salt

Salt	Amman	
ḥukūma	*ḥukūme*	'government'
bawwāba	*bawwābe*	'gate'
ġurfa	*ġurfe*	'room'
mimlaka	*mamlake*	'kingdom'
gahwa	*ʔahwe* ~ *gahwe*	'coffee'

3.2.2.1.2. The Allomorphs of *-a*

-it

The main allomorph of *-a* is *-it* in the construct state. The construct form refers to the shape taken by a noun when modified by another noun. In Arabic, it marks the head of NPs when modified by a noun, a possessive suffix or the dual marker *-ēn*:

nabʕ-a 'spring'	*nabʕ-it ṃayye* 'water spring'
ǧidd-e 'grandmother'	*ǧidd-it-i* 'my grandmother'
šagg-a 'apartment'	*šagg-t-ēn* 'two apartments'

The vowel /i/ of *-it* is elided in unstressed open syllables (*šagg-t-ēn*), except between a geminate and a consonant, if they are homorganic (*ǧidditi*).

-t

Words ending in *-a* (< **-ā*) or the feminine ending are realised *-ā* in Salt. In the construct state, the feminine morpheme surfaces as *-t:*

ḥayā 'life'	*ḥayā-t-na* 'our life'
ṣalā 'prayer'	*ṣalā-t iğ-ğumʕa* 'Friday prayer'
ʕaṣā 'stick'	*ʕaṣā-t il-gaššāṭa* 'the mop stick'
ʕabā 'overgarment'	*ʕabā-t il-ʕamm* 'the uncle's overgarment'
waṭā 'land'	*waṭā-t ngūḷa* 'Ngūla's land'

-at

In …aCaC-a sequences, the feminine morpheme is realised *-at* in all construct contexts (unstressed medial /a/ undergoes elision). In …aC-a sequences, only vowel-initial suffixes trigger the use of the allomorph *-at*, as shown in Table 18.

Table 18: Allomorph *-at* in the construct state

Vowel-initial suffix	Consonant-initial suffix	Genitive construction
bagr-at-ēn 'two cows' (< *bagar-at-ēn*)	*zalm-at-ku* 'your (PL) man' (< *zalam-at-ku*)	*marg-at ʕadas* 'lentil soup' (< *marag-at ʕadas*)
miḥram-at-i 'my tissue'	*miṣṭab-it-ha* 'her terrace'	*madras-t is-salṭ* 'the school of Salt' (< madras-it is-salṭ)
mar-at-i 'my wife'	(unattested)	*mar-t ibn-i* 'my son's wife'

Other instances of *-at* are construct forms of *luġa* 'language' and *manṭiga* 'area': *luġ-at-o* 'his language', *luġ-at-na* 'our language', *luġ-at is-salṭ* 'the dialect of Salt', *manṭig-at il-karak* 'the area around Kerak', and also one instance in *šōrab-at ʕadas* 'lentil soup'.

-īt

The construct form of words ending in *-iyy-e* is maximally *-iyy-it*, as in *kāziyyit ryāḏ* 'Riyad's petrol station'. In normal speech, however, *iyyit-* is often reduced to *iyt-* and *īt-*:

kāziyye 'petrol station' *kāziyy-it ryāḏ* 'Riyad's petrol station'
diyye 'blood money' *diyt-o* 'blood money owed to him'
maniyye 'destiny, death' *manī-t-o* 'his death'

A peculiarity of the dialects of central and northern Jordan is the use of the allomorph *-īt* of the feminine ending when it is suffixed to active participles augmented with bound object or dative pronouns:

mistagill + -a + -o *mistagill-īt-o* 'she underestimates it'
ǧārr + -a + -ni *ǧārr-īt-ni* 'she has dragged me'
wāgif + -a + ilha *wāgf-īt-lha* 'she does not let her get away with it'
kātib + -a + ilha *kātb-īt-ilha* 'she has written to her'

3.2.2.2. Number

3.2.2.2.1. Plural *-īn*

Nouns rely on non-concatenative morphology for plural marking. Plural marking on nouns by means of the suffix *-īn* is limited to nouns which lexicalised from adjectives and participles, as illustrated below. The use of *-īn* is restricted to masculine referents. As such, it is often described as a masculine plural suffix.

falasṭīni 'Palestinian' *falasṭīniyy-īn* 'Palestinians'
mislim 'Muslim' *misəlm-īn* 'Muslims'

mwaḏḏaf 'employee' *mwaḏḏaf-īn* 'employees'
ṭawwāf ḥrāš 'forest warden' *ṭawwāf-īn ḥrāš* 'forest wardens'

3.2.2.2.2. Plural *-iyye*

The suffix *-a*, also used as a feminine marker and a singulative marker, serves to pluralise some nouns ending in *-i*, which may be adjectives with human reference used as nouns. The combination of *-i* + *-e* yields *-iyye*. The use of *-a* as a plural marker mostly surfaces with collective nouns with human reference:

fḥēṣi 'from Fḥēṣ' PL *fḥēṣiyye*
salṭi 'from Salt' PL *ṣalṭiyye*
masīḥi 'Christian' PL *masīḥiyye*
fidāʔi 'freedom fighter' PL *fidāʔiyye*

Interestingly, the segment *iyye* has been reinterpreted as a plural marker which can attach to other nouns:

xtyār 'old person' PL *xtyāriyye* (~ *xatāyre*)
šufēr 'driver' PL *šufēriyye*
mʕallim 'teacher' PL *mʕallimiyye*

3.2.2.2.3. Plural *-āt*

The morpheme *-āt*, although primarily associated with feminine referents and therefore historically described as feminine plural marker, is much more productive than *-īn*. It marks nouns which lexicalised from adjectives and participles denoting female referents.

baddāwiyye 'Bedouin woman' *baddāwiyyāt* 'Bedouin women'
ṣāḥbe 'female friend' *ṣāhbāt* 'female friends'

Nouns ending in the feminine morpheme *-a* often form their plural with *-āt*:

xāḷa 'maternal aunt' *xāḷāt* 'maternal aunts'
ḥanafiyye 'tap' *ḥanafiyyāt* 'taps'

There are also nouns that are masculine in the singular which are marked *-āt* in the plural:

zgāg 'alley' *zgāgāt* 'alleys'
nhār 'day' *nhārāt* 'days'

Borrowed nouns also pluralise in *-āt*:

šwāl 'sack' (< Turkish *çuval*) *šwālāt* 'sacks'
banṭalōn 'trousers' (< French *pantalon*) *banṭalōnāt* 'trousers'

Many clan names form their plural with *-āt*: *ʕarabiyyāt, xrēsāt, ḥyāṣāt, ḥyārāt, nʕēmāt, xlēfāt, bšārāt, ʕaṭiyyāt, ġnēmāt, ḥwēṭāt, ṣwēṣāt, zēdāt, gṭēšāt*...

Diminutives form their plural with *-āt*: *wlēd* 'little boy', *wlēdāt* 'little boys'.

The suffix *-āt* also often surfaces in the plural of substances to denote 'a certain quatity of X'. Given the number of recorded tokens, these formations are quite productive. It can also denote 'the place where X is cultivated', as in *zētūnāt* 'olive fields' (< *zētūn* 'olive') and *tīnāt* 'fig fields' (< *tīn* 'fig'). Some of these forms are plurals of singulatives (see below), but the singulative is not always attested, as in *arḍ* 'land'. The singulative ***arḍ-a* 'one piece of land' is not attested, but *arḍ-āt* is.

gaməḥ 'wheat' *gamḥāt*
dibəs 'syrup' *dibsāt*
xašab 'wood' *xašabāt*

ǧamīd 'dehydrated milk'	*ǧamīdāt*
xubz 'bread'	*xubzāt*
ṭabīx 'cooked food'	*ṭabīxāt*
zbīb 'raisin'	*zbībāt*
arḏ̣ 'earth'	*arḏ̣āt*
ʕadas 'lentil'	*ʕadasāt*
ḥummuṣ 'chickpea'	*ḥummṣāt*
ʕinəb 'grape'	*ʕinbāt*
šʕīr 'barley'	*šʕīrāt*
ṭḥīn 'flour'	*ṭḥīnāt*

3.2.2.2.4. Dual *-ēn*

Like other Levantine varieties, the dialects of central and northern Jordan have a very productive dual morpheme *-ēn* that suffixes to nouns:

ʕurs 'wedding'	*ʕurs-ēn* 'two weddings'
gidər 'pot'	*gidr-ēn* 'two pots'
ʕanz 'goat'	*ʕanz-ēn* 'two goats'
ġurfa 'room'	*ġurəft-ēn* 'two rooms'
bāṣ 'bus'	*bāṣ-ēn* 'two buses'

The only restrictions that seem to apply are words ending in vowels—often foreign items, such as *kīlo* 'kilogram' (***kīlowēn*)—and generally any noun which lexicalised from an adjective: *fḥēṣi* 'inhabitant of Fḥēṣ' (***fḥēṣiyyēn* 'two inhabitants of Fḥēs'), *garīb* 'close' (***garībēn* 'two relatives'). The use of the dual is also disfavoured in genitive constructions that exhibit a certain degree of lexicalisation, such as *bint ʕamm* 'daughter of paternal uncle, cousin': ***bint-ēn il-ʕamm* 'the two cousins'. In these cases, speakers have to resort to a periphrastic construction involving the numeral *ṯnēn* (M) or *ṯintēn* (F) 'two' according the gender of the referent and the plural form of the noun: *banāt il-ʕamm iṯ-ṯintēn* 'the two cousins' (lit. 'the two daughters of my paternal uncle'). Otherwise, dualisation of the modified noun in a genitive construction is permitted: *ṯilṯ-ēn il-walad* 'the two thirds of the boy', *gidr-ēn ṃayye* 'two pots full of water'.

3.2.2.2.5. Pseudo-dual

The pseudo-dual marker has the same shape as the dual marker, but is called 'pseudo-' because it is actually a plural. It marks paired body parts such as the eyes, ears, legs, hands and shoulders. The dialects of Arabic vary in the number of items that are eligible for pseudo-dual marking. In the dialect discussed here, pseudo-dual marking is permitted only on two items: *riǧl* ~ *iǧr* 'foot, leg' and *īd* 'hand, arm': *iǧr-ēn* ~ *riǧl-ēn* 'feet, legs' and *īd-ēn* ~ *ad-ēn* 'hands'. A striking morphological difference between dual -*ēn* and pseudo-dual -*ēn* is that bound pronouns can suffix to the pseudo-dual, but not to the dual.

Table 19: Pseudo-dual and bound pronouns

1SG	*īdayye ~ adayye*	*riǧlayye ~ iǧrayye*
2MS	*īdēk ~ adēk*	*riǧlēk ~ iǧrēk*
2FS	*īdēč ~ adēč*	*riǧlēč ~ iǧrēč*
3MS	*īdē ~ adē*	*riǧlē ~ iǧrē*
3FS	*īdēha ~ adēha*	*riǧlēha ~ iǧrēha*
1PL	*īdēna ~ adēna*	*riǧlēna ~ iǧrēna*
2MP	*īdēku ~ adēku*	*riǧlēku ~ iǧrēku*
2FP	*īdēčin ~ adēčin*	*riǧlēčin ~ iǧrēčin*
3MP	*īdēhum ~ adēhum*	*riǧlēhum ~ iǧrēhum*
3FP	*īdēhin adēhin*	*riǧlēhin ~ iǧrēhin*

Final /n/ of *-ēn* normally drops: *īd-ē-k* 'your hands'. A token with /n/ was recorded once in the following example (7). The informant was warning about the fact that the little child in the room was about to get his hands trapped. Speakers identify /n/-forms as a feature of children's language or when an adult talks about or to a child.

(7) *ad-ēn-o* *w* *il-bāb!*
hand-PL-3MS and DEF-door
'His hands and the door (take care his hands do not get trapped in the door)!'

Final /d/ in *īd* 'hand' may geminate when a preposition cliticises to the left: *bi-īd-ē-na* 'with our hands' can surface as [baddeːna]. The plural form *īdayyāt* 'hands' surfaces once in the corpus, but in a poetic passage, so its use in normal speech is hard to assess. Other paired body parts that pluralise with the pseudo-dual marker in other dialects pluralise according to another morphological template: *ʕēn* 'eye' PL *ʕyūn* (not ***ʕinēn*), *ʔiḏən* 'ears' PL *ʔaḏān* 'ears' (not ***dinēn*, ***widnēn*...).

The fact that the suffix *-ēn* in *iǧrēn* ~ *riǧlēn* and *adēn* refers to a plural is evidenced by the fact that it is perfectly grammatical to adjoin a numeral that requires the head to be marked for plurality: *xaməs adēn* 'five hands', *xaməs ʔiǧrēn* 'five feet'. Duality is expressed by suffixing the singulative morpheme to the base, followed by the dual marker: *īd-t-ēn* 'two hands', *iǧər-t-ēn* 'two feet'. This also extends to *iḏən-t-ēn* 'two ears' and *ʕēn-t-ēn* 'two eyes'. It should be noted that there is no agreement amongst speakers as far as the grammaticality of these forms is concerned, with some speakers rejecting them in favour of periphrastic constructions of the type *ʕyūn ṯintēn* 'two eyes' (eyes two.F).

3.2.2.2.6. Collective and Singulative

In all Arabic dialects, the morpheme *-a*, mostly associated with feminine marking, is also a singulative morpheme. The collective form lacks any overt marker or is zero-marked. In other words, *a*-less nouns denote a substance, whereas *a*-forms denote units of the substance. Consider the following pairs:

bagar 'cow'	*bagaṛa* 'one cow'
ġalaṭ 'mistake'	*ġalṭa* 'one mistake'
gišər 'peel'	*gišre* 'peel of one piece of fruit, vegetable'
tīn 'fig'	*tīne* 'one fig'
lēl 'night'	*lēle* 'one night'
baṭṭīx 'watermelon'	*baṭṭīxa* 'one watermelon'

Some singulatives pluralise with the feminine plural marker *-āt*: *laḥme* PL *laḥmāt* 'pieces of meat'; but not all, as ***lēlāt* 'nights' does not exist and only *layāli* is attested.

3.2.2.3. Derivational Morphology

3.2.2.3.1. *-iyye*

The morpheme *-iyye* surfaces in a handful of nouns, such as *šatawiyye* 'winter', *ṣēfiyye* 'summer', *ǧambiyye* 'mat', *tamṯīliyye* 'serial', *šibriyye* 'dagger', *šbūbiyye* 'youth', *miškaliyye* 'problem'. This suffix also surfaces in the word *mirbaʕāniyye*, from the root *r-b-ʕ* 'four', which refers to the forty coldest days of the winter. The formative *iyye* is not a productive derivational device normally used to expand the lexicon.

3.2.2.3.2. *-iyyāt*

The suffix *-iyyāt* attaches to nouns that refer to periods of the day to denote 'sometime during X'. The recorded tokens are listed below:

ṣubəḥ 'morning'	*ṣubḥiyyāt*
ḍuhər 'midday'	*ḍuhriyyāt*
miġrib 'sunset'	*miġərbiyyāt*
masa 'evening'	*maswiyyāt*

3.2.2.3.3. *-ği*

The suffix *-ği*, or other phonetic variants, is commonly used in all the dialects spoken in areas that at some point in their history were under Ottoman rule. Its productivity varies greatly across dialects. In Jordan, a handful of items containing this suffix were recorded. It appears that its productivity is rather limited. It mostly denotes 'someone who does, makes or practices X regularly':

kahraba 'electricity'	*kahrabği* 'electrician'
niswān 'woman'	*niswanği* 'womaniser'
maṣlaḥa 'interest'	*maṣlaḥği* 'someone caring only about his own interest'
sukur 'intoxication'	*sukarği* 'drunkard'
dukkān 'shop'	*dukkanği* 'shopkeeper'
muškile 'problem'	*maškalği* 'troublemaker'
kundara 'shoes'	*kundarği* 'shoemaker'

ḥilu 'sweet'	*ḥalawanǧi* 'pastry chef'
gahwa 'coffee'	*gahwaǧi* 'coffee maker'
xuḏ̣ra 'vegetable'	*xuḏ̣arǧi* 'vegetable seller'
muxayyam '(refugee) camp'	*maxyamǧi* 'refugee camp dweller'

Formally, the syllable to which the suffix *-ǧi* attaches has to be CaC. If the syllable is already of the type CVC, the vowel is simply changed to /a/: (*nis.wān* → *nis.wan, su.kur* → *su.kar*). If the base ends in CVCV, it undergoes reduction to CaC (*maṣlaḥa* → *maṣlaḥ, kahraba* → *kahrab*). An interesting token that also undergoes degemination is *maxyamǧi* '(Palestinian) refugee camp dweller' from *muxayyam* 'refugee camp'. Another option is to add the formative /n/, as in *ḥilu* → *ḥalawan*. This latter option is also found in the word *šawarmanǧi* 'shawarma seller', but this item, known elsewhere in the Levant, does not seem to have much currency in Jordan. An exception is the word *gahwaǧi* 'coffee maker, one who serves coffee' and not ***gahwanǧi*. For a detailed study of the forms and functions of this suffix *-či* across dialects, see Procházka-Eisl (2018).

3.2.2.4. Intrusive *t-*

Like other Levantine dialects, Ḥōrāni and Balgawi Arabic insert what appears to be an intrusive *t-* between numerals from three to ten and a limited set of nouns. The following list was retrieved:

Sg	Pl	
šahər	*t-ušhur*	'month'
yōm	*t-iyyām*	'day'
rġīf	*t-iriġfe*	'loaf of bread'
alf	*t-ālāf*	'thousand'

nafs	*t-unfus*	'spirit'
nahər	*t-unhur*	'river'
rubəʕ	*t-irbāʕ*	'quarter'
lḥāf	*t-uluḥfe*	'duvet'

Descriptively, two solutions are available to account for this intrusive *t-*, depending on which category bears allomorphy: the numeral or the modified noun. Diachronically, it is clear that the intrusive *t-* is reminiscent of the construct allomorph of the suffix *-a* on the numeral: *xaməs t-ušhur* < **xams-at ʔašhur* 'five months'. Synchronically, however, it seems more economical to report the allomorphy on the modified noun and avoid positing a separate paradigm selected by a small set of nouns.

3.3. Adjectives

3.3.1. Non-concatenative Morphology

3.3.1.1. CaCC

Singular *ǧadd* 'serious', *ṣaḥḥ* 'correct', *sahl* 'easy', *faxm* 'superb'

3.3.1.2. CiCC

Singular *bišʕ* 'ugly', *xišn* 'rough', *ḥilw* 'sweet'

3.3.1.3. CuCC

Singular *murr* 'bitter', *ḥurr* 'free'

Plural *ḥumur* 'red', *sumur* 'dark', *xuḏur* 'green', *zurug* 'blue', *šugur* 'blond'

3.3.1.4. CaCiC

Singular *šaris* 'fierce'

3.3.1.5. CuCaCa

Plural *fugara* 'poor'

3.3.1.6. CaCi

Adjectives *gawi* 'strong', *ṭari* 'tender', *radi* 'bad', *ḏaki* 'intelligent'

3.3.1.7. CāCiC

The template is very productive and forms active participles from basic verb stems; see above for a list of tokens.

3.3.1.8. CaCīC

Singular *rawīm* 'thick', *karīm* 'generous', *ṣaḥīḥ* 'correct', *gadīm* 'old', *ʕazīz* 'dear', *ṭawīl* 'long', *saʕīd* 'happy', *waḥīd* 'unique', *naḍ̣īf* 'clean', *xabīṯ* 'cunning', *rahīb* 'terrific', *wasīʕ* 'large', *ʕarīḍ̣* 'large', *galīl* 'little', *garīb* 'close', *ʕanīd* 'stubborn', *ḥabīb* 'beloved', *gaṣīr* 'short', *fagīr* 'poor', *faḍ̣īʕ* 'marvellous', *xafīf* 'light', *marīḍ̣* 'sick', *gadīr* 'powerful', *ʔaxīr* 'last', *šadīd* 'intense', *salīm* 'well', *ġarīb* 'strange', *daxīl* 'foreign'

3.3.1.9. CCīC

Singular *mlīḥ* 'good', *bʕīd* 'far', *kbīr* 'big', *ṯgīl* 'heavy', *zġīr* 'small', *rfīʕ* 'thick', *ǧdīd* 'new', *kṯīr* 'numerous', *gṣīr* 'small', *ḍ̣ʕīf* 'weak', *nḍ̣īf* 'clean', *rxīṣ* 'cheap'

3.3.1.10. CCayyiC

Singular	*kwayyis* 'good', *glayyil* 'few', *zġayyir* 'small'

3.3.1.11. aCCaC

Singular elative, colours and disabilities	*awwal* 'first', *aḥsan* 'better', *aḥmar* 'red', *aġlab* 'most', *asraʕ* 'faster', *akbar* 'bigger', *akṯar* 'more', *ashal* 'easier', *ašṭar* 'cleverer', *agdam* 'older', *ašhar* 'more famous', *aṭwal* 'taller', *abkar* 'earlier', *aʕlam* 'wiser', *aṯgal* 'heavier', *aṭlag* 'more agile', *azrag* 'blue', *azġar* 'smaller', *absaṭ* 'simpler', *axḍar* 'green', *aswad* 'black', *aṣfar* 'yellow', *aḥdaṯ* 'more modern', *aʕraǧ* 'limping', *axras* 'mute', *aṭraš* 'deaf'
C_3 = /y/	*aḥla* 'more beautiful', *agwa* 'stronger', *aʕla* 'higher', *aġla* 'more expensive', *azča* 'tastier', *aʕma* 'blind'

3.3.1.12. CaCCiC (< CaCīC when C_2 = /y/)

Singular	*ṭayyib* 'good', *mayyit* 'dead', *sayyiʔ* 'bad', *ǧayyid* 'good'

3.3.1.13. CaCCān

Singular	*malyān* 'full', *zaʕlān* 'mad', *xalgān* 'born', *fahmān* 'connoisseur', *kabrān* 'old', *xarbān* 'broken', *farḥān* 'happy', *ʕadmān* 'bereft (of something)', *šabʕān* 'replete, sated'

3.3.1.14. CiCCān ~ CuCCān

Plural	*xirsān* 'mutes', *ṭuršān* 'deaf people'

3.3.2. Concatenative Morphology

The number of derivational devices based on concatenation is limited. Only two seems to have some productivity: *-i* and *-āni*.

3.3.2.1. *-i*

This suffix is extremely common in Arabic and is used to form adjectives from nouns. When the feminine suffix *-a* attaches to *-i*, the allomorph of *-a* is *-yye*.

arḍ 'ground'	*arḍ-i*	*arḍ-i-yye*
masīḥ 'Christian'	*masīḥ-i*	*masīḥ-i-yye*
tiǧāra 'trade'	*tiǧār-i*	*tiǧār-i-yye*

3.3.2.2. *-āni*

The suffix *-āni* forms adjectives mostly from nouns denoting spatial relations, but also colours:

awwal 'beginning'	*awwalāni* 'first'
āxir 'end'	*āxrāni* 'last'
barra 'outside'	*barrāni* 'outsider'
ǧuwwa 'inside'	*ǧuwwāni* 'insider'
fōg 'above'	*fōgāni* 'upper'
taḥt 'below'	*taḥtāni* 'lower'
wasaṭ 'middle'	*wasṭāni* 'middle'
ṭaraf 'side'	*ṭarfāni* 'lateral'
asmar 'brown'	*(a)smarāni* 'dark-skinned'
abyaḍ 'white'	*(a)biyaḍāni* 'fair-skinned'
ġōr 'Jordan Valley'	*ġōrāni* 'from the Jordan Valley, black man'

3.4. Verbs

3.4.1. Inflectional Paradigms

Most varieties of Arabic have two main inflectional paradigms reflecting mostly aspectual distinctions. Various labels have been in use in the scholarly literature, such as perfect/imperfect, past/non-past and perfective/imperfective. The pair perfect/imperfect is rather infelicitous, because it already has an accepted usage in general linguistics that does not correspond to the Arabic linguistic facts. The perfect typically "indicates the continuing present relevance of a past action" (Comrie 1976, 52), whereas the imperfect is usually understood as a combination of imperfective aspect and past reference. The distinction past/non-past may sound less inopportune but, at least in the present dialect, one of the core functions of the 'non-past' is the imperfect, that is, a subtype of events located prior to the time of reference. The labels imperfective/perfective are more appropriate because they remain neutral as far as tense is concerned. There is one imperfective stem and one perfective stem, both of which inflect for person, number and gender. There is also an imperative stem, largely derived from the imperfective. As far as non-finite forms of the verb are concerned, there is one active participle and one passive participle, which inflect for number and gender. There are ten derivational templates for three-consonant roots and two derivational templates for four-consonant roots. Weak roots have at least one semi-consonant (/w/ or /y/) as one of the root consonants.

3.4.1.1. Imperfective

In the imperfective, the verbal word contains a maximum of seven morphological slots, as shown in Table 20. The first slot Neg_1 is the disjoint negation prefix *a-*. The indicative slot is filled with the indicative mood prefix *b-* or zero. The prefix slot is filled with the person indexes. The stem is that of the imperfective, which varies according the derivational template. The suffix slot is filled by number and gender indexes. The pronoun slot is filled by either the object bound pronouns or dative bound pronouns. The last slot is the negation suffix *-š*. It marks the right boundary of the verbal word.

Table 20: Morphological layout of the imperfective

Neg_1	Indicative	Prefix	Stem	Suffix	Pronoun	Neg_2	Surface
a	*b*	*i*	*ǧīb*		*hin*	*š*	[abǧi:bɪnnɪʃ] 'he doesn't bring them'
	b	*i*	*ḥuṭṭ*	*u*	*lha*	*š*	[bɪħʊtˤtˤʊ:lha:ʃ] 'they don't put for her'
		yi	*ʕmal*	*u*	*lo*		[yɪʕmalu:lo] 'they used to do for him'

As noted above, the imperfective inflects for person, number and gender. The values are given below:

Table 21: Inflection of the imperfective

	Singular			Plural		
	Prefix	Stem	Suffix	Prefix	Stem	Suffix
1	*a-*	...	Ø	*n-*	...	Ø
2M	*t-*	...	Ø	*t-*	...	*-u*
2F	*t-*	...	*-i*	*t-*	...	*-in*
3M	*t-*	...	Ø	*y-*	...	*-u*
3F	*y-*	...	Ø	*y-*	...	*-in*

3.4.1.2. Perfective

The perfective stem consists of a maximum of four morphological slots, as shown in Table 22. The first slot Neg_1 is not part of the phonological word, because it behaves either as a free morpheme when used alone, or as a clitic when used in combination with Neg_2 *-š*. The stem varies according to the derivational template. Suffixes combine the three inflectional categories: gender, number and person. The Neg_2 slot is filled with zero or *-š*. In the perfective, the marker *-š* cannot appear alone and the first slot has to be filled with *mā*. The descriptive problem is that they do not have the same status: *-š* is affixal and *mā* is either a clitic or a free morpheme (§4.5.1.3).

Table 22: Morphological layout of the perfective

Neg_1	Stem	Suffix	Pronoun	Neg_2	Surface
	waddē	*t*	*lo*		[wadde:tlo] 'I brought for him'
mā	*ḥabb*	*at*	*hū*	*š*	[ma ħabbathu:ʃ] 'She didn't like him'

The inflectional values of the perfective are given below:

Table 23: Inflection of the perfective

	Singular		Plural	
	Stem	Suffix	Stem	Suffix
1	...	*-t*	...	*-na*
2M	...	*-t*	...	*-tu*
2F	...	*-ti*	...	*-tin*
3M	...	Ø	...	*-u*
3F	...	*-at*	...	*-in*

3.4.1.3. Imperative

The morphological layout of the imperative is given in Table 24. The imperative is used for positive commands. Negative commands require the subjunctive.

Table 24: Morphological layout of the imperative

Stem	Suffix	Pronoun	Surface
ḥaḏḏir	*u*	*li*	[ħaðˤðˤruːlɪ] 'prepare for me'
anṭi		*ni*	[antˤiːnɪ] 'give me'

The imperative inflects for gender and number only. The values are the following:

Table 25: Inflection of the imperative

	Singular		Plural	
	Stem	Suffix	Stem	Suffix
2M	...	Ø	...	*-u*
2F	...	*-i*	...	*-in*

3.4.2. Three-consonant Roots

As noted above, there are ten derivational templates for three-consonant roots. These templates are traditionally called 'forms' or 'measures' and are assigned a number:

Table 26: Derivational templates for three-consonant roots

	Perfective	Imperfective
I	CvCvC	CCvC
II	CaCCaC	CaCCiC
III	CāCaC	CāCiC
IV	aCCaC	CCiC
V	tCaCCaC	tCaCCaC
VI	tCāCaC	tCāCaC
VII	nCaCaC	nCaCiC
VIII	CtaCaC	CtaCiC
IX	$C_1C_2aC_3C_3$	$C_1C_2aC_3C_3$
X	staCCaC	staCCiC

3.4.2.1. Form I CvCvC

3.4.2.1.1. Strong Roots

There are two perfective stems: CaCaC and CiCiC; and three imperfective stems: CCaC, CCiC and CCuC. For CaCaC stems, the imperfective can be CCaC, CCiC or CCuC. For CiCiC, only CCaC and CCiC are attested. Consequently, the vowel distribution is loosely predictable. The following combinations are attested:

CaCaC–CCaC: *ḥaṣal–yiḥṣal* 'happen', *gaṭaʕ–yigṭaʕ* 'cut', *ṭalaʕ–yiṭlaʕ* 'go out', *raḥal–yirḥal* 'move out', *ḏ̣ahar–yiḏ̣har* 'appear', *saḥab–yisḥab* 'withdraw', *fataḥ–yiftaḥ* 'open', *ḏabaḥ–yiḏbaḥ* 'slaughter', *laḥag–yilḥag* 'follow', *gaḏ̣ab–yigḏ̣ab* ~ *yigḏ̣ib* 'grasp', *dafaʕ–yidfaʕ* 'pay', *nağaḥ–yinğaḥ* 'succeed', *raḥam–yirḥam* 'have mercy', *fazaʕ–yifzaʕ* 'support', *rağaʕ–yirğaʕ* 'return'

CaCaC–CCuC: *marag–yumrug* 'pass by', *gaʕad–yugʕud* 'stay', *xaṭab–yuxṭub* 'engage', *sakat–yuskut* 'quiet', *sakan–yuskun* 'dwell', *ṭalab–yuṭlub* 'ask', *ḍarab–yuḍrub* 'hit', *tarak–yutruk* 'leave', *ḥaṣad–yuḥṣud* 'harvest', *ḥakam–yuḥkum* 'judge', *nagal–yungul* 'move'

CaCaC–CCiC: *ʕazam–yiʕzim* 'invite', *kasar–yiksir* 'break', *ḥalaf–yiḥlif* 'swear', *katal–yiktil* 'kill, beat', *ḥağaz–yiḥğiz* 'book', *balas–yiblis* 'steal', *xadam–yixdim* 'serve', *halak–yihlik* 'destroy'

CiCiC–CCaC: *kibir–yikbar* 'grow up', *ṭiliʕ–yiṭlaʕ* 'get out', *ziʕil–yizʕal* 'be upset', *fihim–yifham* 'understand', *ričib–yirčab* 'ride', *simiʕ–yismaʕ* 'hear', *gibil–yigbal* 'accept', *gidir–yigdar* 'be able', *niğiḥ–yinğaḥ* 'succeed', *libis–yilbas* 'wear', *riğiʕ–yirğaʕ* 'return', *liḥig–yilḥag* 'follow', *širib–yišrab* 'drink', *ṯigil–yiṯgal* 'be heavy', *fišil–yifšal* 'fail', *kiṯir–yikṯar* 'multiply', *xilig–yixlag* 'be born', *hilik–yihlak* 'be exhausted'

CiCiC–CCiC: *nizil–yinzil* 'descend', *ʕirif–yiʕrif* 'know', *ḥibil–yiḥbil* 'be pregnant'

Remnants of apophonic passive include the following pairs: *xalag* 'he created' vs *xilig* 'he was born' and *halak* 'he exhausted' vs *hilik* 'he was exhausted'. Vowel alternation can also differentiate homophonous roots: *gibil* 'accept' vs *gabal* 'go forward'. Variation was recorded in the following items in the imperfective: *yiktib* ~ *yiktub* 'he writes', *yigḍib* ~ *yigḍab* 'he grasps', *yiʕrif* ~ *yiʕraf* 'he knows'. In the perfective, the following variations were recorded: *ṭalaʕ* ~ *ṭiliʕ* 'he went out', *rağaʕ* ~ *riğiʕ* 'he came back', *laḥag* ~ *liḥig* 'he followed', *nağaḥ* ~ *niğiḥ* 'he succeeded'.

The verbs *ḏabaḥ* 'he slaughtered' and *ričib* 'he rode' inflect as follows in the perfective:

Table 27: Perfective of *ḏabaḥ–yiḏbaḥ* 'slaughter'

	Singular	Plural
1	*ḏabaḥt*	*ḏabaḥna*
2M	*ḏabaḥt*	*ḏabaḥtu*
2F	*ḏabaḥti*	*ḏabaḥtin*
3M	*ḏabaḥ*	*ḏabaḥu*
3F	*ḏabḥat*	*ḏabaḥin*

Table 28: Perfective of *ričib–yirčab* 'ride'

	Singular	Plural
1	*rčibt*	*rčibna*
2M	*rčibt*	*rčibtu*
2F	*rčibti*	*rčibtin*
3M	*ričib*	*ričbu*
3F	*ričbat*	*ričbin*

Note the elision of /a/ in *ḏabḥat,* as explained above for unstressed medial /a/ in CaCaCaC sequences. The stem alternations *rčib-* and *ričb-* are caused by the elision of /i/ in unstressed open syllables: **ričíbt* → *rčíbt* and **ríčibin* → *ríčbin.*

In the imperfective, the following paradigms were recorded for *yirčab* 'he rides', *yinzil* 'he goes down' and *yumrug* 'he passes':

Table 29: Imperfective of *ričib–yirčab* 'ride'

	b-imperfective		Bare imperfective	
	Singular	Plural	Singular	Plural
1	*barčab*	*mnirčab*	*arčab*	*nirčab*
2M	*btirčab*	*btirčabu*	*tirčab*	*tirčabu*
2F	*btirčabi*	*btirčabin*	*tirčabi*	*tirčabin*
3M	*birčab*	*birčabu*	*yirčab*	*yirčabu*
3F	*btirčab*	*birčabin*	*tirčab*	*yirčabin*

Table 30: Imperfective of *nizil–yinzil* 'go down'

	b-imperfective		Bare imperfective	
	Singular	Plural	Singular	Plural
1	*banzil*	*mninzil*	*anzil*	*ninzil*
2M	*btinzil*	*btinizlu*	*tinzil*	*tinizlu*
2F	*btinizli*	*btinizlin*	*tinizli*	*tinizlin*
3M	*binzil*	*binizlu*	*yinzil*	*yinizlu*
3F	*btinzil*	*binizlin*	*tinzil*	*yinizlin*

Table 31: Imperfective of *marag–yumrug* 'pass by'

	b-imperfective		Bare imperfective	
	Singular	Plural	Singular	Plural
1	*bamrug*	*mnumrug*	*amrug*	*numrug*
2M	*btumrug*	*btumurgu*	*tumrug*	*tumurgu*
2F	*btumurgi*	*btumurgin*	*tumurgi*	*tumurgin*
3M	*bumrug*	*bumurgu*	*yumrug*	*yumurgu*
3F	*btumrug*	*bumurgin*	*tumrug*	*yumurgin*

The medial /a/ stems remain stable, as expected, whereas medial /i/ and /u/ stems undergo vowel elision and epenthesis insertion between the first and the second consonant when suffixes are added: *nzil* → *nzl* → *nizl*; *mrug* → *mrg* → *murg*. It is also noticeable in these paradigms that /y/ in third-person prefixes is deleted after the indicative marker *b*-: *yirčab* vs *birčab*. The deletion of /y/ in this form is found in all sedentary Jordanian dialects. On the other hand, in other Levantine dialects /y/ is deleted in open syllables only (*birūḥ* 'he goes' but *byinzal* 'he descends'). In the imperative, a prosthetic vowel is inserted:

Table 32: Imperative of *ričib–yirčab* 'ride', *nizil–yinzil* 'descend' and *marag–yumrug* 'pass by'

2MS	*írčab*	*ínzil*	*úmrug*
2FS	*írčabi*	*ínizli*	*úmurgi*
2MP	*írčabu*	*ínizlu*	*úmurgu*
2FP	*írčabin*	*ínizlin*	*úmurgin*

The template of the active participle is CāCiC and of the passive participle is maCCūC. They both inflect for gender and number:

Table 33: Active participle and passive participle of *ričib–yirčab* 'ride'

	Active	Passive
MS	*rāčib*	*markūb*
FS	*rāčbe*	*markūba*
MP	*rāčbīn*	*markūbīn*
FP	*rāčbāt*	*markūbāt*

3.4.2.1.2. *ʔaxaḏ* 'he took' and *ʔakal* 'he ate'

The perfective inflects normally. Idiosyncrasies arise in the imperfective, as shown below. Contrast between the 1SG and the 3MS in the *b*-imperfective is neutralised, because of the /y/-deletion after *b*-: *bōkil* 'I eat, he eats'. Contrast is restored in the bare forms: *ōkil* 'I eat' and *yōkil* 'he eats'. The same phenomenon is observed with *ʔaxaḏ* 'he took'.

Table 34: Imperfective of *akal–yōkil* 'eat' and *axaḏ–yōxuḏ* 'take'

	akal–yōkil 'eat'				*axaḏ–yōxuḏ* 'take'			
	b-imperfective		Bare imperfective		*b*-imperfective		Bare imperfective	
	SG	PL	SG	PL	SG	PL	SG	PL
1	*bōkil*	*mnōkil*	*ōkil*	*nōkil*	*bōxuḏ*	*mnōxuḏ*	*ōxuḏ*	*nōxuḏ*
2M	*btōkil*	*btōklu*	*tōkil*	*tōklu*	*btōxuḏ*	*btōxḏu*	*tōxuḏ*	*tōxḏu*
2F	*btōkli*	*btōklin*	*tōkli*	*tōklin*	*btōxḏi*	*btōxḏin*	*tōxḏi*	*tōxḏin*
3M	*bōkil*	*bōklu*	*yōkil*	*yōklu*	*bōxuḏ*	*btōxḏu*	*yōxuḏ*	*yōxḏu*
3F	*btōkil*	*bōklin*	*tōkil*	*yōklin*	*btōxuḏ*	*btōxḏin*	*tōxuḏ*	*tōxḏin*

The template of the active participle of these two verbs is māC_2iC_3. Passive derivations with the template maCCūC, such as *maʔkūl* and *maʔxūḏ*, are borrowed from the standard dialect. The normal convention in the dialect is to use the active participle of the Form VIII derivation *mittākil* and *mittāxiḏ* (see below).

Table 35: Active participle of *akal–yōkil* 'eat' and *axaḏ–yōxuḏ* 'take'

MS	*mākil*	*māxiḏ*
FS	*mākle*	*māxḏe*
MP	*māklīn*	*māxḏīn*
FP	*māklāt*	*māxḏāt*

In the imperative, Central Jordanian dialects exhibit forms common to most Arabic dialects, whereas Northern Jordanian dialects add a prosthetic /u/:

Table 36: Imperative of *akal–yōkil* 'eat' and *axaḏ–yōxuḏ* 'take'

	Central		Northern	
2MS	*kul*	*xuḏ*	*ukul*	*uxuḏ*
2FS	*kuli*	*xuḏi*	*ukli*	*uxḏi*
2MP	*kuli*	*xuḏu*	*uklu*	*uxḏu*
2FP	*kulin*	*xuḏin*	*uklin*	*uxḏin*

In addition to this, many dialects have a suppletive imperative for *ʔaxaḏ*, involving the deictic formative *hā-*, to which second-person bound pronouns suffix, yielding the following paradigm:

Table 37: Suppletive imperative of *axaḏ–yōxuḏ* 'take'

MS	*hā-k*
FS	*hā-č*
MP	*hā-ku*
FP	*hā-čin*

The fact that *hā-* is a real predicate is evidenced by its argument structure, as shown in (8), where the theme argument is coded like an object, as it is carried by the pronominal object host *iyyā-*.

(8) *ʔil-ak ʕalayye ʕašartālāf dular hā-k iyyā-hin*
for-2MS on.1SG ten_thousand dollar take.IMP-2MS OBJ-3FP
'I owe you ten thousand dollars, take them'

3.4.2.1.3. C_1 = /w/ or /y/

Recorded verbs are *wiṣil* 'arrive', *wigiʕ* 'fall', *wigif* 'stand', *wilid* 'give birth' or 'be born', *wirid* 'get water', *wirim* 'swell', *wiriṯ* 'inherit'. While the perfective paradigm of these verbs is completely regular, the imperfective exhibits a fair amount of variation, which corresponds roughly to three stages in the dialect: traditional, innovative I and innovative II.

Table 38: Traditional imperfective of *wiṣil–yaṣal* 'arrive'

	b-imperfective		Bare imperfective	
	Singular	Plural	Singular	Plural
1	*baṣal*	*mnaṣal*	*aṣal*	*naṣal*
2M	*btaṣal*	*btaṣlu*	*taṣal*	*taṣlu*
2F	*btaṣli*	*btaṣlin*	*taṣli*	*taṣlin*
3M	*baṣal*	*baṣlu*	*yaṣal*	*yaṣlu*
3F	*btaṣal*	*baṣlin*	*taṣal*	*yaṣlin*

In the traditional paradigm, the vowel of the prefix is /a/. This is the situation documented by Cantineau (1946, 245) for Ḥōrāni dialects in the thirties of last century, hence the label 'traditional'. Two things ought to be noticed. First, there is homophony between the 1SG and 3MS *baṣal* 'I arrive, he arrives' (also, incidentally, 'onion'). Exactly like *axaḏ* and *akal*, contrast is restored in the bare imperfective. Second, /a/ drops in unstressed open syllables, which is unexpected in these dialects: *yaṣal* 'he arrives' vs *yaṣlu* 'they arrive', although one instance in which /a/ was maintained was recorded: *taṣali* 'you (F) arrive'.

Table 39: Innovative I imperfective of *wiṣil–yiṣal* 'arrive'

	b-imperfective		Bare imperfective	
	Singular	Plural	Singular	Plural
1	*baṣal*	*mniṣal*	*aṣal*	*niṣal*
2M	*btiṣal*	*btiṣalu*	*tiṣal*	*tiṣalu*
2F	*btiṣali*	*btiṣalin*	*tiṣali*	*tiṣalin*
3M	*biṣal*	*biṣalu*	*yiṣal*	*yiṣalu*
3F	*btiṣal*	*biṣalin*	*tiṣal*	*yiṣalin*

In this paradigm, the vowel in the prefix has shifted to /i/, which has the advantage of restoring the contrast between the 1SG and 3MS: *baṣal* 'I arrive' vs *biṣal* 'he arrives'. Medial /a/ does not drop in unstressed open syllables: *biṣal* 'he arrives' vs *biṣalu* 'they arrive'.

Table 40: Innovative II imperfective of *wiṣil–yūṣal* 'arrive'

	b-imperfective		Bare imperfective	
	Singular	Plural	Singular	Plural
1	*bawṣal*	*mnūṣal*	*awṣal*	*niṣal*
2M	*btūṣal*	*btūṣalu*	*tūṣal*	*tūṣalu*
2F	*btūṣali*	*btūṣalin*	*tūṣali*	*tūṣalin*
3M	*būṣal*	*būṣalu*	*yūṣal*	*yūṣalu*
3F	*btūṣal*	*būṣalin*	*tūṣal*	*yūṣalin*

In the Innovative II paradigm, the first consonant is restored in all positions, which can be interpreted as an innovation motivated by transparency. This innovation is likely not to be an internal development but rather contact-induced, because most urban dialects in the area maintain C_1 in the imperfective. Speakers who use this paradigm are also likely to have lost gender distinction in the plural and merged these forms in favour of the masculine.

Medial /i/ verbs such as *wirid–yarid* 'get water' behave like /a/ verbs, but they also exhibit additional variation in the maintenance of the stem vowel: *yardin* ~ *yirdin* ~ *yiridin* 'they used to get water'.

Only one C_3 = /y/ verb has been recorded: *yibis–yabas* 'get dry'. It behaves like C_3 = /w/ verbs in the traditional and innovative I paradigms, but a slight difference arises in the innovative II paradigm.

Table 41: Traditional imperfective of *yibis–yabas* 'get dry'

	b-imperfective		Bare imperfective	
	Singular	Plural	Singular	Plural
1	*babas*	*mnabas*	*abas*	*nabas*
2M	*btabas*	*btabsu*	*tabas*	*tabsu*
2F	*btabsi*	*btabsin*	*tabsi*	*tabsin*
3M	*babas*	*babsu*	*yabas*	*yabsu*
3F	*btabas*	*babsin*	*tabas*	*yabsin*

In this case too, there is homophony between 1SG and 3MS *babas* 'I get dry, he gets dry' and /a/ also drops in unstressed open syllables: *tabas* 'you (M) get dry' vs *tabsi* 'you (F) get dry'.

Table 42: Innovative I imperfective of *yibis–yibas* 'get dry'

	b-imperfective		Bare imperfective	
	Singular	Plural	Singular	Plural
1	*babas*	*mnibas*	*abas*	*nibas*
2M	*btibas*	*btibasu*	*tibas*	*tibasu*
2F	*btibasi*	*btibasin*	*tibasi*	*tibasin*
3M	*bibas*	*bibasu*	*yibas*	*yibasu*
3F	*btibas*	*bibasin*	*tibas*	*yibasin*

Here again, contrast is restored between 1SG *babas* 'I get dry' and 3MS *bibas* 'he gets dry'. Medial /a/ is also maintained in unstressed open syllables: *tibas* 'you (M) get dry' vs *tibasi* 'you (F) get dry'.

Table 43: Innovative II imperfective of *yibis–yības* 'get dry'

	b-imperfective		Bare imperfective	
	Singular	Plural	Singular	Plural
1	*baybas*	*mnības*	*aybas*	*nības*
2M	*btības*	*btībasu*	*tības*	*tībasu*
2F	*btībasi*	*btībasin*	*tībasi*	*tībasin*
3M	*bības*	*bībasu*	*yības*	*yībasu*
3F	*btības*	*bībasin*	*tības*	*yībasin*

In this paradigm, the weak element has been restored through long /ī/. Innovative II speakers are also likely to have lost gender distinction in the plural in favour of the masculine forms.

In the imperative, as in the Northern imperatives of *akal* and *axad̠*, the prothetic vowel /a/ is inserted:

Table 44: Imperative of *wigif–yagaf* 'stand', *wirid–yarid* 'fetch water', *yibis–yabas* 'get dry'

	Central and Northern		
	wigif–yagaf 'stand'	*wirid–yarid* 'fetch water'[2]	*yibis–yabas* 'get dry'
2MS	*agaf*	*arid*	*abas*
2FS	*agfi*	*ardi*	*absi*
2MP	*agfu*	*ardu*	*absu*
2FP	*agfin*	*ardin*	*absin*

In the current state of the dialect, broad speakers alternate between the traditional paradigm and the Innovative I paradigm, in both spontaneous speech and elicitation.

3.4.2.1.4. C_2=/w/ or /y/

There are plenty of roots whose second element is weak. These verbs behave similarly to in other varieties. Consider the inflections of *rāḥ–yrūḥ* 'go' (*r-w-ḥ*), *xāf–yxāf* 'be scared' (*x-w-f*) and *ṭāḥ–yṭīḥ* 'go (descend)' (*ṭ-y-ḥ*) in the perfective. The underlying templates are the following:

[2] This term refers specifically to fetching water from a spring, which used to be a part of women's daily chores in villages before tap water became available.

rāḥ–yrūḥ	:	CaCaC–CCuC
xāf–yxāf	:	CaCaC–CCaC
ṭāḥ–yṭīḥ	:	CaCaC–CCiC

Table 45: Perfective of *rāḥ–yrūḥ* 'go', *xāf–yxāf* 'be scared', *ṭāḥ–yṭīḥ* 'go (descend)'

	rāḥ–yrūḥ 'go'		*xāf–yxāf* 'be afraid'		*ṭāḥ–yṭīḥ* 'fall'	
	Singular	Plural	Singular	Plural	Singular	Plural
1	*ruḥt*	*ruḥna*	*xift*	*xifna*	*ṭiḥt*	*ṭiḥna*
2M	*ruḥt*	*ruḥtu*	*xift*	*xiftu*	*ṭiḥt*	*ṭiḥtu*
2F	*ruḥti*	*ruḥtin*	*xifti*	*xiftin*	*ṭiḥti*	*ṭiḥti*
3M	*rāḥ*	*rāḥu*	*xāf*	*xāfu*	*ṭāḥ*	*ṭāḥu*
3F	*rāḥat*	*rāḥin*	*xāfat*	*xāfin*	*ṭāḥat*	*ṭāḥin*

In the imperfective, the following paradigms were recorded:

Table 46: Imperfective of *rāḥ–yrūḥ* 'go'

	b-imperfective		Bare imperfective	
	Singular	Plural	Singular	Plural
1	*barūḥ*	*minrūḥ*	*arūḥ*	*nrūḥ*
2M	*bitrūḥ*	*bitrūḥu*	*trūḥ*	*trūḥu*
2F	*bitrūḥi*	*bitrūḥin*	*trūḥi*	*trūḥin*
3M	*birūḥ*	*birūḥu*	*yrūḥ*	*yrūḥu*
3F	*bitrūḥ*	*birūḥin*	*trūḥ*	*yrūḥin*

Table 47: Imperfective of *xāf–yxāf* 'be scared'

	b-imperfective		Bare imperfective	
	Singular	Plural	Singular	Plural
1	*baxāf*	*minxāf*	*axāf*	*nxāf*
2M	*bitxāf*	*bitxāfu*	*txāf*	*txāfu*
2F	*bitxāfi*	*bitxāfin*	*txāfi*	*txāfin*
3M	*bixāf*	*bixāfu*	*yxāf*	*yxāfu*
3F	*bitxāf*	*bixāfin*	*txāf*	*yxāfin*

Table 48: Imperfective of *ṭāḥ–yṭīḥ* 'go (descend)'

	b-imperfective		Bare imperfective	
	Singular	Plural	Singular	Plural
1	*baṭīḥ*	*minṭīḥ*	*aṭīḥ*	*nṭīḥ*
2M	*biṭṭīḥ*	*biṭṭīḥu*	*ṭṭīḥ*	*ṭṭīḥu*
2F	*biṭṭīḥi*	*biṭṭīḥin*	*ṭṭīḥi*	*ṭṭīḥin*
3M	*biṭīḥ*	*biṭīḥu*	*yṭīḥ*	*yṭīḥu*
3F	*biṭṭīḥ*	*biṭīḥin*	*ṭṭīḥ*	*yṭīḥin*

The imperative paradigms are as follows:

Table 49: Imperative of *rāḥ–yrūḥ* 'go', *xāf–yxāf* 'be scared', *ṭāḥ–yṭīḥ* 'go (descend)'

2MS	*rūḥ*	*xāf*	*ṭīḥ*
2FS	*rūḥi*	*xāfi*	*ṭīḥi*
2MP	*rūḥu*	*xāfu*	*ṭīḥu*
2FP	*rūḥin*	*xāfin*	*ṭīḥin*

The active participle is as follows:

Table 50: Active participle of *ṭāḥ–yṭīḥ* 'go', *xāf–yxāf* 'be scared', *ṭāḥ–yṭīḥ* 'go (descend)'

MS	*rāyiḥ*	*xāyif*	*ṭāyiḥ*
FS	*rāyḥa*	*xāyfe*	*ṭāyḥa*
MP	*rāyḥīn*	*xāyfīn*	*ṭāyḥīn*
FP	*rāyḥāt*	*xāyfāt*	*ṭāyḥāt*

Contrary to what is observed in the standard dialect, the glide is restored in the passive participle of weak-middle-consonant verbs, here exemplified by the verb *bāʕ–ybīʕ*:

Table 51: Passive participle of *bāʕ–ybīʕ* 'sell'

MS	*mabyūʕ*
FS	*mabyūʕa*
MP	*mabyūʕīn*
FP	*mabyūʕāt*

3.4.2.1.5. C_3 = /y/

When C_3 is weak, two templates are available in both the perfective and the imperfective: CaCa / CiCi and CCi / CCa.

The following combinations are attested:

CaCa–CCi : *bača–yibči* 'cry', *bana–yibni* 'build', *ḥama–yiḥmi* 'protect'

CaCa–CCa : *gara–yigra* 'study', *saʕa–yisʕa* 'strive'

CiCi–CCa : *nisi–yinsa* 'forget', *ṣiḥi–yiṣḥa* 'wake up', *ḥimi–yiḥma* 'get hot', *ribi–yirba* 'grow', *riḏ̣i–yirḏ̣a* 'be satisfied'

CiCi–CCi : *diri–yidri* 'know'

In the perfective, CaCa and CiCi verbs inflect as follows:

Table 52: Perfective of *gara–yigra* 'study' and *nisi–yinsa* 'forget'

	gara–yigra 'study'		*nisi–yinsa* 'forget'	
	Singular	Plural	Singular	Plural
1	*garēt*	*garēna*	*nsīt*	*nsīna*
2M	*garēt*	*garētu*	*nsīt*	*nsītu*
2F	*garēti*	*garēti*	*nsīti*	*nsītin*
3M	*gara*	*garu*	*nisi*	*nisyu*
3F	*garat*	*garin*	*nisyat*	*nisyin*

In CaCa, C_3 surfaces as /ē/ (< */ay/) in the first and second persons, but is deleted in the third-person forms. In CiCi, C_3 surfaces as /ī/ (< */iy/) and is totally restored in the third person. Some variation is observed for some verbs: *giri* 'he read' instead of *gara*, *nasa* instead of *nisi*.

In the imperfective, CCa and CCi verbs inflect as follows:

Table 53: Imperfective of *diri–yidri* 'know', *nisi–yinsa* 'forget'

	diri–yidri 'know'				*nisi–yinsa* 'forget'			
	b-imperfective		Bare imperfective		*b*-imperfective		Bare imperfective	
	SG	PL	SG	PL	SG	PL	SG	PL
1	*badri*	*mnidri*	*adri*	*nidri*	*bansa*	*mninsa*	*ansa*	*ninsa*
2M	*btidri*	*btidru*	*tidri*	*tidru*	*btinsa*	*btinu*	*tinsa*	*tinsu*
2F	*btidri*	*btidrin*	*tidri*	*tidrin*	*btinsi*	*btinsin*	*tinsi*	*tinsin*
3M	*bidri*	*bidru*	*yidri*	*yidru*	*binsa*	*binsu*	*yinsa*	*yinsu*
3F	*btidri*	*bidrin*	*tidri*	*yidrin*	*btinsa*	*binsin*	*tinsa*	*yinsin*

When vocalic suffixes are added, the final vowel in the stem is deleted: *b-tidri* + *-u* yields *b-ti-dr-u*, *b-ti-nsa* + *-i* yields *b-ti-ns-i* and *btidri* + *-i* yields *b-ti-dr-i*. The 2MS and 2FS forms of CCi verbs are therefore homophonous: *b-ti-dri* 'you (M) know' and *b-ti-dr-i* 'you (F) know'.

In the imperative, these verbs inflect as follows (the examples below are derivations of the verbs *bana–yibni* 'build' and *nisi–yinsa* 'forget'; no examples of the imperative of *diri–yidri* 'know' were recorded):

Table 54: Imperative of *bana–yibni* 'build' and *nisi–yinsa* 'forget'

2MS	*ibni*	*insa*
2FS	*ibni*	*insi*
2MP	*ibnu*	*insu*
2FP	*ibnin*	*insin*

The active and passive particples of *nisi–yinsa* 'forget' inflect as follows:

Table 55: Active and passive participle of *nisi–yinsa* 'forget'

	Active	Passive
MS	*nāsi*	*mansi*
FS	*nāsye*	*mansiyye*
MP	*nās(y)īn*	*mansiyyīn*
FP	*nāsyāt*	*mansiyyāt*

3.4.2.1.6. $C_2 = C_3$

In the perfective, $C_2 = C_3$ verbs fit into the template CaCC. In the imperfective, CaCC, CiCC and CuCC are attested, as shown below.

CaCC : *yḏall* 'stay'

CiCC : *yliff* 'turn', *yṭill* 'oversee', *ylimm* 'collect', *yḥibb* 'love, kiss', *yšidd* 'make tight', *ylidd* 'watch', *yšimm* 'smell', *yʕidd* 'count', *yfitt* 'crumble', *yḏinn* 'think', *ydill* 'point', *yzimm* 'carry', *ymidd* 'extend'[3]

CuCC : *ymurr* 'pass', *ynuṭṭ* 'jump', *yḥuṭṭ* 'put', *yrudd* 'answer', *ymudd* 'extend', *yḥukk* 'scrape', *yfukk* 'untie', *yṣuff* 'put aside', *ydugg* 'beat', *ykubb* 'throw' *yxumm* 'bully', *yguḥḥ* 'cough'

The perfective, here exemplified by *ladd–ylidd* 'look', inflects as follows:

---

[3] Many of these forms are realised with /u/ in the Northern dialects: *yluff* 'turn', *ylumm* 'collect', *yzumm* 'carry', *ymudd* 'extend', *yšumm* 'smell'.

Table 56: Perfective of *ladd–ylidd* 'look'

	Singular	Plural
1	*laddēt*	*laddēna*
2M	*laddēt*	*laddētu*
2F	*laddēti*	*laddētin*
3M	*ladd*	*laddu*
3F	*laddat*	*laddin*

To the best of our knowledge, all present-day Arabic dialects insert some kind of long vowel between the stem and the suffix, by analogy with the perfective of C_3=/y/ verbs (cf. *sawwēt* 'I did', below).

The imperfective inflects as follows. Verbs with medial /a/ and /u/ behave the same.

Table 57: Imperfective of *ladd–ylidd* 'look'

	b-imperfective		Bare imperfective	
	Singular	Plural	Singular	Plural
1	*balidd*	*minlidd*	*alidd*	*minlidd*
2M	*bitlidd*	*bitliddu*	*tlidd*	*bitliddu*
2F	*bitliddi*	*bitliddin*	*tliddi*	*tliddin*
3M	*bilidd*	*biliddu*	*ylidd*	*yliddu*
3F	*bitlidd*	*biliddin*	*ytlidd*	*yliddin*

The active participle fits into the template $C_1āC_2C_3$ instead of the $C_1āC_2iC_3$ more commonly found in the Levantine area. The passive participle is formed regularly with the template maCCūC, here exemplified by *ḥaṭṭ–yḥuṭṭ* 'put':

Table 58: Active and passive participle of *ḥaṭṭ–yḥuṭṭ* 'put'

	Active	Passive
MS	*ḥāṭṭ*	*maḥṭūṭ*
FS	*ḥāṭṭa*	*maḥṭūṭa*
MP	*ḥāṭṭīn*	*maḥṭūṭīn*
FP	*ḥāṭṭāt*	*maḥṭūṭāt*

The imperative inflects as follows:

Table 59: Imperative of *ladd–ylidd* 'look'

2MS	*lidd*
2FS	*liddi*
2MP	*liddu*
2FP	*liddin*

3.4.2.1.7. *ağa–yīği* 'come'

This verb, presumably from the classical root *ğ-y-ʔ* 'come' (*ğāʔa–yağīʔu*), has been reinterpreted as being from *ʔ-ğ-y*. The perfective paradigm is as follows.

Table 60: Perfective of *ağa–yīği* 'come'

	Singular	Plural
1	*ğīt*	*ğīna*
2M	*ğīt*	*ğītu*
2F	*ğīti*	*ğītin*
3M	*ağa*	*ağu*
3F	*ağat*	*ağin*

In the first and second persons, a prosthetic /i/ or /a/ is often added: *ağīt* ~ *iğīt* 'I came'. In the third person, /a/ alternates with /i/ in initial position: *ağa* ~ *iğa* 'he came'.

The imperfective is shown below. The most salient feature is the long vowel /ī/, common to most southern Levantine dialects, as opposed to northern dialects, which have short /i/:

Table 61: Imperfective of *aǧa–yīǧi* 'come'

	b-imperfective		Bare imperfective	
	Singular	Plural	Singular	Plural
1	*bāǧi*	*mnīǧi*	*āǧi*	*nīǧi*
2M	*btīǧi*	*btīǧu*	*tīǧi*	*tīǧu*
2F	*btīǧi*	*btīǧin*	*tīǧi*	*tīǧin*
3M	*bīǧi*	*bīǧu*	*yīǧi*	*yīǧu*
3F	*btīǧi*	*btīǧu*	*tīǧi*	*yīǧu*

Only the active participle is attested:

Table 62: Active participle of *aǧa–yīǧi* 'come'

MS	*ǧāy*
FS	*ǧāyye*
MP	*ǧāyyīn*
FP	*ǧāyyāt*

In the imperative, as in most varieties of Arabic (with the exception of those that have undergone heavy restructuring), there is a suppletive stem, often reduced to *taʕ*.

Table 63: Imperative of *aǧa–yīǧi* 'come'

2MS	*taʕāl* ~ *taʕ*
2FS	*taʕāli* ~ *taʕi*
2MP	*taʕālu* ~ *taʕu*
2FP	*taʕālin* ~ *taʕin*

3.4.2.2. Form II CaCCaC

3.4.2.2.1. Strong Roots

This template, as in other dialects of Arabic, often expresses a causative or intensive meaning. It can be used to derive verbs from the bare form CvCvC, such as *ḥamal–yiḥmil* 'carry' vs *ḥammal–yḥammil* 'load'. Intensive derivation is exemplified by *gaṭaʕ–yigṭaʕ* 'cut' vs *gaṭṭaʕ–ygaṭṭiʕ* 'cut into small pieces'. It is also used to derive verbs from nominal roots: *kallal–ykallil* 'wreathe, marry' (< *klīl* 'wreath, Christian wedding ceremony'), *ġarram–yġarrim* 'fine' (< *ġarāma* 'penalty'). Due to semantic shift, the derivational link may be blurred (in this case, probably intensive): *dār–ydūr* 'turn' vs *dawwar* 'search, turn in full circle' (not 'turn repeatedly'). Sometimes the derivational process leads to multiple different meanings: *rāḥ–yrūḥ* 'go', but *rawwaḥ–yrawwiḥ* means both 'go home' and 'cause someone to go'. This template is very productive and frequently used to expand the lexicon: *nukte* 'joke' vs *nakkat–ynakkit* 'make jokes'.

The perfective inflects as follows:

Table 64: Perfective of *čammal–yčammil* 'complete, continue'

	Singular	Plural
1	*čammalt*	*čammalna*
2M	*čammalt*	*čammaltu*
2F	*čammalti*	*čammaltin*
3M	*čammal*	*čammalu*
3F	*čammalat*	*čammalin*

The imperfective inflects as follows:

Table 65: Imperfective of *čammal–yčammil* 'complete, continue'

	b-imperfective		Bare imperfective	
	Singular	Plural	Singular	Plural
1	*bačammil*	*minčammil*	*ačammil*	*nčammil*
2M	*bitčammil*	*bitčammlu*	*tčammil*	*tčammlu*
2F	*bitčammli*	*bitčammlin*	*tčammli*	*tčammlin*
3M	*bičammil*	*bičammlu*	*yčammil*	*yčammlu*
3F	*bitčammil*	*bičammlin*	*yčammil*	*yčammlin*

The imperative inflects as follows:

Table 66: Imperative of *čammal–yčammil* 'complete, continue'

2MS	*čammil*
2FS	*čammli*
2MP	*čammlu*
2FP	*čammlin*

Because these verbs are mostly transitive, the passive participle is attested. The template of the active particple is mCaCCiC and the passive is mCaCCaC, here exemplified by *ḥammal–yḥammil* 'load'.

Table 67: Active and passive participle of *ḥammal–yḥammil* 'load'

	Active	Passive
MS	*mḥammil*	*mḥammal*
FS	*mḥammle*	*mḥammale*
MP	*mḥammlīn*	*mḥammalīn*
FP	*mḥammlāt*	*mḥammalāt*

3.4.2.2.2. C_3 = /y/

Only roots whose third consonant is weak are irregular, as in the verb *sawwa–ysawwi* 'do, make'. The perfective behaves like

Form I C_3 = /y/ verbs, in which the weak consonant is restored in the first and second persons: *sawwē-t* < **sawway-t*. The base vowel is deleted when vowel-initial morphemes attach to the stem: *saww-u*.

Table 68: Perfective of *sawwa–ysawwi* 'do, make'

	Singular	Plural
1	*sawwēt*	*sawwēna*
2M	*sawwēt*	*sawwētu*
2F	*sawwēti*	*sawwētin*
3M	*sawwa*	*sawwu*
3F	*sawwat*	*sawwin*

Table 69: Imperfective of *sawwa–ysawwi* 'do, make'

	b-imperfective		Bare imperfective	
	Singular	Plural	Singular	Plural
1	*basawwi*	*minsawwi*	*asawwi*	*nsawwi*
2M	*bitsawwi*	*bitsawwu*	*tsawwi*	*tsawwu*
2F	*bitsawwi*	*bitsawwin*	*tsawwi*	*tsawwin*
3M	*bisawwi*	*bisawwu*	*ysawwi*	*ysawwu*
3F	*bitsawwi*	*bisawwin*	*tsawwi*	*ysawwin*

The imperative inflects as follows:

Table 70: Imperative of *sawwa–ysawwi* 'do, make'

2MS	*sawwi*
2FS	*sawwi*
2MP	*sawwu*
2FP	*sawwin*

The active and passive participles have the templates mCaCCi and mCaCCa, here exemplified by *nagga–ynaggi* 'choose':

Table 71: Imperative of *nagga–ynaggi* 'choose'

	Active	Passive
MS	*mnaggi*	*mnagga*
FS	*mnaggye*	*mnaggaye*
MP	*mnagg(y)īn*	*mnaggayīn*
FP	*mnaggyāt*	*mnaggayāt*

3.4.2.3. Form III CāCaC

3.4.2.3.1. Strong Roots

Form III verbs are usually transitive. As noted by Larcher (1999, 22), the primary semantics of the pattern are, for Arab grammarians, those of *mušāraka* 'involvement', whereas for scholars of Arabic, the core semantics of this pattern are conative. He further notes that the fundamental value of CāCaC is neither participative nor conative, but insistence. Some verbs in this group are *sāʕad–ysāʕid* 'help', *hāǧar–yhāǧir* 'migrate', *ʕākas–yʕākis* 'go against', *xābaṭ–yxābiṭ* 'do things in a disorderly manner', *sāfar–ysāfir* 'travel', *nāwaš–ynāwiš* 'give', *hāwaš–yhāwiš* 'quarrel', *gāsam–ygāsim* 'divide', *ʕāwan–yʕāwin* 'help', *dāwam–ydāwim* 'be at work', *sāyar–ysāyir* 'go along with', *ǧāwab–yǧāwib* 'answer', *ḥāfaḏ̣–yhāfiḏ̣* 'preserve', *dāfaʕ–ydāfiʕ* 'defend', *gābal–ygābil* 'meet', *ǧāfal–ygāfil* 'surprise', *ḏ̣ārab–yḏ̣ārib* 'rival'.

The verb *sāʕad* 'help' inflects as follows in the perfective. As shown above, /t/ assimilates to /d/, yielding [tt]: *sāʕadt* 'I helped' [saːʕatt].

Table 72: Perfective of *sāʕad–ysāʕid* 'help'

	Singular	Plural
1	*sāʕadt*	*sāʕadna*
2M	*sāʕadt*	*sāʕadtu*
2F	*sāʕadti*	*sāʕadtin*
3M	*sāʕad*	*sāʕadu*
3F	*sāʕadat*	*sāʕadin*

The imperfective paradigm is shown below:

Table 73: Imperfective of *sāʕad–ysāʕid* 'help'

	b-imperfective		Bare imperfective	
	Singular	Plural	Singular	Plural
1	*basāʕid*	*minsāʕid*	*asāʕid*	*nsāʕid*
2M	*bitsāʕid*	*bitsāʕdu*	*tsāʕid*	*tsāʕdu*
2F	*bitsāʕdi*	*bitsāʕdin*	*tsāʕdi*	*tsāʕdin*
3M	*bisāʕid*	*bisāʕdu*	*ysāʕid*	*ysāʕdu*
3F	*bitsāʕid*	*bisāʕdin*	*tsāʕid*	*tsāʕdin*

Only the active participle was recorded for this pattern. The template is mCāCiC. The passive participle derivation, although not attested in the data, is accepted by native speakers with the template mCāCaC: *msāʕad* 'helped' (F *msāʕade*, PL *msāʕadīn*, FP *msāʕadāt*).

Table 74: Active participle of *sāʕad–ysāʕid* 'help'

MS	*msāʕid*
FS	*msāʕde*
MP	*msāʕdīn*
FP	*msāʕdāt*

The imperative inflects as follows:

Table 75: Imperative of *sāʕad–ysāʕid* 'help'

2MS	*sāʕid*
2FS	*sāʕdi*
2MP	*sāʕdu*
2FP	*sāʕdin*

3.4.2.3.2. C_3 = /y/

Verbs of this type include *nāda–ynādi* 'call', *sāwa–ysāwi* 'do, make' (which alternates with Form II *sawwa–ysawwi*) and *lāga–ylāgi* 'find', although the Form I variant *ligi–yilga* has also been recorded.

The perfective inflects as follows:

Table 76: Perfective of *nāda–ynādi* 'call'

	Singular	Plural
1	*nādēt*	*nādēna*
2M	*nādēt*	*nādētu*
2F	*nādēti*	*nādētin*
3M	*nāda*	*nādu*
3F	*nādat*	*nādin*

The imperfective inflects as follows:

Table 77: Imperfective of *nāda–ynādi* 'call'

	b-imperfective		Bare imperfective	
	Singular	Plural	Singular	Plural
1	*banādi*	*minnādi*	*anādi*	*nnādi*
2M	*bitnādi*	*bitnādu*	*tnādi*	*tnādu*
2F	*bitnādi*	*bitnādin*	*tnādi*	*tnādin*
3M	*binādi*	*binādi*	*ynādi*	*ynādi*
3F	*bitnādi*	*binādin*	*tnādi*	*ynādin*

Only the active participle is attested:

Table 78: Active participle of *nāda–ynādi* 'call'

MS	*mnādi*
FS	*mnādye*
MP	*mnād(y)īn*
FP	*mnādyāt*

The imperative, as expected, inflects as follows:

Table 79: Imperative of *nāda–ynādi* 'call'

2MS	*nādi*
2FS	*nādi*
2MP	*nādu*
2FP	*nādin*

3.4.2.4. Form IV aCCaC

One of the most conservative features of the dialects of central and northern Jordan is the maintenance of the template aCCaC, refered to as Form IV in Arabic studies. Form IV has a causative meaning. In the history of Arabic, Form II and Form IV have long been competing as causative derivational devices. In all present-day dialects, Form IV has either been supplanted totally, as in the urban dialects of the Levant, or marginalised, as in the traditional rural and Bedouin varieties. In this regard, Form IV cannot be said to be productive any more, because it cannot be used to create new verbs and expand the lexicon. What we have are remnants of older derivational patterns. In spite of this lack of productivity, Form IV is still clearly identifiable on morphological grounds because it kept a separate template. In the dialects where Form IV was supplanted, it merged with either Form I or Form II. The different derivational relations are shown in Table 80.

Table 80: Form IV

	Source	Derived form
Derived from verbs	*ṭalaʕ–yiṭla* 'go out'	*ṭlaʕ–yiṭliʕ* 'move out'
	riğiʕ–yirğaʕ 'return'	*rğaʕ–yirğiʕ* 'bring back'
	zaʕal–yizʕal 'be upset'	*zʕal–yizʕil* 'upset'
	gaʕad–yigʕud 'sit down'	*gʕad–yigʕid* 'wake up'
	nišif–yinšaf 'dry up'	*nšaf–yinšif* 'dry'
Derived from non-verbs	*w-g-d* 'ignition'	*ōgad–yōgiʕ* 'ignite'
	w-ğ-ʕ 'pain'	*ōğaʕ–yōğiʕ* 'hurt'
	f-ṭ-r 'breakfast'	*fṭar–yifṭir* 'take breakfast'
	ṣ-l-ḥ 'peace'	*ṣlaḥ–yiṣliḥ* 'make peace'
	ṭ-ʕ-m 'food'	*ṭʕam–yiṭʕim* 'provide'
	ḏ̣-w-y 'light'	*ōḏ̣a–yōḏ̣i* 'lighten'
	b-ʕ-d 'remote'	*bʕad–yibʕid* 'move off'
	k-s-y 'cloth'	*ksa–yiksi* 'clothe'
Meteorological	*š-t-y* 'rain'	*štat–tišti* 'rain'
	ṯ-l-ğ 'ice'	*ṯlağat–tiṯliğ* 'snow'
	ġ-r-b 'sunset'	*ġrabat–tiġrib* 'get dark'
Other	*n-ṭ-y* ~ *ʕ-ṭ-y*	*nṭa–yinṭi* ~ *ʕṭa–yiʕṭi* 'give'

There are only a handful of Form IV verbs that can be securely identified as being derived from verbs of Form I. Interestingly, the majority of these Form I verbs are monovalent. In the current state of the dialects, Form II verbs derive from both monovalent and bivalent Form I verbs. It cannot be excluded that the system of derived stems was sensitive to transitivity and that the two templates might have been in complementary distribution as valency-expanding devices at earlier stages: Form II derives causatives from Form I verbs whose valency value is two, and Form IV derives causatives from Form I verbs whose valency value is one.

Form IV also derives verbs from non-verbs. For some of these items, the meaning was narrowed down and became more specific than a causative. The verb *ṭʕam–yiṭʕim*, derived from the root *ṭ-ʕ-m* 'food, taste', does not have the general meaning 'feed', but more specifically God's granting or providing, as exemplified in (9). The general meaning 'feed' is conveyed by Form I of the same root *taʕam–yiṭʕam*.

(9) a. *aḷḷa biṭʕim*
God provide.IPFV.3MS
'God provides'

b. *aḷḷa ṭʕam-na walad*
God provide.PFV.3MS-1PL boy
'God granted us a son'

Another example is the verb *gʕad–yigʕid*, whose meaning specialised into 'wake up', not 'cause someone to sit', the latter being conveyed by Form II *gaʕʕad–ygaʕʕid*.

The verb *bʕad–yibʕid* 'move off' is not attested in our data as a causative 'move something away', as it only surfaced in one utterance describing a one-participant event (10), although Cantineau (1946, 260–62) gives both meanings for the Ḥōrāni dialects in the thirties of last century.

(10) *rāḥat bʕadat ʕan-na*
go.PFV.3FS move_away.PFV.3FS from-1PL
'She went away, she moved away from us'

As shown above, meteorological verbs are expressed using the (a)CCaC template. One restriction arises with weak-second-consonant roots such as *l-y-l* 'night'. In this case, Form II CaCCaC is used: *layyalat id-dinya* 'it became night' (night.PFV.3FS DEF-world).

3.4.2.4.1. Strong Roots

Strong roots inflect as below, here exemplified by *ṭlaʕ–yiṭliʕ* 'take out'. Prothetic /a/ is optional.

Table 81: Perfective of *(a)ṭlaʕ–yiṭliʕ* 'take out'

	Singular	Plural
1	*(a)ṭlaʕt*	*(a)ṭlaʕna*
2M	*(a)ṭlaʕt*	*(a)ṭlaʕtu*
2F	*(a)ṭlaʕti*	*(a)ṭlaʕtin*
3M	*(a)ṭlaʕ*	*(a)ṭlaʕu*
3F	*(a)ṭlaʕat*	*(a)ṭlaʕin*

In the imperfective, inflections are identical to those of medial /i/ Form I verbs:

Table 82: Imperfective of *(a)ṭlaʕ–yiṭliʕ* 'take out'

	b-imperfective		Bare imperfective	
	Singular	Plural	Singular	Plural
1	*baṭliʕ*	*mniṭliʕ*	*aṭliʕ*	*niṭliʕ*
2M	*btiṭliʕ*	*btiṭilʕu*	*tiṭliʕ*	*tiṭilʕu*
2F	*btiṭilʕi*	*btiṭilʕin*	*tiṭilʕi*	*tiṭilʕin*
3M	*biṭliʕ*	*biṭilʕu*	*yiṭliʕ*	*yiṭilʕu*
3F	*btiṭliʕ*	*biṭilʕin*	*tiṭliʕ*	*yiṭilʕin*

The template of the active participle is miCCiC. No passive participle was recorded.

Table 83: Active participle of *(a)ṭlaʕ–yiṭliʕ* 'take out'

MS	*miṭliʕ*
FS	*miṭilʕa*
MP	*miṭilʕīn*
FP	*miṭilʕāt*

The imperative inflects as follows.

Table 84: Imperative of *(a)ṭlaʕ–yiṭliʕ* 'take out'

MS	*iṭliʕ*
FS	*iṭilʕi*
MP	*iṭilʕu*
FP	*iṭilʕin*

3.4.2.4.2. C_1 = /w/

These verbs inflect as follows in the perfective. Initial /ō/ comes from the monophthongisation of /aw/: **awǧaʕ* → *ōǧaʕ*.

Table 85: Perfective of *ōǧaʕ–yōǧiʕ* 'hurt'

	Singular	Plural
1	*ōǧaʕt*	*ōǧaʕna*
2M	*ōǧaʕt*	*ōǧaʕtu*
2F	*ōǧaʕti*	*ōǧaʕtin*
3M	*ōǧaʕ*	*ōǧaʕu*
3F	*ōǧaʕat*	*ōǧaʕin*

The first segment of the imperfective is unexpectedly /ō/, as in *yōǧiʕ* 'it hurts', as if it harked back to **yawǧiʕ*. The template yiCCiC should have yielded ***yīǧiʕ* (< **yiwǧiʕ*). The most probable explanation is an analogy with the perfective stem. The inflections were recorded as in the table below. The first singular and the third masculine singular are homophonous in the *b*-imperfective, as in *ʔakal* and *ʔaxaḏ* (see above).

Table 86: Imperfective of *ōǧaʕ–yōǧiʕ* 'it hurts'

	b-imperfective		Bare imperfective	
	Singular	Plural	Singular	Plural
1	*bōǧiʕ*	*mnōǧiʕ*	*ōǧiʕ*	*nōǧiʕ*
2M	*btōǧiʕ*	*btōǧʕu*	*tōǧiʕ*	*tōǧʕu*
2F	*btōǧʕi*	*btōǧʕin*	*tōǧʕi*	*tōǧʕin*
3M	*bōǧiʕ*	*bōǧʕu*	*yōǧiʕ*	*yōǧʕu*
3F	*btōǧiʕ*	*bōǧʕin*	*tōǧiʕ*	*yōǧʕin*

Only the active participle of *ōǧaʕ* 'hurt' is attested:

Table 87: Active participle of *ōǧaʕ–yōǧiʕ* 'hurt'

MS	*mōǧiʕ*
FS	*mōǧʕa*
MP	*mōǧʕīn*
FP	*mōǧʕāt*

The imperative was elicited as follows. It exhibits a prosthetic /i/, similar to the prosthetic vowel of weak-first-consonant Form I verbs. The verb is *ōgad–yōgid* 'kindle (fire)'.

Table 88: Imperative of *ōgad–yōgid* 'kindle'

2MS	*igid*
2FS	*igdi*
2MP	*igdu*
2FP	*igdin*

3.4.2.4.3. C_2 = /w/ or /y/

No verb of this type was recorded. There are, however, at least three verbs that are historically causative derivations from weak-second-consonant Form I verbs. Consider the following pairs:

gām–ygūm 'get up'	*gām–ygīm* 'remove'
dār–ydūr 'turn'	*dār–ydīr* 'operate'
fār–yfūr 'boil'	*fār–yfīr*[4] 'cause to boil'

The causative meaning is rather straightforward and all the CīC verbs are apparently derived from CūC verbs, but the fact that they were all reinterpreted as Form I verbs is evident from the shape of the active participle, which if from Form IV should be miCCiC (***mgīm*, ***mdīr* and ***mfīr*). For all these verbs, the active participle is the same as it is for Form I verbs, having the shape CāyiC: *gāyim* 'standing' or 'having taken away'; *dāyir* 'turning' or 'having run'; *fāyir* 'boiling' or 'having caused to boil'.

3.4.2.4.4. C_3 = /y/

The verbs *(a)nṭa–yinṭi* ~ *aʕṭa–yiʕṭi* 'give' and *(a)ksa–yiksi* 'clothe' belong to this category. They predictably inflect as follows in the perfective:

Table 89: Perfective of *(a)nṭa–yinṭi* 'give'

	Singular	Plural
1	*(a)nṭēt*	*(a)nṭēna*
2M	*(a)nṭēt*	*(a)nṭētu*
2F	*(a)nṭēti*	*(a)nṭētin*
3M	*(a)nṭa*	*(a)nṭu*
3F	*(a)nṭat*	*(a)nṭin*

[4] The usual form is *fawwar–yfawwir*, but some older speakers retained this rather unusual form.

In the imperfective, the following paradigm was recorded:

Table 90: Imperfective of *(a)nṭa–yinṭi* 'give'

	b-imperfective		Bare imperfective	
	Singular	Plural	Singular	Plural
1	*banṭi*	*mninṭi*	*inṭi*	*ninṭi*
2M	*btinṭi*	*btinṭu*	*tinṭi*	*tinṭu*
2F	*btinṭi*	*btinṭin*	*tinṭi*	*tinṭin*
3M	*binṭi*	*binṭu*	*yinṭi*	*yinṭu*
3F	*btinṭi*	*binṭin*	*tinṭi*	*yinṭin*

Only the active participle is attested:

Table 91: Active participle of *(a)nṭa–yinṭi* 'give'

MS	*minṭi*
FS	*minṭiyye*
MP	*minṭiyyīn*
FP	*minṭiyyāt*

The imperative was recorded as follows:

Table 92: Imperative of *(a)nṭa–yinṭi* 'give'

2MS	*(a)nṭi*
2FS	*(a)nṭi*
2MP	*(a)nṭu*
2FP	*(a)nṭin*

3.4.2.4.5. C_1 and C_3 = /w/ or /y/

Apparently only one verb belongs to this category: *ōḏa–yōḏi* 'light'. It behaves as follows in the perfective:

Table 93: Perfective of *ōḍa–yōḍi* 'light'

	Singular	Plural
1	*ōḍēt*	*ōḍēna*
2M	*ōḍēt*	*ōḍētu*
2F	*ōḍēti*	*ōḍētin*
3M	*ōḍa*	*ōḍu*
3F	*ōḍat*	*ōḍin*

In the imperfective, the following forms were elicited:

Table 94: Imperfective of *ōḍa–yōḍi* 'light'

	b-imperfective		Bare imperfective	
	Singular	Plural	Singular	Plural
1	*bōḍi*	*mnōḍi*	*ōḍi*	*nōḍi*
2M	*btōḍi*	*btōḍu*	*tōḍi*	*tōḍu*
2F	*btōḍi*	*btōḍin*	*tōḍi*	*tōḍin*
3M	*bōḍi*	*bōḍu*	*yōḍi*	*yōḍu*
3F	*btōḍi*	*bōḍin*	*tōḍi*	*yōḍin*

The active participle is inflected as follows:

Table 95: Active participle of *ōḍa–yōḍi* 'light'

MS	*mōḍi*
FS	*mōḍye*
MP	*mōḍ(y)īn*
FP	*mōḍyāt*

Elicitation of the imperative paradigm unexpectedly yielded a prothetic /ā/:

Table 96: Imperative of *ōḍa–yōḍi* 'light'

2MS	*āḍi*
2FS	*āḍi*
2MP	*āḍu*
2FP	*āḍin*

3.4.2.5. Form V tCaCCaC

3.4.2.5.1. Strong Roots

Form V tCaCCaC is often described as the middle, reflexive or passive of Form II CaCCaC. Whatever the semantics, the prefix *t-* is a morphological valency-decreasing device. The perfective behaves as follows:

Table 97: Perfective of *tḥammal–yitḥammal* 'endure'

	Singular	Plural
1	*tḥammalt*	*tḥammalna*
2M	*tḥammalt*	*tḥammaltu*
2F	*tḥammalti*	*tḥammaltin*
3M	*tḥammal*	*tḥammalu*
3F	*tḥammalat*	*tḥammalin*

The imperfective paradigm is as follows:

Table 98: Imperfective of *tḥammal–yitḥammal* 'endure'

	b-imperfective		Bare imperfective	
	Singular	Plural	Singular	Plural
1	*batḥammal*	*mnitḥammal*	*atḥammal*	*nitḥammal*
2M	*btitḥammal*	*btitḥammalu*	*titḥammal*	*titḥammalu*
2F	*btitḥammali*	*btitḥammalin*	*titḥammali*	*titḥammalin*
3M	*bitḥammal*	*bitḥammalu*	*yitḥammal*	*yitḥammalu*
3F	*btitḥammal*	*bitḥammalin*	*titḥammal*	*yitḥammalin*

Only the active participle is attested:

Table 99: Active participle of *tḥammal–yitḥammal* 'endure'

MS	*mitḥammil*
FS	*mitḥammle*
MP	*mitḥammlīn*
FP	*mitḥammlāt*

The imperative inflects as follows:

Table 100: Imperative of *tḥammal– yitḥammal* 'endure'

2MS	*tḥammal*
2FS	*tḥammali*
2MP	*tḥammalu*
2FP	*tḥammalin*

3.4.2.5.2. C_3 = /y/

This is the only kind of verb that behaves irregularly in Form V. Some verbs in this category are *tġadda* 'have lunch', *twaffa* 'die', *tʕadda* 'attack, encroach', *tʕašša* 'have dinner', *txabba* 'hide'. The perfective of *txabba* 'hide' inflects as follows:

Table 101: Perfective of *txabba–yitxabba* 'hide'

	Singular	Plural
1	*txabbēt*	*txabbēna*
2M	*txabbēt*	*txabbētu*
2F	*txabbēti*	*txabbētin*
3M	*txabba*	*txabbu*
3F	*txabbat*	*txabbin*

The imperfective paradigm was recorded as follows:

Table 102: Imperfective of *txabba–yitxabba* 'hide'

	b-imperfective		Bare imperfective	
	Singular	Plural	Singular	Plural
1	*batxabba*	*mnitxabba*	*atxabba*	*nitxabba*
2M	*btitxabba*	*btitxabbu*	*titxabba*	*titxabbu*
2F	*btitxabbi*	*btitxabbin*	*titxabbi*	*titxabbin*
3M	*bitxabba*	*bitxabbu*	*yitxabba*	*yitxabbu*
3F	*btitxabba*	*bitxabbin*	*titxabba*	*yitxabbin*

Only the active participle is attested:

Table 103: Active participle of *txabba–yitxabba* 'hide'

MS	*mitxabbi*
FS	*mitxabbye*
MP	*mitxabb(y)īn*
FP	*mitxabbyāt*

The imperative was recorded as follows:

Table 104: Imperative of *txabba–yitxabba* 'hide'

2MS	*txabba*
2FS	*txabbi*
2MP	*txabbu*
2FP	*txabbin*

3.4.2.6. Form VI tCāCaC

3.4.2.6.1. Strong Roots

Form VI is described as the reciprocal of Form III. Some verbs in this group are *tḥārab–yitḥārab* 'wage war against one another', *txānag–yitxānag* ~ *thāwaš–yithāwaš* ~ *ṭṭāwaš–yiṭṭāwaš* 'quarrel with one another', *tḥālaf–yitḥālaf* 'ally', *tšāġab* 'cause trouble', *twāsaṭ–yitwāsaṭ* 'mediate'. The perfective of *thāwaš–yithāwaš* 'quarrel' was recorded as follows:

Table 105: Perfective of *thāwaš–yithāwaš* 'quarrel'

	Singular	Plural
1	*thāwašt*	*thāwašna*
2M	*thāwašt*	*thāwaštu*
2F	*thāwašti*	*thāwaštin*
3M	*thāwaš*	*thāwašu*
3F	*thāwašat*	*thāwašin*

The imperfective paradigm is as follows:

Table 106: Imperfective of *thāwaš–yithāwaš* 'quarrel'

	b-imperfective		Bare imperfective	
	Singular	Plural	Singular	Plural
1	*bathāwaš*	*mnithāwaš*	*athāwaš*	*nithāwaš*
2M	*btithāwaš*	*btithāwašu*	*tithāwaš*	*tithāwašu*
2F	*btithāwaši*	*btithāwašin*	*tithāwaši*	*tithāwašin*
3M	*bithāwaš*	*bithāwašu*	*yithāwaš*	*yithāwašu*
3F	*btithāwaš*	*bithāwašin*	*tithāwaš*	*yithāwašin*

Only the active participle is attested:

Table 107: Active participle of *thāwaš–yithāwaš* 'quarrel'

MS	*mithāwiš*
FS	*mithāwše*
MP	*mithāwšīn*
FP	*mithāwšāt*

The imperative paradigm was recorded as follows:

Table 108: Imperative of *thāwaš–yithāwaš* 'quarrel'

2MS	*thāwaš*
2FS	*thāwaši*
2MP	*thāwašu*
2FP	*thāwašin*

3.4.2.6.2. C_3 = /y/

The following verbs belong to this category: *tlāga–yitlāga* 'meet', *tgāḍa–yitgāḍa* 'arbitrate', *txāwa–yitxāwa* 'become like brothers'. The perfective inflects as follows:

Table 109: Perfective of *tlāga–yitlāga* 'meet'

	Singular	Plural
1	*tlāgēt*	*tlāgēna*
2M	*tlāgēt*	*tlāgētu*
2F	*tlāgēti*	*tlāgētin*
3M	*tlāga*	*tlāgu*
3F	*tlāgat*	*tlāgin*

The imperfective inflects as follows:

Table 110: Imperfective of *tlāga–yitlāga* 'meet'

	b-imperfective		Bare imperfective	
	Singular	Plural	Singular	Plural
1	*batlāga*	*mnitlāga*	*atlāga*	*nitlāga*
2M	*btitlāga*	*btitlāgu*	*titlāga*	*titlāgu*
2F	*btitlāgi*	*btitlāgin*	*titlāgi*	*titlāgin*
3M	*bitlāga*	*bitlāgu*	*yitlāga*	*yitlāgu*
3F	*btitlāga*	*bitlāgin*	*titlāga*	*yitlāgin*

The active participle was recorded as follows:

Table 111: Active participle of *tlāga–yitlāga* 'meet'

MS	*mitlāgi*
FS	*mitlāgye*
MP	*mitlāg(y)īn*
FP	*mitlāgyāt*

In the imperative, the following forms were elicited:

Table 112: Imperative of *tlāga–yitlāga* 'meet'

2MS	*tlāga*
2FS	*tlāgi*
2MP	*tlāgu*
2FP	*tlāgin*

3.4.2.7. Form VII nCaCaC

Form VII is described as a passive, middle or reflexive derivation of Form I. This derivation is very productive. It includes verbs such as *nkatal–yinkatil* 'be killed, beaten up', *nḥabas–yinḥabis* 'be imprisoned', *nḏabaḥ–yinḏabiḥ* 'be slaughtered', *nʕazam–yinʕazim* 'be invited', *nfataḥ–yinfatiḥ* 'be opened', *nhazam–yinhazim* 'be beaten', *nkasar–yinkasir* 'be broken', *nsaḥab–yinsaḥib* 'withdraw', *nsağan–yinsağin* 'be imprisoned', *nḍarab–yinḍarib* 'be beaten up', *nbasaṭ–yinbasiṭ* 'be happy', *nṭarad–yinṭarid* 'be expelled', *ntarak–yintarik* 'be abandoned', *nʕadd–yinʕadd* 'be considered', *nṭaxx–yinṭaxx* 'be shot'. As noted above, there are remnants of the apophonic passive in pairs such as *hilik* 'be exhausted' vs *halak* 'exhaust' or *xilig* 'be born' vs *xalag* 'create'. Even these remnants, however, are being supplanted by the Form VII pattern, as suggested by the competing verb *nxalag* 'be born'. The corpus also contains one instance of *n-* prefixation to the verb *sāwa* 'do, make', formally belonging to Form III: *n-sāwa* 'be done' (although *tsawwa* ~ *tsāwa* 'be done' is the normally accepted form). The only restriction on forming verbs with this pattern arises with /n/-initial roots such as *nisi–yinsa* 'forget'. The *n-* derivation would yield something like ***n-nasa*, which is seemingly unacceptable to speakers. For this kind of root, speakers resort to the infixation of /t/ between the first and second consonants: *n-t-asa–yin-t-asi* 'be forgotten'. An exception to this is the verb *n-našar* 'be published' from *našar* 'publish', possibly because the infixal /t/ derivation *n-t-ašar* is used to mean 'to spread'.

3.4.2.7.1. Strong Roots

The perfective inflects as follows:

Table 113: Perfective of *nkatal–yinkatal* 'be killed, beaten up'

	Singular	Plural
1	*nkatalt*	*nkatalna*
2M	*nkatalt*	*nkataltu*
2F	*nkatalti*	*nkataltin*
3M	*nkatal*	*nkatalu*
3F	*nkatlat*	*nkatalin*

The imperfective inflects as follows:

Table 114: Imperfective of *nkatal–yinkatal* 'be killed, beaten up'

	b-imperfective		Bare imperfective	
	Singular	Plural	Singular	Plural
1	*bankatil*	*mninkatil*	*ankatil*	*ninkatil*
2M	*btinkatil*	*btinkatlu*	*tinkatil*	*tinkatlu*
2F	*btinkatli*	*btinkatlin*	*tinkatli*	*tinkatlin*
3M	*binkatil*	*binkatlu*	*yinkatil*	*yinkatlu*
3F	*btinkatil*	*binkatlin*	*tinkatil*	*yinkatlin*

Speakers resort to the passive participle of Form I, maCCūC, rather than the active participle of Form VII: *nkatal* 'be killed' → *maktūl*, *nʕazam* 'be invited' → *maʕzūm*, *nḥabas* 'be jailed' → *maḥbūs*, *nzalaṭ* 'be scratched (wounded)' → *mazlūṭ*. The template minCaCiC is attested for the roots *b-s-ṭ* and *s-ḥ-b*: *minbasiṭ* 'flat (land)' and *minsaḥib* 'having withdrawn'.

Imperative forms were elicited for the verb *nʕazam* 'be invited':

Table 115: Imperative of *nʕazam–yinʕazim* 'be invited'

2MS	*inʕazim*
2FS	*nʕazmi*
2MP	*nʕazmu*
2FP	*nʕazmin*

3.4.2.7.2. $C_2 = C_3$

This category includes verbs such as *nǧann–yinǧann* 'become crazy' and *nṭaxx–yinṭaxx* 'be shot'. The perfective was recorded as follows. Note the vowel /ē/ inserted between the stem and the suffix.

Table 116: Perfective of *nṭaxx–yinṭaxx* 'be shot'

	Singular	Plural
1	*nṭaxxēt*	*nṭaxxēna*
2M	*nṭaxxēt*	*nṭaxxētu*
2F	*nṭaxxēti*	*nṭaxxētin*
3M	*nṭaxx*	*nṭaxxu*
3F	*nṭaxxat*	*nṭaxxin*

The imperfective inflects as follows:

Table 117: Imperfective of *nṭaxx–yinṭaxx* 'be shot'

	b-imperfective		Bare imperfective	
	Singular	Plural	Singular	Plural
1	*banṭaxx*	*mninṭaxx*	*anṭaxx*	*ninṭaxx*
2M	*btinṭaxx*	*btinṭaxxu*	*tinṭaxx*	*tinṭaxxu*
2F	*btinṭaxxi*	*btinṭaxxin*	*tinṭaxxi*	*tinṭaxxin*
3M	*binṭaxx*	*binṭaxxu*	*yinṭaxx*	*yinṭaxxu*
3F	*btinṭaxx*	*binṭaxxin*	*tinṭaxx*	*yinṭaxxin*

The active participle was elicited as follows:

Table 118: Active participle of *nṭaxx–yinṭaxx* 'be shot'

MS	*minṭaxx*
FS	*minṭaxxa*
MP	*minṭaxxīn*
FP	*minṭaxxāt*

The imperative was elicited as follows:

Table 119: Imperative of *nṭaxx–yinṭaxx* 'be shot'

2MS	*inṭaxx*
2FS	*inṭaxxi*
2MP	*inṭaxxu*
2FP	*inṭaxxin*

3.4.2.7.3. C_2 = /w/ or /y/

This category includes verbs such as *ndās–yindās* 'be humiliated, stepped on', *nṣāb–yinṣāb* 'be afflicted', *ngāl–yingāl* 'be said', *nbāʕ–yinbāʕ* 'be sold'. The *n-* derivation of the root *ʕ-w-r* 'be one-eyed' retains medial /w/: *nʕawar* 'be one-eyed'. The perfective forms of *nbāʕ* were elicited as follows:

Table 120: Perfective of *nbāʕ–yinbāʕ* 'be sold'

	Singular	Plural
1	*nbaʕt ~ nbiʕt*	*nbaʕna ~ nbiʕna*
2M	*nbaʕt ~ nbiʕt*	*nbaʕtu ~ nbiʕtu*
2F	*nbaʕti ~ nbiʕti*	*nbaʕtin ~ nbiʕtin*
3M	*nbāʕ*	*nbāʕu*
3F	*nbāʕat*	*nbāʕin*

The imperfective was elicited as follows:

Table 121: Imperfective of *nbāʕ–yinbāʕ* 'be sold'

	b-imperfective		Bare imperfective	
	Singular	Plural	Singular	Plural
1	*banbāʕ*	*mninbāʕ*	*anbāʕ*	*ninbāʕ*
2M	*btinbāʕ*	*btinbāʕu*	*tinbāʕ*	*tinbāʕu*
2F	*btinbāʕi*	*btinbāʕin*	*tinbāʕi*	*tinbāʕin*
3M	*binbāʕ*	*binbāʕu*	*yinbāʕ*	*yinbāʕu*
3F	*btinbāʕ*	*binbāʕin*	*tinbāʕ*	*yinbāʕin*

The active participle inflects as follows:

Table 122: Active participle of *nbāʕ–yinbāʕ* 'be sold'

MS	*minbāʕ*
FS	*minbāʕa*
MP	*minbāʕīn*
FP	*minbāʕāt*

The imperative was recorded as follows:

Table 123: Imperative of *nbāʕ–yinbāʕ* 'be sold'

2MS	*inbāʕ*
2FS	*inbāʕi*
2MP	*inbāʕu*
2FP	*inbāʕin*

3.4.2.7.4. C_3 = /y/

Verbs belonging to this category are *nʕama–yiʕami* 'be blind', *ngara–yingara* 'be read', *nḥača–yinḥača* 'be spoken'.

The perfective inflects as follows.

Table 124: Perfective of *nʕama–yiʕami* 'be blind'

	Singular	Plural
1	*nʕamēt*	*nʕamēna*
2M	*nʕamēt*	*nʕamētu*
2F	*nʕamēti*	*nʕamētin*
3M	*nʕama*	*nʕamu*
3F	*nʕamat*	*nʕamin*

In the imperfective, the template of the stem is either nCCaCi or nCCaCa depending on the verb, exemplified by *yinʕami* 'he becomes blind' and *yingara* 'it is read'. These forms were elicited, because they are pragmatically unexpected and as such barely found in naturally occurring speech.

Table 125: Imperfective of *nʕama–yiʕami* 'be blind' and *ngara–yingara* 'be read'

	b-imperfective		Bare imperfective	
	Singular	Plural	Singular	Plural
1	*banʕami*	*mninʕami*	*anʕami*	*mninʕami*
	bangara	*mningara*	*angara*	*mningara*
2M	*btinʕami*	*btinʕamu*	*tinʕami*	*tinʕamu*
	btingara	*btingaru*	*tingara*	*tingaru*
2F	*btinʕami*	*btinʕamin*	*tinʕami*	*tinʕamin*
	btingari	*btingarin*	*tingari*	*tingarin*
3M	*binʕami*	*binʕamu*	*yinʕami*	*yinʕamu*
	bingara	*bingaru*	*yingara*	*yingaru*
3F	*btinʕami*	*binʕamin*	*tinʕami*	*inʕamin*
	btingara	*bingarin*	*tingara*	*ingarin*

The active participle inflects as follows. Note the gemination of /y/ with suffixed forms.

Table 126: Active participle of *nʕama–yiʕami* 'be blind'

MS	*minʕami*
FS	*minʕamiyye*
MP	*minʕamiyyīn*
FP	*minʕamiyyāt*

The imperative inflects as follows.

Table 127: Imperative of *nʕama–yiʕami* 'be blind'

2MS	*inʕami*
2FS	*inʕami*
2MP	*inʕamu*
2FP	*inʕamin*

3.4.2.8. Form VIII CtaCaC

The meaning of this form is often middle or reflexive when a derivational link can be established with a Form I verb: *xalaṭ* 'mix' vs *xtalaṭ* 'mixed (itself)', or sometimes with a Form II verb: *sawwa* 'do' vs *stawa* 'be cooked', *sallam* 'hand over' vs *stalam* 'receive'. In many cases, though, at least synchronically, no derivational link with any other verb can be established: *štaġal* 'work', *štara* 'buy'.

3.4.2.8.1. Strong Roots

The perfective inflects as follows. Note the resyllabification in the 3FS *štaġlat* (< *štaġalat*), in which medial /a/ drops from CaCaCaC.

Table 128: Perfective of *štaġal–yištaġil* 'work'

	Singular	Plural
1	*štaġalt*	*štaġalna*
2M	*štaġalt*	*štaġaltu*
2F	*štaġalti*	*štaġaltin*
3M	*štaġal*	*štaġalu*
3F	*štaġlat*	*štaġalin*

The stem template in the imperfective is CtaCiC, a feature shared between Central and Northern Jordanian (Ḥōrāni) dialects. Because of dialect contact, CtiCiC can be heard in Central Jordan, but much less so in Ḥōrāni.

Table 129: Imperfective of *štaġal–yištaġil* 'work'

	b-imperfective		Bare imperfective	
	Singular	Plural	Singular	Plural
1	*baštaġil*	*mništaġil*	*aštaġil*	*ništaġil*
2M	*btištaġil*	*btištaġlu*	*tištaġil*	*tištaġlu*
2F	*btištaġli*	*btištaġlin*	*tištaġli*	*tištaġlin*
3M	*bištaġil*	*bištaġlu*	*yištaġil*	*yištaġlu*
3F	*btištaġil*	*bištaġlin*	*tištaġil*	*yištaġlin*

The active participle of *štaġal* is based on the template CaCCāC: *šaġġāl*. A proper Form VIII active participle is attested for other roots, such as *l-z-m*: *miltazim* 'commited':

Table 130: Active participle of *ltazam–yiltazim* 'be committed'

MS	*miltazim*
FS	*miltazme*
MP	*miltazmīn*
FP	*miltazmāt*

The imperative inflects as follows.

Table 131: Imperative of *štȧgal–yištȧgil* 'work'

2MS	*ištȧgil*
2FS	*štȧgli*
2MP	*štȧglu*
2FP	*štȧglin*

3.4.2.8.2. C_1 = /w/ or /ʔ/

The verb *ttaṣal–yittaṣil* 'get in touch' is in all likelihood borrowed from the standard dialect. Except for the assimilation of /w/ to /t/, it inflects normally in all the paradigms. Autochthonous derivations of weak-first-consonant roots are inflected according to the template ttāC_2aC_3 in both the perfective and the imperfective. Formally, these verbs inflect like Form VI tCāCaC verbs.

ttākal–yittākal	'be eaten'	< *ʔakal* 'eat'
ttāxaḏ–yittāxaḏ	'be taken'	< *ʔaxaḏ* 'take'
ttāgad–yittāgad	'be ignited'	< *ʔōgad* 'ignite'
ttāǧaʕ–yittāǧaʕ	'be in pain'	< *ʔōǧaʕ* 'cause pain'

The active participle inflects as follows.

Table 132: Active participle of *ttākal–yittākal* 'be eaten', *ttāxaḏ–yittāxaḏ* 'be taken', *ttāgad–yittāgad* 'be ignited' and *ttāǧaʕ–yittāǧaʕ* 'be in pain'

MS	*mittākil*	*mittāxiḏ*	*mittāgid*	*mittāǧiʕ*
FS	*mittākle*	*mittāxḏe*	*mittāgde*	*mittāǧʕe*
MP	*mittāklīn*	*mittāxḏīn*	*mittāgdīn*	*mittāǧʕīn*
FP	*mittāklāt*	*mittāxḏāt*	*mittāgdāt*	*mittāǧʕāt*

3.4.2.8.3. C_2 = /w/ or /y/

Some verbs in this category are *ḥtāǧ–yiḥtāǧ* 'need', *rtāḥ–yirtāḥ* 'rest', *xtār–yixtār* 'choose' and *štāg–yištāg* 'miss'.

The perfective inflects as follows. Long /ā/ in the stem undergoes reduction to /a/ when consonant-initial suffixes attach.

Table 133: Perfective of *xtār–yixtār* 'choose'

	Singular	Plural
1	*xtart*	*xtarna*
2M	*xtart*	*xtartu*
2F	*xtarti*	*xtartin*
3M	*xtār*	*xtāru*
3F	*xtārat*	*xtārin*

The imperfective inflects as follows.

Table 134: Imperfective of *xtār–yixtār* 'choose'

	b-imperfective		Bare imperfective	
	Singular	Plural	Singular	Plural
1	*baxtār*	*mnixtār*	*axtār*	*nixtār*
2M	*btixtār*	*btixtāru*	*tixtār*	*tixtāru*
2F	*btixtāri*	*btixtārin*	*tixtāri*	*tixtārin*
3M	*bixtār*	*bixtāru*	*yixtār*	*yixtāru*
3F	*btixtār*	*bixtārin*	*tixtār*	*yixtārin*

Active and passive participles are undifferentiated—when the passive participle is available, as in the case of *xtār*:

Table 135: Active and passive participles of *xtār–yixtār* 'choose'

MS	*mixtār*
FS	*mixtāra*
MP	*mixtārīn*
FP	*mixtārāt*

The imperative inflects as follows.

Table 136: Imperative of *xtār–yixtār* 'choose'

2MS	*xtār*
2FS	*xtāri*
2MP	*xtāru*
2FP	*xtārin*

3.4.2.8.4. C_3 = /y/

Verbs of this kind are *stawa–yistawi* 'be cooked', *štara–yištari* 'buy', *ʕtada–yiʕtadi* 'aggress', *ltaga–yiltagi* 'meet'.

The perfective inflects as follows.

Table 137: Perfective of *štara–yištari* 'buy'

	Singular	Plural
1	*štarēt*	*štarēna*
2M	*štarēt*	*štarētu*
2F	*štarēti*	*štarētin*
3M	*štara*	*štaru*
3F	*štarat*	*štarin*

The imperfective inflects as follows.

Table 138: Imperfective of *štara–yištari* 'buy'

	b-imperfective		Bare imperfective	
	Singular	Plural	Singular	Plural
1	*baštari*	*mništari*	*aštari*	*ništari*
2M	*btištari*	*btištaru*	*tištari*	*tištaru*
2F	*btištari*	*btištarin*	*tištari*	*tištarin*
3M	*bištari*	*bištaru*	*yištari*	*yištaru*
3F	*btištari*	*bištarin*	*tištari*	*yištarin*

Speakers of the traditional dialect tend to use the active participle of Form I *šara–yišri* alongside *štara–yištari*: *šāri*. The active participle of the verb *ltaga* 'meet' was elicited as follows. Note the gemination of /y/ when suffixes attach to the stem.

Table 139: Active participle of *ltaga–yiltagi* 'meet'

MS	*miltagi*
FS	*miltagiyye*
MP	*miltagiyyīn*
FP	*miltagiyyāt*

There is no passive participle for *štara* but speakers use the active participle of the passive derivation *nšara* 'be bought': *minšari*.

The imperative inflects as follows.

Table 140: Active participle of *štara–yištari* 'buy'

2MS	*ištari*
2FS	*ištari*
2MP	*ištaru*
2FP	*ištarin*

3.4.2.9. Form IX $C_1C_2aC_3C_3$

This derivation seems to be limited to colour adjectives: *aḥmar* 'red' vs *ḥmarr* 'become red'. No instances of this template were recorded in spontaneous speech. Speakers favour the use of the construction *ṣār* 'become' + adjective. The following paradigms were all elicited.

Table 141: Perfective of *ḥmarr–yiḥmarr* 'become red'

	Singular	Plural
1	*ḥmarrēt*	*ḥmarrēna*
2M	*ḥmarrēt*	*ḥmarrētu*
2F	*ḥmarrēti*	*ḥmarrētin*
3M	*ḥmarr*	*ḥmarru*
3F	*ḥmarrat*	*ḥmarrin*

Table 142: Imperfective of *ḥmarr–yiḥmarr* 'become red'

	b-imperfective		Bare imperfective	
	Singular	Plural	Singular	Plural
1	*baḥmarr*	*mniḥmarr*	*aḥmarr*	*niḥmarr*
2M	*btiḥmarr*	*btiḥmarru*	*tiḥmarr*	*tiḥmarru*
2F	*btiḥmarri*	*btiḥmarrin*	*tiḥmarri*	*tiḥmarrin*
3M	*biḥmarr*	*biḥmarru*	*yiḥmarr*	*yiḥmarru*
3F	*btiḥmarr*	*biḥmarrin*	*tiḥmarr*	*yiḥmarrin*

Table 143: Active participle of *ḥmarr–yiḥmarr* 'become red'

MS	*miḥmarr*
FS	*miḥmarra*
MP	*miḥmarrīn*
FP	*miḥmarrāt*

Table 144: Imperative of *ḥmarr–yiḥmarr* 'become red'

2MS	*ḥmarr*
2FS	*ḥmarri*
2MP	*ḥmarru*
2FP	*ḥmarrin*

3.4.2.10. Form X staCCaC

This pattern has limited productivity in the vernacular. Many items are borrowings from the standard dialect: *stawṭan–yistawṭin* 'settle', *stahlak–yistahlik* 'consume', *staʕmal–yistaʕmil* 'utilise', *staʔǧar–yistaʔǧir* 'rent', *stawla–yistawli* 'take control', *starāḥ–yistarīḥ* 'rest'. Some realisations are plainly colloquial, such as *standạr–yistandạir* 'wait' (cf. standard *intaḏ̣ar–yantaḏ̣ir*), *stagnaʕ–yistagniʕ* 'be convinced' (cf. standard *iqtanaʕ–yaqtaniʕ*), *staʕǧal–yistaʕǧil* 'be in a hurry'. Formally, the verb *stanna–yistanna* 'wait', known to all Arabic dialects, is a blend between Form V and Form X (cf. standard *istaʔnā*). Form X is truly productive insofar as it derives verbs from nouns and adjectives denoting a property to express 'pass off X as Y', as illustrated below.

staṭwal–yistaṭwil 'pass off X as long'	< *ṭawīl* 'long'
stahbal–yistahbil 'pass off X as stupid'	< *ahbal* 'stupid'
stagall–yistagill 'pass off X as little'	< *galīl* 'few'
staḏraṭ–yistaḏriṭ 'pass off X as a fart'	< *ḏrāṭ* 'fart'
staxra–yistaxri 'pass off X as crap'	< *xara* 'crap'

3.4.2.10.1. Strong Roots

The perfective inflects as follows:

Table 145: Perfective of *staʕmal–yistaʕmil* 'utilise'

	Singular	Plural
1	*staʕmalt*	*staʕmalna*
2M	*staʕmalt*	*staʕmaltu*
2F	*staʕmalti*	*staʕmaltin*
3M	*staʕmal*	*staʕmalu*
3F	*staʕmalat*	*staʕmalin*

The imperfective stem is staCCiC. Medial /i/ is elided in unstressed position. The three-consonant cluster is resolved by epenthetic insertion between the first and second consonant.

Table 146: Imperfective of *staʕmal–yistaʕmil* 'utilise'

	b-imperfective		Bare imperfective	
	Singular	Plural	Singular	Plural
1	*bastaʕmil*	*mnistaʕmil*	*astaʕmil*	*nistaʕmil*
2M	*btistaʕmil*	*btistaʕimlu*	*tistaʕmil*	*tistaʕimlu*
2F	*btistaʕimli*	*btistaʕimlin*	*tistaʕimli*	*tistaʕimlin*
3M	*bistaʕmil*	*bistaʕimlu*	*yistaʕmil*	*yistaʕimlu*
3F	*btistaʕmil*	*bistaʕimlin*	*tistaʕmil*	*yistaʕimlin*

The participles inflect as follows. The passive participle in *mu-* is likely to be borrowed from the standard variety. Forms in *mi-* are vernacular: *mistaʕmal, mistaʕmale, mistaʕmalīn, mistaʕmalāt.*

Table 147: Active and passive participles of *staʕmal–yistaʕmil* 'utilise'

	Active	Passive
MS	*mistaʕmil*	*mustaʕmal*
FS	*mistaʕimle*	*mustaʕamale*
MP	*mistaʕimlīn*	*mustaʕmalīn*
FP	*mistaʕimlāt*	*mustaʕmalāt*

The imperative inflects as follows:

Table 148: Imperative of *staʕmal–yistaʕmil* 'utilise'

2MS	*staʕmil*
2FS	*staʕimli*
2MP	*staʕimlu*
2FP	*staʕimlin*

3.4.2.10.2. $C_2 = C_3$

Verbs belonging to this category are *stagall–yistagill* 'belittle' and *staġall–yistaġill* 'exploit'.

The following paradigm was recorded in the perfective. The perfective stem is staCaCC. As in other roots of this kind, a long /ē/ is inserted between the stem and consonant-initial suffixes.

Table 149: Perfective of *staġall–yistaġill* 'exploit'

	Singular	Plural
1	*staġallēt*	*staġallēna*
2M	*staġallēt*	*staġallētu*
2F	*staġallēti*	*staġallētin*
3M	*staġall*	*staġallu*
3F	*staġallat*	*staġallin*

The imperfective stem is staCiCC and inflects as follows:

Table 150: Imperfective of *staġall–yistaġill* 'exploit'

	b-imperfective		Bare imperfective	
	Singular	Plural	Singular	Plural
1	*bastaġill*	*mnistaġill*	*astaġill*	*nistaġill*
2M	*btistaġill*	*btistaġillu*	*tistaġill*	*tistaġillu*
2F	*btistaġilli*	*btistaġillin*	*tistaġilli*	*tistaġillin*
3M	*bistaġill*	*bistaġillu*	*yistaġill*	*yistaġillu*
3F	*btistaġill*	*bistaġillin*	*tistaġill*	*yistaġillin*

Only the active participle genuinely belongs to the spoken variety. The passive participle is most probably borrowed from the standard dialect.

Table 151: Active and passive participles of *staġall* 'exploit'

	Active	Passive
MS	*mistaġill*	*mustaġall*
FS	*mistaġille*	*mustaġalle*
MP	*mistaġillīn*	*mustaġallīn*
FP	*mistaġillāt*	*mustaġallāt*

The imperative inflects as follows:

Table 152: Imperative of *staġall* 'exploit'

2MS	*staġill*
2FS	*staġilli*
2MP	*staġillu*
2FP	*staġillin*

3.4.2.10.3. C_2 = /y/

C_2 = /w/ verbs like *staṭwal–yistaṭwil* 'perceive as long' are regular. Only C_2 = /y/ verbs, such as *starāḥ–yistarīḥ* 'rest', are weak. The perfective behaves as follows. Final /ā/ shortens to /a/ when consonantal suffixes are added.

Table 153: Perfective of *starāḥ–yistarīḥ* 'rest'

	Singular	Plural
1	*staraḥt*	*staraḥna*
2M	*staraḥt*	*staraḥtu*
2F	*staraḥti*	*staraḥtin*
3M	*starāḥ*	*starāḥu*
3F	*starāḥat*	*starāḥin*

The stem of the imperfective is staCīC:

Table 154: Imperfective of *starāḥ–yistarīḥ* 'rest'

	b-imperfective		Bare imperfective	
	Singular	Plural	Singular	Plural
1	*bastarīḥ*	*mnistarīḥ*	*astarīḥ*	*nistarīḥ*
2M	*btistarīḥ*	*btistarīḥu*	*tistarīḥ*	*tistarīḥu*
2F	*btistarīḥi*	*btistarīḥin*	*tistarīḥi*	*tistarīḥin*
3M	*bistarīḥ*	*bistarīḥu*	*yistarīḥ*	*yistarīḥu*
3F	*btistarīḥ*	*bistarīḥin*	*tistarīḥ*	*yistarīḥin*

The active participle inflects as follows:

Table 155: Active participle of *starāḥ–yistarīḥ* 'rest'

MS	*mistarīḥ*
FS	*mistarīḥa*
MP	*mistarīḥīn*
FP	*mistarīḥāt*

The imperative inflects as follows:

Table 156: Imperative of *starāḥ–yistarīḥ* 'rest'

2MS	*starīḥ*
2FS	*starīḥi*
2MP	*starīḥu*
2FP	*starīḥin*

3.4.2.10.4. C_3 = /y/

The verb *starğa–yistarği* ‘dare’ belongs to this category. In the perfective, it inflects as follows:

Table 157: Perfective of *starğa–yistarği* ‘dare’

	Singular	Plural
1	*starğēt*	*starğēna*
2M	*starğēt*	*starğētu*
2F	*starğēti*	*starğētin*
3M	*starğa*	*starğu*
3F	*starğat*	*starğin*

The imperfective inflects as follows:

Table 158: Imperfective of *starğa–yistarği* ‘dare’

	b-imperfective		Bare imperfective	
	Singular	Plural	Singular	Plural
1	*bastarği*	*mnistarği*	*astarği*	*nistarği*
2M	*btistarği*	*btistarğu*	*tistarği*	*tistarğu*
2F	*btistarği*	*btistarğin*	*tistarği*	*tistarğin*
3M	*bistarği*	*bistarğu*	*yistarği*	*yistarğu*
3F	*btistarği*	*bistarğin*	*tistarği*	*yistarğin*

The active participle was recorded as follows.

Table 159: Active participle of *starğa–yistarği* ‘dare’

MS	*mistarği*
FS	*mistarğye*
MP	*mistarğ(y)īn*
FP	*mistarğyāt*

3.4.2.10.5. *stanna* ‘wait’

This verb, likely historically derived on the basis of the pattern staCCaC (St. *istaʔnā–yastaʔnī* ‘wait’), formally behaves like a

Form V tCaCCaC verb: *stanna–yistanna*. Another vestigial variant, *ttanna–yittanna*, is not used in the present-day dialect. The perfective inflects as follows:

Table 160: Perfective of *stanna–yistanna* 'wait'

	Singular	Plural
1	*stannēt*	*stannēna*
2M	*stannēt*	*stannētu*
2F	*stannēti*	*stannētin*
3M	*stanna*	*stannu*
3F	*stannat*	*stannin*

The imperfective inflects as follows:

Table 161: Imperfective of *stanna–yistanna* 'wait'

	b-imperfective		Bare imperfective	
	Singular	Plural	Singular	Plural
1	*bastanna*	*mnistanna*	*astanna*	*nistanna*
2M	*btistanna*	*btistannu*	*tistanna*	*tistannu*
2F	*btistanni*	*btistannin*	*tistanni*	*tistannin*
3M	*bistanna*	*bistannu*	*yistanna*	*yistannu*
3F	*btistanna*	*bistannin*	*tistanna*	*yistannin*

The active participle inflects as follows:

Table 162: Active participle of *stanna–yistanna* 'wait'

MS	*mistanni*
FS	*mistannye*
MP	*mistann(y)īn*
FP	*mistannyāt*

The imperative inflects as follows:

Table 163: Imperative of *stanna–yistanna* 'wait'

2MS	*stanna*
2FS	*stanni*
2MP	*stannu*
2FP	*stannin*

3.4.2.10.6. C_2 and C_3 are weak

The verb *staḥa–yistaḥi* 'be shy' belongs to this category. No other such verb has been recorded. Historically, it comes from the root *ḥ-y-y*. The noun is *ḥaya* 'decency'. This verb inflects like C_3 = /y/ verbs.

3.4.3. Four-consonant Roots

Although not as numerous as three-consonant roots, four-consonant roots form a substantial part of the lexicon. Many verbs belonging to this category are derived from three-consonant roots by various processes of insertion, doubling or blending. Examples of /n/-insertions are *waldan–ywaldin* 'behave like a child' (< *walad* 'child'), *ḥamran–yḥamrin* 'behave like a donkey' (< *ḥmār* 'donkey'). Doubling occurs most prominently with C_2 = C_3 roots, yielding $C_1aC_2C_1aC_2$: *šabšab* 'act like a youngster' (< *šabb* 'youngster'), *lamlam–ylamlim* 'collect with care' (< *lamm–ylimm* 'collect'), *ḥabḥab–yḥabḥib* 'kiss repeatedly' (< *ḥabb* 'kiss'). An example of C_1 doubling occurs in *baḥbaš–ybaḥbiš* 'dig repeatedly' (< *b-ḥ-š* 'dig'). Blending occurs in *xarbaṭ–yxarbiṭ* 'confuse', seemingly a blend between *x-r-b* 'damage' and *x-b-ṭ* 'hit'. Other verbs are simply derived from four-consonant nouns: *xatyar–yxatyir* 'become old' (< *xityār* 'old'), *talfan–ytalfin* 'phone' (< *talafōn* 'telephone'). Other four-consonant verbs are *faḥlaṭ–yfaḥliṭ* 'stumble', *balṭaš–ybalṭiš* 'cheat', *dagmaš–ydagmiš* 'cut (wood)', *falfal–yfalfil* 'cook rice',[5] *ʕangar–yʕangir* 'position one's headdress to express pride and joy', *bahdal–ybahdil* 'reprimand', *farfad–yfarfid* 'spread, loosen'. There are only two derivational templates: CaCCaC and prefixed *t*-CaCCaC.

3.4.3.1. CaCCaC

3.4.3.1.1. Strong Verbs

The following paradigm was recorded in the perfective of the verb *falfal–yfalfil* 'cook rice':

Table 164: Perfective of *falfal–yfalfil* 'cook rice'

	Singular	Plural
1	*falfalt*	*falfalna*
2M	*falfalt*	*falfaltu*
2F	*falfalti*	*falfaltin*
3M	*falfal*	*falfalu*
3F	*falfalat*	*falfalin*

The imperfective was recorded as follows:

Table 165: Imperfective of *falfal–yfalfil* 'cook rice'

	b-imperfective		Bare imperfective	
	Singular	Plural	Singular	Plural
1	*bafalfil*	*minfalfil*	*afalfil*	*nfalfil*
2M	*bitfalfil*	*bitfalfəlu*	*tfalfil*	*tfaləflu*
2F	*bitfaləfli*	*bitfaləflin*	*tfaləfli*	*tfaləflin*
3M	*bifalfil*	*bifaləflu*	*yfalfil*	*yfaləflu*
3F	*bitfalfil*	*bifaləflin*	*tfalfil*	*yfaləflin*

[5] The term *falfal* to refer to the method of cooking rice derives from *filfil* 'pepper' or *falfal* 'add pepper', although, intriguingly, no pepper is used in cooking rice.

The templates of the active and passive participles are mCaCCiC and mCaCCaC:

Table 166: Active and passive participles of *falfal–yfalfil* 'cook rice'

	Active	Passive
MS	*mfalfil*	*mfalfal*
FS	*mfaləfle*	*mfalfale*
MP	*mfaləflīn*	*mfalfalīn*
FP	*mfaləflāt*	*mfalfalāt*

The imperative inflects as follows:

Table 167: Imperative of *falfal–yfalfil* 'cook rice'

2MS	*falfil*
2FS	*faləfli*
2MP	*faləflu*
2FP	*faləflin*

3.4.3.1.2. C_2 = /w/ or /y/

These verbs do not behave irregularly but, because of monophthongisation, they have a peculiar shape: *CawCaC → CōCaC and *CayCaC → CēCaC. C_2 = /w/ verbs are more common than C_2 = /y/, for which only two verbs were recorded: *hēğan–yhēğin* 'sing *hğēni*, a folkloric tune' and *dēwan–ydēwin* 'spend time leisurely'. C_2 = /w/ verbs are *sōlaf–ysōlif* 'narrate (a story)', *gōṭar–ygōṭir* 'depart, leave', *bōrad–ybōrid* 'refresh, cool off', *dōzan–ydōzin* 'tune (a musical instrument)', *ḥōrab–yḥōrib* 'be on bad terms with someone'. The perfective is shown below:

Table 168: Perfective of *sōlaf–ysōlif* 'narrate'

	Singular	Plural
1	*sōlaft*	*sōlafna*
2M	*sōlaft*	*sōlaftu*
2F	*sōlafti*	*sōlaftin*
3M	*sōlaf*	*sōlafu*
3F	*sōlafat*	*sōlafin*

The imperfective inflects as follows:

Table 169: Imperfective of *sōlaf–ysōlif* 'narrate'

	b-imperfective		Bare imperfective	
	Singular	Plural	Singular	Plural
1	*basōlif*	*minsōlif*	*asōlif*	*nsōlif*
2M	*bitsōlif*	*bitsōlfu*	*tsōlif*	*tsōlfu*
2F	*bitsōlfi*	*bitsōlfin*	*tsōlfi*	*tsōlfin*
3M	*bisōlif*	*bisōlfu*	*ysōlif*	*ysōlfu*
3F	*bitsōlif*	*bisōlfin*	*tsōlif*	*ysōlfin*

The active participle inflects as follows. The passive participle was not recorded in spontaneous speech, although the forms *msōlaf*, *msōlafe*, *msōlafīn* and *msōlafāt* are regular.

Table 170: Active participle of *sōlaf–ysōlif* 'narrate'

MS	*msōlif*
FS	*msōlfe*
MP	*msōlfīn*
FP	*msōlfāt*

The imperative was recorded as follows:

Table 171: Imperative of *sōlaf–ysōlif* 'narrate'

2MS	*sōlif*
2FS	*sōlfi*
2MP	*sōlfu*
2FP	*sōlfin*

3.4.3.1.3. C_4 = /y/

The most common verb in this category is *warǧa–ywarǧi* 'show'. The variant *farǧa–yfarǧi* is less frequent. This verb appears to be a blend between the root *w-r-y* in the verb *warra* 'show' and *f-r-ǧ* (cf. *tfarraǧ* 'look'). The verb inflects as follows in the perfective:

Table 172: Perfective of *warǧa–ywarǧi* 'show'

	Singular	Plural
1	*warǧēt*	*warǧēna*
2M	*warǧēt*	*warǧētu*
2F	*warǧēti*	*warǧēti*
3M	*warǧa*	*warǧu*
3F	*warǧat*	*warǧin*

The following inflections were recorded in the imperfective.

Table 173: Perfective of *warǧa–ywarǧi* 'show'

	b-imperfective		Bare imperfective	
	Singular	Plural	Singular	Plural
1	*bawarǧi*	*minwarǧi*	*awarǧi*	*nwarǧi*
2M	*bitwarǧi*	*bitwarǧu*	*twarǧi*	*twarǧu*
2F	*bitwarǧi*	*bitwarǧin*	*twarǧi*	*twarǧin*
3M	*biwarǧi*	*biwarǧu*	*ywarǧi*	*ywarǧu*
3F	*biwarǧi*	*bitwarǧin*	*tiwarǧi*	*ywarǧin*

Only the active participle is attested:

Table 174: Active participle of *warǧa–ywarǧi* 'show'

MS	*mwarǧi*
FS	*mwarǧye*
MP	*mwarǧ(y)īn*
FP	*mwarǧyāt*

The imperative inflects as follows:

Table 175: Imperative of *warǧa–ywarǧi* 'show'

2MS	*warǧi*
2FS	*warǧi*
2MP	*warǧu*
2FP	*warǧin*

3.4.3.1.4. tCaCCaC

As noted above, the morpheme *t-*, whether prefixed or infixed, is a valency-decreasing device. It can have a passive meaning, as in *bahdal* 'reprimand' vs *tbahdal* 'be reprimanded', or reflexive, as in *farfad* 'spread, loosen' vs *tfarfad* 'spread or loosen oneself, relax'. The verb *tfakfak* 'disjoin itself in several pieces' derives from the transitive verb *fakfak* 'disjoin in several pieces', itself an intensive quadriliteral derivation through doubling of *fakk–yfukk* 'disassemble'. Another verb is *tḥarkaš* 'provoke', which inflects as follows in the perfective:

Table 176: Perfective of *tḥarkaš–yitḥarkaš* 'provoke'

	Singular	Plural
1	*tḥarkašt*	*tḥarkašna*
2M	*tḥarkašt*	*tḥarkaštu*
2F	*tḥarkašti*	*tḥarkaštin*
3M	*tḥarkaš*	*tḥarkašu*
3F	*tḥarkašat*	*tḥarkašin*

The imperfective inflects as follows:

Table 177: Imperfective of *ṯharkaš–yiṯharkaš* 'provoke'

	b-imperfective		Bare imperfective	
	Singular	Plural	Singular	Plural
1	*baṯharkaš*	*mniṯharkaš*	*aṯharkaš*	*niṯharkaš*
2M	*btiṯharkaš*	*btiṯharkašu*	*tiṯharkaš*	*tiṯharkašu*
2F	*btiṯharkaši*	*btiṯharkašin*	*tiṯharkaši*	*tiṯharkašin*
3M	*biṯharkaš*	*biṯharkašu*	*yiṯharkaš*	*yiṯharkašu*
3F	*btiṯharkaš*	*biṯharkašin*	*tiṯharkaš*	*yiṯharkašin*

The active participle inflects as follows:

Table 178: Active participle of *ṯharkaš–yiṯharkaš* 'provoke'

MS	*miṯharkiš*
FS	*miṯharəkše*
MP	*miṯharəkšīn*
FP	*miṯharəkšāt*

The imperative was recorded as follows:

Table 179: Imperative of *ṯharkaš–yiṯharkaš* 'provoke'

2MS	*ṯharkaš*
2FS	*ṯharkaši*
2MP	*ṯharkašu*
2FP	*ṯharkašin*

3.4.4. Masdars

Like most Arabic dialects, the variety discussed here has productive and systematic ways of deriving verbal nouns from some of the forms. Verbs belonging to Form I all have a masdar, but their shape is not always predictable: *saṭaḥ* 'lay (on flat ground)' → *misṭāḥ* 'laying', *simiʕ* 'listen' → *simʕ* 'listening', *maras* 'soak' →

mars ‘soaking’,[6] *ḥaraṯ* ‘plough’ → *ḥrāṯ* ‘ploughing’. Only Form I verbs whose second consonant is weak have a predictable masdar. If the second consonant is /w/, the template of the masdar is CōC and if the consonant is /y/, the template of the masdar is CēC, as shown below:

Table 180: Masdars of hollow verbs

C_2 = /w/		C_2 = /y/	
rāḥ–yrūḥ ‘go’	*rōḥ*	*bāʕ–ybīʕ* ‘sell’	*bēʕ*
nāl–ynūl ‘obtain’	*nōl*	*ṭāḥ–yṭīḥ* ‘go down’	*ṭēḥ*
šāf–yšūf ‘see’	*šōf*	*čāl–yčīl* ‘weight’	*čēl*

Form II masdars are formed using the template taCCīC: *ḥammaṣ* ‘roast’ → *taḥmīṣ* ‘roasting’, *gaddar* ‘estimate’ → *tagdīr* ‘estimation’. The masdar of *xallaf* ‘give birth’, however, is *xilfe* and not ***taxlīf*. Form II verbs whose last consonant is weak use the template tiC_1C_2āye: *rabba* ‘bring (someone) up’ → *tirbāye* ‘upbringing’, *salla* ‘entertain’ → *tislāye* ‘entertainment’, *xabba* ‘hide’ → *tixbāye* ‘hiding’, *nagga* ‘choose’ → *tingāye* ‘choosing’. Only two instances of tCiCCiC (cognate with the Form V Standard Arabic template taCaCCuC) used for the masdar of a Form II verb occurred in the corpus: *tgiṭṭiʕ* < *gaṭṭaʕ* ‘cut into pieces’ and *thillil*[7] < *hallal* / *thallal* ‘exult’.

Form III masdars are formed using the template mCāCaCa. Only sound roots seem to be eligible for this formation: *gāsam* ‘separate’ → *mgāsame* ‘separation’, *nāwaš* ‘lend, give’ → *mnāwaše*

---

[6] This verb is used to describe the process of rehydrating dried buttermilk (*ǧamīd*). The hydrated substance is called *marīs*.

[7] Also found in the saying *kuṯr it-thilil* ~ *it-thilli biǧīb iḍ-ḍēf ir-radi* ‘excessive glorification brings bad guests’.

'giving', *hāwaš* 'quarrel' → *mhāwaše* 'quarrelling', *ǧāwab* 'answer' → *mǧāwaba* 'answering', *xābaṭ* 'do things in disorder' → *mxābaṭa* 'doing things in disorder'.

Above Form III, masdar derivation is not productive any more. Speakers can still rely on standard derivations, but these are not part of the local stock. To overcome these morphological restrictions, speakers normally resort to masdar derivations of forms that are morphologically linked. Typically, Form V verbs will select Form II masdars, and Form VI verbs will select Form III masdars: *tsalla* 'have fun' → *tislāye* (< *salla*), *tbāṭaḥ* 'wrestle' → *mbāṭaḥa* (< *bāṭaḥ*). If these are not available, speakers will use the Form I masdar: *twāsaṭ* 'mediate' → *wāsṭa* 'pulling strings, mediation'.

Quadriliteral verbs productively form their masdar with the template CaCCaCa, whether Form I CaCCaC or Form II tCaCCaC: *bahdal* 'reprimand' / *tbahdal* 'be reprimanded' → *bahdale*. For verbs obviously derived from nouns, the masdar is the noun it was derived from: *dīwān* 'guest room', *dēwan* 'pass time leisurely' (root *d-y-w-n*).[8] In the traditional dialect, masdars are used primarily in constructions called *mafʕūl muṭlaq* in Arabic grammar, the so-called cognate object construction (see §4.4.3.1).

3.4.5. Summary of Verbal Morphology

Table 181 summarises the derivational possibilities of the verb. Only the perfective, the imperfective and the active participle can be said to be fully productive. The passive participle is attested

---

[8] As in the example *adēwin ʕind-hum dīwān* 'I used to pass time leisurely at their place'.

only for Forms I, II and III and Form I of four-consonant roots, and transparent masdar derivation is only fully available for Forms II and III and Form I of quadrilateral verbs. This constrasts sharply with standard Arabic, in which all the slots are filled.

Table 181: Morphology of the verb

		Perfective	Imperfecctive	Active	Passive	Masdar
Triliteral	I	CvCvC	CCvC	CāCiC	maCCūC	CvCC, C(v)Cv̄C,....
	II	CaCCaC	CaCCiC	mCaCCiC	mCaCCaC	taCCīl ~ tCiCCiC/ tiCCāye
	III	CāCaC	CāCiC	mCāCiC	-	mCāCaCa
	IV	(a)CCaC	CCiC	miCCiC	-	-
	V	tCaCCaC	tCaCCaC	mitCaCCiC	-	taCCīl ~ tCiCCiC/ tiCCāye
	VI	tCāCaC	tCāCaC	mitCāCiC	-	mCāCaCa
	VII	nCaCaC	nCaCiC	minCaCiC	-	CvCC, C(v)Cv̄C,....
	VIII	CtaCaC	CtaCiC	miCtaCiC	-	CvCC, C(v)Cv̄C,....
	IX	$C_1C_2aC_3C_3$	$C_1C_2aC_3C_3$	mi$C_1C_2aC_3C_3$	-	-
	X	staCCaC	staCCiC	mistaCCiC	-	-
Quadriliteral	I	CaCCaC	CaCCiC	mCaCCiC	mCaCCaC	CaCCaCa
	II	tCaCCaC	tCaCCaC	mitCaCCiC	-	CaCCaCa

3.5. Pronouns

Arabic has at minimum a set of free pronouns and a set of bound pronouns, usually functioning as possessive and object indices. Dative pronouns are not found in all varieties and their identification as a separate set is often not straightforward.

3.5.1. Free Pronouns

Table 182: Free pronouns

	Singular	Plural
1	*ana*	*iḥna*
2M	*int ~ inte*	*intu*
2F	*inti*	*intin*
3M	*hū ~ huwwa*	*hummu*
3F	*hī ~ hiyye*	*hinne*

One of the most salient features in the forms presented in Table 182 is gender distinction in the plural: *intu* vs *intin* and *hummu* vs *hinne*. Gender distinction in the plural is maintained in all the traditional dialects of Jordan.

Variation is found in the first-person singular in Jordan. Central Jordanian dialects mostly have *ana*, while Ḥōrāni is known for using *ani*. Interestingly, *ani* was also sporadically recorded in the village of Fḥēṣ, close to Salt, although the most common form is overwhelmingly *ana*. On closer scrutiny, it appears that the use of *ani* in Central Jordan is a recessive feature of the traditional dialect, whose use is limited to marked speech acts. Consider the following example:

(11) *ani ʕārif čēf id-dinya rāḥat*

1SG know.AP.MS how DEF-world go.PFV.3FS

'I have no idea how things have changed!'

The dialects discussed here also have apocopated variants for the 2MS *int*, 3MS *hū* and 3FS *hī*. While the short form *int* is less frequent than *inte*, the apocopated forms of the third person are far more frequent in the corpus than the long forms, as shown in Table 183, which lists the number of tokens. The 3MP *hummu* seems to occur in most Central varieties (Palva 1989 reports it for Kerak). Ḥōrāni dialects usually exhibit *huṃṃa*. The quality of final /a/ in both *huwwa* and *hiyye* follows the rules of the phonology and phonetics of the feminine morpheme *-a* (§3.2.2.1.1): *-a* raises to [ɛ] after the coronal /y/ in *hiyye* and raising is inhibited after the bilabial approximant /w/ in *huwwa*.

Table 183: Frequency of short and long forms

int	16	*hū*	217	*hī*	83
inte	45	*huwwa*	13	*hiyye*	25

3.5.2. Bound Pronouns

Table 184: Bound pronouns

	Singular			Plural		
	C_	V_	_-*š*	C_	V_	_-*š*
1	*-i* ; *-ni*	V:*-y(e)* ; V:*-ni*	*-ī*, *-yī* ; *-nī*	*-na*	V:*-na*	*-nā*
2M	*-ak*	V:*-k*	*-kī*	*-ku*	V:*-ku*	*-kū*
2F	*-ič*	V:*-č*	*-čī*	*-čin*	V:*-čin*	*-činn*
3M	*-o*	V:	*-hū*	*-hum*	V:*-hum*	*-humm*
3F	*-ha*	V:*-ha*	*-hā*	*-hin*	V:*-hin*	*-hinn*

As shown in Table 184, gender distinction is also maintained in the plural in the set of bound pronouns. Allomorphic variation broadly depends on three contexts: after a consonant (C_), after a vowel (V_) and before the negation marker *-š*. After a vowel, the suffixation of bound pronouns triggers the lengthening of the contact vowel (V:). The suffixation of the negation marker *-š* triggers vowel lengthening or consonant gemination.

In the 1SG, the form *-i* is used as a possessive, whereas *-ni* is an object form: *ahl-i* 'my family' vs *biʕrif-ni* 'he knows me'. After a vowel, lengthening occurs: *axū-y* 'my brother', *ḍarabū-ni* 'they hit me'. Before *-š*, lengthening and, as expected, stress shift onto /ī/ occur: *bidd-ī-š* 'I don't want', *maʕā-yī-š* 'I don't have', *(ma) tiʕzim-nī-š* 'don't invite me'.

In the 2MS, the allomorph *-ak* appears after a consonant, as in *wlād-ak* 'your children'; *-k* after a vowel, as in *axū-k* 'your brother'. The allomorph *-kī* occurs before the negator *-š*, as in *maʕ-kī-š* 'you (M) don't have'. It contrasts with feminine *-čī*: *maʕ-čī-š* 'you (F) don't have' (see below). The form *-kī* is surprising from a pan-dialectal perspective, because in most dialects, *-ki* is a feminine form. Indeed, this is what happened in Amman, where the levelling of /č/ resulted in the neutralisation of gender distinction: *maʕ-kī-š* came to be used for both male and female addressees. It seems that an increasing number of speakers in Amman tend to restore gender distinction, by using the form *maʕ-kā-š* for the masculine and *maʕ-kī-š* for the feminine.

In the 2FS, *-ič* occurs after consonants, as in *wlād-ič* 'your (F) children', and *-č* after vowels, as in *abū-č* 'your (F) father'. The allomorph *-čī* is selected before *-š*: *mniʕrif-čī-š* 'we don't know you'.

In the 3MS, *-o* appears after a consonant: *ḥamūlt-o* 'his clan'. After a vowel, lengthening occurs: *abū* 'his father'. The allomorph *-hū* is selected before *-š*: *mā ykubbin-hū-š* 'they would not throw it' (NEG throw.SBJV.3FP-3MS-NEG).

In the 1PL, Ḥōrāni dialects exhibit the allomorph *-ana* after a two-consonant cluster: *ʕind-ana* 'at ours', as opposed to Central Jordanian *ʕin-na*. Stress normally falls on the first syllable [ˈʕɪndana]. This allomorph is reminiscent of Najdi "trochaic" Bedouin dialects (Ingham 1994, 30).

In the 3FS, 2PL and 2MP, the contact vowel is lengthened, as in *yiǧī-ha* 'it comes to her', *ʕašā-na* 'our dinner', *mniʕṭī-ku* 'we give you'. Before *-š*, the final vowel is lengthened (and stressed): *ma badd-hā-š* 'she doesn't want', *btiʕrif-nā-š* 'you don't know us', *badd-kū-š* 'you don't want'.

In the 2FP, 3MP and 3FP, the most salient feature, besides vowel lengthening after a vowel, is the gemination of the contact consonant when the negation marker *-š* suffixes to the base:

mniʕriff-(h)umm-əš [mnɪʕrɪffʊmmʊʃ] 'we don't know them'
a-b(i)ǧīb-(h)inn-əš [abʤiːbɪnnɪʃ] 'he doesn't bring them (F)'

In casual speech, initial /h/ in *-ha*, *-hum* and *-hin* often undergoes deletion before a vowel or a voiced consonant, as illustrated in the preceding example *a-b(i)ǧīb-(h)inn-əš* [abʤiːbɪnnɪʃ] 'he doesn't bring them (F)'. Other instances are *min-(h)um* [ˈmɪnʊm] 'from them (M)', *il-(h)in* [ˈʔɪlɪn] 'they (F) have', *gadd-(h)a* [ˈgadda] 'as much as her'.

Bound pronouns can also attach to proper names to mark endearment. This was mostly recorded in the speech of the older generation when speaking about younger close relatives such as sons and grandsons, as in (12), where a grandmother refers to her grandson Aḥmad using the 1PL bound pronoun *-na*.

(12)	*hayy-o*	*(a)ḥmad-na*	*bʕayyi*	*yitġaṭṭa*
	DEM-3MS	Aḥmad-1PL	refuse.IPFV.3MS	cover.SBJV.3MS

ġēr	*bi*	*ḥrām*
except	with	blanket

‘There, (our) Aḥmad, he refuses to cover himself except with a (woollen) blanket’

3.5.3. Dative Pronouns

Table 185: Dative pronouns

	Singular				Plural			
	C_; V_	CC_	C_-š	CC_-š	C_; V_	CC_	C_-š	CC_-š
1	*-li*		*-lī*		*-lna*	*-ilna*	*-lnā*	*-ilnā*
2M	*-lak*		*-lkī*		*-lku*	*-ilku*	*-lkū*	*-ilkū*
2F	*-lič*		*-lčī*		*-lčin*	*-ilčin*	*-lčinn*	*-ilčinn*
3M	*-lo*		*-lhū*	*-ilhū*	*-lhum*	*-ilhum*	*-lhumm*	*-ilhumm*
3F	*-lha*	*-ilha*	*-lhā*	*-ilhā*	*-lhin*	*-lhinn*	*-lhinn*	*-ilhin*

The dialects investigated here and many other Levantine varieties developed a set of dative pronouns from the grammaticalisation of the preposition *la* ‘for, to’ and bound pronouns. The kind of allomorphic variation seen in these dative pronouns is therefore the same as for bound pronouns: *xuḏ-lak* ‘take for you’ vs *mā lkī-š* ‘you don’t have’; *waddēt-lo* ‘I sent to him’ vs *mā ṭāliʕ-ilhū-š* ‘he is not entitled (to get anthing)’ (NEG go_out.AP.MS-3MS.DAT-NEG).

The recognition of a grammaticalised set of dative pronouns is warranted by the fact that their phonological and morphological behaviour is similar, albeit not identical, to that of object pronouns, rather than to that of a preposition to which bound forms are added.

When a dative pronoun attaches to a vowel-final base, it creates a new phonological word, because there is only one primary stress. In this case, it behaves like an object pronoun (see also §3.1 for one attested exception).

wigfū-lhum	[wʊgfˈuːlhʊm]	'they stood against them'
alāgī-lič	[alaːˈgiːlɪʧ]	'I find for you (F)'

Interestingly, things are different when it attaches to a base ending in a consonant. In the examples below, if the verb and the attached pronoun had formed a single phonological word, stress would have fallen on the penultimate syllable. Consequently, dative pronouns behave like suffixes when they attach to a vowel-final base and like clitics when they attach to a consonant-final base.

asōlif-lič	[aˈsoːlɪflɪʧ]	'I tell you (F)'
sōlaf-li	[ˈsoːlaflɪ]	'He told me'
baḏḏakkar-lak	[baðˈðakkarlak]	'I remember for you'

This clitic behaviour is still different, though, from that of a normal preposition. In that case there are two primary stresses, indicative of two phonological words, as shown below:

ağu ʕalē-hum	[ˈʔaʤʊ ʕaˈleːhʊm]	'they came down to them'
yikḥatu bī-hum	[ˈyɪkħatʊ ˈbiːhʊm]	'they drag them'

In addition to this, the rightward morphological boundary of the verb is the negation marker *-š*. When dative pronouns attach to the right of the verb, they do so within the morphological boundary, that is, right before the marker *-š*: *biğīb-lī-š* 'he doesn't bring to me'. Moreover, in Levantine Arabic and elsewhere in the Asian part of the Arabic-speaking world, the verb has only one morphological slot at its right boundary, filled either by an object pronoun or a dative pronoun. If an object pronoun (*-ha*) and a dative pronoun (*-lič*) co-occur, the morphological slot will be filled by the dative pronoun, and the object pronoun will be hosted by the morpheme *iyyā-* outside of the verb, as illustrated in (13).

(13) *badd-ič awaṣṣif-lič iyyā-ha*
want-2FS describe.SBJV.1SG-2FS.DAT OBJ-3FS
'Do you want me to describe it to you?'

Another argument is the allomorph of the feminine marker *-a* when a dative pronoun suffixes to an active participle. In this case, the allomorph *-īt* is the same as in the case of the suffixation of object pronouns:

(14) a. *kātb īt ilha*
write.AP F 3FS.DAT
[kaːtbiːtɪlha]
'she has written to her'

b. *kātb īt ha*
write.AP F 3FS.OBJ
[kaːtbiːtha]
'she has written it'

Consequently, there are solid phonological and morphological grounds to posit the existence of a grammaticalised set of dative pronouns.

3.5.4. The Pronominal Host *iyyā-*

The primary function of *iyyā-* is to host a pronominal object when no morphological slot is available on the predicate. There are three cases in which this occurs:

- Pronominal theme and recipient in ditransitive verbs (§4.4.2.4)

(15) *nṭā-hum* *iyyā-ha*
give.PFV.3MS-3MP OBJ-3FS
'He gave it to them'

- Pronominal object and pronominal dative in monotransitive verbs (§3.5.3)

(16) *išraḥ-lo* *yyā-ha*
explain.IMP.MS-DAT.3MS OBJ-3FS
'Explain it to him'

- Pronominal object of prepositional predicates *ʕind-* 'at' (§4.4.1.2.2) and *badd-* 'want' (§4.4.1.2.4)

(17) *bisawwi* *illi* *badd-o* *yyā*
do.IPFV.3MS REL want-3MS OBJ.3MS
'He does what he wants'

The morpheme *iyyā* is also selected when two free pronouns are coordinated with *w* 'and': *iḥna w iyyā-ku* 'we and you (PL)', *ana w iyyā-č* 'me and you (F)', *hū w iyyā* 'him and him', *hū w iyyā-ha* 'him and her', *hī w iyyā* 'her and him'. First-person pronouns have to occur first: *ana w iyyā* 'me and him', leaving ***hū w iyyā-ni* strongly dispreferred.

The 1SG is *iyyā-ni*, not ***iyyā-y*. Its use is mostly attested in object position with *badd-*: *badd-o yyā-ni* 'he wants me' (want-3MS OBJ-1SG).

Table 186: Inflections of *iyyā-*

	Singular	Plural
1	*iyyā-ni*	*iyyā-na*
2M	*iyyā-k*	*iyyā-ku*
2F	*iyyā-č*	*iyyā-čin*
3M	*iyyā*	*iyyā-hum*
3F	*iyyā-ha*	*iyyā-hin*

3.5.5. Indefinites

3.5.5.1. *wāḥad* 'someone'

The numeral *wāḥad* 'one' and its feminine equivalent *waḥade* are used as indefinite pronouns meaning 'someone'. Unlike in other varieties, there is no morphological plural of *wāḥad*.

(18) *bī wāḥad biḥibb waḥade*
EXIST one.M love.IPFV.3MS one.F
'(if) someone (a boy) loves someone (a girl)'

3.5.5.2. *il-wāḥad* 'one'

The difference between *wāḥad* 'someone' and *il-wāḥad* 'one' is that the latter is non-referential. In (19), *il-wāḥad* is generic and does not refer to any specific individual.

(19) *il-yōm il-wāḥad miš māyin ʕa bn-o*
DEF-day DEF-one NEG control.AP.MS on son-3SG
'Nowadays, one doesn't even control his son'

3.5.5.3. *ḥada* 'anyone' and *maḥada* 'no one'

In positive polarity, *ḥada* is used in interrogative and conditional clauses. The difference between *ḥada* and *wāḥad* is one of specificity: the use of *ḥada* forces a generic reading, whereas *wāḥad* implies specificity.

(20) *ḥada* *wiṣil*

someone arrive.PFV.3MS

'Did someone arrive?'

(21) *šifət* *ḥada*

see.PFV.2MS someone

'Did you see someone?'

In negative polarity, it combines most often with the negation marker *mā* and tends to form with it one single phonological unit, as suggested by stress assignment on the first syllable and the shortening of initial /ā/: *mā ḥada* [maː ˈħada] > *maḥada* [ˈmaħada] 'no one'. The former realisation is a feature of hyper-articulated speech (see §4.5.1.10.2 for more on the negation of indefinites).

3.5.5.4. *nās* ~ *nāsāt* 'someone, some'

The lexical meaning of *nās* is 'people'. It normally triggers plural or feminine agreement according to the level of individuation. The morpheme is also used as an indefinite pronoun, interpretable as a suppletive plural of *wāḥad* 'someone'. The grammaticalisation of *nās* as an indefinite pronoun is evident from the fact that it triggers masculine singular agreement, as shown in (22), and not feminine singular or masculine plural, as it does when it refers to its lexical meaning.

(22) *fī* *nās* *mā* *biḥibb-əš* *yrūḥ*
EXIST some NEG like.IPFV.3MS-NEG go.SBJV.3MS
'Some don't like to go'

In negative polarity, it means 'no one', as exemplified in (23).

(23) *il-yōm* *amērka* *baṭṭal* *nās* *yrūḥ*
DEF-day America stop.PFV.3MS some go.SBJV.3MS
'These days no one goes to America any more'

3.5.5.5. *il-kull* 'everyone'

The indefinite *il-kull*, composed of the article *il-* and the quantifier *kull* 'all', triggers singular agreement, not plural. It remains neutral as far as gender assignment is concerned, because it depends on the gender of the referent. In (24), the referent is a male, whereas in (25), the referent is a female.

(24) *il-kull* *badd-o* *zalmat-o*
DEF-all want-3MS man-3MS
'Everyone wants his own man (whom he supports)'

(25) *il-kull* *badd-ha* *tihǧim* *ʕalē*
DEF-all want-3FS attack.SBJV.3FS on.3SG
'Everyone (F) wanted to jump on him'

3.5.5.6. *kull wāḥad, kull waḥade* 'everyone'

The indefinite *kull wāḥad* (feminine *kull waḥade*) combines the quantifier *kull* 'each, all' and indefinite *wāḥad* 'someone':

(26) *wallāhi kull wāḥad bisōlif šikəl, ʕammō*

by_God each one.M tell.IPFV.3MS shape uncle

'Everyone has his own version of the story man!'

(27) *šaggt-ēn mʔaǧǧarāt kull waḥade b-ṯalaṯ mīt lēra*

flat-DU rented.FP each one.F with-three hundred dinar

'Two flats are rented, three hundred dinars each'

3.5.5.7. *kull man* 'everyone'

This indefinite, composed of the quantifier *kull* 'each, all' and the interrogative *man* 'who', is rare in the corpus (only three tokens). Semantically, the difference from *kull wāḥad* is that *kull man* is restricted to human referents. It seems to belong to an archaic register that is not making its way into the speech of the younger generations.

(28) *kull man ʕārif ʕašīrt-o*

each who know.AP.MS clan-3MS

'Everyone knows his own clan'

3.5.5.8. *man* 'anyone'

The morpheme *man* is primarily an interrogative 'who', but it also occurs as an indefinite pronoun in the frozen idiom:

(29) *ḥēša man simiʕ*

no_offence who hear.PFV.3MS

'No offence to those who listen'

3.5.5.9. *flān* 'so-and-so'

The Arabic word *flān* 'so-and-so', and its feminine *flāne*, is not referential. The speaker has no specific entity in mind at the time of utterance. It closely corresponds to French *untel*. The adjective *flāni* is regularly derived, with the suffix *-i*. It is only used as a noun modifier (not a predicate) and indicates that the entity the noun refers to is non-specific: *in-nhār lə-flāni* 'that (non-specific) day'.

(30)

wēnta	*minrūḥ*	*ana*	*wiyyā-č*	*yā*	*flāne*
when	go.IPFV.1PL	1SG	and-2FS	VOC	so-and-so.F

'When shall we go, you and I, dear so-and-so'

3.5.5.10. *il-xāyir* and *il-māxūḏ* 'thingy'

Both *il-xāyir* and *il-māxūḏ* are used when the speaker has difficulties retrieving the appellation of the entity. The use of *il-māxūḏ* is affective, whereas *il-xāyir* is neutral. The plural *il-xāyrāt* is also in use.

(31)

wēn	*ḥaṭṭēt*	*ha-l-māxūḏ*	~	*il-xāyir*
where	put.PFV.2MS	DEM-DEF-thingy		DEF-thingy

'Where did you put that thing (whose name I can't recall)'

3.5.5.11. *baʕḏ̣* 'some'

The morpheme *baʕḏ̣* refers to a part-of-a-whole relation with another entity. Morphosyntactically, it behaves like a noun, because it can be modified by another noun (32) and bound pronouns can suffix to it (33). The construction *baʕəḏ̣ min* + noun is also attested: *baʕəḏ̣ min il-masīḥiyye* 'some of the Christians' (some from DEF-Christians).

(32)

gāmu	*baʕḏ̣*	*il-ʕašāyir*	*min*	*ʕabbād*
stand_up.PFV.3MP	some	DEF-clans	from	Abbad

'Some ʕAbbādi clans stood up (rebelled)'

(33) *baʕəḏ̣-hum sātir ʕōrt-o baʕəḏ̣-hum laʔ*
some-3MP cover.AP.MS genital-3MS some-3MS no
'Some of them are decently dressed, some of them aren't'

3.5.5.12. *(ʔi)ši* 'something'

The morpheme *(ʔi)ši* 'something' has two realisations, *ʔiši* with prothetic *ʔi* and monosyllabic *ši*. The former is common to most Palestinian and Jordanian varieties, whereas the latter is common in Northern Levantine varieties. In terms of corpus distribution, the prothetised variant significantly outnumbers the monosyllabic one, with a ratio of three to one. It also occurs in adverbial collocations such as *ʔawwal ʔiši* 'first of all', *āxir ʔiši* 'lastly', *akṯar ʔiši* 'above all'. The phrase *ʔiši hēč* (~ *(ʔi)ši hēk*) 'something like that' can also be realised *hēk (ʔi)ši*, in which case the affrication of /k/ seems to be inhibited by the presence of contiguous /š/. Ellipsis often occurs, leaving *(ʔi)ši* alone, coordinated either with *w* 'and' or *aw* 'or' and placed clause-finally.

(34) *bsawwu šaġḷāt la l-wlād iz-zġār w iši hēč*
do.IPFV.3MP things for DEF-kids DEF-small and thing so
'They do things for small kids and stuff like that'

(35) *biǧū-hum dāyman ḏ̣yūf aǧānib w iši*
come.IPFV.3MP-3MP always guests foreigners and thing
'They always have foreign guests and things like that'

An interesting structure involves the use of *ʔiši* to refer to indefinite collective human entities in asyndetically coordinated clauses. It conveys the idea of commotion and a certain degree of messiness:

(36) *mʕabbaye l-balad! iši bilʕab iši*
full.F DEF-town thing play.IPFV.3MS thing
biṭlaʕ ʕa š-šağara!
go_up.IPFV.3MS on DEF-tree
'It's full of people downtown! Some play, others climb trees!'

3.6. Demonstratives

3.6.1. Pronominal and Adnominal

Only forms are discussed in this section (for more on the syntactic behaviour of demonstratives, see §4.1.5). Demonstratives are either pronominal or adnominal. The dialect of Salt and its surroundings, like most dialects, has a two-way distance contrast: proximal and distal.

Table 187: Demonstratives

	Proximal	Distal
Masculine	*hāḏa*	*haḏāk*
Feminine	*hāḏi* ~ *hāy*	*haḏīč*
Plural	*haḏōl*	*haḏolāk*

These demonstratives are most often velarised: *hāḏ̣(a)*, *hāḏ̣ōl*, *haḏ̣āk*, *haḏ̣(o)lāk*. Even *haḏīč* was recorded once as *haḏ̣īč*.

There is another set, almost identical to the one presented in Table 187, that is used either pronominally or post-nominally but not pre-nominally: *hāḏa z-zalame* ~ *iz-zalame hāḏ̣* 'this man' but not *haḏ̣ iz-zalame*. Formally, it consists of the base form augmented with the formative *-a*, except the masculine proximal form *hāḏ̣*, which is the apocopated version of *hāḏa*.

Table 188: Pronominal and post-nominal demonstratives

	Proximal	Distal
Masculine	*hāḏ̣*	*haḏ̣āka*
Feminine	*hāye*	*haḏīče*
Plural	*haḏōḷa*	*haḏolāka*

There is also an apocopated allomorph *ha-* that does not inflect for gender and number. It can occur alone, or alongside post-nominal full demonstratives: *ha-l-midrase hāy* 'this school' (DEM-DEF-school DEM).

There are agreement mismatches in some phrases involving a demonstrative and a noun denoting a temporal element. A recurrent pattern is the use of *haḏīkt* or *haḏīčt* followed by a masculine time-denoting noun. The form *haḏīkt* ~ *haḏīčt* in itself is interesting, because the intrusive final /t/ looks like the construct allomorph of the feminine marker *-a*: *hadīkt in-nhār* (M) 'that day'. This intrusive /t/ also surfaces without agreement mismatch in *haḏīčt il-marra* (F) 'that time' and *haḏīčt il-lēle* (F) 'that night'. The corpus also contains instances of masculine demonstratives and feminine or plural heads: *haḏ̣āk l-iyyām* 'those days', *haḏ̣āk il-lēle* 'that night'. The plural form *l-iyyām* is expected to trigger feminine agreement (see §4.3), and so is the feminine noun *lēle* 'night'. These agreement mismatches and the construct-like /t/ of the feminine marker *-a* tend to suggest that speakers are reinterpreting these phrases as genitive constructions.

3.6.2. Sentential Demonstratives

Sentential demonstratives, also called presentatives, are deictic demonstratives that are used predicatively or as subjects of nonverbal predicate clauses (Diessel 1999; Manfredi 2014). Gender and distal constrast is lost, although gender can be restored by affixing bound pronouns.

3.6.2.1. *hāy*

In the current state of the dialect, the most common presentative is *hāy* (glossed 'there'), as illustrated in (37). It is homophonous with the proximal feminine demonstrative. When bound pronouns attach to *hāy*, /ā/ is realised short and /y/ geminates, as shown in (38). The use of *(h)iyyā-* as a presentative also occurs, but this was not recorded in spontaneous speech: *hiyyā-ha* 'there she is'. The presentative usage of *iyyā-* is not unknown in other dialects, such as coastal Palestinian, where it still has some currency.

(37) *hāy rubəʕ lēra waḷḷa mā btitgayyad*

DEM quarter dinar I_swear NEG be_recorded.IPFV.2MS

'Here is a quarter of a dinar, you don't have to give it back (to me)'

(38) *hayy-ič bitḥaṭṭbi*

DEM-2FS collect_wood.IPFV.2FS

'There you are collecting wood!'

Table 189: Inflections of *hāy*

	Singular	Plural
1	*hayy-ni*	*hayy-na*
2M	*hayy-ak*	*hayy-ku*
2F	*hayy-ič*	*hayy-čin*
3M	*hayy-o*	*hayy-hum*
3F	*hayy-ha*	*hayy-hin*

3.6.2.2. *hari*

The form *hari* is considered by most speakers to belong to the old dialect. In Labovian terms, it seems to be a stereotype. Etymologically, it harks back to the deictic formative *h-* and the root *r-ʔ-y* 'see', which makes it one of the three remnants of that root in the dialect (the other ones being the discourse marker *tara* and the verb *warra–ywarri* 'show'). A variant *harwi* was also recorded, as exemplified in (41).

(39) *hari wlād il-maʕārif fakku*

DEM children DEF-schools release.PFV.3MP

'Here are the school children, they went out'

(40) *ʔil-o mazraʕa harī-ha ʕala ṭarīg is-salṭ*

for-3MS farm DEM-3FS on way DEF-Salt

'He has a farm, there it is on the way to Salt'

(41) *harwī-ha l-bagara rūḥu ǧībū-ha*

DEM-3FS DEF-cow go.IMP.MP bring.IMP.MP-3FS

'There is the cow, go and fetch it'

Table 190: Inflections of *hari*

	Singular	Plural
1	*harī-ni*	*harī-na*
2M	*harī-k*	*harī-ku*
2F	*harī-č*	*harī-čin*
3M	*harī*	*harī-hum*
3F	*harī-ha*	*harī-hin*

3.7. Interrogative Proforms

Some grammars distinguish between interrogative pronouns and interrogative adverbs. Pronouns are usually understood as substitutes for noun phrases and adverbs are predicate- or clause-modifying lexical(ised) formations. In practice, any kind of substitute is often labelled pronominal. Consequently, interrogative adverbs are also pronominal. To avoid any ambiguity, we decided to use the term proform, which remains agnostic about the kind of constituent that it replaces. The list of these proforms is given in Table 191. The dialects of central and northern Jordan exhibit slight differences compared to other Levantine dialects.

Table 191: Interrogatives

šū, (wi)ššū, ēš	'what'	*čēf, šlōn*	'how'
man	'who'	*gaddēš*	'how much'
wēn	'where'	*bēš*	'how much'
wēnta, (a)mēt	'when'	*čam*	'how many'
lēš, lawēš	'why'	*ayy(a)*	'which'

3.7.1. *šū, (wi)ššū, ēš* 'what'

The form *šū* is found almost everywhere in the Levant. The geminated variants *ššū* and *wiššū* are much more localised and only surface in the speech of the broadest informants, as illustrated in (42).

(42) *xarrab il-bāb u mā baʕrif wiššū*
damage.PFV.3MS DEF-door and NEG know.IPFV.1SG what
'He damaged the door and I don't know what (else)'

The interrogative also optionally inflects for gender: *šī* (who.F).

(43) *šī l-ʕālam hāy illi ʕind-ak?*
what.F DEF-people DEM REL at-2MS
'What sort of people are at your place?!'

The variants *ēš* and *šū* are in near-complementary distribution. While *ēš* can broadly be used instead of *šū*, its usage also extends to noun modifier and object of a preposition. At least in the traditional dialect, the use of *šū* as a noun modifier in a genitive construction or as an object of a preposition is dispreferred. This is also reflected in the interrogatives *lēš* 'why', *gaddēš* 'how much' and *bēš* 'for how much', all of which combine a preposition with *ēš*.

abu ēš int	'what is your name?' (father what 2SG)	(***abu šū int*)
miššān ēš	'what for?'	(***miššān šū*)
miṯəl ēš	'like what?'	(***miṯəl šū*)

3.7.2. *man* 'who'

The interrogative *man* is the indigenous form in Central and Northern Jordan, although pan-Levantine *mīn* can be heard. Speakers tend to favour the use of gender-inflected forms when asking a question, leaving *man* for indirect questions. The most common gender-inflected forms are *manu* (M) and *mani* (F). There are also some inflected forms that were obtained by elicitation: *manummu* 'who.MP' and *maninne* 'who.FP'. There are also emphatic forms which involve various degrees of coalescence with the pronouns *hū* and *hī*: *manū* ~ *manu hū*, *manī* ~ *mani hī*.

(44) *in ana mā satart ibn axū-y manu badd-o*
if 1SG NEG protect.PFV.1SG son father-1SG who.M want-3MS
yusutr-o mani badd-ha tōxḏ-o
protect.SBJV.3MS-3MS who.F want-3FS take.SBJV.3FS-3MS
'If I don't protect my nephew, who will? Who will take him? (If I don't find a wife for my nephew, who will? What woman will marry him?)'

3.7.3. *wēn* 'where'

The interrogative *wēn* 'where' is found across the Levant. It can combine with the prepositions *la* and *min*: *la wēn* 'where to', *min wēn* 'where from'. The latter can also be contracted to *minnēn* and *mnēn*. Bound pronouns can attach to *wēn*: *mnēn-hum* 'where are they from?' (where_from-3MP), unless focused:

(45) *wēn hī hassa*
where 3FS now
'Where is she now?'

3.7.4. *wēnta ~ (a)mēt(a)* 'when'

The morpheme *wēnta* is an assimilated form of **w-ēmta* (< **wa-ay-mata*). It was recorded consistently in Salt (46). As for *(a)mēt(a)*, it was recorded in Fḥēṣ (47). In Salt, the morpheme *mēt(a)* appears only in the conjunction *mēta-ma* 'when'.

(46) *wēnta minrūḥ ana wiyyā-č*
when go.IPFV.1PL 1SG and-2FS
'When shall we go, you and me?'

(47) *mēt aǧa l-farrāz*
when come.PFV.3MS DEF-land_surveyor
'When did the land surveyor come?'

3.7.5. *čēf, šlōn* 'how'

The most common form is *čēf* (48) and its unaffricated variant *kēf*.

(48) *čēf banēt gaṣər bī-ha*
how build.PFV.2MS farmhouse in-3FS
'How did you build a farmhouse in it?'

In our data, the use of *šlōn* is mostly restricted to 'how is X' or 'how do you see X', which may suggest that *šlōn* and *čēf* are or were in near-complementary distribution, with *šlōn* limited to adjectival predicative expressions. These can be primary predicates as in (49) or secondary predicates as in (50). Both *čēf* ~ *kēf* and *šlōn* permit the suffixation of bound pronouns: *šlōn-ak* ~ *kēf-ak* ~ *čēf-ak* 'How are you?'.

(49) *mḥammad šlōn-o*

Muhammad how-3MS

'Muhammad, how is he?'

(50) *šlōn šāyif id-dinya*

how see.AP.MS DEF-world

'How do you see the world?'

There is also some degree of idiomisation: *čēf ḥāl-ak* 'how are you' is common, but not *šlōn ḥāl-ak* (although *šlōn ṣiḥḥt-ak* 'how is your health' is possible).

3.7.6. *lēš, lawēš* 'why'

Combining the preposition *la* 'for, to' and *ēš* 'what', *lēš* is found in most Levantine dialects; *lawēš* is much more localised. It is recessive in the dialect and found only in the speech of the broadest informants. On the whole, our data exhibit a ratio of 1 to 4 in favour of *lēš*.

(51) *int lēš miḍḍāyig*

2SG why annoyed

'Why are you annoyed?'

(52) *yī ġabra lawēš baḥurr ḥāl-i*

oh EXCLAM why torture.IPFV.1SG REFL-1SG

'Blimey, why am I torturing myself?'

3.7.7. *gaddēš* 'how much'

The interrogative *gaddēš* (or a variant thereof) is pan-Levantine. It combines the nominal *gadd* 'quantity' and *ēš* 'what' and is used for quantities. Unlike *čam* ~ *kam* 'how many' (see below), it is a real pronoun in that it interrogates a quantified full NP.

(53) *gaddēš inbāʕat*

how_much be_sold.PFV.3FS

'How much was (the land) sold for?'

(54) *gaddēš il-baraka inte*

how_much DEF-benediction 2MS

'How old are you?'

3.7.8. *bēš* 'for how much'

The interrogative *bēš* 'for how much' lexicalised from the preposition *b-*, to which the interrogative *ēš* 'what' was added. The preposition *b-* has both a locative 'in' and an instrumental 'with' meaning. While *b-ēš* can also mean 'with what', it reflects here an extension of the instrumental meaning of *b-*, because the semantics of *bēš* are restricted to questioning the price of something (which can also be conveyed by *gaddēš* 'how much'). In (55), the speaker is asking a rhetorical question, which explains the in-situ syntax of the interrogative.

(55) *šārīn arbaʕa! šārīn-ha bēš? sittīn ʕanz!*
buy.AP.PL four buy.AP.PL-3FS for_how_much sixty goat
'Four of them had bought (this land)! How much had they paid for it? Sixty goats!'

3.7.9. *čam* 'how many'

The morpheme *čam* 'how many' is also used for quantities, but unlike *gaddēš*, it is not a pronoun, but rather a pro-numeral that needs a head noun. It is placed to the left of the head noun, which has to be in the singular. If the speaker does not want to specify the quantified element, the indefinite pronoun *wāḥad* has to be used: *čam wāḥad* 'how many?' (F *čam waḥade*). In this sense, it is more like an interrogative determiner. Other variants are *čamm* ~ *ačamm* ~ *ačamman*, or, with the preposition *min*, *(a)čam(m) min* ~ *ačamm min*. The affricate /č/ often undergoes deaffrication, so all the variants presented here also surface with /k/. Speakers extend the use of *čam* to a prenominal quantifier meaning 'a couple of' (§4.1.1.2).

(56) *čam safaṭ əbtišrab inte*
how_many pack drink.IPFV.2MS 2MS
'How many packs (of cigarettes) do you smoke (a day)?'

3.7.10. *ayy(a)* 'which'

The interrogative *ayy(a)* is also a determiner, because it modifies an NP: *ʔayy(a) yōm* 'what day?'. There is also another allomorph *ayyāt*, used with bound pronouns: *ayyāt-o* 'which one?'.

(57) *miš ʕārif ayyāt-o*
NEG know.AP.MS which-3MS
'I don't know which one'

Another interrogative determiner common in the area, but not one recorded frequently in our data, is *anu* (M), *ani* (F): *anu wāḥad, ani waḥade* 'which one'.

3.8. Other Proforms

3.8.1. *hēč* 'so, in this way'

The proform *hēč* 'so, in this way' is often realised without affrication: *hēk*. It can be augmented with what looks like the feminine morpheme *-a*: *hēče* ~ *hēča* ~ *hēke* ~ *hēka*. This form is common to most Levantine dialects and is a substitute for expressions denoting manner and shape.

(58) *iḥna kull-na hēč mitʕawwdāt min ʔumm-na*
1PL all-1PL so used.FP from mother-1PL
'We are all like that, used (to it) from our mother'

3.8.2. *ha-l-gadd(e)* 'that much'

The proform *ha-l-gadd(e)* is formed from the nominal *gadd* 'size', to which the article *il-* and the apocopated demonstrative *ha-* attach. Unlike *hēk*, which refers to shape and manner, *ha-al-gadd* is a substitute for expressions referring to size and quantity:

(59) *tlidd* *ʕa* *rummānit* *čitiff-(h)a*

look.SBJV.2MS on pomegranate(?) shoulder-3FS

ha-l-gadd *əmdabbara*

that_much bruised.PP.FS

'(If) you look at her shoulder (humerus), (you would see) that she got a bruise that big'

3.8.3. *kaḏa* 'things like that'

The morpheme *kaḏa* (seemingly from *ka* 'like' and *ḏa* 'this') is used when speakers want to mark off the final boundary of an item enumeration. In (60), the speaker is describing an old administrative building in Salt called *is-sarāya*, used in Ottoman times for various legal and administrative procedures.

(60) *bāgī-ha* *mā* *bāgī-ha* *muddaʕi* *ʕām*

rest-3FS NEG rest-3FS prosecutor general

u *maḥākim* *ṣuləḥ* *u* *kaḏa*

and courts peace and things_like_that

'The rest (of the *sarāya*) consisted of one prosecutor and magistrates courts and things like that'

3.9. Prepositions

Most dialects of Arabic have two sets of prepositions. The first one is composed of items that are core prepositions, i.e., they need an object. The second set is composed of preposition-like nominals that can be used on their own, or be modified by a noun. There are also complex prepositions composed of a preposition and a noun.

3.9.1. Core Prepositions

3.9.1.1. *b(i)* ~ *fi* 'in'

The preposition *bi* has locative, instrumental and comitative meanings: *bi l-ʔurduniyye* 'in the University of Jordan' (in DEF-Jordanian.F), *b-adē-hum* 'with their hands' (with-hands-3MP). The comitative meaning is restricted to motion events, as illustrated in (61).

(61) *wēn* *ruḥt* *bi* *ṣ-ṣalīb*
where go.PFV.2MS with DEF-cross
'Where did you go with the cross?'

The object of some verbs is marked with the preposition *b-*, such as *tʕarraf bi* 'get acquainted with someone', *fakkar bi* 'think of'.

In the current state of the dialect, *bi* is interchangeable with *fi*, although the traditional dialect only had *bi*. The intrusion of *fi* is a contact-induced change, from Amman and ultimately from other Levantine varieties.[9]

When bound pronouns suffix to *bi*, the contact vowel is lengthened.

Table 192: Inflections of *bi* ~ *fi*

	Singular	Plural
1	*biyye* ~ *fiyye*	*bī-na* ~ *fī-na*
2M	*bī-k* ~ *fī-k*	*bī-ku* ~ *fī-ku*
2F	*bī-č* ~ *fī-č*	*bī-čin* ~ *fī-čin*
3M	*bī* ~ *fī*	*bī-hum* ~ *fī-hum*
3F	*bī-ha* ~ *fī-ha*	*bī-hin* ~ *fī-hin*

[9] Southern Levantine (Muʔābi) varieties, e.g., Kerak, use *fi* consistently. This is one of the main distinguishing features between Central-Northern and Southern Jordanian.

3.9.1.2. *min* 'from'

The primary meaning of this preposition is ablative: *min hōn* 'from here'. In unstressed position, /i/ elides: *mn ahəl-ha* 'from her family'. When followed by the article *il-*, it is not uncommon for final /n/ to drop: *m-iḓ-ḓiffe il-ġarbiyye* 'from the West Bank'. Some instances of a partitive reading are also attested, in combination with the apocopated demonstrative *ha-*: *ağīb min ha-z-zibde* (bring.SBJV.1SG from DEM-DEF-butter) 'I used to bring some butter'; *bifittu min ha-l-xubəz* (crumble from DEM-DEF-bread) 'they crumble some bread'.

The object of some verbs is also marked with *min*, as shown in (62).

(62) *wēnta ban-na nuxluṣ min ha-š-šaġla*
when want-1PL end.SBJV.1PL from DEM-DEF-thing
'When will we be done with this thing?'

When bound pronouns attach to *min*, final /n/ is geminated before vowel-initial segments:

Table 193: Inflections of *min*

	Singular	Plural
1	*minn-i*	*min-na*
2M	*minn-ak*	*min-ku*
2F	*minn-ič*	*min-čin*
3M	*minn-o*	*min-hum*
3F	*min-ha*	*min-hin*

3.9.1.3. *ʕan* 'from'

The preposition *ʕan* is also usually translated as 'from', but the main difference from *min* is that it conveys an idea of remoteness 'away from', as shown in (63).

(63) *kull il-ʕālam naglat ʕan-ha*
all DEF-people move.PFV.3FS from-3FS
'All the people moved away from it'

Another common meaning conveyed by *ʕan* is 'about' (64).

(64) *isʔalī-ni ʕan illi ṣār əmbāriḥ*
ask.IMP.FS-1SG about REL happen.PFV.3MS yesterday
'Ask me about what happened yesterday'

As expected, final /n/ geminates when vowel-initial pronouns are suffixed.

Table 194: Inflections of *ʕan*

	Singular	Plural
1	*ʕann-i*	*ʕan-na*
2M	*ʕann-ak*	*ʕan-ku*
2F	*ʕann-ič*	*ʕan-čin*
3M	*ʕann-o*	*ʕan-hum*
3F	*ʕan-ha*	*ʕan-hin*

3.9.1.4. *la* 'to, for'

The core meanings of *la* are allative and benefactive: *la ʕammān* 'to Amman', *la ǧ-ǧēš* 'for the army'. This preposition is also used in predicative possessive constructions of the type *il-i arḍ* 'I have a piece of land' (for-1SG land) and in genitive constructions involving kinship relations: *ibən xāl-ha la umm-i* 'the cousin of my mother' (son maternal_uncle-3FS for mother-1SG). Northern Levantine dialects also use *la* as a differential object marker. This construction is not attested in the traditional dialects of Jordan. When bound pronouns attach to *la*, the allomorph *il-* is used. The allomorph *il-* also surfaces in combination with the interrogative *man* 'who': *il-man* 'to whom?'. This is seemingly a contact-induced form, borrowed from the Bedouin dialect of the ʕAdwān, which exhibits *il-min*.

Table 195: Inflections of *la*

	Singular	Plural
1	*il-i*	*il-na*
2M	*il-ak*	*il-ku*
2F	*il-ič*	*il-čin*
3M	*il-o*	*il-hum*
3F	*il-ha*	*il-hin*

3.9.1.5. *maʕ* 'with'

The core meaning of *maʕ* is comitative: *maʕ umm-ha* 'with her mother'. An interesting feature of the traditional dialect is that *maʕ* can also be used with a locative meaning, as shown in (65). Some speakers exhibit a heavily velarised initial /m/: *ṃaʕ* [mˤɑʕ].

(65) *timši* *maʕ* *is-šāriʕ*
walk.SBJV.2MS with DEF-street
'You walk along the street'

When bound pronouns attach to the preposition, two sets are available, one with the allomorph *maʕ* and one with the allomorph *maʕa*, in which case final /a/ lengthens when bound pronouns are added.

Table 196: Inflections of *maʕ*

	Singular			Plural		
1	*maʕ-i*	~	*maʕā-y*	*maʕ-na*	~	*maʕā-na*
2M	*maʕ-ak*	~	*maʕā-k*	*maʕ-ku*	~	*maʕā-ku*
2F	*maʕ-ič*	~	*maʕā-č*	*maʕ-čin*	~	*maʕā-čin*
3M	*maʕ-o*	~	*maʕā*	*maʕ-hum (maḥḥum)*	~	*maʕā-hum*
3F	*maʕ-ha (maḥḥa)*	~	*maʕā-ha*	*maʕ-hin (maḥḥin)*	~	*maʕā-hin*

3.9.1.6. *ʕala* 'on'

The preposition *ʕala* has two core meanings: allative 'to' and superessive 'on'. While the superessive meaning is found cross-dialectally, the allative use is largely restricted to the Levantine area. This meaning is also conveyed by *la* and they are often interchangeable: *ʕa l-bēt* ~ *la l-bēt* 'home'. Some verbs require an object marked with *ʕala*: *ṭall ʕala* 'look at', *ḥāfaḏ̣ ʕala* 'keep'. The preposition takes the following forms when bound pronouns attach to it:

Table 197: Inflections of *ʕala*

	Singular	Plural
1	*ʕalay-ye*	*ʕalē-na*
2M	*ʕalē-k*	*ʕalē-ku*
2F	*ʕalē-č*	*ʕalē-čin*
3M	*ʕalē*	*ʕalē-hum*
3F	*ʕalē-ha*	*ʕalē-hin*

3.9.1.7. *ʕind* 'at'

The main use of *ʕind* is adessive 'at': *yitgāḏ̣a ʕind šēx* (seek_justice.SBJV.3MS at sheikh) 'he would seek justice from a sheikh'. The preposition is also used in predicative possessive clauses: *ʕindhum maktabe* (at-3MP library) 'they have a library'. For bound pronouns attached to *ʕind,* the following forms were recorded. Note that Ḥōrāni dialects have *ʕind-ana* instead of *ʕin-na* ‘at ours’, which is a Central Jordanian form.

Table 198: Inflections of *ʕind*

	Singular	Plural
1	*ʕind-i*	*ʕin-na*
2M	*ʕind-ak*	*ʕind-ku*
2F	*ʕind-ič*	*ʕind-čin*
3M	*ʕind-o*	*ʕind-hum*
3F	*ʕind-ha*	*ʕind-hin*

3.9.1.8. *dūn, bala* ‘without’

The morpheme *dūn* can be used alone, as in *dūn mʔāxaḏe* ‘no offence’, but surfaces most often in combination with the prepositions *bi* and *min*: *bdūn laḥme* ‘without meat’, *min dūn ḏanb* ‘without fault’.

(66) *lissa baʕətt-(h)a btigra l-ğarīde*

still still-3FS read.IPFV.3FS DEF-newspaper

mindūn naḏḏārāt

without glasses

‘She still reads the newspaper without glasses’

The morpheme *bala* has the same meaning but has much less currency: *bala wağəʕ ha-r-rās* ‘without racking your brain’ (without pain DEM-DEF-head).

(67) *mā biṭlaʕ bala fṭūr*

NEG exit.IPFV.3MS without breakfast

‘He doesn’t leave the house without eating breakfast’

3.9.1.9. *mšān* and *ʕašān* 'for'

The morpheme *mšān* comes from the contraction of *minšān*. Only contracted variants are attested. The geminated form *miššān* is also common: *miššān ḥalāl-hum* 'for their livestock'. The morpheme *ʕašān* has the same meaning but is less frequent than *mšān* (7 tokens of *ʕašān* in the corpus vs 74 tokens of *mšān* and its variant *miššān*). It can also be used as a conjunction 'in order to'. Although *ʕašān* is often used as a conjunction in Levantine dialects, this is seemingly not shared by traditional Central and Northern Jordanian, where it is only used as a preposition.

(68) *ḏabəḥ u saləx yṣīr ʕašān-hin*
slaughter and skinning become.SBJV.3MS for-3FP
'They would slaughter and skin each other for them (the women they kidnapped)'

3.9.1.10. *ǧamb* and *ḥadd* 'next to'

Both prepositions have the same meaning and they have equal currency in the dialect: *ǧamb il-bēt* 'next to the house', *ḥadd dār slēmān* 'next to Suleiman's house'. They are also augmented with the preposition *b-* 'in': *b-ḥadd dēr dibwān* 'next to Dēr Dibwān', *b-ǧamb ir-ruǧum* 'next to the cairn'. The realisation *b-ǧanəb* was also recorded: *b-ǧanəb-hin* 'next to them (F)'.

3.9.1.11. *gbāl* 'in front of'

This word also has a velarised variant *g̣ḅāḷ* [gbɑːɫ]. It was recorded only once without a complement, so it is probably best categorised as a preposition: *gbāl il-galʕa* 'in front of the castle'.

It can also be marked with *min*: *min gbāl arḏ̣ ʕīsā-na* 'in front of the land of our Issa'.

3.9.1.12. *ʕugub* and *baʕəd* 'after'

The most common way to express 'after' is *baʕəd*:

(69) *baʕəd il-walad ǧābat binət*

after DEF-boy bring.PFV.3FS girl

'After the boy, she had a girl'

As with *gabl* 'before', a formative /ī/ is inserted between the preposition and bound pronouns.

Table 199: Inflections of *baʕd*

	Singular	Plural
1	*baʕdiy-ye*	*baʕdī-na*
2M	*baʕdī-k*	*baʕdī-ku*
2F	*baʕdī-č*	*baʕdī-čin*
3M	*baʕdī*	*baʕdī-hum*
3F	*baʕdī-ha*	*baʕdī-hin*

The form *ʕugub* was presumably borrowed from neighbouring Bedouin varieties, in which it is extremely common. In the current state of the dialect, *ʕugub* is extremely recessive and has been almost completely supplanted by *baʕəd*. Contrary to *baʕəd*, with *ʕugub*, /ī/ does not normally occur between the preposition and bound pronouns: *ʕugub-ha* 'after it', although *ʕugbī-ha* may be heard.

(70) *winn ʕugb is-sitte*

DM after DEF-six

'It was after six o'clock'

3.9.1.13. *miṯl* and *zayy* 'like'

Both prepositions are in use and they are to a large extent interchangeable, as suggested by their relatively even distribution (95 tokens of *zayy* and 104 tokens of *miṯl*): *zayy il-yōm* 'like today', *miṯəl-hin* 'like them (F)'. A common construction is *zayy* X *zayy* Y or *miṯl* X *miṯl* Y 'X and Y are the same': *miṯl-i miṯəl abu z-zalame hāḏa* (like-1SG like father man DEM) 'Me and the father of this man are the same'.

3.9.1.14. *badāl* 'instead'

This preposition is widely attested across the Levant.

(71) *badāl is-sabt mumkin il-xamīs*
instead DEF-Saturday maybe DEF-Thursday
'Instead of Saturday, maybe Thursday'

3.9.1.15. *ġādī* ~ *ġādiyye* 'beyond'

This preposition, etymologically linked to the adverb *ġād* 'there', belongs to the traditional dialect. It has two variants, *ġādī* and *ġādiyye*: *ġādī ǧaraš* 'beyond Jerash', *ġādiyye nāʕūr* 'beyond Naour'.

3.9.1.16. *tala* 'towards, in the direction of'

The preposition *tala* belongs to the old dialect. Only two tokens occur in the corpus. Example (72) was recorded from an elderly informant from Fḥēṣ.

(72) *əb-ǧāl illi tala l-ḳaṃṃ*
in-side REL towards DEF-camp
'On the side towards the military camp'

3.9.1.17. *yamm* 'next to'

Like *tala* 'towards', the preposition *yamm* belongs to an archaic register; only one token was recorded.

(73)

gāl	*yōmin*	*ṭabbēna*	*miṯəl-mā*	*tgūl*
say.PFV.3SG	when	arrived.PFV.1PL	as	say.SBJV.2SG

yamm	*ʔumm yanbūte*	*tala*	*čifər hūda…*
next_to	Umm Yanbuteh	towards	Kufr Hūda

gāl	*winn*	*id-dinya*	*ṯalǧ*
say.PFV.3SG	DM	DEF-worl	ice

'He said when we got there, next to Umm Yanbuteh towards Kufr Hūda, it was snowing'

3.9.1.18. *gadd* 'as much as'

This preposition arose from the grammaticalisation of the noun *gadd* 'size'.

(74)

tbīʕ	*gadd*	*is-sūg*	*kull-o*
sell.IPFV.3FS	as_much_as	DEF-market	all-3MS

'She alone used to sell has much as the whole market'

3.9.1.19. *ḥawāla* and *bīǧi* 'around'

The preposition *ḥawāla* primarily has a spatial meaning: *ḥawāla l-balad* 'around the town'. It is also often used in the sense 'approximately'. The syntax remains the same and has to be followed by a noun: *ḥawāla alfēn dulum* 'around two thousand dunams (decares)'.

The morpheme *bīǧi*, equivalent to *ḥawāla* in its meaning of 'approximately', comes from the grammaticalisation of the inflected form *biǧi* 'he comes' (third masculine singular imperfective of *aǧa* 'come'). It has lost its inflectional properties and remains invariable. Syntactically, it surfaces mostly to the left of an NP (75), hence its classification as a preposition, although it was recorded once to the right of the noun, as shown in (76):

(75) *afitt* *bīǧi* *ʕašar* *xaməsṭaʕšar* *əšrāk*
crumble.SBJV.1SG around ten fifteen loaf
b-ha-l-lagən *hāḏ*
in-DEM-DEF-bowl DEM
'I used to crumble around ten to fifteen loaves in that bowl'

(76) *bitġaddu* *ha-n-nās* *...bīǧi...*
have_lunch.IPFV.3MP DEM-DEF-people ...around...
xaməs *mīt* *wāḥad* *bīǧi*
five hundred one around
'These people have lunch, around... 500 of them'

The speaker inserted a pause to recall the right number, and then uttered *bīǧi* after the NP, suggesting that rightward placement is possible.

3.9.1.20. *abu* 'quantity'

The morpheme *abu*, whose lexical meaning stretches from 'father' to 'owner', is also being grammaticalised into what looks like a preposition to denote vagueness when expressing a quantified referent.

(77) *il-ʕašāyir* *il-ʔaṣliyye* *abu* *xaməs* *sitt* *ʕašāyir*
DEF-clans DEF-original around five six clans
'The original clans are around five or six'

(78) *bī-ha siǧən siǧən əmwakkat yaʕni hōn abu sāʕt-ēn*

in-3FS prison prison temporary meaning here around hours-DU

'There was a prison, that is a custody prison, around two or three hours'

3.9.1.21. *ka* 'as'

The preposition *ka*, which may have been borrowed from Standard Arabic, is used as a functive preposition 'in the quality of'.

(79) *badd-hum yiḏbaḥū-na ka naṣāra*

want-3MP slaughter.SBJV.3MP-1PL as Christians

'They want to slaughter us, as Christians'

3.9.1.22. *xlāf* 'beside'

This preposition *xlāf* belongs to the traditional dialect. Only a handful of tokens were recorded, as exemplified in (80).

(80) *ṭagm-ēn kanabayāt… xlāf illi ǧāb-o*

set-DU sofas beside REL bring.PFV.3MS-3MS

'Two sets of sofas… beside the one he brought'

3.9.2. Preposition-like Morphemes

These are morphemes that indicate for the most part spatial relations and whose origin is mostly nominal. A property they have in common is that their complement can be omitted.

3.9.2.1. *tiḥt* and *ḥādir* 'under'

The traditional form is *tiḥt*, although *taḥt* can be heard: *kān bī-ha sāḥa tiḥət* 'there was a yard below' (be.PFV.3MS in-3FS yard below), *tiḥət dār-ku* 'below your house'. When bound pronouns suffix to *tiḥt*, the vowel /ī/ is inserted between the base and the suffix:

Table 200: Inflections of *tiḥt*

	Singular	Plural
1	*tiḥtiyye*	*tiḥtī-na*
2M	*tiḥtī-k*	*tiḥtī-ku*
2F	*tiḥtī-č*	*tiḥtī-čin*
3M	*tiḥtī*	*tiḥtī-hum*
3F	*tiḥtī-ha*	*tiḥtī-hin*

The morpheme *ḥādir* is recessive and can only be found in the speech of the broadest speakers: *tiḥət dār-ku min ḥādir* (under house-2MP from below) 'down below your house'.

3.9.2.2. *barra* 'outside'

This form is common to most Levantine dialects: *mā ḏ̣all-əš ʔiši barra* (NEG remain.PFV.3MS-NEG thing outside) 'there is nothing left outside'. The construct form is *barrīt* or *barrāt*: *barrīt il-balad* 'out of town'.

3.9.2.3. *ǧuwwa* 'inside'

The morpheme *ǧuwwa* is well attested in most varieties of Arabic. An example is *hī ǧuwwa* (3FS inside) 'she is inside'. The construct form is *ǧuwwīt*: *ǧuwwīt il-bēt* 'inside the house'.

3.9.2.4. *fōg* 'above'

The morpheme *fōg* is common to most Arabic dialects: *ʕumr-o fōg it-tisʕīn* (age-3MS above DEF-ninety) 'he is more than ninety years old'. When bound pronouns attach to *fōg*, /ī/ is inserted between the base and the suffix:

Table 201: Inflections of *fōg*

	Singular	Plural
1	*fōgiy-ye*	*fōgī-na*
2M	*fōgī-k*	*fōgī-ku*
2F	*fōgī-č*	*fōgī-čin*
3M	*fōgī*	*fōgī-hum*
3F	*fōgī-ha*	*fōgī-hin*

3.9.2.5. *gabəl* 'before'

The morpheme *gabəl* is sometimes velarised [gɑbɨɫ]. Examples are *gabl iḍ-ḍuhər* 'before midday' and (81).

(81) *gabəl mudde ʕāmlīt-li xall arbaʕ ganāni*

before period do.AP.FM-1SG.DAT vinegar four bottles

'Some time ago, she had made four bottles of vinegar for me'

A vowel /ī/ is inserted between *gabəl* and bound pronouns:

Table 202: Inflections of *gabl*

	Singular	Plural
1	*gabliy-ye*	*gablī-na*
2M	*gablī-k*	*gablī-ku*
2F	*gablī-č*	*gablī-čin*
3M	*gablī*	*gablī-hum*
3F	*gablī-ha*	*gablī-hin*

3.9.2.6. *giddām* 'in front of'

Unlike *gbāl*, *giddām* can appear on its own, or be modified by a noun: *is-sčāfiyye la giddām* (DEF-Skāfiyye to front) 'the Skāfiyye market is in front', *giddām əwlād-o* (in_front_of children-3MS) 'in front of his children'.

Table 203: Inflections of *giddām*

	Singular	Plural
1	*giddām-i*	*giddām-na*
2M	*giddām-ak*	*giddām-ku*
2F	*giddām-ič*	*giddām-čin*
3M	*giddām-o*	*giddām-hum*
3F	*giddām-ha*	*giddām-hin*

3.9.2.7. *wara* 'behind'

The morpheme *wara* is common to most Arabic dialects: *ugʕud wara* 'sit on the back', *wara ha-ṭ-ṭāwle* (behind DEM-DEF-table) 'behind this table'. Final /a/ is lengthened when bound pronouns suffix to the base:

Table 204: Inflections of *wara*

	Singular	Plural
1	*warā-ye*	*warā-na*
2M	*warā-k*	*warā-ku*
2F	*warā-č*	*warā-čin*
3M	*warā*	*warā-hum*
3F	*warā-ha*	*warā-hin*

3.9.2.8. *ḥasab* 'according to'

This morpheme exhibits peculiar behaviour. Bound pronouns cannot attach to it: ***ḥasab-o* 'according to him', and it has to be followed by a full noun phrase: *ḥasab il-mudīr* 'according to the boss'. Headless relative clauses are also accepted: *ḥasab illi smiʕt-o* (according_to REL hear.PFV.1MS-3MS) 'according to what I heard'. Used alone, it means 'it depends'.

3.9.3. Complex Prepositions

These prepositions are composed of a simplex preposition and a noun.

3.9.3.1. *la-ḥadd*

This preposition is composed of *la* ‘to’ and the noun *ḥadd* ‘limit’. It surfaces mostly in the phrase *la-ḥadd il-ʔān* ‘until now’, as well as in one instance of *la-ḥadd il-yōm* ‘until this day’.

3.9.3.2. *b-gāʕ* ‘down’

This preposition is composed of *b-* ‘in’ and *gāʕ* ‘bottom’.

(82)	*ṣaffat*	*əhnāk*	*b-gāʕ*	*tīnit*	*kassāb*
	park.PFV.3FS	there	below	fig	Kassāb

‘(The car) parked there, below Kassāb’s fig tree’

3.9.3.3. *b-wasṭ* ‘in the middle’

The preposition can be realised in various ways: *b-wasaṭ*, *b-wasṭ*. Emphasis can propagate leftward and /w/ partially assimilates to preceding /b/, yielding the surface form [ƀƀʷɑsˤtˤ]. When bound pronouns attach, /ī/ is inserted: *ḅḅʷaṣṭī-hum* ‘in the middle of them’.

3.9.3.4. *bi-ḥḏa* ‘next to’

This complex preposition combines the preposition *bi-* ‘in’ and the nominal *ḥḏa* ‘side’. It belongs to an archaic register and is only used by broad speakers. The root *ḥ-ḏ-y* is also attested in the verb *tḥaḏḏa* 'approach'. Example (83) is a traditional saying in sedentary Jordanian.

(83)	*badd-ī-š*	*anām*	*bi-ḥḏā-k*
	want-1SG-NEG	sleep.SBJV.1SG	in-side-2MS

'I don't want to sleep next to you!'

bitrayyiḥ-ni	*min*	*rīḥt*	*əfsā-k*
relax.IPFV.2MS-1SG	from	smell	fart-2MS

'(Good!) I'll take a break from the stench of your fart!'

3.9.3.5. *ʕa-rās* 'after'

This preposition is composed of *ʕa* 'on' and *rās* 'head': *ʕa rās-o* 'after him'. Its use seems limited to the succession of pregnancies. Interestingly, it has not totally lexicalised, because it keeps inflectional properties, as shown in (84), where the plural *rūs* 'heads' is used because it modifies a plural head.

(84)	*ǧibət*	*sabəʕ*	*banāt*	*ʕa-rūs*	*baʕəḍ-hin*
	bring.PFV.1SG	seven	girls	on-heads	RECP-3FP

'I gave birth to seven girls one after the other'

3.10. Numerals

3.10.1. Cardinals

The cardinal numbers in sedentary Jordanian do not differ a great deal from other Levantine dialects. Gender distinction is maintained only for 'one' and 'two', as shown below. Sedentary Jordanian stands out with respect to the form *waḥade*, as opposed to *waḥde* elsewhere in the Levant.

Table 205: Inflections of *wāḥad* and *ṯnēn*

	Masculine	Feminine
'one'	*wāḥad*	*waḥade*
'two'	*ṯnēn*	*ṯintēn*

From three to ten, gender distinction has been reallocated. The suffix *-a* does not mark gender any more and the distribution of the bare forms and the suffixed forms is sensitive to syntax and semantics. The general rule is that bare forms are used when a counted item immeditately follows the numeral. Suffixed forms are used when the numeral stands on its own or follows the counted item (see §4.1.6 for the syntax of numerals): *ṯaman kfūf* 'eight slaps'. Exceptions to this rule occur with recent loanwords: *ṯalāṯe kīlo* 'three kilograms', *ʕašara santi* 'ten centimetres'.

Table 206: Numerals 1–10

	Bare	-*a*		Bare	-*a*
'three'	*ṯalāṯ*	*ṯalāṯe*	'seven'	*sabʕ*	*sabʕa*
'four'	*arbaʕ*	*arbaʕa*	'eight'	*ṯaman*	*ṯamānye*
'five'	*xams*	*xamse*	'nine'	*tisʕ*	*tisʕa*
'six'	*sitt*	*sitte*	'ten'	*ʕašar*	*ʕašara*

From eleven to nineteen, there are also two sets: one bare set and one with the ending *-ar*, which is used when the numeral is followed by a counted item: *ṯnaʕš-ar girš* 'twelve piasters'.[10]

[10] This is another distinguishing feature between Central–Northern and Southern Jordanian, where *-ar* forms are not used.

Table 207: Numerals 11–19

	Bare	-ar		Bare	-ar
'eleven'	*ḥdaʕš*	*ḥdaʕšar*	'sixteen'	*sittaʕš*	*sittaʕšar*
'twelve'	*ṭnaʕš*	*ṭnaʕšar*	'seventeen'	*sabəʕṭaʕš*	*sabəʕṭaʕšar*
'thirteen'	*ṯalaṯṭaʕš*	*ṯalaṯṭaʕšar*	'eighteen'	*ṯamanṭaʕš*	*ṯamanṭaʕšar*
'fourteen'	*arbaʕṭaʕš*	*arbaʕṭaʕšar*	'nineteen'	*tisəʕṭaʕš*	*tisəʕṭaʕšar*
'fifteen'	*xaməsṭaʕš*	*xaməsṭaʕšar*			

Tens are mostly similar across dialects:

Table 208: Tens

'twenty'	*ʕišrīn*	'sixty'	*sittīn*
'thirty'	*ṯalāṯīn*	'seventy'	*sabʕīn*
'forty'	*arbʕīn*	'eighty'	*ṯamānīn*
'fifty'	*xamsīn*	'ninety'	*tisʕīn*

Hundreds are normally formed using a numeral followed by *miyye* 'one hundred'. When followed by a counted item, the construct form *mīt* is employed:

Table 209: Hundreds

	Standalone	Construct
'one hundred'	*miyye*	*mīt*
'two hundred'	*mītēn*	*mītēn*
'three hundred'	*ṯalāṯ miyye*	*ṯalāṯ mīt*
'four hundred'	*arbaʕ miyye*	*arbaʕ mīt*
'five hundred'	*xaməs miyye*	*xaməs mīt*
'six hundred'	*sitt miyye*	*sitt mīt*
'seven hundred'	*sabəʕ miyye*	*sabəʕ mīt*
'eight hundred'	*ṯaman miyye*	*ṯaman mīt*
'nine hundred'	*tisəʕ miyye*	*tisəʕ mīt*

Thousands are formed using a numeral followed by the plural *t-ālāf*:

Table 210: Thousands

'one thousand'	*alf*	'six thousand'	*sitt t-ālāf*
'two thousand'	*alfēn*	'seven thousand'	*sabəʕ t-ālāf*
'three thousand'	*ṯ(a)lat t-ālāf*	'eight thousand'	*ṯaman t-ālāf*
'four thousand'	*arbaʕ t-ālāf*	'nine thousand'	*tisəʕ t-ālāf*
'five thousand'	*xaməs t-ālāf*		

Millions, although not common in daily speech, are normally expressed with the word *malyōn*, the dual *malyōnēn* 'two million' and the plural *malāyīn* 'millions' with numerals from three to nine: *ṯalaṯ malāyīn* 'three million', *arbaʕ malāyīn* 'four million', *xames malāyīn* 'five million', *sitt malāyīn* 'six million', *sabəʕ malāyīn* 'seven million', *ṯaman malāyīn* 'eight million', *tisəʕ malāyīn* 'nine million'.

3.10.2. Ordinals

As in standard Arabic, ordinals from two to ten are formed with the pattern CāCiC. 'First' has a suppletive root and pattern. From two to ten, the feminine is normally formed by adding the morpheme *-a*. The plural of *awwal* 'first' was recorded as *ʔawāla*: *il-ʕašara l-ʔawāla* 'the first ten'.

Table 211: Ordinals

	Masculine	Feminine		Masculine	Feminine
'first'	*awwal*	*ʔūla*	'sixth'	*sādis*	*sādse*
'second'	*ṯāni*	*ṯānye*	'seventh'	*sābiʕ*	*sābʕa*
'third'	*ṯāliṯ*	*ṯālṯe*	'eighth'	*ṯāmin*	*ṯāmne*
'fourth'	*rābiʕ*	*rābʕa*	'nineth'	*tāsiʕ*	*tāsʕa*
'fifth'	*xāmis*	*xāmse*	'tenth'	*ʕāšir*	*ʕāšre*

Above ten, using cardinal numbers is the only option, but speakers express doubts about these constructions: *id-dars lə-ḥdaʕš* 'the eleventh lesson'.

3.10.3. Fractions

Like other Levantine dialects, sedentary Jordanian uses *nuṣṣ* for 'half': *nuṣṣ nhār* 'half a day'. The pattern CuCC is used for higher fractions: *t̠ilt̠* ~ *t̠ult̠* 'third', *rubʕ* 'quarter' (plural *rbāʕ* < *arbaʕa* 'four'), *xums* 'fifth' (< *xamse* 'five'). There seem to be restrictions on forming fractions above five, and *suds* 'sixth', *subʕ* 'seventh' and *tusʕ* 'ninth', although attested in Standard Arabic, are only reluctantly accepted as part of the native stock. According to speakers' own judgements, this is not the case with *t̠umn* 'eighth' and *ʕušr* 'tenth', which are claimed to have more currency because of their common use in inheritance legislation. There are no morphological means of forming fractions above ten.

3.11. Adverbs

We discuss here adverbs as a word class (for adverbial modification as a strategy, see §4.4.3). Adverbs are often seen as a catch-all category for all lexemes or morphemes that belong to minor word classes. On the whole, there are two approaches to adverbs: narrow and broad. We first discuss the narrow approach, followed by the broad approach.

Functional views on language entertain the idea that basic word classes can be identified through the combination of three prototypical semantic classes (properties, actions and objects) and three discourse functions (reference, predication and modification).

Table 212: Functional views on word classes (Croft 2001, 89)

	Reference	Predication	Modification
Objects	Nouns		
Actions		Verbs	
Properties			Adjectives

Nouns are the expression of objects used referentially, verbs are the expression of actions used predicatively and adjectives are the expression of properties used modificatively. The theory predicts that any other combination will prototypically lead to more overt coding: nouns used modificatively will receive some kind of genitive marking, actions used modificatively will be coded either as non-finite forms (participles, converbs, gerunds) or relative clauses, and so forth. Adverbs are absent from this typology. Since adjectives are seen as property words that "narrow the reference of a noun" (Haspelmath 2010, 670), Hallonsten Halling (2017, 40) suggests that prototypical adverbs should be seen as property words that "narrow the predication of a verb." This is the narrow approach to adverbs, which corresponds more or less to the adverbs of manner of traditional grammar.

Dialectal Arabic does not use any overt coding when a lexeme denoting a property narrows the predication of a verb, as shown in (85), where *mlīḥ* 'good' can modify both a noun and a verb. Spoken Arabic would therefore cluster with the "languages with simple modifiers," that is, those that "have exactly the same non-derived lexeme functioning both adjectivally and adverbially" (Hallonsten Halling 2017, 45).

(85) a. *šuġl əmlīḥ*
work good
'A good job'

b. *baʕrif-ha mlīḥ*
know.IPFV.1SG-3FS good
'I know her well'

However, the ability of bare adjectives to modify a predicate is very limited in Arabic, with *mlīḥ* and its synomyms (*kwayyis*, *ṭayyib*) being among the rare candidates. Much more common is to use a prepositional phrase (which is a kind of overt coding) such as *b-surʕa* 'with speed', *ʕa ṣ-ṣaḥīḥ* 'correctly' (on DEF-correct) or the so-called cognate object construction (Arabic *al-mafʕūl al-muṭlaq* 'the absolute complement', see §4.4.3.1 for more). Consequently, there is very little ground to posit the existence of a separate word class of adverbs in dialectal Arabic. This is probably as far as the discussion would go under the narrow approach.

Under the broad approach, an adverb is any lexicalised formation that operates at the level of the predicate (= narrow view) or at the clausal level, or put differently, formations that have scope over the predicate or the clause. Among clause-level adverbs, one should further distinguish between substitutes for noun phrases used adverbially and lexemes that do not substitute for anything, i.e., between proforms and non-proforms (Creissels 1988). Typically, items that are labelled adverbs of time and place are substitutes for noun phrases, whereas modal adverbs are not. This is the classification we will adopt here.

3.11.1. Predicate-level Adverbs

As noted above, very few adjectives can be used to modify predicates. Beside *mlīḥ* and its synonyms *kwayyis* and *ṭayyib*, only *kṯīr* 'many' can be safely classified as an adjective.

3.11.1.1. *kṯīr* 'much'

The word *kṯīr* or a variant thereof is found in all Levantine dialects. It modifies adjectives—in which case it can appear to the right or to the left: *kṯīr naḏ̣īf* 'very clean', *ḥilwa kṯīr* 'very nice'—and verbs, as shown in (86). Unless focused, it appears to the right of the predicate.

(86) *futt* *əkṯīr*

enter.PFV.1SG much

'I often entered (the Sarāya—an old administrative building)'

3.11.1.2. *šwayye* 'little'

Found in many dialects of Arabic, *šwayy* is the diminutive derivation of *ši* 'thing'. Like *kṯīr*, *šwayy(e)* modifies both adjectives and verbs. It appears before or after the adjective it modifies: *šwayye šaṭṭūra* 'somewhat skilled', *kbār əšwayy* 'a bit old'. Like *kṯīr*, it is placed after the predicate, unless focused.

(87) *tʔaxxart* *šwayy*

be_late.PFV.1SG little

'I was a bit late'

3.11.1.3. *galīl-mā* 'rarely'

The adverb *galīl-mā* is attested only as a predicate modifier. Two formatives can be identified: *galīl* 'few' and *mā,* which in other varieties may function as an indefinite marker (cf. Standard Arabic *qalīl-an mā* 'rarely'). The latter formative *mā* has no productivity as a marker of indefiniteness in sedentary Jordanian and seems to occur only in this lexicalised formation.

(88) *galīl-mā bīğu ʕa lə-fḥēṣ*
rarely come.IPFV.3MP to DEF-Fḥēṣ
'They rarely come to Fḥēṣ'

3.11.1.4. *šwayy šwayy* 'slowly'

The adverb *šwayy šwayy* is known to most spoken dialects of Arabic, so its presence in Central and Northern Jordan comes as no surprise.

(89) *šwayy əšwayy sakanu lə-fḥēṣ*
slowly dwell.IPFV.3MP DEF-Fḥēṣ
'They slowly settled in Fḥēṣ'

3.11.1.5. *tay tay* 'slowly'

This adverb is a hapax in the corpus. It was recorded in example (90). This adverb is so uncommon that it is not recognised by all speakers. During the recording session, the host even felt the need to mark a pause and explain the meaning of *tay tay*, which he glossed as *šwayy šwayy* 'slowly'.

(90) *gabalo* *l-ǧamal* *tay tay* *la* *bēt* *ahl-o*

straight_forward DEF-camel slowly to house owner-3SG

'The camel (walked) slowly straight forward to the house of its owner'

3.11.1.6. *yāḷḷa* 'barely'

The adverb *yāḷḷa* 'barely' lexicalised from the vocative particle *yā* and *aḷḷa* 'God'. It clearly differs from the interjection *yaḷḷa* 'let's go' in vowel length.

(91) *xamsṭaʕšar* *yōm* *bi* *d-dūr* *nās* *mā* *tiṭlaʕ-əš*

fifteen day in DEF-houses people NEG exit.SBJV.3FS-NEG

yāḷḷa *tiʕǧin* *tixbiz* *badd-ha*

barely knead.IPFV.3FS make_bread.SBJV.3FS want-3FS

iši *ḥilu*

something sweet

'(During the winter), people wouldn't go out for fifteen days, they would barely knead and bake bread (but would still) want something sweet'

3.11.1.7. *yā dōb* 'hardly'

The etymology of *yā dōb* remains uncertain. It is seemingly formed from the vocative particle *yā* and the nominal derivation of a verbal root (either *d-ʔ-b* 'persistence' or *d-w-b* 'be worn out'). Only a couple of tokens are attested in our dataset, but it is widely attested in other dialects of the Levant and beyond.

(92) *nās* *yā dōb* *kānat* *ʕāyše*

people hardly be.PFV.3FS living.F

'People were barely surviving'

3.11.2. Clause-level Adverbs

3.11.2.1. Proforms

3.11.2.1.1. Time

hassaʕ 'now'

This lexeme combines a feminine demonstrative *hāḏi* or *hāy* (or the apocopated form *ha*) and *sāʕa* 'hour'. Many variants are attested: *hassāʕ*, *hissaʕ*, *hissāʕ*, *issāʕ*, *issaʕ* and also *hassa*. Amman normally has pan-Levantine *halla*, which may surface in the speech of some speakers.

(93) *hassaʕ abṣar šū ʕāmil*
now I_wonder what do.AP.MS
'Now, I don't know what he is up to'

lassāʕ and *baʕd* 'until now, still, yet'

The morpheme *lassāʕ* seemingly comes from the lexicalisation of the preposition *la* 'to' and *hassaʕ* 'now'. It can still surface as two separate morphemes: *mawǧūde la hissaʕ* 'until now it's there' (present.F to now). Interestingly, *lassāʕ* often collocates with *baʕəd* 'still', which is often classified as a phasal adverb.

(94) *lassāʕ baʕəd-hum bī-ha bass gallu*
until_now still-3MP in-3FS but be_little.PFV.3MP
'They are still in it up to now but only few of them are left'

In negative polarity, *baʕd* translates as 'yet', but the core meaning is still 'until the moment of reference':

(95) *waḷḷāhi baʕd-ha mā rǧaʕat-o lassāʕ*

By_God still-3FS NEG bring_back.PFV.3FS-3MS until_now

'She hasn't brought it back yet'

The morpheme *baʕd* may surface without any bound pronoun, in which case it tends to occur clause-finally, as shown in (96), in which it translates as 'also':

(96) *abū… laḥḥagt-o baʕəd*

his_father… follow.PFV.1SG-3FS also

'I also knew his father'

Constituent order in Arabic is sensitive to information structure. Consequently, *baʕd* + suffix may surface clause-finally with a focused element placed clause-initially. In (97), the lexeme *wlād* is focused and is placed before the adverb:

(97) *ā badukr-o… wlād baʕəd-na*

yes remember.IPFV.1SG-3MS… kids still-1PL

'Yes I remember him, we were still kids'

There is no restriction with unmarked *baʕəd* in non-verbal predicate clauses, as illustrated in (98):

(98) *ṭarābīš ḏ̣allin əb-ha-s-salṭ… ḥabaṭraš baʕəd*

tarboush.PL stay.PFV.3FP in-DEM-DEF-Salt… many still

'There were people wearing the fez in Salt… they were still numerous'

The adverb is homophonous with the preposition *baʕd* 'after', but a morphological difference surfaces when bound pronouns attach to them. In the first-person adverbial *baʕd* selects the allomorph *-ni*: *baʕd-ni* 'I am still…', whereas the preposition selects the allomorph *-i* /*-y(e)* and /ī/ is inserted between the base and the suffix: *baʕdiyye* 'after me'.

Pan-Levantine *lissa* 'still, yet' was recorded only marginally (five tokens in the whole corpus).

taww- 'right now'

The morpheme *taww-*[11] is rather recessive in the dialects of central and northern Jordan, as suggested by the number of tokens we recorded—only one, as illustrated in (99). It cannot stand on its own and needs a bound pronoun: *taww-ni wāṣle* (right_now.1SG arrive.AP.FS) 'I have just arrived'. Active participles of verbs of motion can have a past, present or future reading and *taww-* perfectly accommodates that. It can therefore mean equally a very short time before or a very short time after the moment of reference. The morpheme *taww-* is well attested in Najdi Arabic, in which it has the same syntax and semantics (Sowayan 1995).

(99) *iḥna taww-na mrawwḥīn min lə-ġmāra*
1PL right_now-1PL come_back.AP.MP from DEF-harvest
'We have just come back from harvesting'

mbāriḥ 'yesterday'

The adverb *mbāriḥ* is found across the Levant. It is also the normal form found in most parts of central and northern Jordan.

(100) *hāḏa ğāy ʕalay-ye mbāriḥ*
DEM come.AP.MS on-1SG yesterday
'He came to me yesterday'

---

[11] A variant of *taww-* is *tōb*, as in *tōb-ni ṭābxa* 'I have just cooked'.

awwal əmbāriḥ and *mbāriḥit lūla* 'the day before yesterday'

The phrase *awwal əmbāriḥ* 'the day before yesterday', found across most of the Levant, was also recorded in Salt:

(101) *awwal əmbāriḥ* *sawwū-lna* *ʕaša*
the_day_before_yesterday do.PFV.3MP-1PL.DAT dinner
'The day before yesterday they cooked dinner for us'

Our corpus of data from Amman suggests that *awwal əmbāriḥ* is being replaced by *ʾabl əmbāriḥ* 'the day before yesterday' by the younger generation. The elicited phrase *mbāriḥit lūla*, seemingly borrowed from neighbouring Bedouin dialects, may come from *il-bāriḥa l-ʔūla* (DEF-yesterday-F DEF-first.F). Final /t/ in *mbāriḥit* shows that speakers have reinterpreted this sequence as a genitive construction. No instances of *awwal-t əmbāriḥ*, found elsewhere in the Levant, were recorded, although it occurs frequently in Amman.

bukra 'tomorrow'

The form *bukra* is also common in much of the region.

(102) *ǧāyy-ak* *bukra* *wāḥad* *min* *lə-fḥēṣ*
come.AP.MS-2MS tomorrow someone from DEF-Fḥēṣ
'Tomorrow someone from Fḥēṣ will come to you'

Although the primary meaning of *bukra* is 'tomorrow', it can also be used figuratively in the sense of 'in the future' (see also *ġadd* below):

(103) *bukra* *yīǧin-na* *ha-s-salṭiyyāt* *yibkin*
tomorrow come.SBJV.3FP-1PL DEM-DEF-Salti_women cry.IPFV.3FP
'In the future, these women from Salt would come to us and whinge'

baʕəd bukra 'after tomorrow'

To express 'after tomorrow', most Levantine dialects use the phrase *baʕəd bukra*, and so do northern and central sedentary Jordanian dialects. Abū Ǧābir (1992, 89) also mentions the phrase عقب باكر in Arabic script, which should be read *ʕugub bāčir*. This form, common in neighbouring Bedouin varieties, was not recorded in spontaneous speech. Speakers rejected it in elicitation and only accepted *baʕəd bukra*. Other hypothetical combinations such as ***ʕugub bukra*, ***ʕugub ġadd* and ***baʕəd ġadd* were also rejected.

(awwal) ams 'lately'

The presence of the morpheme *ams* has already been noted in the area by both Cantineau (1946, 394) and Palva (2008, 54, 64). Cantineau heard it in Irbid but considered it a borrowing from the standard dialect. Palva, writing about Salt and Karak, notes that *ams* and *mbāriḥ*, both meaning 'yesterday', are competing forms. He further suggests that *ams* was borrowed from neighbouring Bedouin varieties. As far as Ḥōrān is concerned, elicitation suggests that both *ams* and *mbāriḥ* mean 'yesterday' and are part of the local stock. Whether *ams* was borrowed from Bedouin dialects is hard to determine with certainty. As for Salt, both corpus data and elicitation agree in restricting *mbāriḥ* to 'yesterday' and *ams* to 'some time ago, lately'. Also reported is the adverb *msāt* 'back in the day', in all likelihood formed from *ams* and the feminine plural -*āt*, but it was not attested in spontaneous speech, suggesting that the form may have disappeared from the modern-day dialect.

Examples (104) and (105) feature the use of *ams* in the sense of 'lately', used in collocation with *awwal*. In (104), there is little doubt about the meaning the speaker had in mind when using *ams*, because he added the phrase *gabəl šahər* 'a month ago'.

(104) *awwal ams gabəl šahər ruḥt*
lately before month go.PFV.1SG
xayyaṭt il-lbās hāḏ̣ ʕa tukkānit-ku
sew.PFV.1SG DEF-garment DEM to shop-2MP
'Some time ago, a month ago, I went to your shop and had this garment sewed'

(105) *hāḏ̣a lli waffa (a)wwal aməs*
DEM REL die.PFV.3MS lately
'The one who died some time ago'

ġadd 'in the future'

What was noted for *ams* and *mbāriḥ* also holds true for *bukra* and *ġadd*. Cantineau (1946, 394) already noted that *l'expression véritablement ḥôrānaise pour 'demain' est* ġadd 'The true way of expressing "tomorrow" in Ḥōrāni dialects is *ġadd*'. The morpheme *ġadd* surfaced only twice in the corpus, in a recording from 1987 by a Salti female speaker whose idiolect was one of the broadest recorded. Both corpus data and elicitation agree in assigning the meaning 'in the future' to *ġadd* in Salt. In Ḥōrān, *ġadd* means both 'tomorrow' and 'in the future'.

(106) *ġadd waḥade btizʕal*

future one.F get_angry.IPFV.3FS

'In the future, one (of them) might get angry'

(107) *ġadd biṭmaʕ biyye*

future be_greedy.IPFV.3MS in.1SG

'Next thing you know, he'll get greedy with me'

il-ʕām 'last year'

In the standard variety, the lexeme *ʕām* is used more or less as a synonym of *sana* 'year'. In most Levantine varieties, it occurs only in the string *il-ʕām* with the meaning of 'last year'. In Amman, the younger generation tend to use the expression *il-ʕām il-māḍi* ~ *is-sane l-māḍye* instead of *il-ʕām*, whose use is decreasing.

(108) *aǧa ʕazam-ni lamma tǧawwaz*

come.PFV.3MS invite.PFV.3MS-1SG when marry.PFV.3MS

ibn-o l-ʕām

son-3MS last_year

'He invited me when his son got married last year'

il-ʕām l-awwal 'two years ago'

The phrase *il-ʕām l-awwal* may lexicalise in various ways cross-dialectally, but in Sedentary Jordanian, it does not undergo any reduction. The meaning is 'two years ago', unlike in other varieties (e.g., North African dialects), in which it means 'last year'.

(109) *il-ʕām l-awwal rāḥat la rūsya*

two_years_ago go.PFV.3FS to Russia

'Two years ago, she went to Russia'

bakkīr 'soon, early'

The lexeme *bakkīr* is found in many parts of the Levant. Palva (2008, 64) also gives *badri, bidri* and *mbaddir* with a similar meaning. While *badri* was found perfectly acceptable by our speakers, *bidri* was judged to be 'not Jordanian'. As for *mbaddir*, it is the active participle of the verb *baddar–ybaddir* 'come early', more or less equivalent to *bakkar–ybakkir*. Accordingly, the form *mbaddir* is used when someone arrives earlier than expected: *wa̤l̤la mbaddir!* 'you have come early! (i.e., I wasn't expecting you now)'.

(110)	*ǧīna*	*bakkīr...*	*wāḥad*	*u*	*ṯamānīn*	*banēt*
	come.PFV.1PL	early	one	and	eighty	build.PFV.1SG

'We came here early, I built (this house) in 1981'

sant il-ǧāy 'next year'

The phrase *sant il-ǧāy* 'next year' is undergoing lexicalisation, as evidenced by the lack of feminine agreement on the active participle *ǧāy* (< *aǧa* 'he came') and the construct form *sant* of *sane* 'year', which suggests that speakers are reinterpreting this as a compound.

ṯāni yōm 'the next day'

The phrase *ṯāni yōm* (lit. 'second day') is lexicalised, because it can be modified by a definite NP, as shown in (111). The adjective *ṯāni* is the ordinal derivation of *iṯnēn* 'two'. Ordinals in Arabic can only be modified by an indefinite NP, with which they form a genitive construction (***ṯāni l-yōm* is not grammatical).

(111) *ṯāni yōm il-ʕurs min-ha lli*
second day DEF-wedding from-3FP REL
biǧi la ha-l-walad baǧīb-lak
come.IPFV.3MS to DEM-DEF-boy bring.IPFV.1SG-3MS.DAT
'The day after the wedding, I'll bring you (what I owe you), from the boy's (the groom's) share'

Interestingly, this construction made it into the dialect of the second generation of Ammanis, but has not been transmitted to the younger generation, as noted by Al-Wer (2011):

> ...*yaʕni bitsāfri ṯāni yōm ʕīd mīlād-ik?* 'So you'll be travelling the day after your birthday?'... The younger generation in Amman do not generally parse this expression correctly... they interpret the date of the birthday to be after the day travelling takes place.

In other words, younger Ammanis interpret the sequence [*ṯāni yōm*]$_{\text{PRED}}$ [*ʕīd mīlād-ik*]$_{\text{SUBJ}}$ (second day feast birth-2FS) as a clause 'your birthday is the next day'.

awwal, zamān 'before'

Both *awwal* 'first' and *zamān* 'time' are nominals that can be used adverbially to express 'before, in the past'. They seem to be ellipses for phrases such as *ʕala dōr awwal* (on era before) or *ʕala zamān awwal* (on time before), both of which mean 'back in the day'.

(112) *ana ʕayyu ygarrū-ni gālu*
1SG refuse.PFV.3MP teach.SBJV.3MP-1SG say.PFV.3MP
ʕēb il-bint awwal tigra
shame DEF-girl before study.SBJV.3FS
'They refused to send me to school. Before, it was shameful to send a girl to school'

The word *zamān* can also surface as an ellipsis of the phrase *min zamān* 'for a long time':

(113) *zamān əbtišrab titin*
time drink.IPFV.2MS tobacco
'Have you been smoking for a long time?'

dāyman and *dōm* 'always'

The adverb *dāyman* is found in most eastern varieties of Arabic. It is in all likelihood a relexification from Standard Arabic, as suggested by the suffix *-an*, which has no productivity in the vernacular. The morpheme *dōm* is found across the region and probably predates *dāyman* in the dialect, as shown in (115), which is a common saying. In practice, though, *dāyman* has much more currency in the present-day dialect.

(114) *haḏ̣ōl yištaġlu dāyman maʕ-o*
DEM.PL work.SBJV.3MP always with-3MS
'They used to work with him all the time'

(115) *akbar minn-ak yōm aʕraf minn-ak dōm*
older from-2MS day wiser from-2MS always
'One day older, forever wiser'

kulsaʕ ‘always, often’

This form comes from the lexicalisation of *kull sāʕa* ‘every hour’. Only one token was recorded in spontaneous speech, reproduced below:

(116)

ana	*waḷḷa*	*kulsaʕ*	*bāǧi*	*basʔal*	*ʕan*	*ǧōrǧ*
1SG	by_God	always	come.IPFV.1SG	ask.IPFV.1SG	about	Georges

‘I often come and ask about Georges’

bsāʕ ‘quickly’

This adverb comes from the lexicalisation of the preposition *b-* ‘in’ and the noun *sāʕa* ‘hour’. It belongs to the traditional dialect and has little currency in present-day usage, as suggested by the very few tokens we recorded in spontaneous speech (117).

(117)

ʕilm-ak	*haḏ̣āk*	*il-ḥīn*	*ana*	*walad*
knowledge-2MS	DEM	DEF-time	1SG	boy

fa	*bsāʕ*	*winn-i*	*wāṣil*
so	quickly	DM-1SG	arrive.AP.MS

‘Keep in mind that back then I was a kid, so I had got there in no time’

il-yōm ‘today’, *il-lēle* ‘tonight’…

Nouns or more complex NPs referring to temporal distinctions can be used adverbially. They are marked with the article *il-*: *is-sane* ‘this year’, *il-yom* ‘today’, *il-lēle* ‘tonight’, *il-masa* ‘this evening’, *iṣ-ṣubəḥ* ‘this evening’, *il-ʕaṣər* ‘in the late afternoon’, *iḏ̣-ḏ̣uhər* ‘at noon’. Examples of local expressions are *iṣ-ṣubəḥ sarwa* ‘in the morning before sunrise’, *tāli l-lēl* ‘late at night’ (*tāli* means ‘end, last'). One should keep in mind that these are not technically lexical adverbs because they show no signs of lexicalisation.

The Suffix *-ha*

The morpheme *-ha* suffixes to nouns denoting time relations, such as *sant-ha* 'that year', *lēlit-ha* 'that night', *sāʕit-ha* 'at that time'. It can also suffix to the prepositions *baʕd* 'after' and *gabəl* 'before', in which case /ī/ is inserted between the base and the suffix: *baʕdī-ha* 'after that', *gablī-ha* 'before that'.

(118) *ḏugna l-murr sant-ha*
taste.PFV.1PL DEF-bitter year-ADV
'We suffered that year'

This morpheme can be interpreted as the third-person feminine bound pronoun *-ha*, but it may well be an apocopated form of the demonstrative, as suggested in example (119), where the speaker used the plain feminine demonstrative *hāye*. The noun occurs in its construct form *sant* (< *sane* 'year'), which implies that the speaker interprets this as a genitive construction.

(119) *ḍallēna ʕind dār ʕamm-i ʕīd*
stay.PFV.1PL at house uncle-1SG ʕīd
ninzil… sant hāye b-ḥarb is-sitte
descend.SBJV.1SG year DEM in-war DEF-six
'We used to stay at my Uncle ʕīd's that year during the Six-Day War'

3.11.2.1.2. Space

hōn 'here'

The morpheme *hōn* is found in most Levantine dialects. Another variant is *hōna,* and less frequently *hōne.* It can combine with *min* 'from', *la* 'to' or *la ʕind* 'towards': *min hōn* 'from here', *la hōn* 'to here', *la ʕind hōn* 'to this place'. Another marginal reflex is *hān,* which only occurred once in the corpus.

hnāk 'there'

The common form in Central and Northern Jordan is *hnāk* and its variant *hnāka* (120). It combines with different prepositions: *min əhnāk* 'from there', *la hnāk* 'until there'.

(120) *gaʕadu* *hnāka* *ḥawāla* *sabəʕ* *tušhur*
stay.PFV.3MP there around seven months
'They stayed there about seven months'

ġād 'over there'

Jordanian dialects, like other rural and Bedouin varieties in the area, have two deictic adverbs whose translation is roughly the same: *hnāk* 'there' and *ġād* 'over there' or variants thereof. In Southern Sinai, for example, de Jong (2003, 171) also notes that there is a two-way contrast between *hnāk* 'there' and *ġādiy* 'over there'. In sedentary Jordanian, both morphemes are semantically equivalent: *rūḥ la ġād* ~ *ruḥ la hnāk* 'go there', although *ġād* is more likely to imply the notion of 'beyond vision'. The morpheme *ġādī,* and its variant *ġādiyye,* does convey the meaning of 'beyond', but it is a preposition, not a deictic adverb (see §3.9.1.15).

In addition to this, *ġād* is pragmatically marked, because it is used in many collocations in which it is not interchangeable with *hnāk*: *ġād ʕanni!* 'away from me!', *ʔayy ġād!* 'get out of my sight', *šī(l) ġād* 'get off my back', *zīḥ ġād* 'move off, stand aside'.

(121)

hassāʕ	*muntāz*	*bi-hū-š*	*bala*
now	great	in-3MS-NEG	problem
umman	*awwal*	*ġād*	*ʕaglīt-o*
but	before	there	spirit-3MS

'Now he's OK, he doesn't cause trouble anymore, but before, he was just crazy'

The morpheme *ġād* also occurs in the construction (*min*) X *u ġād* in the sense of 'beyond X', where X refers to any expression denoting a place: *min ǧaraš u ġād* 'from Jerash and beyond', *il-madīne ir-riyāḍiyye u ġād* 'from the sports city and beyond'. Like *hnāk*, it can combine with the prepositions *min* and *la*: *min ġād* 'from there', *la ġād* 'until there'.

ǧāy 'this way'

The adverb *ǧāy*, etymologically the active participle of the verb *aǧa* 'he came', is found in many rural and Bedouin dialects of the Levant and beyond. It lexicalised into an adverb whose meaning is 'this way', as shown in (122). It is clear from this example that *ǧāy* has lost all its inflectional properties. One would expect plural agreement with the subject, had it been used as a participle.

(122)

gāʕdīn	*kull-hum*	*birḥalu*	*ǧāy*
stay.AP.PL	all-3MP	leave.IPFV.3MP	this_way

'They are all coming this way'

It can be used in both local and temporal expressions: *min ṯalāṯīn sane u ğāy* 'for thirty years onwards' (from thirty year and this_way).

ḥādir 'below'

The adverb *ḥādir*, etymologically the active participle of the root *ḥ-d-r* 'go down', is also attested in other rural and Bedouin varieties of the southern Levant. The root *ḥ-d-r*, common in the standard variety, is recessive in sedentary Jordanian and belongs to a conservative register. On one occasion, *ḥādir* appeared as the object of the preposition *min* (123).

(123) *dār-o* *tiḥət* *dār-ku* *min* *ḥādir*
house-3MS under house-2MP from below
'His house is under yours, from below'

(124) *hummu* *bʕād* *ʕan* *il-ḥumra* *ḥādir*
3MP far.PL from il-Ḥumra below
'They are below, far from il-Ḥumra'

3.11.2.2. Non-proforms

3.11.2.2.1. *xāfaḷḷa*, *yimkin* and *biğūz* 'maybe'

The morpheme *xāfaḷḷa*, commonly found in neighbouring Bedouin dialects, is a lexicalisation of *xāf* 'he fears' and *aḷḷa* 'God'. Its frequency is low and it belongs to an archaic register.

(125) *hassaʕ ʕumər-ha biǧi xamse u arbʕīn*

now age-3FS around five and forty

xāfaḷḷa mawālīd ṯalāṯ u sittīn

maybe born.PL three and sixty

'She must be around forty-five now, she was born maybe in 1963'

The morpheme *yimkin* is the lexicalisation of the 3MS imperfective of the aCCaC derivation of the root *m-k-n*. In Standard Arabic, *ʔamkana-yumkinu* 'be possible' is already impersonal, because it only inflects in the 3MS, but the difference is that the perfective form *ʔamkan* exists, contrary to dialectal Arabic, in which ***amkan* is not found.

(126) *bi s-sane kull-ha yimkin yistahlik*

in DEF-year all-3FS maybe consume.SBJV.3MS

raṭl-ēn sukkar

pound-DU sugar

'In one year they used to consume maybe two pounds of sugar'

The form *biǧūz* is also a lexicalisation, from the 3MS imperfective form of the root *ǧ-w-z* 'permit'. The surface form is most often realised *bǧūz* because of the elision of /i/ in unstressed open syllables.

(127) *bǧūz laḥḥagt-o ana*

maybe know.PFV.1SG-3MS 1SG

'I may have known him'

3.11.2.2.2. *wakād* 'exactly'

The adverb *wakād*, from the root *w-k-d* ~ *ʔ-k-d* 'sure', is a hapax, as exemplified in (128). It belongs to a very archaic register and did not make it to the younger generations. Its classification as a non-proform clause-level modifier is a default option, because it seems to have scope over the clause [*kann-o gbāl-i hassaʕ*] as in example (128).

(128)	*baʕirf-o*	*wal̤l̤a*	*mitəl*	*wakād*	*kann-o*
	know.IPFV.1SG-3MS	by_God	like	exactly	as_if-3SG
	gbāl-i	*hassaʕ*			
	front-1SG	now			

'I remember him, as if he was in front of me right now'

3.11.2.2.3. *akīd* 'surely'

The morpheme *akīd* is the adverbial use of the CaCīC derivation of the root *ʔ-k-d*, whose usual cognate in the present dialects is *w-k-d*. Given the paucity of its occurrence across the corpus (five tokens from two speakers), its inclusion in the inventory of the traditional dialect remains uncertain.

(129)	*akīd*	*biğū-hum*	*dāyman*	*ḍyūf*	*ağānib*	*u*	*iši*
	surely	come.IPFV.3MP-3MP	always	guests	foreigners	and	thing

'For sure they always have foreign guests and everything'

3.11.3. The Suffix *-an*

Although the standard Arabic adverbial suffix *-an* is not part of the dialectal stock, it appears in many borrowings from the standard dialect. These are now fully integrated into the spoken variety: *dāyman* 'always', *tagrīban* 'almost', *maṯalan* 'for example', *ṭabʕan* 'of course', *aṣlan* 'basically', *abadan* 'never, at all, really'. Other instances recorded in spontaneous speech are *ḥāliyyan* 'currently', *maǧǧānan* 'free', *ġāliban* 'often', *sābiqan* 'previously', *ʕādatan* 'usually' and *xāṣṣatan* 'especially', but these are not part of the vernacular. Additionally, *-an* occurred in the form of *-it* or *-in* in the expression *ġaṣbit* ~ *ġaṣbin ʕan* 'by force' instead of *ġaṣban ʕan*.

3.12. Other Minor Parts of Speech

3.12.1. Interjections and Exclamations

3.12.1.1. *wa̤l̤la* 'I swear'

The interjection *wa̤l̤lāhi*, literally 'by God', is extremely common in spontaneous speech and has many different realisations: *wa̤l̤la*, *wa̤l̤lā*, *wa̤l̤lāh*, *wa̤l̤lāhi*, *billāh(i)*, *ba̤l̤la*. Our corpus contains several hundred instances of it. Its frequency suggests that its semantics have bleached to the point that it has simply become a declarative marker.

(130) *wa̤l̤la ṃṃāʕīn-ak illi ʕa ḏ̣ahr-ak*
I_swear clothes-2MS REL on back-2MS
at̠gal min ṭalabīt-na ʕind-ak
heavier from request-1PL at-2MS
'The clothes you are wearing are heavier than our request (i.e., our request is easy to fulfil)'

(131) *waggaft* *billāhi* *l-karīm* *mā* *maʕ-i*
stop.PFV.1SG by_God DEF-generous NEG with-1SG
ʕašar *əgrūš* *bi* *ǧ-ǧēb*
ten piasters in DEF-pocket
'I stopped, I swear I didn't have ten piasters in my pocket'

Example (132) shows that *waḷḷa* has predicative properties, because it can be complemented with a clause introduced by the complementiser *inn(o)*:

(132) *waḷḷa* *inn-ku* *ġālyīn* *ǧīrān* *ʕazīzīn*
I_swear COMP-2MP expensive.MP neighbours dear.MP
'I swear you are dear neighbours to us'

As for *baḷḷa*, it also occurs in interrogative clauses (whether sarcastically or as a challenge): *baḷḷa ṣaḥīḥ?* 'is it really true?' (by_God true), *baḷḷa badd-ič titǧawwazi* 'do you really want to get married?' (by_God want-2FS marry.SBJV.2FS), *baḷḷa šū!* 'no kidding!'. It is also used to soften a request: *ǧībī-li naḏḏārāt-i baḷḷa* 'bring me my glasses please' (bring.IMP.FS glasses-1SG by_God)

3.12.1.2. *māši* 'OK'

The interjection *māši* comes from the lexicalisation of the active participle of the verb *maša–yimši* 'walk'. It is common to many spoken varieties of Arabic: *gal-lo māši* 'he told him OK!'.

3.12.1.3. *ṭayyib* ~ *ṭab* 'well'

The adjective *ṭayyib* 'good' is also used as an interjection when the speaker wants to add an assertion or a request consequent to the state of affairs previously depicted. In (133), the speaker asked the addressee how old he was. After being given the answer, he concludes that there is a ten-year difference between them using *ṭayyib*. Example (134) illustrates the use of the contracted form *ṭab*.

(133) *ṭayyib bī ʕašar əsnīn bēn-i u bēn-ak*
well EXIST ten years between-1SG and between-2MS
'Well, there is a ten-year difference between you and me'

(134) *ṭab lēš mā ruḥət?*
well why NEG go.PFV.2MS
'Well, why didn't you go?'

3.12.1.4. *aywa* 'yes'

The most common way of saying 'yes' in many Arabic dialects is *aywa*. In narrative style, *aywa* is used as a resumptive device after an interruption. Consider the excerpt in (135). The speaker pauses for a while after *ʕašīratin-mā*, then resumes his narrative with *aywa*. This strategy is not an idiolectal feature, since it was observed in the speech of multiple speakers.

(135) *kān maṯalan tagālītt-(h)um*
be.PFV.3MS example customs-3MP
yitwaffa wāḥad min ʕašīratin-mā
die.SBJV.3MS one from clan-INDEF
aywa…
yes
bagīt il-ʕašāyir əssawwī-lo akəl u tiʕzim-hum
rest DEF-clans do.SBJV.3FS-3MS food and invite.SBJV.3FS-3MP
'According to the traditional custom, when someone from a clan dies, yes… other clans would cook food and invite the clan of the deceased'

3.12.1.5. *ā* 'yes'

Within the Levant, Jordanians and Palestinians are known for their back realisation in the use of a long back vowel [ɑ:] meaning 'yes'. It constitutes a sort of shibboleth, especially for Lebanese and Syrian speakers who tend to use a higher realisation [e:].

(136) *inti sākne bi s-salṭ?*
2FS dwell.AP.FS in DEF-Salt
ā ana sākin bi s-salṭ
yes 1SG dwell.AP.MS in DEF-Salt
'Do you live in Salt? Yes, I live in Salt'

3.12.1.6. *la(ʔ)* 'no'

The morpheme *la(ʔ)* 'no' is found in all dialects of Arabic.

(137) *laʔ laʔ hassa bī-š mustašfa*
no no now EXIST-NEG hospital
'No, no, now there is no hospital'

One speaker uttered the morpheme with a final [ʕa]: *laʕa wal!* 'No really!'. The shift from [ʔ] to [ʕ] is not unknown elsewhere in the area.

3.12.1.7. *yaḷḷa* 'let's go, come on'

The interjection *yaḷḷa* is also widespread across the Arabic-speaking world:

(138) *yaḷḷa yā (u)xt-i xan-na nnazzl-ič ʕa t-taktōr*
come_on VOC sister-1SG let-1PL bring.SBJV.1SG-2FS to DEF-doctor
'Come on my sister, let us take you to the doctor'

3.12.1.8. *yī* 'oh!'

The interjection *yī* is used by speakers to express surprise. In (139), the informant reports the reaction of the nurses working in the hospital when they learnt she had delivered a girl:

(139)	*yā*	*ḥarām*	*ǧābat*	*bint*	*yī*	*yī*	*yī*	*yī*
	VOC	illicit	bring.PFV.3FS	girl	oh	oh	oh	oh

'Oh, it's so bad, she had a girl'

3.12.1.9. *ġabra* and *ġabṣa*

Our data also attests the exclamative *ġabra*. It belongs to an archaic register, and is seemingly a feature of elderly female register, in order to express astonishment and surprise. Both elicitation and corpus data yielded collocations with *yā* and the variant *ġabṣa* (*yā ġabra* ~ *yā ġabṣa*). In (140), the speaker reacts to a previous utterance about the divorce of a woman.

(140) Speaker 1:

rawwaḥat	*ṭṭallagat*
leave.PFV.3FS	divorce.PFV.3FS

'She left, she divorced'

Speaker 2:

yā	*ġabra*	*lēš*
Oh	EXCLAM	why

'Oh my dear, why?"

3.12.1.10. *wēl* 'woe'

The interjection *wēl* conveys an idea of emphasis, as shown in (141), here in combination with *yī*.

(141) *yī yī yī wēl mā (a)ʕazz-o ʕabdirraḥīm*
oh oh oh woe so dearer-3MS Abdelrahīm
'My god, Abdelrahim is so dear'

3.12.1.11. Vocative *yā*

As in most Arabic dialects, *yā* is used as a vocative particle.

(142) *yā mēmt-i kul it-tuffāḥa*
VOC mother-1SG eat.IMP.MS DEF-apple
'Eat the apple, my son'

3.12.1.12. Vocative *wal-*

The morpheme *wal-*, possibly segmentable as the conjunction *wa* 'and' and the preposition *l(a)* 'for, to', is used to call out to the addressee and flag an emotional state of discomfort, such as fear, annoyance, loss of patience or wrath, towards the situation at the time of utterance. Consequently, only second-person bound pronouns attach to *wal-*: *wal-ak* (2MS), *wal-ič* ~ *wal-ik* (2FS), *wal-ku* (2MP), *wal-čin* (2FP).

(143) *wal-ič yā bint uguʕdi*
VOC-2FS VOC girl sit.IMP.FS
'Hey girl, sit down!'

3.12.2. Discourse Markers

3.12.2.1. *(la)ʕād*

The morpheme *(la)ʕād* is a sequential marker used to connect two events in a sequence, as shown below (glossed 'then'). It may have lexicalised from the verb *ʕād* 'come back' or be cognate with

Semitic *ʕād 'still, again' (found also in other Arabic dialects, such as Maltese *għad* 'still', and also Hebrew *ʕōd*). In (144), the speaker talks about two events. The first one is a group of fighters escaping from the battlefield and the second is a fighter coming to their place with trousers filled with grenades. The two events are formally linked with *ʕād*. *(la)ʕād* differs from a coordination conjunction because of its rather floating syntax, as in (145), where the full form *laʕād* is placed clause-finally. The full form *laʕād* is less frequent, as suggested by the presence of only three tokens in the corpus. The reflex *ʕādat* is also attested, albeit in only three tokens (146).

(144) *hummu hārbīn ḏābḥīn u hārbīn* ***ʕād*** *marag*
3MP flee.AP.MP fight.AP.MP and flee.AP.MP then pass.PFV.3MS
ʕalē-na wāḥad gāṣṣ il-banṭalōn la hōn
on-1PL one cut.AP.MS DEF-trousers to here
u mmalli ǧyāb-o ganābil
and fill.AP.MS pockets-3MS grenades
'They were escaping, escaping and fighting, then someone showed up at our place, who had cut his trousers and filled his pockets with grenades'

(145) *m(ā) ōxḏ-əš minn-o čēf asawwi* ***laʕād***
NEG take.SBJV.1SG-NEG from-3SG how do.SBJV.1SG so
'I (can't) take (money) from him, so what (can) I do'

(146) *twaffa ibn il-ḥaǧǧ lə-kbīr w iz-zalame*
die.PFV.3MS son DEF-elder DEF-big and DEF-man
ʕādat *kibir*
so get_old.PFV.3MS
'The elder son of (my) man died, and he (my man) got old'

3.12.2.2. *baga*

The use of reflexes of **baqa* as discourse markers is well attested in many Levantine dialects (Germanos 2008). It seems to be extremely marginal in Jordanian dialects, as only one clear use of *baga* as a discourse marker was recorded in spontaneous speech (147). It flags the utterance as a conclusion. In Jordan, *baga* is mostly used as a verb 'be, stay' and an imperfect auxiliary.

(147)	***baga***	*hāy*	*giṣṣa*	*kamān*
	so	DEM.F	story	also

'So this also was a story'

3.12.2.3. *tara*

The morpheme *tara* is etymologically linked to the root *r-ʔ-y* 'see'. It comes from the lexicalisation of the second-person masculine singular imperfective inflection *tara* 'you see'. It is used as an attention-catcher device when the speaker wants to inform the addressee about the relative significance of the utterance. It can surface either clause-initially (148) or clause-finally (149). Although *tara* is mostly attested in its bare form, one token with the 1SG bound pronoun was recorded: *tarā-ni*. We glossed it 'you see', which roughly seems to capture its meaning. It ranges from 'keep in mind' to 'pay attention'.

(148)	*tara*	*bisağğil*	*dīri*	*bāl-ič*
	you_see	record.IPFV.3MS	turn.IMP.FS	mind-2FS

'He is recording, pay attention (to what you say)'

(149) *xaḏ-ha* *ʕa* *kabar* *tara*

take.PFV.3MS-3FS on old_age you_see

'(Keep in mind that) he married her when he was old'

3.12.2.4. *yamm(abdan)* 'absolutely'

The morpheme *yammabdan* belongs to the traditional dialect and does not seem to be part of the inventory of younger generations, although they are still able to parse its meaning correctly. It surfaced in its short reflex *yamm* in recordings from 1987, 2007 and 2012. The full reflex *yammabdan* was only mentioned in passing in metalinguistic commentaries by some consultants, until we got hold of a short recording from the sixties, in which one can hear Issa Al-Wer, the father of one the present authors, born in 1902 in Salt, utter the long reflex *yammabdan*, as shown in (150). The use of the short reflex is illustrated in (151). Semantically, *yamm(abdan)* is used as an intensifying device 'absolutely, completely'. It could be considered a predicate-modifying adverb, but its classification as a discourse marker is motivated by its function of linking between two utterances, as suggested by (151) and (152). While the etymology of the second formative *abdan* is obviously the adverb *abadan* 'absolutely, at all', the etymology of *yamm* remains opaque.

(150) *ā* *yammabdan,* *ʕa* *ṭūl* *yammabdan*

yes absolutely on length absolutely

ana *ma* *fī-š* *māniʕ* *abadan*

1SG NEG exist-NEG hindrance at_all

'Yes absolutely, there is no hindrance at all'

(151) *ṭayyaḥt-lo* *biǧi* *xamsīn* *kīs* *yamm*

send.PFV.1SG-DAT.3SG around fifty bag absolutely

axatt *lə-grūš* *min* *əlyās*

take.PFV.1SG DEF-piasters from Ilyas

'I sent him around fifty bags, and took the money from Ilyas'

(152) *tdaxxal* *bī-ha* *l-malik* *yamm*

intervene.PFV.3MS in-3FS DEF-king absolutely

ṣār *badd-o* *ysakkir-ha*

become.PFV.3MS want-3MS close.SBJV.3MS-3FS

'The king got involved to the point that he wanted to close it down (the university)'

3.12.2.5. *winn-*

Although the morpheme *winn* belongs to an archaic register and is not making it into the speech of younger generations, it is extremely frequent in the speech of broad speakers (more than one hundred tokens occurred across the corpus). It is obviously cognate with the standard Arabic focus marker *ʔinna* and lexicalised from the conjunctor *w* 'and' and the complementiser *inn-*. In sedentary Jordanian, *winn-* is a narrative device used to flag an unexpected turn or foreground an event: 'suddenly, next thing you know'. It can appear augmented with bound pronouns, as in (153), bare, as in (154), or with the 3MS allomorph *-o* used as an expletive element, as in (155).

(153) *ma xallū-hā-š* *tʕabbi* *ṃayye*
NEG let.PFV.3MP-3FS-NEG fill.SBJV.3FS water
rağʕat ***winn-ha*** *bitʕayyiṭ*
return.PFV.3FS DM-3FS cry.IPFV.3FS
'(She wanted to get water but) they didn't let her, she came back crying!'

(154) *ʕind-i walad marra thāwaš* *hū u š-šurṭa*
at-1SG son once quarrel.PFV.3MS 3MS and DEF-police
ʕa l-muṯallaṯ ***winn*** *ṭarag* *iš-šurṭi sabəʕ ṯaman*
on DEF-crossroad DM hit.PFV.3MS DEF-police seven eight
əkfūf w axaḏ *fard-o*
palms and take.PFV.3MS pistol-3MS
'One of my sons once quarrelled with a police man, at the crossroad. He slapped him seven or eight times and took his gun.'

(155) *ha-l-walad ənhazam* *min il-midrase ʕād yōm*
DEM-DEF-boy leave.PFV.3MS from DEF-school then day
winno *ṭalabū* *la ğ-ğēš*
DM ask.PFV.3PL.OBJ.3MS to DEF-army
'The boy dropped out of school, and one day, they called him (to serve) in the army'

3.12.2.6. *willa*

Like *winn*, the morpheme *willa* is used as a narrative device to signal an unexpected turn or bring an event to the foreground. It has a very low usage rate compared to *winn*, as only five tokens were recorded in the corpus.

(156) *šwayy hēk sāʕt-ēn zamān* ***willa*** *hū kāsir il-ʕadu*
bit so hour-DU time DM 3SG break.AP.MS DEF-enemy
'After two hours or so, he had already defeated the enemy'

3.12.2.7. *gāl* 'it seems, apparently'

The verb *gāl* 'he said' lexicalised into an evidentiality marker. A recent study suggests that, at least in Irbid, *gāl*, when used as a discourse marker, has three pragmatic functions, namely "expressing the speaker's mental state, signalling indirect evidentiality, and revealing the speaker's incredulity towards the accompanying utterance" (Al-Shawashreh, Jarrah and Zuraikat 2021). In our data, *gāl* is used as a hearsay evidential or reportative marker, implying that the speaker acquired the information indirectly, typically through conversation. It does not seem, however, to flag any intention on the part of the speaker to distance himself from the propositional content of the utterance. This is shown in example (157), where the speaker simply reports that he heard the newcomers (i.e., the refugees) are in fact indigent.

(157) *iṭṭallaʕi ʕa lli ağū-na hassāʕa*
look.IMP.FS on REL come.PFV.3MP-1PL now
haḏōl illi biğu ***gāl*** *fugara*
DEM REL come.IPFV.3MP DM poor
'Look at these people who came now (as refugees). Those are, I heard, poor'

3.12.2.8. *aṯāri* 'it turned out'

The morpheme *aṯāri*, which has reflexes in other neighbouring dialects, is used in narrations to introduce a state of affairs that contradicts an assumption inferred by the previous statement. Example (158) refers to a Christian woman who bought a piece of land from a fellow Christian. The assumption was that her husband was also a Christian, because interreligious unions are strongly disfavoured. Contrary to that expectation, her huband turned out to be a Muslim, which triggers the use of *aṯāri*.

(158) *il-mara ʕala asās inn-ha masīḥiyye*
DEF-woman on ground COMP-3FS Christian
w ***aṯāri*** *ǧōz-ha mislim*
and it_turned_out husband-3FS Muslim
'The woman (managed to buy land) on the basis that she was Christian and it turned out that her husband was a Muslim'

(159) *ṣawwarū-na* ***aṯrīt-ni*** *hummu mṣawwrīn*
film.PFV.3MP-1PL it_turns_out-1SG 3MP film.AP.MP
w ana dāyir hēč
and 1SG turn.AP.MS so
'They filmed us, it turned out that as they were filming, I was turning like this'

Bound pronouns can attach to *aṯāri*. The allomorph *aṯrīt-* can also be selected.

Table 213: *aṯārī* ~ *aṯrīt* and bound pronouns

	Singular	Plural
1	*aṯārī-ni* ~ *aṯrīt-ni*	*aṯārī-na* ~ *aṯrīt-na*
2M	*aṯārī-k* ~ *aṯrīt-ak*	*aṯārī-ku* ~ *aṯrīt-ku*
2F	*aṯārī-č*	*aṯārī-čin* ~ *aṯrīt-čin*
3M	*aṯārī* ~ *aṯrīt-o*	*aṯārī-hum* ~ *aṯrīt-hum*
3F	*aṯārī-ha* ~ *aṯrīt-ha*	*aṯārī-hin* ~ *aṯrīt-hin*

3.12.3. Focus-sensitive Particles

Focus-sensitive particles are morphemes that do not mark focus per se, but require a focused constituent in their scope (van der Wal 2016). The following morphemes are discussed below: *ḥatta* 'even', *kamān* 'also', *uxra* 'also', *bardo* 'also' and *bass* 'only'.

3.12.3.1. *ḥatta* 'even'

The particle *ḥatta* 'even' is a scalar-additive focus-sensitive particle. In (160), the constituent under focus is the noun phrase *lə-bwāb* 'the doors', marked as expected with a rising pitch. In (161), the focused constituent is the whole clause *ʕalē guṣṣāde*. If the focused constituent were *ʕalē*, it would imply a dislocation beyond the clausal boundaries, in which case the existential marker *bī* ~ *fī* would be needed for the clause to be grammatical: *ḥatta ʕalē bī guṣṣāde*.

(160) *kull ši rāyiḥ* ***ḥatta*** *lə-bwāb*
all thing go.AP.MS even DEF-doors
bāgīn yišlaʕu l-bāb ʕan id-dār
be.AP.MP take_off.SBJV.3MP DEF-door from DEF-house
'Everything was going, even the doors, they were taking the door off the house'

(161) ***ḥatta*** *ʕalē guṣṣāde*
even on.3SG little_poem
'There is even a little poem about him'

The particle *ḥatta* can also surface to the right, as in (162). Here, *waḥade min-hin* 'one of them' is left-dislocated and the particle *ḥatta* has scope over the whole clause *ǧawwazətt-(h)a hōn*.

(162) *ʕind-i ṯalaṯ wlād u bint-ēn waḥade*

at-1SG three kids and girl-DU one.F

min-hin ǧawwazətt-(h)a hōn ḥatta

from-3FP marry.PFV.1SG-3FS here even

'I have three kids and two daughters, I even married off one of them here'

3.12.3.2. *kamān* 'also'

The morpheme *kamān* is an additive focus particle and has currency in many eastern dialects of Arabic. It is usually placed after the constituent over which it has scope, as in (163), although left placement is also permitted: *kamān abū-y* 'my father too'. It is common in the area to use *kamān* as a prenominal modifier: *kamān sāʕa* 'another hour'. This usage is unattested in our data, which seem to restrict this function to *uxra* (see §3.12.3.4).

(163) *fī-ha migbara kamān*

in-3FS cemetery too

'There is a cemetery in it too'

3.12.3.3. *barḏo* 'also'

Corpus data suggest that the morpheme *barḏo* 'also' mostly has scope over clausal constituents, as in (165) and (166). One speaker also uttered the inflected form *barəḏ-ni* (also-1SG), in (164), but it is a hapax in the corpus. This suggests that it is very marginal in sedentary Jordan, although it does have some currency elsewhere (Woidich 2006, 161).

(164) *ḥbilət* *ʕa* *rās-o* *b-walad*
be_pregnant.PFV.1SG on head-3MS with-boy
barəḏ̣-ni *ṭaraḥt-o*
also-1SG push.PFV.1SG-3MS
'After him, I got pregnant with a boy (but) I miscarried it as well'

(165) *ağu* *l-ʕadwān* *ṭāyrīn* *bi* *ḏ̣hūr*
come.PFV.3MP DEF-Adwan flight.AP.MP in backs
xēl-hum ***barḏ̣o***
horses-3MP too
'Men from the ʕAdwān came, racing on the back of their horses too'

(166) *axū* *nāṣir* *kān* *yištaġil*
brother.3SG Nasser be.PFV.3MS work.SBJV.3MS
bi *l-mafrag* ***barḏ̣o***
in DEF-Mafrag too
'Nāṣir's brother was working in Mafrag as well'

3.12.3.4. *uxra* 'also'

The morpheme *uxra* is the only remnant of the adjective *ʔāxar* (masculine), *ʔuxra* (feminine) 'other', known in standard Arabic and other spoken varieties. In the southern Levant, the feminine form *uxra* lexicalised, losing all its inflectional properties, and was reinterpreted as a focus-sensitive particle. The morpheme is quite common and occurred especially frequently in the speech of our broadest informants. Other elicited variants are *luxur* and also *ruxra*. There does not seem to be any restriction on the type of constituents over which *uxra* can have scope. In (167), it has scope over *galīl* 'few'.

(167) *basmaʕ ġēr ṣāyir samaʕ-i galīl* ***uxra***
hear.IPFV.1SG except become.AP.MS hearing-1SG few too
'I can hear, but my hearing is becoming weak too'

Interestingly, the steps that led to the grammaticalisation of *uxra* into an additive focus-sensitive particle are still attested in the language. Originally an adjectival modifier, it was first reinterpreted as a quantifier 'another', but keeping the original rightward order, as shown in (168). Because the adjectival nature of the word was lost, leftward syntax became permissible (169), as in the case of other quantifiers.

(168) *ištara mīt dulum* ***uxra*** *fōg*
buy.PFV.3MS hundred dunum too up
il-bī-hin gaṣər iš-šarīf zēd
REL-in-3FP palace DEF-Sharif Zēd
'He further bought a hundred dunums uphill where the palace of the Sharif Zēd is located'

(169) *law ṣaddām yʕīš bass* ***uxra*** *xaməs tiyyām*
if Saddam live.SBJV.3MS only another five days
'If only Saddam could live for another five days'

3.12.3.5. *bass* 'only'

The morpheme *bass* 'only', found in many varieties of Arabic, is a restrictive focus-sensitive particle. It can appear to the left of the constituent it modifies, as in (170), or to the right, as in (171):

(170) *haḏolāk kānu yīǧu* ***bass*** *bi ṣ-ṣēfiyye*

DEM.PL be.PFV.3MP come.SBJV.3MP only in DEF-summer

'Those people used to come only in the summer'

(171) *waḷḷāhi raʔīs ḥukūmt-ak mā*

by_God president government-2MS NEG

burbuṭṭ-(h)um sayyid-na ***bass***

tie.IPFV.3MS-3MP lord-1PL only

'(Even) your prime minister can't tie them up, only the king (can)'

4. SYNTAX

In this chapter, we first discuss the syntax of phrases (noun and verb), before moving on to clauses (simple and complex). Because agreement is a phenomenon that operates both within and between phrases, it is dealt with across the sections on phrases and clauses. Linear order within each constituent type is discussed at the beginning of each section. Although relative clauses are usually treated under complex clauses, they are discussed here within the noun phrase section, because they act primarily as noun modifiers.

4.1. The Noun Phrase

Minimally, a noun phrase consists of a free pronoun, or a noun. In (172), the 3FP free pronoun *hinne* coreferences the right-dislocated noun *il-banāt* 'the girls', followed by another adjectival predicate *kwayysāt*.

(172) *yā sīd-i hinne ḥilwāt il-banāt kwayysāt*
VOC sir-1SG 3FP nice.FP DEF-girls good.FP
'My friend, they are nice, the girls, (they are) good'

The linear order within the noun phrase is the following:

(determiners) noun (noun)* (demonstrative) (adjective)* (relative)*

Complex NPs are rare in spontaneous speech. Most often, they occur when the speaker adds right-adjoined modifiers to further narrow the reference of the head, and to increase retrievability

 https://doi.org/10.11647/OBP.0410.04

on the part of the addressee. Example (173) illustrates the order DETERMINER NOUN DEMONSTRATIVE ADJECTIVE RELATIVE:

(173) *il-kafkīr hāḏa lə-kbīr illi binišlu bī*
DEF-ladle DEM DEF-big REL snatch.IPFV.3MS with.3MS
l-laḥme min iṭ-ṭunǧara
DEF-meat from DEF-pot
'This big ladle with which they take the meat out of the pot'

Three kinds of syntactic relation between a head and its modifiers can be identified:

(a) Determination
Determination primarily involves a disparate set of premodifiers that arose from the grammaticalisation of elements of different origins and which do not display a unified syntactic behaviour. We include in this category the definite article *il-*, *uxra* 'another', *min* 'some of', *čam* 'some' and prenominal demonstratives. The kind of dependency at play between the head and these preposed elements can be represented this way: [[DETERMINERS] NOUN]

(b) Construct state
The construct state consists minimally of a genitive construction with a nominal modifier and a modified noun. In theory, the number of nouns is recursive. The dependency between the elements can be represented as follows: [NOUN [NOUN]]

(c) Apposition
There are other modifiers that occur rightward of the head. These are postnominal demonstratives, adjectives,

> and relative clauses. The linear order of these right-adjoined modifiers is rather flexible and as such, they are best characterised as appositive, exhibiting loose syntactic integration with their head. The syntactic dependency can be represented as follows: [[NOUN] [POSTMODIFIERS]].

In addition to this, there is a hybrid class of modifiers, which can be characterised as syntactic heads but semantic modifiers. These are nominals that head the noun they semantically modify in a construct state relation, referred to in this description as 'modifying heads'.

We first discuss determiners, followed by the construct state and other genitive constructions, including modifying heads. Adjective phrases and relative clauses are treated separately, because, although they belong to the same class of appositive postnominal modifiers, they have different internal structures. Demonstratives and numerals are also discussed separately, because they do not have a unified behaviour. The last section is on the expression of comparison.

4.1.1. Determiners

4.1.1.1. The Article *il-*

Nouns can be augmented with the definite article *il-*, which either flags the entity as being identifiable or denotes the whole class (174). As noted in §3.1, the article, like any left-adjoined morpheme, does not exhibit strict affixal behaviour, because, except in rare cases, it does not modify the position of stress.

(174) *il-kalb niǧis... amma l-biss taqi*

DEF-dog impure... whereas DEF-cat devout

'Dogs are impure whereas cats are immaculate'

4.1.1.2. *(a)čam(m) ~ (a)kam(m)* 'a couple of'

The morpheme *čam(m)* (< *kamm*) is originally a noun whose meaning is 'quantity'. It is often homophonous with the interrogative *čam ~ kam* 'how much', with which it shares cognacy. It often collocates with the preposition *min* 'from', with different levels of coalescence. It can, further, be realised with or without affrication, which doubles the total number of surface forms. Example (175) illustrates the use of the variant *akamman*, in which the vowel of *min* has undergone vowel harmony with the preceding /a/. The modified noun is always in the singular.

(175) *kān bī ʕin-na* ***akamman*** *zalame*

be.PFV.3MS EXIST at-1PL a_couple_of man

maʕā-hum bārūd

with-3MP rifle

'We had a few men who had rifles'

4.1.1.3. *uxra* 'another'

The morpheme *uxra* can be interpreted both as an additive focus-sensitive particle 'also' (§3.12.3.4), and as a prenominal modifier, as shown in (176):

(176) *badd-ak tḥuṭṭ uxra xamse miṯəl-hin*

want-2MS put.SBJV.2MS another five like-3FP

'You have to put another five (items) like these ones'

It can also co-occur with *(a)čam (min)* 'a couple of':

(177) *il-na uxra ačammin sane*
for-1PL another few year
'We still have an extra few years'

4.1.1.4. *min* 'some of'

Although the morpheme *min* is mostly an ablative preposition, it can have a partitive meaning and be interpreted as a prenominal modifier, as exemplified in (178) and (179). These could also be the result of ellipsis, but the source construction has not been identified. The use of a quantifier, such as a numeral, is possible in (178) (*arbaʕa min ha-š-šhēbiyyāt* 'four of these sweets'), but not (179), because *xubz* 'bread' is a collective (***arbaʕa min ha-l-xubəz* 'four of these breads').

(178) *gaḥaf min ha-š-šhēbiyyāt u šarad*
swallow.PFV.3MS from DEM-DEF-sweet and run.PFV.3MS
'He swallowed some of these sweets and ran away'

(179) *bifittu min ha-l-xubəz u bōklū*
crumble.IPFV.3MP from DEM-DEF-bread and eat.IPFV.3MP.OBJ.3MS
'They cut up some of that bread and eat it'

4.1.2. Genitive Constructions

4.1.2.1. Construct State

As in standard Arabic, when a noun is used in a modification function, the order is head–modifier and the head noun is in a construct form. The construct state is well-known in Semitic linguistics, in which it refers to the shape of a nominal head when it is modified by another noun, a bound pronoun or, in languages such as Akkadian, a relative clause (Huehnergard 2008). The notion of the construct form of nouns has recently been extended to the morphological marking that a head noun takes in a noun-modifier construction, without any kind of cross-referencing of the modifier on the head (Creissels and Good 2018). In Arabic, the only morpheme that exhibits allomorphy in the construct state is the feminine ending *-a*, which surfaces as *-Vt*. In the dialect considered here, the main allomorph is *-it* (see §3.2.2.1.2). No other modifier can be inserted between the head and the modifier. Only the last noun of the construction is marked for definiteness, which holds for the whole phrase (the article *il-* or *zero*).

(180) a. *sukkān is-salṭ*
inhabitants DEF-Salt
'the inhabitants of Salt'

b. *giṭʕ-it ʔarḍ*
piece-F land
'a piece of land'

c. *āxir sūg is-skāfiyye*
end market DEF-Skāfiyye
'the end of the Skāfiyye market'

No modifier can be inserted between the head and the modifier. In (181), the adjective *gadīm-e* 'old-F' modifies *ḥayāt* 'life', but has to be placed at the right edge of the construction. Without context, such a NP is ambiguous: the adjective could equally modify *ḥayāt* 'life' or *is-salṭiyye* 'the Saltis', because *is-salṭiyye* is a collective human noun that can trigger feminine agreement (§4.3.3): [*ḥayāt* [*is-salṭiyye*] [*l-gadīm-e*]] or [*ḥayāt* [*is-salṭiyye* [*l-gadīm-e*]].

Although this is not attested in our dataset, the number of adjectives that can be adjoined is recursive, but they must have the same head.

(181) *ḥayāt is-salṭiyye l-gadīm-e*
life DEF-Saltis DEF-old-F
'The old life of the inhabitants of Salt' (also 'the life of the old inhabitants of Salt')

Although no adjectival modifers can be inserted between the head and the modifier noun, the two terms do not form a tight compound, because ellipsis of the modifier and coordination of the heads are possible:

(182) a. *gahwit iṣ-ṣubəḥ w sakārt iṣ-ṣubəḥ*
coffee DEF-morning and cigarette DEF-morning
'The morning coffee and the morning cigarette'

b. *gahwit ~~iṣ-ṣubəḥ~~ u sakārt iṣ-ṣubəḥ*
coffee DEF-morning and cigarette DEF-morning
'The morning coffee and cigarette'

In theory, there is no restriction on the number of nouns that can be concatenated, but in practice, constructions involving more than three nouns are avoided. In cases of syntactically more complex or semantically marked NPs, the dialect has various linking strategies including the linkers *tabaʕ*, *giyy* and *šiyy* (§4.1.2.2) and the preposition *la* 'for' (§4.1.2.3)

4.1.2.2. The Linkers *tabaʕ*, *giyy* and *šiyy*

Many Arabic dialects developed linkers used in cases of syntactically complex NPs or semantically marked genitive constructions.

The dialects of Arabic vary in the level of markedness of these constructions. At the one end of the spectrum, one finds varieties where these linkers have very limited use, and at the other end, varieties in which these constructions have become the unmarked strategy. The sedentary dialects of Jordan belong to the first type.

In present-day Amman and the Levant in general, the forms commonly encountered are *tabaʕ* and to a lesser extent *tāʕ*. Both *tabaʕ* and *tāʕ* inflect for gender and number, yielding the following paradigms.

Table 214: *tabaʕ* and *tāʕ* in Amman

MS	*tabaʕ*	*tāʕ*
FS	*tabaʕ-it*	*tāʕ-it*
MP	*tabaʕ-īn* ~ *tabaʕ-ūn*	*tāʕ-īn* ~ *tāʕ-ūn*
FP	*tabaʕ-āt*	*tāʕ-āt*

In the current state of the dialects of Central and Northern Jordan, *tabaʕ* is by far the most common. Apocopated *tāʕ* was recorded only once, which suggests that its use is rather marginal. The masculine plural allomorph *-ūn* is not available in traditional dialects and the feminine singular usually resyllabifies into *tabʕat* when followed by a vowel, as shown in Table 215.

Table 215: *tabaʕ* in Salt and Ḥōrāni

MS	*tabaʕ*
FS	*tabaʕ-it, tabʕ-at*
MP	*tabaʕ-īn*
FP	*tabaʕ-āt*

Example (183) illustrates the use of the feminine plural form *tabaʕāt*, which is only available to speakers who have kept gender distinction in the plural. Speakers who have neutralised gender distinction in the plural select the masculine plural form *tabaʕīn* (or *tabaʕūn* ~ *tāʕūn* in Amman).

(183) *bi ẓ-ẓrūf is-sūd hadōl tabaʕ-āt is-sūg*
in DEF-paper_bags DEF-black.PL DEM.PL GEN-FP DEF-market
'In these black paper bags, the ones they use in the market'

The morpheme *giyy* is reported for Ḥōrāni and neighbouring Bedouin dialects (Cleveland 1963, 61; Cantineau 1946, 204; Behnstedt 1997, 498–99). Cantineau (1946, 204) gives a masculine *geyy* ~ *gī*, a feminine *gīt* and a plural *giyyāt* unmarked for gender. As far as our corpus is concerned, very few tokens were recorded in Central Jordan. They all came from the same speaker, an elderly woman recorded in 1987.

(184) *šāhir hāḏ̣a gīt ir-riǧlēn*
Shaher DEM GEN DEF-legs
'Shaher, the one that (mends, treats) legs'

(185) *btismaʕ b-gīt il-ṃayye hāḏ̣a*
hear.IPFV.2MS in-GEN DEF-water DEM
čēf ngul-lo, wazīr il-ṃayye
how say.SBJV.1PL-3MS.DAT minister DEF-water
'You hear about the water guy, what's his name, the minister of water'

(186) *giyyāt it-thillil… waḷḷāhi kull-hin ysaǧǧil-hin*
GEN.PL DEF-song by_God all-3FP record.SBJV.3MS-3FP
'The (women) who sing, he would record them all'

When elicited, speakers produce the following paradigm: *giyy* (masculine singular), *gīt* (feminine singular), *giyyīn* (masculine plural) and *giyyāt* (feminine plural). Interestingly, this contradicts corpus data, which contains the presumably feminine form *gīt* for masculine referents, as in (184) and (185). No instances of masculine plural referents were found in the corpus, only feminine plural. It is therefore possible that gender distinction is neutralised with respect to *giyy* in Salt, unlike in Ḥōrāni, where gender is neutralised only in the plural. The following table summarises elicitation and corpus data. The mismatch between elicitation and corpus data is due to the fact that these morphemes have fallen into obscurity and speakers have little or no intuition regarding their use.

Table 216: The linker *giyy*

<table>
<tr><th></th><th>Elicited</th><th>Ḥōrān (Cantineau 1946)</th><th>Salt (Corpus)</th></tr>
<tr><td>MS</td><td>giyy</td><td>giyy</td><td rowspan="2">gīt</td></tr>
<tr><td>FS</td><td>gīt</td><td>gīt</td></tr>
<tr><td>MP</td><td>giyyīn</td><td rowspan="2">giyyāt</td><td rowspan="2">giyyāt</td></tr>
<tr><td>FP</td><td>giyyāt</td></tr>
</table>

The other genitive linker that was found in the speech of only one speaker is *šiyy*. It occurred four times in a recording from 2007 of a 90-year-old woman from Fḥēṣ. Similar reflexes have been reported in the literature. The form *šēt* is mentioned by Cleveland (1963, 61–62), who associates it with the dialects of Jerusalem and Nablus. It is also found in Palestinian folktales collected by Enno Littman (1905) around Jerusalem. The folktales are in Arabic script and the morpheme is transcribed شيت, which may be read *šīt* or *šēt*. Interestingly, *šēt* seems to have been brought back to life in the coastal Palestinian dialect of Jaffa (Uri Horesh, p.c.).[1] The presence of *šīt* is also reported in Damascus by Lentin (2011) and Behnstedt (1997, 498–99). Lentin (2011) also gives *šiyāt*, but notes that neither *šīt* nor *šiyāt* is marked for gender and number. In Jordan, Palva (2008, 65) gives *šīt* for Salt as unmarked for gender and number, which contradicts our corpus data, as suggested by the tokens presented below.

(187) *waḻḻāhi winn-hum ǧāybīn-o mʕallgīn-o*
by_God DM-3MP bring.AP.MP-3MS hang.AP.MP-3MS
bi l-ǧarra hāy... hāḏa l-... šiyy iǧ-ǧēš
in DEF-jar DEM.F DEM.M DEF- GEN.M DEF-army
'They had brought it and dangled it into that spouted jar, the army thing'

(188) *dār ʕamm-i min hōn šīt is-salṭ*
house uncle-1MS from here GEN.F DEF-Salt
'The house of my uncle, from this road, the one of Salt'

In (187), the speaker has an entity in mind, which she first refers to as feminine *ǧarra* 'clay jar', but then changes the referent using the masculine demonstrative *hāḏa*, and then the genitive linker *šiyy* followed by *iǧ-ǧēš* 'the army'. The form *šiyy* has to be interpreted as a masculine agreeing with *hāḏa*. In (188), the feminine

[1] According to Uri Horesh (p.c.), the pervasiveness of *šēt* in the speech of Arabic–Hebrew bilingual speakers in Jaffa may be attributed in part to its similarity to the Hebrew genitive marker *šel*.

form *šīt* is triggered by the feminine referent *dār* 'house'. Since no plural forms are attested in our data and because elicitation is not reliable for vestigial variants, two paradigms can potentially be inferred (Table 217). Given that gender marking in the plural is neutralised in favour of the feminine form in *giyyāt*, the second paradigm seems more likely.

Table 217: *Šiyy* in Salt

	Option 1	Option 2
MS	*šiyy*	*šiyy*
FS	*šīt*	*šīt*
MP	*šiyyīn*	*šiyyāt*
FP	*šiyyāt*	

Syntactically, the following constructions are attested:

(a) Noun GEN-Bound Pronoun

(b) Noun GEN Noun

- Noun Adjective GEN Noun
- Noun GEN Noun Noun
- Noun Noun GEN Noun

(c) GEN Noun

(a) Noun GEN-Bound Pronoun

(189) *l-amīr il-mihdāwi wēn, ʕala ṭayybit*
DEF-prince DEF-Mihdāwi where to NAME
il-ʕaranki, ʕa ṭ-ṭayybe tabaʕit-na
DEF-Aranki, on DEF-NAME GEN.F-1PL
'Where was the prince Mihdāwi? To the Aranki's *Ṭayybe*, to our *Ṭayybe* (name of a village)'

(190) *bsāʕ winn-i wāṣil, winn-o mayyit bi*

quickly DM-1SG arrive.AP.1SG DM-3SG dead in

l-bēt tabaʕ-o

DEF-house GEN-3MS

'I arrived there quickly, and there he was, dead in his house'

(b) Noun GEN Noun

(191) *ibən ʔil-i bi l-magsam tabaʕ iš-šūne*

son to-1SG in DEF-telephone_exchange GEN DEF-Shune

'A son of mine (works) at the telephone exchange in Shune'

- Noun Adjective GEN Noun

(192) *yǧīb iš-šarḥāt iz-zġār tabaʕāt il-bandōra*

bring.SBJV.3MS DEF-slices DEF-small.PL GEN.FP DEF-tomato

'He used to bring the small slices of tomato'

- Noun GEN Noun Noun

(193) *il-gišre tabaʕit ǧiḏər iš-šaǧara dbāġ bugullū-lo*

DEF-bark GEN.F root DEF-tree *dbāġ* say.IPFV.3MP-3MP.DAT

'The bark of the root of the (oak) tree, they call it *dbāġ*'

- Noun Noun GEN Noun

(194) *xazīn it-tibən tabaʕ id-dawābb ism-o l-matban*

stock DEF-straw GEN DEF-animal name-3MS DEF-*matban*

'The place where they keep the hay for the animals is called *matban*'

(c) GEN Noun

(195) *id-dār il-gadīme baʕəd-ha ʔil-ku willa biʕtū-ha?*

DEF-house DEF-old still-3FS to-2MP or sell.PFV.2MP-3FS

'Does the old house still belong to you or did you sell it?'

tabʕat lə-fḥēṣ? ā biʕət-ha

GEN.F DEF-Fḥēṣ yes sell.PFV.1SG-3FS

'The one in Fḥēṣ? Yes, I sold it'

(196) *il-guṭṭēn… ykūn fākəht iš-štā*

DEF-dried_fig be.SBJV.3MS fruit DEF-winter

tabaʕ iṣ-ṣēf bōklū mistwi

GEN DEF-summer eat.IPFV.3MP.3MS ripe

'The *guṭṭēn* (dried fig) would be a winter fruit, the summer fruit is eaten ripe'

(197) *il-mistašfa kān tabaʕ əl-xirsān*

DEF-hospital be.PFV.3MS GEN DEF-mutes

'The hospital was (one) for mutes'

(198) *haḏ̣ōl tabaʕīn il-ġanāni bġannū-hin*

DEM.PL GEN.PL DEF-songs sing.IPFV.3MP-3FP

'The (men who are in the singing business) sing them'

Normally, the genitive morpheme agrees in number and gender with the referent, but cases of lack of agreement were recorded: *il-ʔarḏ̣ tabaʕ-i* 'my piece of land' instead of *il-arḏ̣ tabʕat-i* (*arḏ̣* 'land' is feminine), *ir-riwāyāt tabaḥ-ḥum* 'their stories' instead of *ir-riwāyāt tabaʕit-hum* or *tabaʕāt-hum* (*riwāyāt* is an inanimate plural and should trigger either feminine singular or feminine plural agreement).

The use of the genitive linker is a marked construction and as such serves specific communicative purposes, whether formal (syntactic), or semantic-pragmatic. In (189), the speaker first uses the phrase *ṭayybit il-ʕaranki* 'Aranki's *Ṭayybe*' and then uses *tabaʕ* and a bound pronoun in *iṭ-ṭayybe tabaʕit-na* 'our land' to mark focus on the possessor. The same applies to (189) and (190), where the speaker marks focus on the possessor by way of the morpheme *tabaʕ* and the bound pronoun *-o*: *il-bēt tabaʕ-o* 'his house', not someone else's house. In (191) *il-magsam tabaʕ iš-šūne* 'the telephone exchange of Shune', the use of *tabaʕ* is motivated by the need felt by the speaker to increase the identifiability of the referent. The phrase *magsam iš-šūne* would refer to an entity that is part of the shared knowledge between the speaker and the addressee. In the case of the complex noun phrases in (192), (193) and (194), the use of the genitive linker is also motivated by a need to bypass the syntactic constraints of the construct state, in which the head noun cannot be marked twice for definiteness. If the speaker has already marked the head with the definite article and wants to add a modifier, the only way to do so and avoid ungrammaticality is to introduce the second modifier with the genitive linker. In a phrase such as *iš-šarḥāt iz-zġār* 'the small slices', any nominal modifier would have to appear between the head and the adjective. In these cases, the genitive linker is best viewed as a discourse planning repair device.

In addition to this, the most frequent use of the genitive linker appears in GEN Noun constructions, as exemplified in (195), (196), (197) and (198). In (195), the referent *id-dār il-gadīme* 'the old house', first introduced into the discourse in the polar question, is recalled in the answer with the morpheme *tabʕat*. The same phenomenon is observed in (196), in which the referent *guṭṭēn* 'dried fig' is defined as a winter fruit. The speaker brings back the referent in the rest of the utterance with *tabaʕ*. In (197), the morpheme *tabaʕ* refers to the subject *il-mistašfa* 'hospital'. In (198), the speaker first refers to the entity he has in mind with the demonstrative *haḏ̣ōl*. Since he fails to retrieve the exact name of that entity, he uses the masculine plural *tabaʕīn* modified by the noun *ġanāni* 'songs': *tabaʕīn il-ġanāni* 'the people (involved in) singing'. This construction is frequently used when the speaker is having difficulties retrieving the exact label of an entity: *tabaʕīn il-mistašfa* 'the people working in the hospital', *tabaʕīn iṭālya* 'the people from Italy', *tabaʕīn bōš* 'the people of Bush, the Americans', *tabaʕīn iš-šurṭa* 'the men working in the police', *tabaʕīn il-baladiyye* 'the people working for the municipality'.

What our data suggest is that the genitive linker is not strickly speaking a genitive morpheme, that is, a morpheme that is recruited to mark a nominal expression used in a modification function towards another nominal expression, which would imply the following dependency: [Noun [GEN Noun]]. The prevalence of the GEN Noun construction in the corpus is evidence that the primary nature of *tabaʕ*, *giyy* and *šiyy* is not to link, but is rather as a pro-form. The internal dependency within a GEN NOUN construction is [GEN [NOUN]], as shown by the selection of the construct allomorph -*Vt* or the feminine ending, as in (199).

(199) *tabʕ-at lə-fḥēṣ*

GEN-F.CSTR DEF-Fḥēṣ

'the one of Fḥēṣ'

It appears, therefore, that these morphemes are best characterised as the **construct pro-form** of a nominal expression. From there, the development into a genitive linker is not straightforward and needs an intermediary stage, which is illustrated in (200). Here the internal structure is [[Noun DEM] [GEN Noun]].

(200) *šāhir hāḏa gīt ir-riğlēn*

Shaher DEM GEN DEF-legs

'Shaher, the one that (mends, treats) legs'

As shown above, what links the two consitutents *šāhir hāḏa* and *gīt ir-riğlēn* is not dependency, but apposition. At this point, the linker is best viewed as a restrictive appositive marker. The syntactic coalescence of the two noun phrases into one noun phrase occurs at a subsequent stage, leading to the reinterpretation of the morpheme as a genitive linker. The three stages are summarised below:

(a) [GEN [Noun]] *tabʕat lə-fḥēṣ* (construct pro-form)

(b) [[Noun] [GEN [Noun]] *šāhir hāḏa gīt ir-riğlēn* (restrictive appositive marker)

(c) [Noun [GEN [Noun]]] *il-magsam tabaʕ iš-šūne* (genitive linker)

In summary, it appears that what is usually called a genitive linker (or exponent) originates from the apposition of one referring NP and one NP formed of the genitive morpheme used as a construct pro-form of the referring NP and a genitival modifier. The two main functions of these morphemes are as a means of reference disambiguation and discourse planning repair. Both functions aim at increasing the accessibility or identifiability of the referent in the adressee's mind, as compared to the unmarked construct state.

4.1.2.3. The Preposition *la* 'for'

The preposition *la* 'for' is also used as a linker in the case of different definiteness patterns between the head and the modifiers. Recall that the construct state only allows the last noun to bear a mark of definition, whether the article *il-* or *zero* for indefiniteness.

(201) a. *xārṭa la baladīt is-salṭ*
map for municipality DEF-Salt
'a map of the municipality of Salt'

b. *ibən uxt ʔil-i*
son sister for-1SG
'a son of a sister of mine'

This category includes cases of syntactically-governed indefiniteness, as in (202), where indefiniteness is imposed by the ordinal *awwal* 'first', which requires the construction to be indefinite. The last noun has to be zero-marked for definition. In this case, the toponym *lə-fḥēṣ* bears the article, so it cannot be the final noun. To overcome this restriction, speakers have to break the genitive construction using *la*.

(202) *awwal raʔīs baladiyye la lə-fḥēṣ*
first head municipality for DEF-Fḥēṣ
~
awwal raʔīs la baladīt lə-fḥēṣ
first head for municipality DEF-Fḥēṣ
'The first mayor of Fḥēṣ'

The sedentary dialects of Jordan also use *la* 'for' as a linker in what is sometimes labelled the 'clitic-doubling' construction (Souag 2017). It refers at minimum to two separate constructions: one is a genitive construction (203) and the other one is the differential object-marking construction (204), unknown in Jordan but common in northern Levantine and Mesopotamian. Although they are not often discussed, there are other similar constructions which seem to be available only in highly innovative northern Levantine dialects. One of them involves content-interrogative clauses with the interrogative *kīf* 'how' or *wēn* 'where' and a human subject (205).

(203) *ibn-o la mḥammad*
son-3MS to Muhammad
'The son of Muhammad'

(204) *šift-o la mḥammad*
see.PFV.1MS-3MS to mhammad
'I saw Muhammad'

(205) *kīf-o la mḥammad*
how-3MS to Muhammad
'How is Muhammad?'

What these constructions have in common is a right-dislocated noun and a coreferencing bound pronoun which occupies the syntactic slot of the dislocated noun. Grammaticalisation probabably started with nouns denoting kinship relations, before extending to human nouns. Aramaic is often cited as the substratal source of this construction, although internal developments cannot be ruled out, because these commonly occur cross-linguistically (cf. French *son père au gamin*). Some dialects allow all three constructions, some allow the first two, and some allow only the first, yielding the following implicational scale: (203) < (204) < (205). Some dialects also innovate in permitting definite referents. Sedentary Jordanian belongs to the most conservative type in that it only permits (203) in genitive constructions denoting kinship relations, as in (206) and (207). The term 'clitic' in this case is arguably infelicitous, because bound pronouns are best interpreted as affixes (§3.1).

(206) *ibn axū la zalmat-i*
son brother.3MS for man-1SG
'a son of the brother of my husband'

(207) *ibən xāl-ha la ʔumm-i*
son maternal_uncle-3FS for mother-1SG
'the son of the maternal uncle of my mother'

4.1.2.4. Modifying Heads

Modifying heads are nouns that head genitive constructions but narrow the reference of another noun. They are therefore syntactic heads but semantic modifers. The syntactic structure is that of the construct state [NOUN [NOUN]]. The morphemes included in this category are *baʕḏ̣* ‘a part of’, *kull* ‘all, every’, *nafs* ‘same’, *ġēr* ‘other’, *šwayyit* ‘few’ and *ayy(a)* ‘any’.

4.1.2.4.1. *baʕḏ̣* ‘a part of’

The morpheme *baʕḏ̣* is a nominal whose meaning is ‘part’. In addition to its use in reciprocal constructions (§4.4.2.6.3), it expresses a part-to-whole relation.

(208) *baʕəḏ̣-hum sātir ʕōrt-o baʕəḏ̣-hum laʔ*
part-3MP protect.AP.MS genital-3MS part-3MP no
‘Some of them are decently dressed, some of them aren’t’

(209) *biḏ̣all baʕḏ̣ il-maḥallāt fātḥāt*
stay.IPFV.3MS part DEF-places open.AP.FP
‘Some of the shops stay open’

4.1.2.4.2. *kull* ‘all’

The morpheme *kull* ‘all’ is the universal quantifier. The unmarked syntax of *kull* is to precede the head. If it precedes an indefinite noun, it means ‘every’: *kull sane* ‘every year’. If it precedes a definite noun, it means ‘all’: *kull il-ʕālam* ‘all the people’. It can be dislocated, in which case a bound pronoun coreferencing the semantic head attaches to it, as shown in (210), where the bound pronoun *hin* coreferences *karāsī-na u ṭālwāt-na* ‘our chairs and tables’.

(210) *wal̤l̤a inno ʕin-na karāsī-na u ṭāwlāt-na*
by_God COMP at-1PL chairs-1PL and tables-1PL
kull-hin barra
all-3FP outside
‘At ours, all our chairs and tables are outside’

4.1.2.4.3. *nafs* 'same'

The morpheme *nafs*, whose lexical meaning is 'spirit', normally precedes a definite semantic head: *nafs il-wakət* 'same time'. Like *kull*, it can follow the head, in which case it is augmented with a bound pronoun coreferencing the head: *il-ǧamīd nafs-o* 'the same dehydrated buttermilk'.

4.1.2.4.4. *ġēr* 'other'

The morpheme *ġēr*, initially a nominal, took various grammaticalisation paths, from a prenominal modifier, to a hortative particle (§4.2.5.4). In positive polarity, one of the most common phrases is *ġēr šikəl* 'something different', as illustrated in (211). Most often, though, *ġēr* (alongside *ʔilla* and *ʕada*) is used in exceptive constructions (§4.5.1.11) which typically involve negative polarity.

(211)	*intu*	*b-ḥāle*	*ġēr*	*šikəl*	*ʕan-na*
	2MP	in-situation	other	style	from-1PL

'Your situation is different (better) from ours'

4.1.2.4.5. *šwayyit* 'few'

The morpheme *šwayyit* is the construct form of *šwayye* 'few', itself the diminutive derivation of *ši* 'thing'.

(212)	*šwayyit*	*ʕadas*	*u*	*šwayyit*	*ruzz*
	few	lentil	and	few	rice

'a little bit of lentils and a little bit of rice'

Some speakers also use *nitfit*, which is the construct form of *nitfe* 'small amount, tuft of hair':

(213) *bī* *nās* *biṭḥuṭṭ* *nitfit* *mā* *zahər*

EXIST people put.IPFV.3FS few water flower

'Some people add a little bit of rose water'

4.1.2.4.6. *ayy(a)* 'any'

The morpheme *ayy(a)* is both a prenominal determiner and an interrogative determiner (§3.7.10). It precedes an indefinite singular count noun. The nominal nature of *ayya* is suggested by its compatibility with bound pronouns, with which the allomorph *ayyāt* is selected (see example (57) in §3.7.10).

(214) *isʔal-ni* *ʔayya* *suʔāl*

ask.IMP.MS-1SG any question

'Ask me any question'

4.1.3. Adjective Phrases

Adjectives follow the head noun, and agree in definiteness with the head:

walad *zġīr* 'a young boy'

boy.INDEF young.INDEF

ṭabīʕt-o *l-ʔawwalāniyye* 'its initial state'

nature-3MS.DEF DEF-first

Complex adjective phrases have the following syntactic structure: ADJECTIVE NOUN. Most of the examples recorded involve the adjective *galīl* 'few' modified by a noun:

galīl-it *ḥaya* 'indecent.F'

few-F.CSTR decency

galīl *ʔadab* 'impolite'

few politeness

galīl-īn *ʕagəl* 'stupid.MP'
few.MP intelligence

The adjective is in the construct form, as evidenced by the construct allomorph *-it* of the feminine ending which surfaces in this position. Consider the following utterance (215). The adjective *kāmle* (complete.F) agrees with the head *ʕēle* 'family'. In the complex adjective phrase *kāml-it il-waṣāyif*, the head adjective *kāml-it* and the nominal modifier *il-waṣāyif* form a genitive construction. The dependencies can be represented as follows: [*ʕēle* [*kāmlit* [*il-waṣāyif*]]]

(215) *hummu hadōl ʕēle kāmle yaʕni*
3PL dem.PL family.F full-F it_means
kāml-it il-waṣāyif min iṭ-ṭīb min
full-F.CSTR DEF-qualities from DEF-goodness from
id-dakā min il-laṭāfa
DEF-cleverness from DEF-kindness
'These people, they have all the qualities of good-heartedness, cleverness and kindness'

In addition to this, standard Arabic also has complex adjective phrases with a similar linear order, but different dependencies. Here the noun is not a modifier, but an argument of the adjectival predicate.

[rağul [ʔasmar [lawn-u-hu]]] 'a dark-skinned man'
man dark colour-NOM-3MS

Only one instance of this construction was recorded in spontaneous speech, illustrated in example (216). In this example, the complex adjective *l-axḍar lōn-o* obviously modifies *bunn*, because of the lack of feminine agreement that *gahwa* should have triggered. It is debatable as to whether this construction belongs to the vernacular or was replicated from standard Arabic.

(216) *il-bunn alli hū l-gahwa l-axḏ̣ar lōn-o*
DEF-coffee_beans REL 3MS DEF-coffee DEF-green colour-3MS
'unroasted coffee, that is coffee whose colour is (still) green'

4.1.4. Relative Clauses

4.1.4.1. Restrictive Relative Clauses

Relative clauses occur rightward of the relativised noun. With the exception of some dialects of Southern Arabia, non-standard varieties of Arabic usually exhibit an invariable relativiser, which most often takes the shape *illi*. In some dialects, there is no formal difference between the relativiser and the article. Traditionally, the relativiser and the article are described as two separate morphemes, but there is no reason not to treat them as two allomorphs whose selection is governed by the category of the modifier:

(217) Adjective:
il-walad il- xabīṯ
DEF-boy DEF- cunning
'the cunning boy'

(218) Clause:
il-walad illi ǧibt-o
DEF-boy DEF bring.PFV.1SG-3MS
'the boy I gave birth to'

Syntactically, the relative clause is externally-headed and follows the relativised noun, as shown in (218). Arabic has two relativisation strategies, depending on the syntactic role of the relativised noun and the type of predicate (Comrie and Kuteva 2013): the pronoun-retention strategy (resumptive) and the gap strategy. The general strategy is the pronoun-retention one, whereas the gap strategy is limited to relativisation of subjects of non-verbal predicates. Because of the pronoun-retention strategy, Arabic has no restrictions on the syntactic roles that are eligibile for relativisation (Keenan and Comrie 1977). The gap strategy is illustrated in (220), in which the relativised noun occupies the subject position in the non-verbal predicate relative clause, without a resumptive pronoun in that position. It may be argued that (219) is also an instance of the gap strategy, because there is no overt free pronoun. However, the morphological status of the indices has little relevance, and the indexation of the subject on the verb by way of the third-person prefix *y-* and the feminine plural suffix *-in de facto* qualifies this as an instance of the pronoun-retention strategy.

(a) Subject

(219) *kull il-maṣāyib illi yṣīrin…*
all DEF-misfortunes DEF become.SBJV.3FP
kull-hin ʕamm-i mitlaggī-hin
all-3FP uncle-1SG receive.PA.MS-3FP
'My uncle would bear all the misfortunes that would happen'

(220) *is-siğn ir-raʔīsi illi gbāl il-ʔašāra*

DEF-prison DEF-main REL front DEF-light

'The main prison, that is in front of the traffic light'

(b) Object

(221) *il-ḥāle lli ḏugət-ha mā nās*

DEF-situation REL taste.PFV.1SG-3FS NEG people

ḏāg-ha bi d-dinya

taste.PFV.3MS-3FS in DEF-world

'No one in this world went through the situation I went through'

(c) Obliquely coded object

(222) *hāḏa lli ana bafakkir bī*

DEM REL 1SG think.IPFV.1SG in.3MS

'This is what I think/I am thinking about'

(d) Complement of preposition

(223) *hāḏa l-ʕurs illi iḥna mniḥči ʕann-o*

DEM DEF-wedding REL 1PL talk.IPFV.1PL about-2MS

miš ʕan iğ-ğdīd

NEG about DEF-new

'The type of wedding we are talking about is not the new one'

(e) Possessor

(224) *hāḏ illi šaʕr-o šāb sant-ha*

DEM REL hair-3MS turn_gray.PFV.3MS year-3FS

'The one whose hair turned grey that year'

The codifiers of Standard Arabic formalised the well-known rule of definiteness as the only parameter that governs the presence or the absence of the relativiser. The dialects discussed here mostly follow this rule. In all the examples above, the relativised noun is definite, and the relative clause is introduced with the relativiser *illi*. Moreover, there are no instances of a definite relativised noun without *illi* and only indefinite heads seem to permit *illi*-less clauses, as shown in (225) and (226).

(225)	*badd-i*	*asʔal*	*ʕan*	*wāḥad*	*ḥakēt*	*ʕann-o*
	want-1SG	ask.SBJV.1SG	about	one	talk.PFV.2MS	about-3MS

'I want to ask about someone you talked about'

(226)	*yǧību*	*marrāt*	*ašyā*	*mn*	*is-sūg*
	bring.SBJV.3MP	times	things	from	DEF-market
	miš	*mawǧūde*	*hōna*		
	NEG	present	here		

'Sometimes they would bring from the market things we couldn't find here'

However, our data contain numerous instances of *illi*-clauses with indefinite heads. These constructions have been discussed in Brustad (2000, 94), who uses a hierarchy of individuation to predict the presence or the absence of the relativiser *illi*. The bottom line is that the more individuated an item is, the more it will permit the use of *illi*. Definiteness is one parameter of individuation. Other parameters are specificity, animacy and topicality. Consider examples (227) and (228). Both involve an indefinite head and an *illi*-clause. They are perfectly grammatical, although they conflict with the standard rule. Although syntactically indefinite, the head is semantically made more specific by the numerals *sitt mīt* 'six hundred' in (227) and *siṭṭaʕšar* 'sixteen' in (228), which render the use of *illi* permissible.

(227) *ʔil-o hnāk sitt mīt dulum, illi bī-hin*
to-3MS there six hundred dunum REL in-3FP
ǧarītt ir-rāy
newspaper Rai
'He owns six hundred dunums, where Ar-Ray newspaper is located'

(228) *mā ʕāš ġēr ʕala siṭṭaʕšar nēra*
NEG live.PFV.3MS except on sixteen dinar
illi ṭlaʕ-lo yyā-hin ʕabdirraḥīm
REL take_out.PFV.3MS-3MS.DAT OBJ-3FP Abdelraheem
'He only lived off sixteen dinars that Abdelraheem had allocated for him'

In the dialects discussed here, the relativiser, although recorded as *illi* in an overwhelming majority of cases, can also surface as *il-*, like the article. It was noted above that there is no reason to treat the relativiser *illi* and the article *il-* as two distinct morphemes, and they should rather be treated as two allomorphs whose selection is governed by the type of modifier: an adjectival predicate will select the marker *il-*, whereas *illi* will be selected by clausal modifiers. Consequently, it would be possible to interpret *illi* as a definite marker, not a relativiser. Interestingly, the allomorph *il-* can be selected with clausal modifiers, as shown below. Most tokens involve non-verbal prepositional predicates, as illustrated in (229) and (230), although verbal predicates are also attested, as in (231) and (232). Example (231) illustrates a headless relative clause in which the predicate is a participle, which has, as a non-finite verbal form, both adjectival properties (here agreement patterns) and verbal ones (here a pronominal object). It appears from all of this that the short allomorph *il-*, although permitted in all cases, is a marginal option whose complementary distribution with *illi* is either vestigial or incipient.

(229) *il-bukse hāy lə-ṣġayyre il-gadd ṣandūg ir-rāḥa*
DEF-box DEM DEF-small REL-quantity box DEF-lokum
'This small box that is the size of a lokum box'

(230) *hassaʕ bawarrī-ki d-dār il-ʔil-o*
now show.IPFV.1SG-2FS DEF-house REL-to-3MS
'Now I'll show you the house that belongs to him'

(231) *ḥawwalū-ha ana l-xābir-ha la milḥame*
transform.PFV.3MP-3FS 1SG REL-recall.AP.MS-3FS to butchery
'They turned it, from what I recall, into a butchery'

(232) *badd-i lbās la l-walad il-buʕruǧ hāḏa*
want-1SG garment for DEF-walad REL-limp.IPFV.3MS DEM
'I want a garment for this boy who limps'

4.1.4.2. Headless Relative Clauses

Headless relative clauses are relative clauses that have no head on the surface and behave like a noun phrase. They have the same structure as normally headed clauses and are introduced by *illi*. As with headed restrictive relative clauses, there are no restrictions on the syntactic roles that are eligible for relativisation. Example (233) illustrates a headless relative clause as the modifier expression in a genitive construction. The relativised syntactic role is that of a subject.

(233) *nrudd* *niṭəlʕ-o* *ʕa*

return.SBJV.1PL take_out.SBJV.1PL-3MS on

[*dār* [*illi* *yištrī*]]

house REL buy.SBJV.3MS-3MS

'We would take it back again to the house of the one who would buy it'

4.1.4.3. Non-restrictive Relative Clauses

Non-restrictive relative clauses, also known as explicative relative clauses, are non-modifying relative clauses: they do not narrow the reference of a nominal expression. Syntactically, they do not form a consitutent with the relativised noun and are in apposition. In many languages, restrictive and non-restrictive relative clauses are coded in the same way. In the dialects investigated here, non-restrictive relative clauses tend to be coded differently from restrictive clauses. Typically, they attach to the right and are introduced with *illi* followed by a free pronoun that cross-references the relativised noun. In (234), *hū* cross-references *iǧ-ǧēš* 'the army', and in (235), *hī* refers to *sane* 'year'.

(234) *xāfu* *inn-hum* *yigṭaʕu* *xaṭṭ* *ər-rağʕa* *ʕala*

fear.PFV.3MP COMP-3MP cut.SBJV.3MP line DEF-retreat on

ǧ-ǧēš *lə-briṭāni* *illi* *hū* *wiṣil* *əs-salṭ*

DEF-army british REL 3MS arrive.PFV.3MS DEF-Salt

'They were afraid to cut the retreat line of the British forces, which had arrived at Salt'

(235) *gaʕdat* *sane* *santēn* *ʕind-i* *illi*
remain.PFV.3FS year year-DU at-1SG REL
hī *sane* *aḻḻa* *aʕlam* *bī-ha*
3FS year God knowing in-3FS
'(The cow) remained at my place one year, two years, that is one year, God knows best'

4.1.4.4. Summary

Many scholars use the label 'relative pronoun', problably inherited from descriptions of European languages. This is, however, problematic from a descriptive point of view. Cross-linguistically, a relative pronoun has to fulfil two conditions (Creissels 2006a, 228; Comrie and Kuteva 2013). First, it has to reflect in some way or another the syntactic position of the relativised noun within the relative clause. Second, the canonical position of the relativised noun within the relative clause must not be occupied by a regular pronoun. The verdict is therefore undisputable: Arabic has no relative pronoun. The canonical position is occupied by a normal pronoun, and the relativiser does not reflect in any way the syntactic position of the relativised noun within the relative clause. Even Standard Arabic does not fulfil any of the requirements: although the relativiser does inflect for case (although only in the dual), it agrees with the case of the relativised noun in the main clause, not the relative clause.

It was also suggested above that there are good reasons to treat the article *il-* and the relativiser *illi* as two allomorphs that are in quasi-complementary distribution: *il-* is selected by adjectival modifiers and *illi* is selected by clausal modifiers. The short allomorph also surfaces with prepositional phrases, which, like adjectives, can be recruited as non-verbal predicates. It seems, therefore, that the selection parameter between *il-* and *illi* is the verbal or non-verbal nature of the predicate within the relative clause. This would also mean that the adjective phrase in Arabic is a sub-type of the relative clause.

4.1.5. Adnominal Demonstratives

Demonstratives can be placed to the left of the noun (236) or to the right of the noun, in which case adjacency is not a rule. Compare in this regard (237), which has the linear order [NOUN DEMONSTRATIVE ADJECTIVE], and (238), which exhibits [NOUN ADJECTIVE DEMONSTRATIVE].

(236)	*ṣurt*	*aḏḏakkar*	*haḏ̣āk*	*il-walad*
	become.PFV.1SG	remember.SBJV.1SG	DEM	DEF-boy

‘I started remembering that boy’

(237)	*ibn-i*	*haḏ̣āk*	*lə-zġīr*	*baʕd-o*	*bigra*
	son-1SG	DEM	DEF-small	still-3MS	study.IPFV.3MS

‘That young son of mine is still studying’

(238)	*kānin*	*yiḏ̣ḥakin*	*ʕalayye*	*l-banāt*
	be.PFV.3FP	laugh.SBJV.3FP	on.1SG	DEF-girls
	lə-kbār	*əšwayye*	*haḏ̣ōl*	
	DEF-old	few	DEM	

‘These girls who were a bit older were laughing at me’

What this suggests is that, in the varieties considered here, constituency is rather loose between the postnominal demonstrative and the coreferential noun. Consequently, it may be more appropriate to consider that the NP and the demonstrative are in apposition and that postnominal demonstratives are primarily proforms. It appears, therefore, that prenominal demonstratives and postnominal demonstratives do not have the same syntactic status: the former are proper noun dependents whereas the latter are appositive proforms.

The previous examples may suggest that postnominal demonstratives are selected by animate or human-referring nouns, but inanimate nouns can also be found:

(239) *tarak* *il-bēt* *haḏ̣āk* *w* *aǧa*
leave.PFV.3MS DEF-house DEM and come.PFV.3MS
yibni *tiḥt*
build.SBJV.3MS below
'He left that house and built (a new house) below'

Like many Levantine dialects, sedentary Jordanian also has a short demonstrative *ha-*, which, unlike the long form, is bound. Typically, nouns referring to non-topical or discursively distant entities that the speaker considers retrievable to the hearer are marked with the short demonstrative. These referents are identifiable either from the co-text (previously mentioned in the discourse) or the context (part of shared knowledge). Only two instances of possible deictic readings were found in the corpus. In (240), the speaker reports a conversation he was having about a venue he needed for an event and marks the noun *maḥall* 'place', which refers to that venue, with *ha-*. The use of the short demonstrative might be triggered by the reported speech and signals that the referent is accessible to both the hearer and the speaker.

(240) *gal-li* *šūf* ***ha**-l-maḥall* *əkbīr* *willa*
say.PFV.3MS-DAT.1SG look.IMP.MS DEM-DEF-place big or
zġīr *gult-lo* *waḻḻāhi* *bī* *l-baraka*
small say.PFV.1SG-DAT.3MS by_God in.3MS DEF-benediction
'He said look at this place, is it big enough? I said it's perfect'

Another example of a possible deictic reading appears in (241).

(241) *ʔāxir* *dār* *bi* *s-salālim* *kānat*
last house in DEF-Salālim be.PFV.3FS
ṭālla *b-rās* ***ha**-ǧ-ǧabal*
overlook.AP.FS in-head DEM-DEF-mountain
'The last house in Salālim was overlooking the top of the mountain'

This, however, is disputable, because it does not involve strict pointing but seems rather to reflect shared spatial knowledge of the mountain adjacent to the Salālim neighbourhood in Salt. Apart from these uncertain tokens, deictic use is only attested when the short demonstrative is supplemented by a long form placed to the right, as shown in (242).

(242) *ʕimil* ***ha**-l-lawḥa* *hāy*
do.PFV.3MS DEM-DEF-painting DEM
'He did this painting'

In (243), the speaker speaks about dishes, then stops at *mansaf*, which becomes the discursive topic. The first three discursively new entities *ha-l-laḥme* 'the meat', *ha-l-marīse* 'the buttermilk sauce' and *ha-n-nār* 'the fire' are marked with the short demonstrative. Although not part of the co-text, these entities are part of the shared knowledge of all the participants in the speech event, because they are all well-acquainted with *mansaf* and what is required to prepare it. The discursive topic *ha-l-minsaf* 'the *mansaf*' resurfaces in the end, marked with *ha-*, as if its topicality has been lowered after all the newly introduced entities.

(243) *iḥna kunna gabəl... nuṭbux minsaf nḥuṭṭ*
1PL be.PFV.1PL before cook.SBJV.1PL mansaf put.SBJV.1PL
***ha**-l-laḥme w ənḥuṭṭ **ha**-l-marīse*
DEM-def-meat and put.SBJV.1PL DEM-DEF-buttermilk
*fōgī-(h)in u minraččib-hin ʕala **ha**-n-nār*
above-3FP and install.IPFV.1PL-3FP on DEM-DEF-fire
laminn-hin yistwin minfalfil ḥabbāt
until-3FP be_ripe.SBJV.3FP cook_rice.IPFV.1PL grain
*ir-ruzz əb-ğanib-hin u minsawwi **ha**-l-minsaf u*
DEF-rice in-next-3FP and make.IPFV.1PL DEM-DEF-mansaf and
*minḥuṭṭ **ha**-l-laḥmāt ʕalē*
put.IPFV.1PL DEM-DEF-meat on.3MS
'We used to cook mansaf, we would put the meat, and the buttermilk sauce on top of it, and we put it on the fire until it is done, we cook the rice next to it, and cook the mansaf and we put the pieces of meat on it.'

In (244), the speaker speaks about her son who recently dropped out of school, but she refers to him using the short demonstrative *ha-l-walad* 'the boy', although he is clearly the topic. The subsequent entities *ha-lə-grāye* 'the study' and *ha-l-mudīr* 'the school principal' are also introduced into the discourse with the short demonstrative and are retrievable for the hearer because they are part of shared knowledge. Consequently, the short demonstrative *ha-* is a device used by speakers to flag entities that are perceived as retrievable and accessible to the hearer, either from the co-text or as part of shared knowledge. The topical status of these entities is generally low, but example (244) shows that speakers also use *ha-* with topical entities to maintain their topical status.

(244) *yōm rāḥ dafaʕ rusūm it-tawǧīhi **ha**-l-walad*
day go.PFV.3MS pay.PFV.3MS fees DEF-final DEM-DEF-boy
abṣar əššu ʔağa gām bīği sbūʕ u
ignore what come.PFV.3MS then around week and
*nhazam **ha**-l-walad ʕan **ha**-lə-grāye, u yā*
withdraw.PFV.3MS DEM-DEF-boy from DEM-DEF-study and VOC
*walad yā nasl it-ṭayyib, **ha**-l-mudīr hadōle*
boy VOC lineage DEF-good DEM-DEF-head DEM.PL
lə-mʕallimiyye, bigūlu ya ʕgāb int lēš miḏḏāyig
DEF-teachers say.IPFV.3MP VOC ʕgāb 2MS why annoyed
u inte miyaddab u int miḥtaram, xalaṣ,
and 2SG polite and 2SG respectable end
***ha**-l-walad ənhazam min il-midrase*
DEM-DEF-boy withdraw.PFV.3MS from DEF-school
'When he went to pay the fees of the final year, I don't know what happened to the boy, around a week or so, the boy dropped out from school, then the head (of the school) and the teachers said to him, you are a good boy, why are you annoyed, you are well behaved and respectable, that was it, the boy dropped out of school'

When demonstratives are used anaphorically, the distance contrast is reallocated as a referent-tracking device for previously mentioned entities and physical distance is reinterpreted as discursive distance, as exemplified in (245). The speaker talks about the two main areas of Salt, called Ḥāra and Krād, which were dominated by different personalities. The discursively proximal entity is coded with the proximal *hāy* and the discursively more distant entity is coded with distal *hadīk*.

(245) *haḏīk il-galʕa gāṣṣ m-in-nuṣṣ, il-ġēdāni*
DEM DEF-castle cut.AP.MS from-DEF-half, DEF-far_side
la ḏōgān w illi min iǧ-ǧiha hāy la l-ḥaǧǧ falāḥ
for Ḏogan and REL from side DEM for DEF-old Falāḥ
hāy *əkrād u* ***hadīk*** *fī ḥāra*
DEM.F.PROX Krād and DEM.F.DIST EXIST Ḥāra
'The castle was divived in two. The far side belonged to Ḏōgān, and the other side belonged to Ḥaǧǧ Falāḥ and Ḥalīm Al-Nimr, one was Krād and the other one Ḥāra'

4.1.6. Numerals

We deal here with the syntax of numerals (for the morphology of numerals, see §3.10). Numerals do not have a unified syntactic behaviour. Some precede the head, while others follow it.

The numeral *wāḥad* 'one' (feminine *waḥade*) is always placed to the right and agrees in gender with the head: *xilfe waḥade* 'one child', *ṣaff wāḥad* 'one class'. The numeral *wāḥad* shows no sign of grammaticalisation into a marker of indefiniteness, which is zero-marked. The numeral *wāḥad* may precede a noun, but in this case *wāḥad* is pronominal and the noun that follows is in apposition: *wāḥad ḍābiṭ* 'someone (who is) an officer'.

Although the dual *-ēn* is the normal way of marking duality, the numeral *t̲nēn* (feminine *t̲intēn*) can modify a noun in the plural to express duality. The number of nouns that are eligible for this periphrastic dual marking is limited. When dual marking is inhibited because of morphological or phonological reasons, the numeral precedes the head, as in *t̲nēn garāyib* 'two relatives', *t̲nēn fḥēṣiyye* 'two inhabitants of Fḥēṣ', *t̲nēn kīlo* 'two kilograms'. Dual marking is blocked on *garāyib* 'relatives' because it is already morphologically a plural and it does not have a singular to which the dual marker could attach. The putative singular form *garīb* can occur as a noun (*garīb ʔil-i* 'a relative of mine') but occurs more often as an adjective 'close', whose plural is *garībīn*. As noted above, the dual marker *-ēn* cannot attach to adjectives, only to nouns. The same applies to *fḥēṣi* 'inhabitant of Fḥēṣ', which is formed with the adjectiviser suffix *-i* and to which the suffix *-ēn* cannot attach. In the case of *kīlo* 'kilogram', the suffixation of *-ēn* seems dispreferred on phonetic grounds to avoid hiatus (although *kīlīyēn* 'two kilos' is possible, albeit archaic).

In all other cases, the numeral *t̲nēn* (feminine *t̲intēn*) follows the head: *banāt t̲intēn* 'two girls', *wlād t̲nēn* 'two boys', *zlām ət̲nēn* 'two men', *xayyāle t̲nēn* 'two horse-riders', *l-xwān it̲-t̲nēn* 'the two brothers', *il-kanāyis it̲-t̲intēn l-kbār* 'the two big churches', *adēn t̲intēn* 'two hands'. Striking cases of alternation between morphological dual and periphrastic dual occur with *walad* 'son' and *bint* 'daughter'. Compare in this respect (246), in which the speaker uses dual marking on *bint-ēn* (girl-DU), and (247), where the speaker employs the periphrastic construction *banāt t̲intēn* (girls two).

(246) *kān ʕumr-i ṯamanṭaʕš mn il-midrase*

be.PFV.3MS age-1SG eighteen from DEF-school

(a)xaḏū-ni ġaṣbit ʕann-i yaʕni tǧawwazt

take.PFV.3MP-1SG force from-1SG mean marry.PFV.1SG

ana ṣār ʕumr-i ṯnēn u ṯamānīn sane

1SG become.PFV.3MS AGE-1SG two and eighty year

ṣār-lo siṭṭaʕšar sane mayyit ǧōz-i

be.PFV.3MS-DAT.3MS sixteen year dead husband-1SG

w ilḥamədlillāh maʕā-y sabəʕ wlād u ***bint-ēn***

and praise_God with-1SG seven boys and girl-DU

'I was eighteen, they took me from school and I got married unwillingly. I turned 82 and my husband died sixteen years ago. Praise be to God, I have seven sons and two daughters'

(247) *axatt wāḥad min lə-[NAME], axatt-o u*

take.PFV.1SG one from DEF-[NAME] take.PFV.1SG and

aḷḷa ṭʕam-ni ***banāt ṯintēn*** *u ṯalaṯ ūlād,*

God provide.PFV.3MS-1SG girls two.F and three boys

u ʕišət maʕā u ʕāš maʕā-y

and live.PFV.1SG with.3MS and live.PFV.3MS with-1SG

həssāʕ zalame kbīr

now man old

'I took someone from the (name of a clan). I took him and God gave me two girls and three boys. I lived with him and he lived with me, now he is an old man'

Brustad (2000, 49), following Blanc (1970, 43) and Cowell (1964, 367), characterises the dual marking strategy as a way to mark a new topic. As far as the dialects investigated here are concerned, our data suggests rather that the main difference is not so much the discursive status of the entity itself, but the locus of focus within the construction. In the periphrastic construction, the focus is on the class to which the participant belongs, whereas morphological dual marking focuses on number. Consequently, *banāt ṯintēn* focuses on the class 'girl', as opposed to *bint-ēn*, which focuses on the the number 'two'. This can be tested with the question *kam bint ʕind-ik* 'How many girls do you have?' (how_many girl at-2F). The normal answer is the synthetic dual *bint-ēn*, not the periphrastic one *banāt ṯintēn*.

Brustad (2000, 49) further adds that, at least in Lebanese Arabic, only animate referents are eligible for periphrastic dualisation. The example *il-kanāyis iṯ-ṯintēn lə-kbār* 'the two big churches' shows that in sedentary Jordanian, even non-human referents can be dualised periphastically.

The phrase *adēn ṯintēn* 'two hands' is different, because the suffix *-ēn* in *adēn* does not mark dual but plural. Only two nouns are eligible for pseudo-dual marking in sedentary Jordanian: *adēn* 'hands' and *riǧlēn* ~ *iǧrēn* 'feet'. When speakers want to dualise *īd* 'hand' or *riǧl* ~ *iǧr* 'foot', they cannot do so with the suffix *-ēn*. One available strategy is the periphrastic construction: *adēn ṯintēn* 'two hands' and *riǧlēn ṯintēn* 'two feet'. The singulative construction *īd-t-ēn* (hand-SING-DU) 'two hands' and *iǧər-t-ēn* (foot-SING-DU) 'two feet', known in other Levantine dialects, is also available, but the grammaticality judgements of this construction exhibit a wide range of inter-speaker variation, from total rejection to total acceptance.

From three upwards, the numerals precede the head:[2]

(248) *a-bī-hū-š sitt sabəʕ sarāyir ʕašar sarāyir*
NEG-in-3MS-NEG six seven beds ten beds
'There is no more than six seven beds in it, ten beds'

When the head is definite, the numeral remains leftward of the head and the article attaches to the numeral, as in (249). Post-posed numerals do occur, but it seems to be a marked syntax, given the unique token we recorded in spontaneous speech in the phrase *hadīk il-ibtidāʔiyyāt is-sitte* 'those six primary school levels' (DEM primary_levels DEF-six). This might well be a syntax borrowed from the standard language, as the choice of a feminine singular demonstrative probably also is, because the dialectal rule is for nouns modified by a numeral to trigger plural agreement (§4.3.4).

(249) *yaʕgūb arǧaʕ il-arbaʕ mīt ǧnē*
Yaʕgūb bring_back.PFV.3MS DEF-four hundred pound
'Yaʕgūb paid back the four hundred pounds'

The syntax of complex numerals is common to most varieties of Arabic: THOUSANDS *w* HUNDREDS *w* UNITS *w* TENS:

[2] In example (248), the speaker uses *sarīr* in reference to a hospital bed. The normal word for 'bed' in Jordanian is *taxət*. The word *srīr* refers to a 'cot' in the vernacular.

(250) *ağa* *sant* *alf* *u* *tisəʕ* *miyye*
come.PFV.3MS year thousand and nine hundred
w *wāḥad* *u* *ʕišrīn*
and one and twenty
'He came in 1921'

4.1.7. Comparison

4.1.7.1. Comparative

Comparative constructions typically involve a gradable predicate, a comparee and a standard, normally coded as two NPs (Stassen 2013a; Treis 2018). The standard is marked by the ablative preposition *min*. The gradable predicate is derived from an adjective through the elative pattern aCCaC, as in (251), where *aṯgal* 'heavier' is derived from *ṯgīl* 'heavy'. If the elative derivation is not available in the lexicon, syntax comes to the rescue and the elative *akṯar* 'more', derived from *kṯīr* 'much', is placed after the adjective, as in (252).

(251) *waḷḷa* *ṃṃāʕīn-ak* *illi* *ʕa* *ḍahr-ak* *aṯgal*
By_God clothes-2MS REL on back-2MS heavier
min *ṭalabit-na* *ʕind-ak*
from request-1PL at-2MS
'The clothes you are wearing are heavier than what we request from you'

(252) *lāzim* *ykūn* *mrattab* *akṯar*
must be.SBJV.3MS prepared more
'It should be more prepared'

The adjectival predicate can be further narrowed with a prepositional phrase involving the instrumental preposition *bi* and a verbal noun, as in (253). The elative construction can also be used to modify a verbal predicate, as shown in (254).

(253) *ana aṭlag minn-o bi l-maši*
1SG freer from-3MS in DEF-walking
'I walk faster than him'

(254) *ḥabbēt-o bǧūz akṭar mn əʕmām-i*
like.PFV.1SG-3MS maybe more from uncles-1SG
'I probably liked him more than I liked my (paternal) uncles'

4.1.7.2. Superlative

Elatives are also used in superlative constructions. The normal syntax is for the elative to be followed by the NP. The syntactic structure is that of the construct state ([NOUN [NOUN]]) in which the syntactic head is the superlative adjective. If the NP is in the singular, it has to be indefinite.

(255) *kānat [aḥsan [balad]] tūnis*
be.PFV.3FS best country Tunisia
'The best country was Tunis'

(256) *kān [akram [wāḥad]] bi l-balga*
be.PFV.3MS more_generous one in DEF-Balga
'He was the most generous person in the whole Balga district'

Definiteness is permitted only for NPs denoting plural referents, as illustrated in (257):

(257) *inte [aḥla [l-kull] inte*

2SG more_nice DEF-all 2SG

'You are the most handsome of all'

Superlative constructions involving the modification of a predicate for which no elative derivation is avaiblable (such as a participle or a verbal predicate within a relative clause) have the following syntax: ELATIVE NP.INDEF PREDICATE, as exemplified in (258).

(258) *akṯar wāḥad bi l-ʕālam nḥarrēt ʕalē hū*

more one in DEF-world be_upset.PFV.1SG on.3MS 3SG

'He is the person I got the most upset about in the world'

Example (259) is similar, but the phrase *aḥla iši ana baḥibb-o* 'the thing I like most' is discontinuous:

(259) *aḥla ʔiši ṣaddgi lli hū ana baḥibb-o*

nicest thing believe.IMP.FS REL 3MS 1SG like.IPFV.1SG-3SG

hū ḥači l-ʕarab il-ʔaṣliyyīn

3SG speech DEF-Bedouins DEF-traditional

'The nicest thing, believe me, that I like, is the speech of the traditional Bedouins'

4.1.7.3. Equative

Equative constructions are normally formed with the morphemes *miṯəl* ~ *zayy* 'like' and, for quantifiable properties, *gadd* 'quantity'. They are used as prepositions that mark the standard. The parameter of comparison is usually an adjective (260). It can also be nominalised, but this depends on the availability of such a derivation in the lexicon (261).

(260) *hinne gawiyyāt miṯəl ʔumm-(h)in*

3FP skilful.FP like mother-3FP

'They are skilful like their mother'

(261) *ana baʕirf-o... gadd iğ-ğamal kubr-o*

1SG know.IPFV.1SG-3SG quantity DEF-camel size-3SG

'I know him, he is as big as a camel'

4.2. The Verb Phrase

The verb phrase minimally consists of a verb, which may be in the perfective, imperfective, active participle or imperative. We first discuss the values of the perfective, the imperfective and the auxiliaries. There is also a set of tense–aspect–mood modifiers, which are divided into auxiliaries and particles. Auxiliaries inflect for gender and number, whereas particles are uninflected. These modifiers all occur leftward of the verb.

4.2.1. The Perfective

Without any modifier, the perfective typically denotes events that have been completed at the time of reference, whose default value is the time of utterance, as shown in (262).

(262) *lagēna gišrāt burdgān axadnā-hin*

find.PFV.1PL peel orange take.PFV.1PL-3FP

w akalnā-hin m-iğ-ğūʕ

and eat.PFV.1PL-3FP from-DEF-hunger

'We found bits of orange peel, we took them and ate them out of hunger'

Brustad (2000, 168) noted that inceptive verbs and verbs of cognition in the perfective denote an "entry into a state." Our data confirm this observation, as shown in (263), where the use of the perfective forms of the verbs *fakkar* 'he thought' and *ṣiḥi* 'he became aware', both cognition verbs, emphasises the onset of the event.

(263)	*kān*	*miš*	*mfakkir*	*bī-hum*	*amman*
	be.PFV.3MS	NEG	think.AP.MS	in-3MP	but

əssāʕ	*fakkar*	*bī-hum*	*u*	*ṣiḥī-lhum*
now	think.PFV.3MS	in-3MP	and	wake_up.PFV.3MS-DAT.3MP

'He didn't think about (his kids), but recently he started thinking about them and became aware of them'

4.2.2. The Imperfective

The main innovation found across all Levantine dialects, and probably the only one, is the creation of mood distinction in the imperfective between the inherited bare prefix conjugation, and one to which a morpheme *b-* prefixes. The bare imperfective was reinterpreted as a subjunctive, whereas the *b-* imperfective was reassigned the value of the indicative mood.

4.2.2.1. Bare Imperfective

The bare imperfective is mostly an integrative form of the verb used in complex predicates that express various non-indicative modalities, and more generally any kind of syntactic dependency. In (264), *yīǧi* and *yitmallak* form a complex predicate with the modal verb *gidir* 'he could'.

(264) *mā gidr-əš wāḥad niğis yīği*

NEG can.IPFV.3MS-NEG one impure come.SBJV.3MS

yitmallak bī-ha

possess.SBJV.3MS in-3FS

'Not a single bastard was ever able to come and take possession of it'

In interrogative contexts, the use of the bare imperfective implies a modal reading, as in (265), where the speaker expresses a wish.

(265) *yā bint il-ḥalāl mā tḥilli ʕan-na?*

VOC girl DEF-licit NEG untie.SBJV.2FS from-1PL

'Give us a break, woman, will you?'

The bare imperfective is also very commonly used with an imperfect meaning, thus combining imperfective aspect and past tense. It usually depicts habitual or iterative events in the past, as shown in excerpt (266):

(266) *w* ***arūḥ*** ***ʕa-xumm*** *ha-d-dğāğ,*

and go.SBJV.1SG to-coop DEM-DEF-chicken

aḏbaḥ-ḥin *w* ***amʕaṭ-hin*** *w*

slaughter.SBJV.1G-3FP and tear_out.SBJV.1SG-3FP and

aḥuṭṭ-hin *əb-ha-ṣ-ṣāğ* *w* ***agalli*** *w*

put.SBJV.1SG-3FP in-DEM-DEF-saj and fry.SBJV.1SG and

aḥuṭṭ-o *b-ṣāğ-o, gabəl ma* ***tihčal****-š*

put.SBJV.1SG-3MS in-saj-3SG before NEG care.SBJV.2MS-NEG

hamm sūg wala ***tihčal*** *hamm iši*

worry market nor care.SBJV.2MS worry thing

'I used to go to the chicken coop. I would slaughter them, pluck them, put them on the saj, fry them, serve it in the saj,... back in the day, you didn't have to care about going to market or anything'

Both the prospective aspect and the imperfect reading of the bare imperfective are seemingly the result of the grammaticalisation of ellipsis. In the case of the the prospective aspect, it is most probably an ellipsis of the modal auxiliary *badd-* 'want'. The imperfect value arose from the ellipsis of the auxiliary *kān*.

The bare imperfective is also selected with some temporal conjunctions such as *lamma* 'when', *bass* 'as soon as' and *min* 'when'.

(267) *lamma ymūt wāḥad min-hum minʕazzī-hum*
when die.SBJV.3MS one from-3MP mourn.IPFV.1PL-3MP
'When one of them dies, we console them'

(268) *min tiṭlaʕ inte mn is-sūg*
when go_out.SBJV.2MS 2SG from DEF-market
ana aṭīḥ w idē-na šaġġālāt
1SG descend.SBJV.1SG and hands-1PL busy
salām čēf ḥāl-ak u šlōn-ak
peace how situation-2MS and how-2MS
'As soon as you go out of the market, and I go down, we are busy greeting each other (and each of us goes his way)'

Lastly, optative mood is also coded with the bare imperfective, contrary to standard Arabic, which requires the perfective.

Optative clauses are very frequent across the corpus and in spontaneous speech in general. The subject *a̤l̤la* 'God' is usually overtly expressed. Below are some examples:

a̤l̤la	*ytammim*	*ʕalē-hum*	'May God bring it (the matter)
God	complete.SBJV.3MS	on-3MP	to a good end for them'

a̤l̤la	*ysiʕd-ak*	'May God reward her'
God	rejoice.SBJV.3MS-2MS	

a̤l̤la	*yuğbur*	*ʕalē-ha*	'May God keep her well'
God	restore.SBJV.3MS	on-3FS	

a̤l̤la	*yrayyiḥ-ni*	*min-hum*	'May God free me from them'
God	ease.SBJV.3MS-1SG	from-3MP	

a̤l̤la	*yustur*	*ʕalē-ha*	'May God protect her'
God	protect.SBJV.3MS	on-3FS	

a̤l̤la	*yxalli*	*ʕumr-ak*	'May God protect you life'
God	keep.SBJV.3MS	life-2MS	

a̤l̤la	*yxallī-lna*	*yyā-k*	'May God keep you for us'
God	keep.SBJV.3MS-DAT.1PL	OBJ-2MS	

a̤l̤la	*ysahhil*	*ʕalē-ha*	'May God make things easy on her'
God	ease.SBJV.3MS	on-3FS	

a̤l̤la	*yirḍa*	*ʕalē*	'May God be satisfied with him'
God	satisfy.SBJV.3MS	on.3MS	

w-a̤l̤la	*lā*	*yismaḥ*	'God forbid'
and-God	NEG	allow.SBJV.3MS	

a̤l̤la	*lā*	*yṣabbiḥ-ha*	'May God not wake you up the
God	NEG	wake.SBJV.3MS-3FS	next morning'

4.2.2.2. *b*-imperfective

The *b*-imperfective indicates indicative mood. It refers to events that have yet to be completed at the time of reference. The *b*-imperfective primarily denotes habitual/iterative events, as in (269), or progressive aspects (270).

(269)

baṣalli	*baṭlaʕ*	*bōkil-li*	*ḥabbit*
pray.IPFV.1SG	go_out.IPFV.1SG	eat.IPFV.1SG-dat.1SG	grain

ʕinib	*aw*	*tuffāḥ*	*bamši*	*ṯnēn*	*kīlo*
grape	or	apple	walk.IPFV.1SG	two	kilometer

u	*barǧaʕ*	*baʕdēn*	*banām*
and	return.IPFV.1SG	afterwards	sleep.IPFV.1SG

'(Every day) I pray, I go out, I eat some grapes or an apple, I walk two km, I come back and then I sleep'

(270)

biʕrif-ilna	*šū*	*mniḥči?*
know.IPFV.3MS-DAT.1PL	what	talk.IPFV.1PL

'Does he know what we are talking about?'

Tense is loosely grammaticalised, because it can also refer to any event that has yet to occur, as shown in (271).

(271)

hassa	*bawarrī-k*	*iyyā*	*hōn*
now	show.IPFV.1SG-2SG	OBJ.3MS	here

'I'll show it to you right now'

4.2.3. The Active Participle

The active participle in spoken Arabic is also loosely marked for tense. Any temporal specification has to be retrieved from the context or needs to be flagged externally. The value of the active participle is mostly aspectual. It is striking to note that the semantics of the active participle are stable cross-dialectally. As noted by Brustad (2000, 168), it indicates a "resultative state" for all types of verbs,[3] except durative verbs, which give a progressive reading. A progressive aspect reading is also possible for verbs of cognition and motion. In (272) and (273), the active participles *mṭawwig* 'having surrounded' and *mḏayyiʕ* 'having lost', both verbs of action, denote perfect aspect, because the active participle "indicates the continuing relevance of a past action" (Comrie 1976, 52). The participles *rāyiḥ* 'going' in (273) and *mfakkir* 'thinking' in (274), respectively motion and cognition verbs, both denote progressive aspect.

(272)

yōm	*ṭalaʕ*	*in-nhār*	*winn*	*iğ-ğēš*	*mṭawwig-na*
when	go_out.PFV.3MS	DEF-day	DM	DEF-army	surround.AP.MS-1PL

'By the time the day broke, the army had surrounded us'

(273)

walḷa	*mḏayyiʕ*	*bagara*	*u*	*rāyḥ*
by_God	loose.AP.MS	cow	and	go.AP.MS

adawwir	*ʕalē-ha*
search.SBJV.1SG	on-3FS

'I have lost a cow and I'm on my way to look for it'

(274)

šū	*mfakkir*	*ana?*	*mfakkir*	*inno*	*badd-o*
what	think.AP.MS	1SG	think.AP.MS	COMP	want-3MS

yiktil-ni	*hnāk!*
beat.SBJV.3MS-1SG	there

'What was I thinking? I was thinking he wanted to beat me up on the spot!'

---

3 In her own classifications: stative, sensory, psychological, motion, durative, inceptive.

The active participle of verbs of motion is compatible with all temporal distinctions. In (275), *ǧāy* refers to a past action that has relevance at the time of reference (perfect aspect). In (276), it refers to an event expected to happen after the time of reference, as evidenced by the adverb *bukra* 'tomorrow', and contrasts with the perfect reading of the active participle *ḍārib* 'having hit'.

(275) *kān ǧāy əb-tilfizyōn*
be.PFV.3MS come.AP.MS with-television
'He had brought a television'

(276) *ǧāyy-ak bukra wāḥad min lə-fḥēṣ*
come.AP.MS tomorrow one from DEF-Fḥēṣ
ḍārib wāḥad min is-sulṭa l-ʕamīle
beat.AP.MS one from DEF-power DEF-agent
'Tomorrow someone from Fḥēṣ who has hit a police officer will come to you'

The active participle of verbs denoting states, such as *nāyim* 'sleeping', *gāʕid* 'sitting', *wāgif* 'standing' and *sākin* 'dwelling', refers to the universal perfect.

(277) *inti kunti sākne b-šigga*
2FS be.PFV.2FS dwell.AP.FS in-apartment
'Were you living in an apartment?'

The main function of the active participle is therefore to mark perfect aspect, except for verbs of cognition and motion, for which it can have a progressive reading.

4.2.4. Auxiliaries

The spoken varieties of Arabic developed a series of auxiliaries that specifiy further tense–aspect–mood distinctions. Some of these are unique to the dialects investigated here, while others are shared by most varieties.

4.2.4.1. Prospective *badd-*

The etymology of the morpheme *badd-* 'want' is likely *bi-widd* 'it is X's wish that'. It is found across the Levant, but also in Egypt (Woidich 2006, 318). Many Bedouin dialects in the area have the reflex *widd-*. The traditional form in central and northern Jordan is *badd-*, although Amman now mostly has *bidd-*. It is mostly analysed as a pseudo-verb, because, although it does not behave morphologically like a verb, it has the argument structure of a transitive verb (see §4.4.1.2.4). It inflects as follows (Table 218). In the 2MS and 2FS, it can reduce to *bak* and *bač*: *ba-k tibni* 'you want to build' (want-2MS build.SBJV.2MS), *ba-č tiyaddi* 'you want to carry out' (want-2FS carry_out.SBJV.2FS).

Table 218: Inflections of *badd-* 'want'

	Singular	Plural
1	*badd-i*	*badd-na*
2M	*badd-ak*	*badd-ku*
2F	*badd-ič*	*badd-čin*
3M	*badd-o*	*badd-hum*
3F	*badd-ha*	*badd-hin*

Because of its polyfunctionality, it may rightly be considered the jack of all trades of markers of futurity. In (278), the first token is clearly volitional in that it signals the intention of the speaker to convey a message to the hearer. The second *badd-ha* is not volitional, because the subject (here a soap opera on television) is inanimate, and it simply marks the futurity of the event.

(278) *badd-i* *abaššr-ič* *il-lēle* *badd-ha*
want-1SG bring_good_tidings.SBJV.1SG-2FS DEF-night want-3FS
tiği *waḥade* *mit̠əl* *hāy*
come.SBJV.3FS one like dem
'I want to bring you good tidings that tonight they will be showing (a serial) like this one'

In (279), *badd-* expresses epistemic modality, and specifically judgement modality.

(279) *min* *əxligt* *hū* *l-mustašfa* *l-inklīzi* *badd-o*
since be_born.PFV.1SG 3MS DEF-hospital DEF-british want-3MS
ykūn *hāḏ̣a* *ʕahd* *alf* *u* *t̠aman* *miyye*
be.SBJV.3MS DEM time thousand and eight hundred
'Since I was born it has been the British hospital, it must have been around 1800'

The use of the auxiliary *badd-* is also extended to expressing necessity, as shown in (280). Here, the first *badd-* marks futurity and the second has a clear deontic meaning close to 'should, have to, must'.

(280) *kull* *ḥiməl* *badd-na* *niʕṭī-k* *iyyā*
every load want-1PL give.SBJV.1PL-2MS OBJ.3MS
bidd-ak *tğīb* *faras*
want-2MS bring.SBJV.2MS horse
'For every load (of raisins) we'll give you, you will have to bring a horse'

Consequently, the morpheme *badd-* has four core meanings: volitional, future, epistemic and deontic.

4.2.4.2. Future *rāyiḥ*

The most common future marker in Levantine dialects is the particle *raḥ*, which precedes the bare imperfective. This morpheme is not part of the native stock and made its way into the dialect only recently. In our data, only one speaker used it (281). No instances of the contracted form *ḥa-* were recorded.

(281) *id-duktōr hāḏ raḥ kṯīr batṣawwar*
DEF-doctor DEM FUT much imagine.IPFV.1SG
yfīd-ak
be_useful.SBJV.3MS-2MS
'This doctor will, I guess, be very useful to you'

According to speakers' own judgements, the native form in the traditional dialects of central and northen Jordan is *rāyiḥ*, the active participle of *rāḥ* 'he went', from which *raḥ* derives. In the whole corpus, only one token of *rāyiḥ* can be clearly identified as a future marker and not the lexical verb 'to go'. The fact that *rāyiḥ* is permitted with another verb of motion is further evidence that it has grammaticalised into a future marker.

(282) *ana rāyiḥ āǧi yōm is-sabət*
1SG FUT come.SBJV.1SG day DEF-Saturday
'I will come on Saturday'

Given that *rāyiḥ* is a hapax in our corpus, while *raḥ* is clearly a borrowing from neighbouring Levantine dialects, and *badd-* is highly polyfunctional, it appears that futurity is only loosely, if at all, grammaticalised in these dialects.

4.2.4.3. Imperfect

4.2.4.3.1. *kān*

Most, if not all, dialects of Arabic use the auxiliary *kān* 'he was' as an imperfect marker, that is, a combination of past tense and imperfective aspect. Note that, in the dialects of central and northern Jordan, the verb *kān* is never affricated. The affricated reflex *čān* is a conditional conjunction (§4.6.4.11.6). In (283), the auxiliary is followed by the bare imperfective and denotes habitual/iterative aspect.

(283) *iṭ-ṭašṭūš hāḏa in-niswān kānin*
DEF-ṭašṭūš DEM DEF-woman be.PFV.3FP
yfaxxrin-hin
make_from_clay.SBJV.3FP-3FP
'The *ṭašṭūš* (a traditional pot) used to be made by women'

On close scrutiny, virtually all the tokens recorded in spontaneous speech involve a bare imperfective, even when the speaker wants to express progressive aspect, as illustrated in (284).

(284) *miš hū kān yōkil tīn*
NEG 3MS be.PFV.3MS eat.SBJV.3MS fig
'Wasn't he eating some figs?'

Only one instance of *kān* followed by *b*-imperfective was recorded (285). It refers to progressive aspect. Given the paucity of its occurence, this construction, although common in present-day

Amman, is seemingly a recent innovation in the dialects investigated here, which seem to rely on the bare imperfective to express both progressive and iterative aspects (but see §§4.2.4.3.2–4.2.4.3.3).

(285) *šū* *kunt* *baḥči?*
what be.PFV.1SG speak.IPFV.1SG
'What was I saying?'

The auxiliary and the auxiliated verb normally agree in gender and number, but instances of number agreement mismatch were recorded, as shown in (286), in which the auxiliary lacks plural marking. These agreement mismatches are attested elsewhere (for Sinai, see de Jong 2011, 112), but our data only contain examples in the third person. It is therefore difficult to assess the degree of grammaticalisation of *kān* into a past tense particle. Another possibility is that *kān* carries here an impersonal value 'it was (the case that)…'.

(286) *kān* *il-ʕabīd* *ʕind-o* *yṭīḥu* *ʕa* *l-ʕēn*
be.PFV.3MS DEF-servants at-3MS descend.SBJV.3MP to DEF-spring
'The servants were going down to the spring'

The verb *kān* can also auxiliate an active participle, in which case it simply marks past tense (and also, incidentally, pluperfect), without any change in the aspectual value carried by the participle.

(287) *kānu* *mhaḏḏrīn-lo* *yyā-ha*
be.PFV.3MP prepare.AP.MP OBJ-3FS
'They had prepared it for him'

The auxiliary can also surface in the imperfective, in which case it depicts a possible world not attested at the time of utterance. Below, the imperfective form *bitkūn* auxiliates a participle. The aspectual value is that of a perfect in a possible future.

(288) *bitkūni fārme baṣala*

be.IPFV.2FS mince.AP.FS onion

'You will have cut up an onion'

The imperfective of *kān* can also combine with a perfective verb, as in (289), but this seems possible only with verbs whose active participle does not denote perfect aspect, such as cognition verbs. No instances of *kān* in the perfective auxiliating a verb in the perfective, of the type *kān aǧa* 'he had arrived', were recorded in the corpus.

(289) *bitkūn fihmat*

be.IPFV.3FS understand.PFV.3FS

'She will have understood'

The traditional dialect also makes marginal use of the active participle *kāyin*. The tokens suggest that it conveys a durative aspect, as shown in (290). It can auxiliate an active participle, it which case it combines perfect aspect with durative aspect, as exemplified in (291). It is equivalent to *bāgi* (see below).

(290) *ṣadīg hū, kāyin ʕa l-ʕaḏ̣əm*

friend 2SG be.AP.MS to DEF-bone

'He has been an intimate friend of his, to the bone'

(291) *kāyin zāriʕ arḏ̣-ku hōna*

be.AP.MS cultivate.AP.MS land-2MP here

'He had been cultivating your land here'

4.2.4.3.2. *ḍall*

The verb *ḍall*, whose primary lexical meaning is 'stay, remain', is also used as imperfect auxiliary. The aspectual value here is always habitual/iterative (292) or durative (293). No progressive reading is attested; this seems only to be permitted with *kān*.

(292)	*ḍallin*	*yīǧin*	*gufrān*	*mn*	*il-ʕirāg*
	stay.PFV.3FP	come.SBJV.3FP	dry_bread	from	DEF-Iraq

'Dry bread used to come from Iraq'

(293)	*ḍallu*	*yġuǧǧu*	*bī-hum*	*tā*
	stay.PFV.3MP	push.SBJV.3MP	in-3MP	until

fawwatū-hum	*ʕa*	*s-salṭ*
enter.PFV.3MP-3MP	in	DEF-Salt

'They kept pushing them until they got them into Salt'

It can also auxiliate active participles of verbs of motion, in which case only the durative reading is available (294).

(294)	*ḍallēt*	*mʕaddi*
	stay.PFV.1SG	pass.AP.MS

'I kept on going'

The verb *ḍall*, whether used as the main predicate or an auxiliary, can be augmented by bound pronouns in the perfective, the imperfective and the imperative. The inflections are reported below (Table 219). The suffixes *-i*, *-u* and *-in* undergo deletion in all paradigms. The 1PL in the perfective remains unchanged: *ḍallēna* (***ḍallēna-na*).

Table 219: *ḍall* and bound pronouns

	Imperfective		Perfective		Imperative	
	Singular	Plural	Singular	Plural	Singular	Plural
1	*baḍall-ni*	*minḍall-na*	*ḍallēt-ni*	*ḍallēna*		
2M	*biḍḍall-ak*	*biḍḍall-ku*	*ḍallēt-ak*	*ḍallēt-ku*	*ḍall-ak*	*ḍall-ku*
2F	*biḍḍall-ič*	*biḍḍall-čin*	*ḍallēt-ič*	*ḍallēt-čin*	*ḍall-ič*	*ḍall-čin*
3M	*biḍall-o*	*biḍall-hum*	*ḍall-o*	*ḍall-hum*		
3F	*biḍḍall-ha*	*biḍall-hin*	*ḍallat-ha*	*ḍall-hin*		

(295) *baḍall-ni* *mgōṭir* *ʕa* *l-bāṣāt*
stay.IPFV.1SG-1SG go.AP.MS to DEF-buses
'I keep walking towards the bus station'

4.2.4.3.3. *baga*

The etymological meaning of *baga* is also 'stay, remain' but, in the dialects considered here, it is equivalent to the verb *kān* 'to be', as illustrated in (296). This semantic shift from 'remain' to 'be' is also well attested in rural Palestinian, but in those dialects, *baga* tends to replace *kān*, whereas in sedentary Jordanian, the use of *baga* is more limited. When used as an auxiliary, it only conveys habitual/iterative aspect (297).

(296) *iḥna* *bagēna* *ǧīrān-o*
1PL be.PFV.1SG neighbours-3MS
'We were his neighbours'

(297) *bagu* *yfōʕlu* *ʕind-o*
be.PFV.3MP work.SBJV.3MP at-3MS
'They used to do petty jobs at his place'

The active participle *bāgi* is also used as an equivalent to *kāyin*. When employed as a copula, it also denotes durative aspect (298). It can auxiliate a verb in the imperfective, as in (299), or an active participle, as in (300). When used with an imperfective, it has a mixture of iterative/habitual aspect and durative aspect. If the auxiliated verb is a participle, it has a mixture of perfect and durative aspects.

(298) *gabəl bāgi mayākin?*
before be.AP.MS machines
'Have there been machines before?'

(299) *bāgy-āt niswān is-salṭ yṭīḥin*
stay.AP-FP women DEF-Salt descend.SBJV.3FP
yardin bi s-sṭūl
get_water.SBJV.3FP with DEF-buckets
'The women from Salt were going down (repeatedly) to get water using buckets'

(300) *bāgy-āt taḥət mlaggṭāt əmn il-arḍ*
stay.AP-FP below collect.AP.FP from DEF-land
'They had been (repeatedly) collecting (cucumbers and tomatoes) from the field'

It should also be added that *baga* is defective, as it never occurs in the imperfective. Only the imperative *ibga* was elicited, in the clause *ibga murr* 'keep visiting (us)' (remain.IMP.MS pass.IMP.MS).

4.2.4.4. Progressive *gāʕid*

In many dialects of Arabic, progressive aspect is grammaticalised using various reflexes of the active participle of *gaʕad* ‘sit’. Although progressive aspect can be conveyed by the *b*-imperfective, it can be further specified with the active participle *gāʕid*, which inflects for gender and number, as shown in (301) and (302).

(301)	*baʕd-hum*	*mā*	*kammalu*	*gāʕd-īn*	*əbğaddidu*	*bī*
	still-3MP	NEG	finish.PFV.3MP	PROG-MP	renovate.IPFV.3MP	in.3MS

‘They haven’t finished yet, they are (still) renovating it’

(302)	*il-yōm*	*mašaḷḷa*	*gāʕd-īn*	*minḥuṭṭ*	*min*	*əǧyāb-na*
	DEF-day	what_God_wants	PROG-MP	put.IPFV.1PL	from	pockets-1PL

‘Now, we are putting (money) from our own pockets’

The most widespread progressive marker in the Levant is *ʕammāl*. It has many reflexes, the most common of which is *ʕam*. Our corpus only contains two occurences of *ʕam*, which suggests that it is not part of the traditional dialect, but rather a recent borrowing from Amman, or urban Palestinian. On the whole, the use of *gāʕid* as a progressive auxiliary remains rather marginal in the speech of the broadest informants. The distribution of *gāʕid* does not mirror that of *ʕam* in those dialects which have it. A closer look reveals that *gāʕid* is only used with human subjects and always involves some degree of intention. This of course reflects some of the semantic properties of the lexical meaning of *gaʕad* ‘to sit’, which typically requires a volitional/intentional animate subject. Further evidence come from the dialect of Amman, which has both *ʕam* and *gāʕid*. In this dialect, their use is contrastive, as suggested by the following pair (303) (Petra Jones, p.c.):

(303) a. *ʕam bilḥag-ni*
PROG follow.IPFV.3MS-1SG
'he is following me'

b. *gāʕid bilḥag-ni*
PROG follow.IPFV.3MS-1SG
'he is (intentionally) following me'

Nowadays, some speakers accept progressive marking with inanimate subjects and non-intentional events, such as in the meteorological expression *gāʕd-e btišti* (PROG-F rain.IPFV.3FS) 'it's raining'. It seems therefore that the speech of the broadest informants still reflects the first stages of grammaticalisation of *gāʕid*, in which only first-stage semantic bleaching had occurred (i.e., the loss of the lexical meaning 'to sit'). Moreover, the auxiliated verb is always in the *b*-imperfective, which is a non-integrative form of the verb, and material can be inserted between *gāʕid* and the verb, as shown in (304). There is therefore almost no morphosyntactic integration between the auxiliary and the auxiliated verb.

(304) *gāʕdīn kull-hum birḥalu ǧāy*
stay.AP.PL all-3MP leave.IPFV.3MP this_way
'They are all coming this way'

Consequently, the lack of syntactic integration and the maintenance of the peripheral semantic properties of the lexical verb *gaʕad* (animate subject and intention) confirm that *gāʕid* is still in an early phase of grammaticalisation, at least as reflected in the speech of the broadest speakers.

4.2.4.5. Inchoative *ṣār*

The verb *ṣār*, whose lexical meanings are 'become' and 'happen', is used in many dialects of Arabic as an inchoative auxiliary. The auxiliary *ṣār* combines inchoativity with durativity. It also implies a change of state and that the event is taking place for the first time. In (305), the speaker states that people started to miss a traditional pot called *ṭašṭūš*, but only recently. In (306), the speaker describes how women go out in the night to pray for God to send rain (*ṭalab il-ġēṯ*). The use of *ṣār* highlights the duration of the process (it is not punctual) and that they started doing so but were not before (change of state).

(305) *ṣārat* *in-nās* *tištāg-lo*
become.PFV.3FS DEF-people miss.SBJV.3FS-3MS
'People started missing it'

(306) *bi l-lēl* *yiṭlaʕin* *yṣīrin*
in DEF-night exit.SBJV.3FP become.SBJV.3FP
yimšin *bi š-šawāriʕ*
walk.SBJV.3FP in DEF-streets
'In the night, (women) would go out and start walking in the streets'

4.2.4.6. Ingressive *ballaš*

The verb *ballaš* 'start' also highlights the onset of an event, but unlike *ṣār*, it is dynamic and combines with punctual aspect, as shown in (307), in which the referent is seated and starts eating. The event is considered not to last in time (punctual), and may be a recurrence of a previous event (iterative), which is impossible with *ṣār*. In addition to this, the verb *ballaš* is also used in a construction not attested with *ṣār* involving the masdar of the auxiliated verb in the object position, as in (308), where *buna* 'act of building' is the masdar of *bana* 'he built', and (309), where *ṭaxx* 'act of shooting' is the masdar of *ṭaxx* 'he shot'.

(307)

ballaš	*yōkil*
start.PFV.3MS	eat.SBJV.3MS

'He started eating'

(308)

ballaš	*buna*
start.PFV.3MS	building

'He started building'

(309)

ballaš	*fi-hum*	*ṭaxx*
start.PFV.3MS	in-3MP	shooting

'He started shooting at them'

4.2.4.7. Ingressive *ağa*

The verb *ağa* 'he came' is also used as an auxiliary marking ingressive aspect with verbs of motion. The auxiliated verb is in the active participle form. This construction belongs to the traditional narrative register. The auxiliary can be in either the perfective, as in (310), or the (bare) imperfective, as in (311).

(310)

waḷḷa	*ğīna*	*mrawwḥīn*
by_God	come.PFV.1SG	return.AP.MP

'We got on the road back home'

(311)

w	*asḥab*	*ḥāl-i*	*w*	*āği*	*mʕaddi*
and	pull_out.SBJV.1SG	REFL-1SG	and	come.SBJV.1SG	pass.AP.MS

'I withdrew and started moving off'

4.2.4.8. Ingressive *gām*

The verb *gām* 'he stood' can also be used as an ingressive auxiliary. In this case, it has lost much of its lexical meaning except that it highlights the abrupt onset of an event. It inflects for aspect, person and number (see §3.4.2.1.4 for the inflection pattern of *gām–ygūm*). The auxiliated verb is in the bare imperfective.

(312) *yōm māt māǧid gumna nimʕad ʕalē*
when die.PFV.3MS Māǧid stand.PFV.1PL recite.SBJV.1PL on.3MS
'When Māǧid (il-ʕadwān) died, we decided to compose and recite poetry to celebrate his life'

Instances of gender and number neutralisation in the third person are recorded, which echoes the neutralisation of agreement observed when *gām* is used as a sequentialiser (§4.2.4.9).

(313) *sant il-ḥamāyde kān ṣāʕ il-gaməḥ əb-ʕašar*
year DEF-NAME be.PFV.3MS sa DEF-wheat with-ten
ṭnaʕšar girš laḥḥag lēra gām
twelve piaster reach.PFV.3MS dinar stand.PFV.3MS
agwa n-nās mā tōkil ġēr ʕaǧwa
strongest DEF-people NEG eat.SBJV.3FS except dried_date
'The year of the great drought, the *sa* (local volume measure, 2.5–3 kg) of wheat cost ten or twelve piasters. It reached a dinar, so (even) the richest people would only eat dried dates.'

4.2.4.9. Sequential *gām*

The lexical meaning of *gām* is 'he stood', but in many dialects, it has lost its lexical meaning and grammaticalised into a marker of sequence in the narration of past events. In the present variety, grammaticalisation is still under way, because *gām* partially retains its inflectional properties, showing optional subject agreement in the third person, as in (314). The grammaticalisation of *gām* is further confirmed by its co-occurrence with other posture verbs such as *rakʕat* 'she knelt'. Adjacency between *gām* and the verb is not a rule, as material can appear between them, as exemplified in (315).

(314) *kān ibn-(h)a bi s-siǧən gāmat*
be.PFV.3MS son-3FS in DEF-prison stand.PFV.3FS
rakʕat giddām-o
kneel.PFV.3FS in_front-3MS
'Her son was in prison, so she knelt in front of him (to implore him)'

(315) *badd-ha trawwiḥ əzyāra gāmat*
want-3FS go.SBJV.3FS visit stand.PFV.3FS
umm-ha dazzat-ilha maṣāri
mother-3FS send.PFV.3FS-DAT.3FS money
'She wanted to go back home for a visit, so her mother sent her money'

(316) *ʕayyu yōxḏū-ha wlād-o*
refuse.PFV.3MP take.SBJV.3MP-3FS children-3MS
gām hū axaḏ-ha, lə-xtyār
stand.PFV.3SG 3SG take.PFV.3MS-3FS DEF-elderly
'His sons refused to marry her, so he, the old man, married her'

In many cases, though, agreement is neutralised, in which case *gām* is best interpreted as a coordinator, as in (317), though it is still glossed as a verb for the sake of clarity.

(317) *ağu* *tā* *yiṣilḥu* *u* *gām*
come.PFV.3MP to reconcile.SBJV.3MP and stand.PFV.3MS
wugfū-lhum *wlād* *iṭ-ṭaʕāmne*
stop.PFV.3MP-DAT.3MP sons DEF-Taʕāmne
'They came to reconcile with one another and the sons of the Taʕāmne clan stopped them'

As noted above, there is aspect agreement between the sequentialiser and the verb that follows. The perfective form of *gām* is selected if the verb that follows is in the perfective, as shown above, and the active participle *gāyim* is selected if the verb that follows is an active participle. The number of tokens in the active participle is too limited to see whether agreement neutralisation is under way.

(318) *hāy* *il-bint* *habša...* *gāyim* *ğōz-ha* *mdaššir-ha*
DEM DEF-girl Habša... stand.AP.MP husband-3FS leave.AP.MP-3FS
'That girl Habša... her husband had left her'

4.2.4.10. (Re)iterative *radd* and *riğiʕ*

In most Levantine dialects, the marker of reiterativity is the verb *riğiʕ* 'he came back'. This auxiliary does occur in our data, but the native way of marking reiterativity in sedentary Jordanian is with the verb *radd* 'reply'. The auxiliary can be used in both the perfective and the imperfective. In the perfective, the auxiliated verb is also in the perfective, as in (319). If *radd* is in the imperfective, the auxiliated verb mostly surfaces in the bare imperfective (320), although the *b*-imperfective is not judged ungrammatical.

(319) *raddēna* *šarēna* *d-dār* *b-wād* *lə-krād*
reply.PFV.1PL buy.PFV.1PL DEF-house in-valley DEF-Krād
'We bought the house in the Krād neighbourhood again'

(320) *biruddu* *yiʕfu* *ʕann-o*
reply.PFV.3MP forgive.SBJV.3MP from-3MS
'They will grant amnesty to him again'

4.2.4.11. Jussive *xalli*

The morpheme *xalli* is the imperative of *xalla* 'he let' and is used as a jussive marker. It can be in the singular, as in (321), or the plural, as in (322). Masculine singular and feminine singular have the same surface form *xalli*. No instances of feminine plural *xallin* were recorded. In the case of a pronominal subject, *xalli* can be augmented with bound pronouns coreferential with the subject. The auxiliated verb is in the bare imperfective.

(321) *xalli* *umm-ič* *tiṭlaʕ*
let.IMP.MS mother-2FS exit.SBJV.3FS
'Let your mother go out'

(322) *xallu* *raḏ̣a* *thāhi*
let.IMP.MP Raḏ̣a recite.SBJV.2MS
'Let Raḏ̣a recite (a mourning hymn)'

The paradigm of *xalli* augmented with bound pronouns is as below (Table 220). Phonetic contraction occurs in the first person and the /h/-initial third person. The form can further reduce to *xan* in the 1PL because of the contiguity of the 1PL /n/ prefix of the bare imperfective: *xan nrūḥ* 'let's go' (< *xan-na nrūḥ*), *xan ngul-lak* 'let us tell you' (< *xan-na ngul-lak*).

Table 220: Inflections of *xalli*

	Singular	Plural
1	*xallī-ni* ~ *xan-ni*	*xallī-na* ~ *xan-na*
2M	*xallī-k*	*xallī-ku*
2F	*xallī-č*	*xallī-čin*
3M	*xallī*	*xallī-hum* ~ *xal-hum*
3F	*xallī-ha* ~ *xal-ha*	*xallī-hin* ~ *xal-hin*

(323) *ṭubxī-lhin xal-(h)in yōklin yā bint il-ḥalāl*
cook.IMP.FS-DAT.3FP let-3FP eat.SBJV.3FP VOC daughter DEF-licit
'Cook for them, let them eat, woman!'

4.2.4.12. Cessative *baṭṭal* and *mā ʕād*

There are two strategies for encoding cessative aspect (i.e., 'stop doing something'). The most common one is to use the verb *baṭṭal* 'he stopped' followed by a verb in the bare imperfective:

(324) *āxir usbūʕ ʕādatan bibaṭṭlu yōxḏu muḥāḏarāt*
last week usually stop.IPFV.3MP take.SBJV.3MP classes
'In the last week they stop having classes'

(325) *baṭṭalat tōǧiʕ-ha miʕdit-ha*
stop.PFV.3FS hurt.SBJV.3FS-3FS stomach-3FS
'Her stomach stopped aching'

The other strategy is to use the verb phrase *mā ʕād*, whose etymological meaning is 'he/it didn't return' (NEG return.PFV.3MS), as an auxiliary followed by a verb in the perfective or the bare imperfective. This construction is found in many dialects of Arabic and shows various degrees of lexicalisation across varieties. In the southern Levant, it normally still inflects for person and number, as shown in (326).

(326) *mā ʕudnā-š* *nšūf-o*

NEG return.PFV.1PL-NEG see.SBJV.1PL-3MS

'We stopped seeing him'

No instances of *mā ʕād* were recorded in spontaneous speech but elicited forms were judged perfectly grammatical. All the elicited examples were with the split negation morpheme *-š*. Negative evidence is never straightforwardly interpretable, but it could suggest that the native strategy is to encode cessative aspect with *baṭṭal* and that *mā ʕād* was borrowed from neighbouring varieties.

4.2.4.13. Defective *rāḥ mā*

An interesting case of grammaticalisation of the verb *rāḥ* 'he went' involves the perfective form of the verb followed by the negator *mā* to encode defective aspect ('have almost done something'). This construction seems to be available only in the southern Levant (Jordan and Palestine). Evidence for the grammaticalisation of *rāḥ* is found in the compatibility of the auxiliary with the lexical verb *rāḥ* itself: *rāḥ mā yrūḥ* 'he was about to go (i.e., he was about to die)' (go.PFV.3MS NEG go.SBJV.3MS).

(327) *ruḥt* *mā* *ašuxx* *taḥt-i*

go.PFV.1SG NEG pee.SBJV.1SG under-1SG

'I was about to pee in my pants'

(328) *gadd-mā* *ngaharət* *rāḥ* *mā*

size-COMP be_vexed.PFV.1SG go.PFV.3MS NEG

yṣīb-ni *ǧalṭa*

hit.SBJV.3MS-1SG stroke

'I was so vexed that I almost had a stroke'

It has been argued by some speakers that this construction, although known and used in Amman, tends to be replaced by *kān bidd-* because it is more transparent semantically: *kunt bidd-i agaʕ* 'I was about to fall' (be.PFV.1SG want-1SG fall.SBJV.1SG).

Another construction reported to us involves the verb *ağa* 'he came' followed by *badd- / bidd-* 'want', as exemplified in (329). No instance of this construction was recorded in spontaneous speech.

(329) *iğīt* *bidd-i* *asawwi* *kēk*
come.PFV.1SG want-1SG do.SBJV.1SG cake
lagēt *mā ʕind-ī-š* *xamīre*
find.PFV.1SG NEG at-1SG-NEG baking_powder
'I was about to make a cake when I found that I didn't have baking powder'

4.2.5. Particles

4.2.5.1. Progressive Aspect *ʕam*

As noted above, pan-Levantine *ʕam* is most likely not part of the native stock. The common way to encode progressive aspect is with the prefix *b-* or the auxiliary *gāʕid*, with several semantic constraints on the subject. Nevertheless, the morpheme *ʕam* was recorded twice in our data. It is normally used in Amman as a progressive marker. Maximally realised as *ʕammāl*, it can be reduced to *ʕamma* and *ʕam*. Other variants such as *ʕan* and *ʕa*, found elsewhere in the Levant, were not attested.

(330) *il-ṃayye min taḥt il-ʕrāg ʕam btiṭlaʕ*

DEF-water from below DEF-valley PROG exit.IPFV.3FS

'The water is spewing out from below the valley'

4.2.5.2. Future *raḥ*

Like *ʕam*, the pan-Levantine future marker *raḥ* is most probably not part of the native stock. It surfaces three times in our data, in the speech of a single speaker. Its appearance in the speech of some speakers is best interpreted as a contact-induced feature from the dialect of Amman.

(331) *mā raḥ aḏall sākin fī-ha*

NEG FUT stay.SBJV.1SG dwelling in-3FS

'I won't keep living in it'

4.2.5.3. Optative *ʕalwē(š)* and *yārēt* ~ *yālēt*

The most common optative marker in Levantine dialects and beyond is *yārēt*. A marginal reflex recorded in the speech of one speaker is *yālēt*, obviously cognate with Standard Arabic *layta*. It was only recorded in one incomplete utterance, reproduced in (332). The morpheme is commonly augmented with bound pronouns indexing the subject (333).

(332) *bagūl yālēt gabəḷ…*

say.IPFV.1SG OPT before

'I say, I wish before…'

(333) *yārēt-o ʕāfye ʕa galb-ič*

OPT-3MS health on heart-2FS

'May this keep your heart healthy'

The morpheme *ʕalwē* has a more limited use and seems to be part of an archaic register not used by all speakers. *ʕalwē* occurs with the complementiser *inn-*, with which it exhibits various degrees of coalescence, from *ʕalwe inn-* to *ʕalwē-n-*, as shown in (335). While the etymology of *yārēt* ~ *yālēt* is in all likelihood the vocative marker *yā* followed by a cognate of the classical Arabic optative marker *layta*, the etymology of *ʕalwē* is obscure. One variant that was recorded in our field notes and is also attested in other neighbouring varieties is *ʕalawwā*.

(334) *ʕalwē tōxḏī-na ʕalē-hum*
OPT take.SBJV.2FS-1PL to-3MP
'I wish you could take us to them'

(335) *ʕalwē-n-n(i) mā (a)xatt-(h)a* (< *ʕalwē inn-i mā axatt-ha*)
OPT-COMP-1SG NEG take.PFV.1SG-3FS
'I wish I hadn't taken it'

4.2.5.4. Hortative *ġēr* and *illa*

The morpheme *ġēr* 'other', originally a nominal, may function as a prenominal modifier or an exceptive marker. Its grammaticalisation into a marker of hortative modality is still under way and stems from the ellipsis of the negated predicate in exceptive constructions. The three stages are all still attested in the language: first no ellipsis as in (336), then ellipsis of the predicate but not the negator (337) and finally ellipsis of both the predicate and the negator (338). In terms of frequency, the full ellipsis is by far the most common structure, suggesting that the grammaticalisation of these morphemes is almost complete. The verb is in the bare imperfective, except in the second person, in which the imperative is also permitted, as shown in (337). As a marker that expresses urgency, it often collocates with oaths like *waḷḷa* 'by God', *ḥayāt-ak* 'your life' and the like.

(336) *waḷḷa mā l-ak ġēr tištri miʕza*
by_God NEG to-2MS HORT buy.SBJV.2MS goat
'You have to buy a goat (lit. you can do nothing but buy a goat)'

(337) *mā ġēr nām lēl-ak iṭ-ṭawīl u txāf-əš*
NEG HORT sleep.IMP.MS night-2MS DEF-long and fear.SBJV.2MS-NEG
'Just get a good night's sleep and don't be afraid'

(338) *waḷḷa ḥayāt-ak ġēr ətǧawwz-o*
by_God life-2MS HORT marry.SBJV.2MS-3MS
'You have to marry him off'

The other exceptive morpheme *illa* is also used, albeit much more marginally (only one token was recorded), as shown in (339). One instance of collocation of *ġēr* and *illa* was also recorded, but it may be a hesitation in speech planning (340).

(339) *šāff-(h)a l-ʔamīr gāl illa ōxuḏ̣-ha*
see.PFV.3MS-3FS DEF-prince say.PFV.3MS HORT take.SBJV.1SG-3FS
'The prince saw her and said I have to marry her'

(340) *illa ġēr əḏ̣ḏ̣alli ḥible*
HORT HORT stay.SBJV.2FS pregnant
'You have to be pregnant'

4.2.5.5. Asseverative *la*

The asseverative marker *la*, also called intentive, is used to flag a strong intention on the part of the speaker. As expected with modal particles, it selects a verb in the bare imperfective (341).

(341) *waḷḷa la (a)xalli l-gird yirčab-ak*
by_God ASSER let.SBJV.1SG DEF-monkey mount.SBJV.3MS-2MS
w yirčab-(h)um
and mount.SBJV.3MS-3MP
'I swear I'll make sure a monkey mounts you and mounts them (I'll get you into trouble)'

It often combines with a conditional, either real or unreal. In this case, it can also be interpreted as a marker of apodosis (see also §4.6.4.11). It optionally collocates with the complementiser *inn-*, as in (342).

(342) *law badri inn-i mā badd-ī-š arǧaʕ*
if know.IPFV.1SG COMP-1SG NEG want-1SG return.SBJV.1SG
ʕa balad-i inn-i l(a) awaṣṣil
to country-1SG COMP-1SG ASSER reach.SBJV.1SG
arḏ̣-ku min hōn la masǧid il-ḥusēn
land-2MP from here to mosque DEF-Hussein
'If I knew that I wasn't returning to my country, I would extend your land to the Hussein mosque'

4.2.5.6. *čin*

The particle *čin* belongs to the traditional register of the dialect. The reason for classifying it as a verbal particle is that it always occurs leftward of a verb in the perfective. It is not clear what its etymology is. There are two possible grammaticalisation paths. It may have arisen either from the verb *kān* 'he was' and its affricated reflex *čān* or from the conjunction *kaʔinno* 'as if'. We believe that this morpheme is a borrowing from neighbouring Bedouin dialects, probably from the dialect of the ʕAdwān, which means that its etymology is not to be sought in the sedentary dialects of central and northern Jordan. In the present dialects, *kān* as a verb is never affricated, except in the case of the conditional morpheme *čān* 'if'.

čin most often collocates with the verb *gāl* 'he said', as in (343) and (344), but other verbs are also attested, as in (345). Consistently across the data, it is used after a clause in the bare imperfective, which in this case signals past tense and habitual/iterative aspect. In the second clause, the verb is in the perfective preceded by *čin*, the combination of which signals a punctual aspect. Semantically, it expresses a sudden and abrupt turn within an iterative or habitual backgrounded event. One possible grammaticalisation path is that in the donor dialect (here the dialect of ʕAdwān, as we think it is), *čin* evolved from the verb *čān* 'he was' (which is affricated in Bedouin, unlike in the present varieties), which may have evolved into a kind of clause linker close in meaning to 'and then'. Because of the frequent collocations with a verb in the perfective, it was later reinterpreted as a preverbal particle. The fact that it is not a clause linker any more is suggested in example (343), where it occurs within the second clause between the subject *illi yištri* 'the one who would buy' and the verb *gāl* 'he said', with which it clearly forms an intonational unit. In prosodic terms, *čin* could be regared as a proclitic, because it remains unstressed.

(343) *nbīʕ-o b-ʕišrīn girš illi yištri*
sell.SBJV.1PL-3MS with-twenty piaster REL buy.SBJV.3MS
***čin** gāl yalḷa ṭilʕ-o ʕa d-dār*
čin say.PFV.3MS go bring.IMP.2MS-2MS on DEF-house
'We used to sell it for 20 piasters, the buyer would then say bring it to the house'

(344) *mn əṣ-ṣubḥiyyāt umṃ-i... tiṭʕam-na*
from DEF-morning mother-1SG feed.SBJV.3FS-1PL
***čin** gālat yalḷa xuḏin*
čin say.PFV.3FS go take.IMP.2FP
il-bahāyim w iṭlaʕin israḥin bī-hin
DEF-animals and go_out.IMP.2FP graze.IMP.3FP with-3FP
'(I remember), in the morning, my mother would feed us, then she would say take the animals and go graze them'

(345) *yīği xālid... bičbi* ***čin*** *gaḥaf*
come.SBJV.3MS Khalid lean.IPFV.3MS čin swallow.PFV.3MS
min ha-šhēbiyyāt u šarad
from DEF-sweets and flee.PFV.3MS
'Khalid would turn up, he would pretend to be leaning forward, but then he would snatch some of these sweets and run away'

4.3. Agreement

4.3.1. Indefiniteness and Gender/Number Neutralisation

Generally, there is no difference between grammatical agreement (agreement within a phrase) and anaphoric agreement (when the controller and the target are not in the same phrase). The only type of construction in which there is a difference is existential and possessive predicates, where gender and number agreement is always neutralised, as in (346). This also extends to other stative verbs that are semantically similar to existential constructions. The one-argument or subject of these predicates does not trigger gender and number agreement on the predicate if it is indefinite, although grammatical agreement occurs within the phrase. This is best shown in (347), where *bēʕa* 'sale' triggers feminine agreement on the adjective *mlīḥa* 'good' but not the verb *ṣaḥḥ* 'be able'.

(346)	*kān*	*ʔil-o*	*ḥawāla*	*sitt*	*mīt*	*dulum*
	be.PFV.3MS	for-3MS	around	six	hundred	dunam

'He used to own around six hundred dunams of land'

(347)	*ṣaḥḥ-lo*	*bēʕa*	*mlīḥ-a*
	enable.PFV.3MS-DAT.3MS	sell.F	good-F

'He managed to get a good sale'

In (348), the subject *wlād* 'children' is expected to trigger feminine singular agreement or masculine plural agreement, but the verb is in the masculine singular. In (349), the subject is in the feminine singular but the verb is in the masculine singular.

(348) *mā biǧī-nī-š* *wlād*
NEG come.IPFV.3MS-1SG-NEG children
'I can't have children'

(349) *xāyif* *yilḥag-na* *mas?ūliyye* *bī-ha*
fear.AP.MS follow.SBJV.3MS-1PL responsibility.F in-3FS
'I fear we'll have problems because of this'

This agreement neutralisation is primarily sensitive to the indefiniteness of the subject and not the VS order, which is itself a by-product of indefiniteness (VS order tends to be selected with new referents and new events, see §4.4.2.1). This is best exemplified by the optional neutralisation of gender agreement in (350), when the subject is indefinite (*ḥarb* 'war' is feminine), whereas gender agreement is compulsory when the subject is definite, although the word order is the same (351).

(350) *ṣār* *ḥarb* ~ *ṣārat* *ḥarb*
become.PFV.3MS war become.PFV.3FS war
'(A) war started'

(351) *ṣārat* *il-ḥarb*
become.PFV.3FS DEF-war
***ṣār* *il-ḥarb*
become.PFV.3MS DEF-war
'The war started'

4.3.2. Masculine Plural versus Feminine Plural

The first observation is that nouns denoting human male referents always trigger masculine plural agreement (352) and nouns denoting human female referents always trigger feminine plural agreement (353).

(352) *nādir… illa min iz-zlām il-gadīm-īn*
rare except from DEF-men DEF-old-MP
'It's rare except from old men'

(353) *yā sīd-i hinne ḥilw-āt il-banāt kwayys-āt*
VOC sir-1SG 3PL beautiful-3FP DEF-girls nice-FP
'The girls are nice and beautiful'

Some instances of masculine plural agreement with feminine plural referents occur in the data (354), but they are best interpreted as a grammatical clash between the Ammani system, which does not have a feminine plural, and the local, native grammar, which does. This phenomenon shows that the grammar is slowly undergoing convergence towards the dialect of Amman, which is the main contact variety and the variety that enjoys the greatest diffusion within Jordan (Herin and Al-Wer 2013). These agreement mismatches can be counted on the fingers of one hand, which suggests that the native grammar is still robust in the speech of our informants.

(354) *ǧābat bint-ēn mʕawwag-īn*
bring.PFV.3FS girl-DU disabled-MP
'She gave birth to two disabled girls'

4.3.3. Masculine Plural versus Feminine Singular

All plural nouns, irrespective of whether the referent is human, collective, animate or inanimate, can trigger feminine singular agreement if the speaker considers the entity as a whole and not as individuated entities. Plural agreement is triggered if the speaker conceives the referent as a collection of individuals. Consequently, the kind of agreement chosen signals how the speaker considers the referent on a scale of individuation (Brustad 2000, 88), and, except for human referents, has nothing to do with the gender of the noun in the singular. There are of course semantic and syntactic correlates to individuation: concrete vs abstract, definite vs indefinite, referential vs non-referential, narrowed reference vs non-narrowed reference, quantified vs unquantified, new vs given. The scale goes therefore from abstract, indefinite, non-referential, non-narrowed, unquantified and new nouns to concrete, definite, referential, narrowed, quantified and given nouns. Human collectives can trigger either feminine singular or masculine plural agreement. Feminine singular agreement occurs with lowly individuated referents, as in (355), and masculine plural occurs with highly individuated referents (356).

(355) *il-ʕurbān* *ṭarrat-na*
DEF-Bedouins push_away.PFV.3FS-1PL
'The Bedouins pushed us away'

(356) *gāymīn* *is-salṭiyye* *mhāwšīn-hum*
stand.AP.MS DEF-inhabitants_of_Salt quarrel.AP.MP-3MP
'The inhabitants of Salt had been quarrelling with them'

A consistent pattern for collective human referents is for them to trigger feminine singular agreement when first introduced into the discourse and for subsequent mentions to trigger masculine plural, as shown in (357). This can also occur within the verb phrase between the auxiliary and the verb, as shown in (358). The auxiliary is first marked for feminine singular, the referent is then introduced into the discourse, and the verb is marked for masculine plural.

(357) *ağat* *l-inglīz* *ḥaṭṭat* *īd-ha*
come.PFV.3FS DEF-British put.PFV.3FS hand-3FS
ʕa *ha-lə-blād* *yōm* *ṣār*
on DEM-DEF-country when happen.PFV.3MS
taʕrīb *la* *ğ-ğēš* *l-inglīz* *rāḥu*
arabisation for DEF-army DEF-British go.PFV.3MP
'The British came and occupied this country. When arabisation of the army took place, the British left'

(358) *ḏallat* *il-ʕurbān* *gabəl* *yiṭlaʕu*
stay.PFV.3FS DEF-Bedouins before go_out.SBJV.3MP
ʕa *l-baṭīn*
to DEF-wilderness
'Before, the Bedouins used to go into the wilderness'

There are interesting borderline cases when the speaker obviously hesitates between two agreement patterns, reflecting an uncertainty about the level of individuation of the referent in the mind of the speaker, as illustrated in (359), where the auxiliary is in the masculine plural and the verb in the feminine singular.

(359) *bāg-īn* *minğann-e* *n-nās*
stay.AP-MP go_crazy.AP-FS DEF-people
'The people had gone crazy'

The word *nās* is peculiar in that it also allows a third agreement pattern, namely masculine singular, when it is indefinite. As noted above (§3.5.5.4), in this case, the morpheme *nās* is best interpreted as an indefinite pronoun.

(360) *miš kull-hum mitšawwg-īn la lə-grāye*

NEG all-3MP enthusiastic-MP to DEF-study

nās badd-o nās mā badd-o

people want-3MS people NEG want-3MS

'Not all of them want to study, some want to, some don't'

4.3.4. Feminine Plural vs Feminine Singular

Non-human referents, whether animate or inanimate, trigger feminine singular agreement or feminine plural agreement, irrespective of the gender in the singular. As with human collectives, feminine singular agreement occurs with referents that are conceived of as a whole (lowly individuated), whereas feminine plural is triggered by referents that are perceived as individuals (highly individuated). In (361), *bṭānāt* 'panels (the lining of the saddle)' are conceived of as a single piece of equipment, hence the feminine singular agreement (here the 3FS bound pronoun *-ha* on *fakkū-ha*).

(361) *gāmu lə-fḥēṣiyye ʕala bṭānāt il-xēl*

stand.PFV.3MP DEF-Fḥēsi.PL on saddles DEF-horse

u fakkū-ha

and untie.PFV.3MP-3FS

'The people of Fḥēṣ charged towards the horses and untied the panels'

In (362), the speaker has in mind a specific individuated set of series he used to watch when he was younger, and therefore uses the feminine plural. Gender is not always marked in the plural. This is the case for demonstratives and certain adjectives like *ṭwāl* 'tall', *kbār* 'big', *zġār* 'small', which are unmarked for gender.

(362) *niḥḏ̣ar…* *fī* *tamṯīliyyāt* *haḏōl* *kānin* *yīǧin*
attend.SBJ.1PL EXIST series DEM.PL be.PFV.3FP come.SBJV.3FP
'We use to watch, there used to be series, these would be shown'

Further evidence of the pragmatic basis of agreement is provided in (363). The feminine noun *ṃayye* 'water' triggers feminine singular agreement on the adjective *mawǧūd-e* 'present', and then feminine plural on the bound pronoun *-hin*. It shows that the speaker switched reference from 'water' as a substance to 'quantities of water', most probably in the form of buckets to be carried on the head. The nouns *ḥatabāt* and *ṭḥīnāt* also trigger feminine plural agreement, indicating that the speaker has an individuated reference in mind.

(363) *kānat* *il-ḥayā* *mityassre* *lēš* *il-ṃayye*
be.PFV.3FS DEF-life easy why DEF-water
mawǧūd-e *bitǧīb-hin* *ʕa* *rās-ak* *il-ḥaṭab-āt*
present-F bring.IPFV.2MS-3FP on head-2MS DEF-wood-FP
mawǧūd-āt *il-muhimm* *ykūnin* *iṭ-ṭḥīn-āt* *ʕind-ak*
present-FP DEF-important be.SBJV.3FP DEF-flour-FP at-2MS
'Life was easy. Why? There was water. You carry it on your head, you have wood, the important thing is to have flour'

As noted above, different agreements can surface within the same verb phrase when the speaker perceives the referent as being somewhere in the middle of the individuation scale, as in (364), where *tīǧi yḥūmin* form a complex predicate in which the first verb is in the feminine singular and the second is in the feminine plural. The subject *ḏ̣bāʕ* 'hyenas' is given, because it has already been mentioned previously. The mixed agreement signals that the speaker does not have in mind an entity perceived as a collection of individuals, but still considers it individuated because it is given.

(364) *iḏ̣-ḏ̣bāʕ* *bgul-lak* *iši* *balāwi…* *waḷḷa*
DEF-hyenas say.IPFV.3MS-DAT.2MS thing numerous by_god
gāl *inno* *iš-šīk* *ṯalāṯ* *ṭaragāt* *ʕalē-na*
say.PFV.3MS COMP DEF-fence three layers on-1PL
gāl *inno* *iḏ̣-ḏ̣bāʕ* *tiǧī-hum* *ṭūl*
say.PFV.3MS COMP DEF-hyenas come.SBJV.3FS-3MP length
il-lēl *yḥūmin* *wara* *š-šīk*
DEF-night circle.SBJV.3FP behind DEF-fence
'He said that there were a lot of hyenas, they had three layers of fencing, all night long, the hyenas would come and wander around (in circles) behind the fence'

Quantified nouns, including the dual (365) and coordinated nominals (366), always trigger feminine plural agreement.

(365) *biǧīb* *ʕanz-ēn* *biḏbaḥū-hin*
bring.IPFV.3MS goat-DU slaughter.IPFV.3MP-3FP
bḥuṭṭū-hin *əb-gidr-ēn* *ṃayye*
put.IPFV.3MP-3FP in-pot-DU water
'He brings two goats, they slaughter them and put them in two pots of water'

(366) *il-ḥayāya* *w* *il-ʕagārib* *w* *il-haḏōl…*
DEF-snakes and DEF-scorpions and DEF-DEM.PL
biḏ̣allin *bištin* *mxabbay-āt*
stay.IPFV.3FP winter.IPFV.3FP hide.PP-FP
'Snakes, scorpions and things like that, stay and winter hidden'

4.3.5. Lack of Gender Agreement in the 1SG

A distinctive feature, seemingly shared by all the traditional dialects of central and northern Jordan, is the lack of gender agreement in the first person singular. This seems to happen exclusively with participles, both active and passive, as illustrated in (367) and (368), which come from the speech of an elderly woman. Had gender agreement been applied, one would have expected *mrawwḥa* (returning.F) and *mabsūṭa* (happy.F) respectively. Based on our data from Amman, there is increasing social consciousnes of the lack of gender marking in these constructions. Ammanis in particular mock women who use the masculine forms when referring to themselves. However, our database contains occurrences of the masculine also in the speech of younger women, both in Amman and in Salt. This lack of agreement does not extend to adjectives that do not have participial morphology, as evidenced in (369), uttered by the same speaker who produced (367), and in which *zġīr-e* (small-F) is in the feminine.

(367) *w ana mrawwiḥ mil lə-ġmāra*
and 1SG return.AP.MS from DEF-harvest
'On my way back from the fields'

(368) *ilḥamdilla ana mabsūṭ*
thank_God 1SG happy
'Praise be to God I'm happy'

(369) *bawaččid w ana zġīr-e*
remember.IPFV.1SG and 1SG small-F
'I remember when I was young'

4.3.6. Summary

Table 212 summarises the different agreement patterns in the plural, which seem for the most part common to all the varieties of Arabic that kept gender distinction in the plural (Bettega 2019).

Table 212: Agreement patterns in the plural

<table>
<tr><th></th><th>Human male</th><th>Human female</th><th>Human collective</th><th>Non-human</th></tr>
<tr><td>Individuated</td><td rowspan="2">MP</td><td rowspan="2">FP</td><td>MP</td><td>FP</td></tr>
<tr><td>Non-individuated</td><td colspan="2">FS</td></tr>
</table>

4.4. Simple Clauses

4.4.1. Non-verbal Predication

Two broad non-verbal predicative constructions are discussed. The first one consists of non-verbal predicates proper and the second one consists of prepositional predicates that tend to undergo a 'verbal drift' whereby they exhibit properties that characterise plain verbal predicates, essentially the negators *mā… -š* and argument structure. The pseudo-verb *badd-* 'want' (see §4.2.4.1), although etymologically a prepositional phrase, is fully grammaticalised into a monotransitive predicate and is treated separately.

4.4.1.1. Identification, Qualification and Localisation

As in most varieties of Arabic, the predication of nouns (370), adjectives (371) or adpositional phrases (372), in the absence of any TAM or polarity marking, does not involve any overt coding in the form of a copula or a predicative marker. The unmarked syntax is [SUBJECT PREDICATE].

(370) *hummu ʔasās il-ġōr u ʔasās il-balga*
3PL foundation DEF-Jordan_Valley and foundation DEF-Balga
'They are the foundation of the Jordan Valley and the Balga area'

(371) *intu kull-ku mlāḥ*
2PL all-2PL good.PL
'You are all good (people)'

(372) *dār slēmān tiḥtī-ku*
house Slēmān under-2PL
'Sleiman's house is below yours'

The reverse order [PREDICATE SUBJECT] occurs when the predicate is focused (see §4.5.2.4 for more on fronting and pitch-raising as a focalisation strategy):

(373) *išrabi šāy* [*zāki*]$_{\text{PRED.FOC}}$ [*š-šāy*]$_{\text{SUBJ}}$
drink.IMP.FS tea tasty DEF-tea
'Drink (some) tea, the tea is tasty'

For disambiguation purposes, the subject and the predicate of identificational clauses may be separated by a pronoun coreferential with the subject when both constituents are definite. These are in fact left-dislocated subjects that are indexed in the clause by way of a free pronoun.

(374) *āxir dār hī dār Abu Rašīd*
last house 3FS house Abu Rašīd
'The last house is Abu Rašīd's house'

(375) *illi bīği mn aḷḷa hū lə-mlīḥ*

REL come.IPFV.3MS from God 3SG DEF-good

'Whatever comes from God is good'

4.4.1.2. Prepositional Predicates

4.4.1.2.1. Existential Predicates

Existential constructions typically encode a locational relation between a figure and an optional ground: *there is a man* (figure) *in the house* (ground). The recognition of a separate existential construction is based on syntactic grounds. While the non-verbal predicates discussed above display the structure [ARGUMENT PREDICATE], existential clauses have the reverse syntax [PREDICATE ARGUMENT]. In the traditional dialect, the figure of an existential clause is introduced with the morpheme *bī*, which grammaticalised from the preposition *bi* 'in' augmented with the 3MS bound pronoun.

(376) *lamma ṣṣīr ṭawāri bī*

when become.SBJV.3FS emergencies EXIST

mačān la l-xēl

place for DEF-horses

'When emergencies occur, there is a place for the horses'

Evidence that the existential marker is fully grammaticalised and has lost its inessive meaning is the possibility for it to co-occur with the preposition *bi* 'in':

(377) *bī bi lə-fḥēṣ ʕurs-ēn ʔaw ṯalāṯe l-yōm*

EXIST IN DEF-Fḥēṣ wedding-DU or three DEF-day

'There are two or three weddings in Fḥēṣ today'

Pan-Levantine *fī* is also commonly used and is probably borrowed from neighbouring dialects. Its origin is difficult to trace, because it is found in both the new dialect of Amman and the Bedouin dialects of the Jordan Valley.

(378) *fī wāḥad bisʔal ʕann-ak*
EXIST one ask.IPFV.3MS about-2MS
'There is someone who is asking about you'

4.4.1.2.2. Possessive Existentials: *ʕind, maʕ* and *la*

Initially, possessive predicates were an extension of existential predicates. The possessor is coded obliquely as the ground argument and the possessee is coded as the figure argument. Three markers are used: *ʕind-* 'at', *maʕ-* 'with' and *la* 'for'. The existential marker *bī* ~ *fī* is optional. When it is expressed, there is contiguity between the existential marker and the preposition.

(379) *bī l-na walad bi l-ʕagaba*
EXIST for-1PL son in DEF-Aqaba
'We have a son in Aqaba'

Most often, though, the existential is omitted. If the possessor is a full NP, it is left-adjacent to the predicate and the NP is indexed on the preposition with a bound pronoun.

(380) *ḏ̣all kull wāḥad ʕind-o faras*
stay.PFV.3MS every one at-3MS horse
'Everyone had a horse'

The object of the preposition may surface as a full NP, but the meaning is locational, not possessive, although they may seem to overlap, as in (381).

(381) *fī ʕind əflān bint ḥilwa*

EXIST at so-and-so girl beautiful

'There is at so-and-so's place a beautiful girl (his daughter)'

Further evidence of the reinterpretation of possessive predicates as transitive predicates comes from the objecthood of the possessee. Relativisation (382) and left-dislocation (383) unambiguously show that the possessee is coded like an object, because it is referenced on the pronominal object carrier *iyyā-*.

(382) *il-lōḥa lli ʕind-i yyā-ha*

DEF-painting REL at-1SG OBJ-3FS

'The painting that I have'

(383) *il-lōḥa hāy ʕind-i yyā-ha*

DEF-painting DEM at-1SG OBJ-3FS

'This painting… I have it'

This object-coding property does not extend to the two other possessive predicators *maʕ* 'with' and *la* 'for'. A sentence such as (384) is either rejected or judged questionable, while (385) is rejected altogether.

(384) ***is-sayyāra lli maʕ-i yyā-ha*

DEF-car REL with-1SG OBJ-3FS

'The car I have'

(385) ***id-dār il-ʔil-i yyā-ha*

DEF-house REL-for-3SG OBJ-3FS

'The house I have'

Some Levantine dialects may permit object marking in *maʕ*-clauses, so in these dialects, (384) is perfectly grammatical. Object marking in *la*-clauses does not seem, at least for now, to be available in any dialect. The merger of possessive predication and transitive predication is therefore still under way.

As far as the semantics of the three predicators *ʕind, maʕ* and *la* are concerned, they have all retained their core features. The preposition *la* is primarily a benefactive marker. Accordingly, in possessive predication, it does not have any locational or spatial meaning. It marks ownership, belonging and physical or virtual attachment. On the whole, the use of *la* seems in part lexically restricted. It is most often used to mark real estate ownership, family ties and any kind of direct (physical or virtual) attachment, all of which imply a strong tie between the possessor and the possessee, seemingly reminiscent of inalienable possession.

(386) *kull ʕāʔile masīḥiyye ʔil-ha ʕāʔile islāmiyye*
each family christian for-3FS family Muslim
mutaxāwiyīn maʕ baʕəḏ̣
be_joint.AP.MS with RECP
'Every Christian family has a Muslim family with whom they form a brotherhood'

(387) *kān hōna bī ʕēn, ʕēn il-ha mazārīb*
be.PFV.3MS here EXIST spring spring for-3FS spouts
'There was here a spring, a spring that had spouts'

(388) *kān fī šēx ʔil-o walad wāḥad*
be.PFV.3MS EXIST sheikh for-3MS son one
'There was a sheikh who had one son'

The predicator *ʕind-* is less restricted than *la*. It has partially retained its spatial meaning. Compare in this regard (388) and (389). In (388), no adessivity is implied, unlike in (389), where the speaker implies that father and children are still living under one roof. The preposition *ʕind-* can also mark ownership without adessivity, as in (390), but it does not express a strong tie, unlike *la*.

(389) *ʕind-o walad u bint-ēn min bint xālt-i*
at-3MS son and girl-DU from daughter maternal_aunt-1SG
'He has a son and two daughters with my cousin'

(390) *brāhīm ʕind-o šarikāt*
Ibrahim at-3MS companies
'Ibrahim has companies'

The predicator *maʕ-* has retained much of its comitative meaning. It does not mark strict possession or ownership, but rather physical contiguity, which may be symbolic when the possessee is an offspring, as in (391).

(391) *ḥāmil maḥ-ḥa binət*
pregnant with-3FS girl
'She is pregnant, she has a girl'

(392) *maʕ-hin sayyāra ʔaw ši*
with-3FP car or thing
'Do they have a car or something?'

(393) *maʕ-kī-š duxxān*
with-2MS-NEG smoke
'You don't have cigarettes'

Stassen (2013b), in his typology of predicative possession, distinguishes four types: the *have* type (transitive), the existential type (intransitive), the topic possessive and the conjunctional possessive. Only the *have* type and the existential type are relevant in our discussion. The existential type is itself subdivided into locational and genitive, whereby the possessor is either obliquely coded as a genitive or a locative. Our data shows that, although Arabic primarily belongs to the existential-locational type, a drift towards the transitive *have* type is under way, with various stages of completion in different dialects. In the dialects under discussion here, this drift is complete with the predicative base *ʕind-* but not with *maʕ-* and *il-*.

4.4.1.2.3. Locational Existentials: *bi* ~ *fi* and *ʕala*

The prepositions *bi* ~ *fi* 'in' and *ʕala* are also used predicatively. Unlike existential *bī*, *bi* has kept its inessive meaning, albeit also figuratively. In this case, the co-occurrence of existential *bī* seems dispreferred (*bī bi-hum*??).

(394) *bī-hum ḥēl*
in-3PL strength
'They have strength'

When marked with the 3MS bound pronoun, *bi* becomes homophonous with existential *bī*. Example (395) also shows that, although the one-argument of these predicates is most often indefinite, definite NPs are also permitted:

(395) *bī l-baraka*
in.3MS DEF-blessing
'There is blessing in it (i.e, it's good, it fits)'

(396) *ma-hī mā fī-ha rbāṭ*

TOP-3FS NEG in-3FS link

'There is no link in it (i.e., it doesn't have anything to do with it)'

The use of the preposition *ʕala* 'on' as a predicative base is much more limited. Physical superessivity is reinterpreted abstractly, as shown in (397) and (398) (also repeated in (463) about negation), where it denotes broad deontic modality:

(397) *ʕalē-ha tawǧīhi ha-s-sane hāy*

on-3FS final_exam DEM-DEF-year DEM

'She has to prepare for the secondary education certificate this year'

(398) *nuškur aḷḷa mā ʕalē-kī-š xōf*

thank.SBJV.1PL God NEG on-2MS-NEG fear

'Thank God you have nothing to fear'

4.4.1.2.4. The Pseudo-verb *badd-* 'want'

The morpheme *badd-* ~ *bidd-* 'want', found across the Levant and beyond, does not have the morphological shape of a verb, because it most probably arose from grammaticalisation of the phrase *bi-widd* (in-wish). It it used both as an auxiliary (§4.2.4.1) and as a main predicate. It can inflect only for person, number and gender through obligatory bound pronoun affixation, which indexes the experiencer. TAM inflections have to be carried by an auxiliary. The pseudo-verb *badd-* is compatible with the following auxiliaries:

kān, baga and *ḏall* (imperfect)	*kunt* ~ *bagēt* ~ *ḏallēt badd-i* 'I wanted'
ṣār (inchoative)	*ṣurt badd-i* 'I wanted (onset of the process)'
baṭṭal (cessative)	*baṭṭalt badd-i* ~ *mā ʕudt-əš badd-i* 'I stopped wanting'

The argument structure of *badd-* is that of a monotransitive predicate:

(399) [*badd-o*]$_{PRED}$ [*z-zalame*]$_{SUBJ}$ [*šaġla mrattabe*]$_{OBJ}$
want-3MS DEF-man thing neat
'The man needs something neat'

Evidence that *badd-* has been reinterpreted as a transitive verbal predicate is provided by the verbal negators *mā… -š* (400) and the objecthood of the patient-like argument that is carried by the pronominal object host *iyyā* (401), properties also shared by *ʕind*.

(400) *a-badd-kī-š bagar*
NEG-want-2MS-NEG cow
'You don't need a cow'

(401) *illi badd-(h)um iyyā ʕaggabū*
REL want-3MP OBJ.3MS arrest.PFV.3MP.OBJ.3MS
w it-tāli gallū-lo rawwiḥ
and DEF-next say.PFV.3MP-DAT.3MS go.IMP.MS
'They arrested the one they wanted and they told the next one to go'

4.4.1.2.5. Summary of Prepositional Predicates and their Verbal Drift

Table 222 summarises the verbal properties of prepositional predicates. It shows that *badd-* and *ʕind-* have fully drifted towards becoming monotransitive verb-like predicates. Cross-dialectal evidence suggests that the same process is under way, at least in some dialects, for *maʕ* but not for *il-*, *ʕala* and *bi*. This may suggest that we are witnessing a diachronic process whereby prepositional predicates are drifting towards monotransitive verb-like predicates.

Table 222: The verbal properties of prepositional predicates

	Verbal negators	Monotransitive
badd- (volition)	X	X
ʕind- (adessive)	X	X
maʕ- (comitative)	X	?
il- (benefactive)	X	-
ʕala (superessive)	X	-
bi (inessive)	X	-

4.4.2. Verbal Predication

Typologically, all varieties of Arabic exhibit a strict accusative alignment. Modern-day dialects are head-marking, which means that the verb indexes the subject of intransitive and transitive verbs and that the arguments are not marked for case, whether inflectionally or adpositionally. Objects of intransitive bivalent predicates are marked prepositionally. SV(O) and VS(O) orders are both unmarked. Pronominal subjects can be omitted, because the subject is already indexed on the verb (except in non-verbal predication).

4.4.2.1. Word Order

It has been argued that dialectal Arabic is a SVO language, contrary to Classical Arabic, which exhibits VSO as its basic order (Shlonsky 1997). This proposition has since been mitigated by a series of studies (Dahlgren 1998; Brustad 2000; Owens et al. 2009) in which it appears that both SVO and VSO are unmarked orders in spoken Arabic. While Dahlgren (1998) and Brustad (2000) focus on the discursive status of the subject, Owens et al. (2009) also investigate its morpholexical class. Brustad (2000, 361) summarises her findings by stating that

> VSO represents the dominant typology in event narration, while SVO functions as a topic-prominent typology that is used to describe and converse, contexts in which discourse topics either shift around, or are taken as a frame within which a main sentence predications holds.

As noted above, Owens et al. (2009, 62) go one step further in including the morpholexical class of the subject. They observe that SV order signals a discourse status of available reference, as instantiated by pronouns, pronominals, constrastive nouns, general and generic nouns. VS order is selected for the presentation of new referents and events, typically indefinite nouns and lexically-/discourse-specific nouns, whether definite or indefinite. Sedentary Jordanian behaves similarly to what has been observed by these previous studies. Looking at the distribution of SV and VS orders in the text *il-bagara* (presented in §5.2) confirms that both the discourse status of the subject and its morpholexical class are word order predictors. The story is about the narrator himself, who in the early fifties of the last century got caught in the middle of scuffles with the police while he was looking for a cow which had left its pastures. Background events are coded with SV(O):

(402) *il-maššīni kān yʕallig ʕa ḥizb il-baʕəṯ*

Al-Mashini be.PFV.3MS hang.SBJV.3MS on party DEF-Baath

'Al-Mashini was mocking the Baath party'

(403) *il-ḥağğe kānat ğāybe naḏīr*

DEF-elderly_lady be.PFV.3FS bring.AP.FS Naḏīr

'My wife had given birth to Naḏīr'

Once the background is presented, the discourse topic *il-bagara* 'the cow' is first introduced as an indefinite object:

(404) *štarēt bagara b-wāḥad u ṯalāṯīn dīnār*

buy.PFV.1SG cow with-one and thirty dinar

'I bought a cow for 31 dinars'

The narration goes on with VS(O), as shown below:

(405) *ġrabat id-dinya*

be_dark.PFV.3FS DEF-world

'It got dark'

(406) *rāḥat il-bagara*

go.PFV.3FS DEF-cow

'The cow was gone'

(407) *bgul-li ḍ-ḍābiṭ*

say.IPFV.3MS-DAT.1SG DEF-officer

'The officer tells me'

Towards the end of the narration, the initial discourse topic *il-bagara* 'the cow' is not in the active registry of the speaker and his audience any more, because the topic shifted to the speaker himself who ended up in prison. At the end of the narrative, the speaker uses the order SV to re-introduce the primary topic:

(408) *w il-bagara rawwaḥat laḥāl-ha*
and DEF-cow go_home.PFV.3FS alone-3FS
'And the cow came back on its own!'

The facts presented here confirm the observations made by previous authors that, broadly speaking, SV is selected in cases of topic instability and VS in cases of topic stability, which also correlates with conversation (SV, topic instability) versus narration (VS, topic stability). As noted by Owens et al. (2009), the SV order used at the beginning of the text as a backgrounding device and at the end of the text to reintroduce the primary topic indicates available reference with contrastive nouns. Conversely, the VS order used in the core of the narration reflects the presentation of new referents and events.

4.4.2.2. Intransitive Constructions

4.4.2.2.1. Monovalent

Monovalent intransitive verbs only have one argument, the subject, which is indexed on the verb:

(409) [*ynāmu*]$_{PRED}$ [*hū w il-binət*]$_{SUBJ}$ *əb-farš wāḥad*
sleep.SBJV.3MP 3SG and DEF-girl in-bed one
'He and the girl would sleep in the same bed'

4.4.2.2.2. Bivalent

The subject of a bivalent intransitive construction, normally indexed on the verb, is not overtly marked and the object is coded like an oblique. The only strategy available in dialectal Arabic is adpositional marking. The inessive and instrumental preposition *bi* 'in, with', superessive *ʕa(la)* 'on' and ablative *ʕan* and *min* are the most common, as shown in (410), where the oblique object of the verb *mān–ymūn* 'control' is marked with *ʕa(la)* 'on':

(410) *il-yōm* [*il-wāḥad*]$_{\text{SUBJ}}$ [*miš* *māyin*]$_{\text{PRED}}$ [*ʕa* *(i)bn-o*]$_{\text{OBJ.OBL}}$
DEF-day DEF-one NEG control.AP.MS on son-3MS
'These days, one doesn't even control his son'

4.4.2.3. Monotransitive Constructions

Both the subject and the object of a transitive construction are zero-marked, as shown in (411). Only the subject is indexed on the verb. Note that differential object marking with the preposition *la*, common in northern Levantine and Mesopotamian Arabic, is not available in the dialect under discussion here.

(411) *balki* [*zalmat-na*]$_{\text{SUBJ}}$ [*mā* *ḏ̣arab-əš*]$_{\text{PRED}}$ [*zalmat-ku*]$_{\text{OBJ}}$
maybe man-1SG NEG strike.PFV.3MS-NEG man-2PL
'Maybe our man didn't hit yours'

4.4.2.4. Ditransitive Constructions

Ditransitive constructions have three core arguments: the subject, the theme and the recipient-like argument (Haspelmath 2013). The coding strategy depends on whether the theme and recipient arguments are pronominal or full NPs. If both are full NPs, both the indirect-object construction and the double-object construction are possible. In the double-object construction, no argument is overtly marked. In the indirect-object construction, the benefactive preposition *la* 'to, for' marks the recipient argument. The linear orders are as follows:

Indirective:	[THEME *la* RECIPIENT]
Double-object:	[RECIPIENT THEME]

When elicited, speakers judge the indirective construction and the double-object construction to be equivalent (412).

(412)

aʕṭēt	[*mḥammad*]$_{\text{recipient}}$	[*ktāb*]$_{\text{theme}}$	
give.PFV.1SG	Muhammad	book	
~			
aʕṭēt	[*ktāb*]$_{\text{theme}}$	[*la*	*muḥammad*]$_{\text{recipient}}$
give.PFV.1SG	book	to	Muhammad

'I gave Muhammad a book ~ I gave a book to Muhammad'

Only one instance of a fully nominal theme and recipient was recorded in spontaneous speech, in the double-object construction in (413). The underlying subject is *aḷḷa* 'God':

(413)

yiʕṭi	[*ḥsēn*]$_{\text{RECIPIENT}}$	[*ṭūlt*	*il-ʕumər*	*w*	*il-hēbe*]$_{\text{THEME}}$
give.SBJV.3SG	Hussein	length	DEF-life	and	DEF-respect

'May (God) give (king) Hussein long life and respect'

Interestingly, both the theme argument and the recipient-like argument are eligible for subject promotion with passive predicates, as shown in (414) and (415):

(414)

nʕaṭēt	*muhle*	*la*	*adfaʕ*	*iḏ̣-ḏ̣arāyib*
be.given.PFV.1SG	delay	to	pay.SBJV.1SG	DEF-taxes

'I was given extra time to pay my taxes'

(415) *nʕaṭat-li* *muhle*
be.given.PFV.3FS-DAT.1SG delay
'Extra time was given to me'

It should be added that it is only with 'give'-verbs (*nʕaṭa* 'be given', *nhada* 'be offered') that the recipient-like argument can be promoted to subject through passivisation. This is not permitted with passive derivations of other ditransitive verbs such as *nbāʕ* 'be sold' (passive of ditransitive *bāʕ* 'sell'), as suggested by the grammaticality of (416) and the ungrammaticality of (417).

(416) *nbāʕat* *sayyāra*
be.sold.PFV.3FS car
'A car was sold'

(417) ***nbiʕt* *sayyāra*
be.sold.PFV.1SG car
Intended: 'I was sold a car'

When both the theme and the recipient are pronominal, only the double-object construction is attested. The recipient is coded like an object and indexed on the verb, and the pronominal theme is hosted by the object carrier *iyyā-* (418).

(418) *nṭā* *yyā-ha*
give.PFV.3MS.OBJ.3MS OBJ-3FS
'He gave her to him'

If the theme is pronominal and the recipient is a full NP, the indirect object construction prevails. The theme is coded like an object and indexed on the verb and the recipient is coded obliquely with the preposition *la* (419).

(419) *gāmu* *nṭū-ha* *la ʕabdaḷḷa*

stand.PFV.3MP give.PFV.3PL-3FS to Abdalla

'They gave her to Abdallah'

If the theme is a full NP and the recipient is pronominal, the double-object construction is selected: the recipient is coded like an object indexed on the verb, and the theme is zero-marked like the object of a monotransitive construction (420).

(420) *anṭī-ni* *gahwa*

give.IMP.FS-1SG coffee

'Give me coffee'

Other ditransitive verbs that allow the double-object construction are *warra* and *farǧa* ~ *warǧa* 'show', *garra* ~ *ʕallam* 'teach', *labbas* 'clothe'. Example (421) illustrates the double-object construction with pronominal themes and recipients. Full NPs were not recorded in spontaneous speech but are considered perfectly acceptable when elicited.

(421) *minwarrī-k* *iyyā*

show.IPFV.1PL-2MS OBJ.3MS

'We show it to you'

garrēt-ha *yyā-hin*

teach.PFV.1SG-3FS OBJ-3FP

'I taught them to her'

labbsū *yyā-ha*

clothe.IMP.MS.OBJ.3MS OBJ-3FS

'Clothe him with it'

The verb *bāʕ* 'sell' also has a ditransitive behaviour, because the double-object construction is selected when the recipient-like argument is pronominal, as shown in (422) and (423).

(422) *hāy illi biʕt-ak iyyā-ha*

DEM REL sell.PFV.1SG-2MS OBJ-3FS

'This is (the story) I sold you'

(423) *biʕt-o l-kīs əb-lērt-ēn*

sell.PFV.1SG-3MS DEF-bag with-dinar-DU

'I sold him the bag for two dinars'

Table 223 summarises the coding strategies used according to the pronominal status of the arguments:

Table 223: Ditransitive constructions

	Pronominal theme	Full NP theme
Pronominal recipient	Double-object	Double-object
Full NP recipient	Indirect-object	Mixed

4.4.2.5. Valency-increasing Operations

4.4.2.5.1. Causative

Causative derivation is carried out by morphological means. In most dialects, only the pattern CaCCaC (form II) is available: *ṭiliʕ* 'go out' > *ṭallaʕ* 'take out'. Conservative varieties also have the pattern (a)CCaC (form IV): *ṭiliʕ* 'go out' > *aṭlaʕ* 'take out'. The dialect discussed here has both *ṭallaʕ* ~ *aṭlaʕ*. At first sight, form IV looks like a moribund device with little or no productivity. It was suggested above (§3.4.2.4) that, in earlier stages of the dialect, form IV and form II may have been in complementary distribution, with form IV used to derive causatives from monovalent verbs and form II from bivalent verbs. If the morphological causative derivation is not available in the lexicon or if the degree of control of the causer is low, syntax comes to the rescue. The periphrastic causative employs the control verb *xalla* 'let' complemented by a subordinate clause in the bare imperfective. In (424), the causer has a lesser degree of control than in the morphological derivation *aṭlaʕ* 'take out'.

(424) *hassa baxallī-ha tiṭlaʕ ʕalē-ki*

now let.IPFV.1SG-3FS leave.SBJV.3FS to-2FS

'Now I'll tell her to come to you'

Morphological causative derivation is not recursive. To form the causative of a morphological causative, only the periphrastic construction is permitted, as in (425).

(425) *la (a)xallī-hum ynayymū-k b-frāš-ak*

INT let.SBJV.1SG-3PL make.sleep.3PL-2MS in-bed-2MS

'I'll make them make you sleep in your bed (i.e., I'll make them hurt you)'

4.4.2.5.2. Non-argumental Dative

Dative marking by means of the preposition *la* is also used to code participants whose semantic role is beneficiary/maleficiary or recipient(-like). Interestingly, non-argumental datives have a different syntactic behaviour from argumental datives, as evidenced when they are coreferential with the subject. As shown in (426), coreferential argumental datives are coded with the reflexive morpheme *ḥāl*, to which there attaches a bound pronoun that references the argument. Here, the recipient argument of the verb *ǧāb* 'he brought' must be marked with the preposition *la* 'to, for'.

Since it is coreferential with the subject (1SG), it has to be coded with reflexive *ḥāl*.

(426) *n ražaʕt issāʕ bažīb la*
If come_back.PFV.1SG now bring.IPFV.1SG to
ḥāl-i iš-šibha w ana barī(?)
REFL-1SG DEF-suspicion and 1SG innocent
'If I go back now, I'll bring suspicions on myself although I'm innocent'

With non-argumental participants, reflexive marking is not permitted, as illustrated in (427) *bōkil-li* 'I eat (for myself)' and (428) *xuḏ-lak* 'take (for yourself)', where the pronominal arguments are coded as normal pronominal datives. There are no restrictions on person, gender and number for non-argumental dative marking.

(427) *bōkil-li ḥabbit ʕinəb aw tuffāḥ*
eat.IPFV.1SG-DAT.1SG piece grape or Apple
'I eat (for myself) a grape or some apple'

(428) *xuḏ-lak ha-l-mīt dulum*
take.IMP.MS-DAT.2MS DEM-DEF-hundred dunam
u bnī-lna dār
and build.IMP.MS-DAT.1PL house
'Take these one hundred dunams and build us a house'

Datives of interest are another kind of non-argumental dative. They act as a discursive device available to the narrator in order to engage the interlocutor in the narration. The interlocutor is coded like a beneficiary, although (s)he is not a participant in the narrated event. In (429) and (430), the interlocutor is coded using masculine singular *lak* and feminine singular *lič* respectively, as a device to give an imaginary role to the interlocutor in the narration of the event.

(429) *iṣ-ṣubḥiyyāt winn-o ǧāyib-lak gaṭṭit*
DEF-morning DM-3MS bring.AP.MS-DAT.2MS bunch
fidāʔiyye... yigḏabū-lak abuʕīsa
Fedayins, catch.SBJV.3MP-DAT.2MS Abuʕīsa
'In the morning, he had brought a bunch of Fedayins, there they were arresting Abu ʕīsa'

(430) *ǧāb il-manāšir u daʕas-hin*
bring.PFV.3MS DEF-flyers and trample.IPFV.3MS-3FP
tiḥt-o... w alāgī-lič iyyā
under-3MS and find.SBJV.3MS-DAT.2FS OBJ.3MS
'He brought the flyers and trampled on them... So I went for him (i.e., I gave him a piece of my mind)'

4.4.2.6. Valency-decreasing Operations

4.4.2.6.1. Passivisation

Passivisation is a valency-decreasing morphological operation by which the subject of an active predicate is demoted. Form I verbs are passivised through the prefixation of *n-* (Form VII) or the infixation of *-t-* (Form VIII), as encoded in the lexicon. Form II and form III verbs can only be passivised with the prefix *t-*. There are no consistent formal means of passivising Form IV verbs and speakers have to resort to the prefixation of *t-* on Form II verbs.

Form I	*tarak* 'he left'	*n-tarak* 'he was abandoned'
Form I	*nasa* 'he forgot'	*n-t-asa* 'he was forgotten'

Form II	*rağğaʕ* 'he brought back'	*t-rağğaʕ* 'he was brought back'
Form III	*sāʕad* 'he helped'	*t-sāʕad* 'he was helped'
Form IV	*rğaʕ* 'he took out'	*t-rağğaʕ* 'he was taken out'

Oblique coding of the demoted agent is hardly attested in spontaneous speech, as only one token was found across the recordings. In (431), the verb *nʕazam* 'he was invited' is derived from *ʕazam* 'he invited'. The agent *dār id-dāhūdi* 'the Dāhūdi clan' is coded obliquely by means of the ablative preposition *min*.

(431) *nʕazam* *raḥmit* *il-ʔamīr* *ʕabdaḷḷa*
be_invited.PFV.3MS late DEF-prince Abdallah
min *dār* *id-dāhūdi*
from house DEF-Dāhūdi
'The late prince Abdallah was invited by the Dāhūdi clan'

Semantically, passivisation often refers to the potentiality/ability/possiblity of the event, as shown in (432), where the verb *n-šarab* 'be drunk', derived from *širib* 'he drank', means 'to be drinkable'. The context of the utterance is the speaker's polite refusal to stay for dinner, saying that he would have liked to do so because the host's coffee is good, but unfortunately he cannot (*xanna nʕaššī-k ğīrt aḷḷa!* 'let us offer you dinner, for God's sake').

(432) *gahwit-ku* *btinšarib*
coffee-1PL be_drunk.IPFV.3FS
'Your coffee is worth drinking (your coffee is good)'

Any bivalent predicate is eligible for passivisation, whether transitive or intransitive bivalent (only the former allow promotion of the object). In (433), the verb *marag* 'pass' is intransitive bivalent with an object coded obliquely with the preposition *min* 'from'. The passive derivation yields *nmarag* 'be passed'. The subject is demoted and masculine singular agreement becomes the default agreement. The object remains coded obliquely with ablative *min*. It imposes an impersonal and potential reading.

(433) *iṭ-ṭarīg wiʕre mā binmarig min-ha*
DEF-road rugged NEG be_passed.IPFV.3MS from-3FS
'The road is rugged; it is impassable'

Interestingly, intransitive bivalent verbs that already bear the valency-decreasing affix *t-* are also eligible for passivisation, but because there are no formal means left to derive them, whether affixal or apophonic, the surface form remains identical. In (434), the verb *t-ʕarraf* 'get to know someone', derived from *ʕarraf* 'make known', marks its object with the proposition *ʕala* or *bi*. Passivisation remains possible, but the verb remains identical. This is a clear case of conversion or zero derivation as a morphological process, in which the output form remains identical to the input form.

(434) *hāḏa z-zalame mā bitʕarraf ʕalē*
DEM DEF-man NEG be_met.IPFV.3MS on.3MS
'One should not get to know this man'

Monovalent intransitive verbs are not eligible for passivisation: the hypothetical passive derivation ***n-ṯagal* from *ṯigil* 'become heavy' is not possible. Finally, unlike in Standard Arabic (cf. *muštabah bi-him* 'suspected'), the use of the passive participle is not grammatical: ***iṭ-ṭarīg mamrūg min-ha* (DEF-way pass.PP.MS from-3FS; intended: 'the way can be passed through').

4.4.2.6.2. Reflexivity

The prefixation of *t-* is a general valency-decreasing operation that can be used for passive, middle, reflexive and reciprocal derivations. Examples of reflexive derivation are *gaddam* 'put forward' vs *t-gaddam* 'move forward', *xabba* 'hide (transitive)' vs *t-xabba* 'hide (intransitive)'.

(435) *bixabbu t-tibən la š-šatawiyye*
hide.IPFV.3MP DEF-straw for DEF-winter
'They keep the straw for winter'

(436) *ʕa ṭ-ṭarīg txabbū-lhum*
on DEF-way hide.PFV.3MP-DAT.3MP
'On the way, they hid (themselves) from them (in order to attack them)'

If the lexicon does not allow the prefixation of *t-* to derive reflexives, reflexivisation is expressed by syntactic means, using the morpheme *ḥāl-* 'situation' or more marginally *nafs-* 'soul', augmented with a bound pronoun coreferential with the reflexivised participant and placed in the respective syntactic slot.

(437) *zamm ḥāl-o u raḥal ʕala ʕammān*
carry.PFV.3MS REFL-3MS and depart.PFV.3MS to Amman
'He carried himself and moved to Amman'

(438) *biššuxx ʕala ḥāl-ak*
pee.IPFV.2MS on REFL-2MS
'You pee in your pants (lit. on yourself)'

(439) *mā blāgī-š iši yustur ʕala nafs-o l-wāḥad*
NEG find.IPFV.3MS-NEG thing protect on REFL-3MS DEF-one
'One can't even find something to cover up himself with'

The morpheme *nafs*, unlike *ḥāl*, is also used as an intensifier, as in (440):

(440) *ibn-i ṯ-ṯāni šāhir nafs-o bi l-baladiyye*
son-1SG DEF-second Šāhir INTENS-3MS in DEF-municipality
'My second son, Šāhir himself, (works) for the municipality'

4.4.2.6.3. Reciprocity

As noted above, reciprocity can be expressed morphologically by the prefixation of *t-*: *hāwaš* 'quarrel' vs *t-hāwaš* 'quarrel (with each other)', *laga* 'find' vs *t-lāga* 'meet each other', *sōlaf* 'tell' vs *ssōlaf* (< *t-sōlaf*) 'tell each other'. If these derivations are not lexically available, reciprocal constructions involve the morpheme *baʕḏ̣* placed in the respective syntactic slot. The morpheme *baʕḏ̣* can appear on its own (441), be augmented with a bound pronoun (442) or be further augmented with *il-baʕḏ̣* (443).

(441) *balimm-hin ʕa baʕəḏ̣*
gather.IPFV.1SG-3FP on RECP
'I gather them on top of each other'

(442) *biṣīru ʕād yitlabbadu la baʕəḏ̣-hum*
become.IPFV.3MP DM sit_quietly.SBJV.3MP to RECP-3MP
'They start getting ready to ambush each other'

(443) *in-nās ʕārfe baʕəḏ̣-ha l-baʕəḏ̣*
DEF-people know.AP.FS RECP-3FS DEF-RECP
'People know each other'

4.4.3. Adverbial Modification

As noted above (§3.11), dialectal Arabic does not have any productive means of deriving adverbs from adjectives. To narrow the predication of a verb, three strategies exist. The first is to use an adjective invariably, as shown in (444), where the adjective *mnīḥ* ~ *mlīḥ* is not overtly marked. The number of adjectives that can be used in this position is limited—mostly those meaning 'good', such as *kwayyis*, *mlīḥ* and *ṭayyib*, and also *kṯīr* 'much'.

(444) *kul* *əmnīḥ* *m̦ām̦a*

eat.IMP.MS good mum

'Eat well, my son'

The second strategy is to create prepositional phrases with the preposition *ʕa(la)* 'on' complemented by a definite adjective, such as *ʕa ṣ-ṣaḥīḥ* 'correctly', *ʕa l-maḏ̣būṭ* 'correctly', *ʕa l-ʔaṣli* 'completely', *ʕa l-xafīf* 'lightly', *ʕa s-sarīʕ* 'quickly'. If such formations are not lexically available, speakers use the instrumental preposition *bi* 'with' complemented by a noun: *b-suhūle* 'easily', *b-surʕa* 'quickly', *b-ḥurriyye* 'freely'. Another possibility is to use the phrase *b-šakl* 'with shape' modified by an adjective: *b-šakəl ṭabīʕi* 'normally', *b-šakəl ʕām* 'generally'. The phrase *b-šakl* can also be used without an adjective, as in (445):

(445) *kānu* *fugara* *b-šakəl*

be.PFV.3MP poor.PL in-shape

'They were extremely poor'

4.4.3.1. Cognate Object Construction

The cognate object construction (Arabic *al-mafʕūl al-muṭlaq*) is well attested in both dialectal and Standard Arabic. Formally, it consists of the nominal derivation (masdar) of the verb in what looks superficially like the object position. It is often described as an emphasis device (تأكيد). What it really does is narrow the predication, which is the prototypical function of adverbs. As such, the cognate object construction is an adverbial modification strategy that fulfils specific semantic and pragmatic purposes. It is arguable whether it should be called 'object' at all, because there is little evidence for the objecthood of the constituent. Indeed, the two tests of left dislocation and relativisation yield mixed results. Consider in this regard (446). Relativising the masdar *tanšīf* would yield ***tanšīf ynaššfū-ha (iyyā??)*. Such a sequence, beside being totally ungrammatical, cannot easily be assigned a meaning.

(446) *il-bandora… ynaššfū-ha tanšīf*
DEF-tomtato… dry.SBJV.3MP-3FS drying
'As for tomatoes, they used to dry them properly'

The only case in which relativisation yields positive results is when the cognate object of an intransitive verb is relativised, as shown in (447). Here, the masdar *taʕab* 'fatigue' of the verb *tiʕib* 'he got tired' is relativised and indexed as an object by means of the 3MS bound pronoun *-o* on the verb *tiʕib*. This is also the only case in which indexing an object pronoun on an intransitive verb is permitted.

(447) *wal̤l̤a* *tʕibət* *taʕab* *mā*
by_God be_tired.PFV.1SG fatigue NEG
wāḥad *bi* *l-ʕālam* *tiʕb-o*
one in DEF-world be_tired.PFV.3MS-3MS
'I got tired in a way no one ever experienced in the world'

Shachmon and Marmorstein (2018) distinguish two sub-types of the cognate object construction: syntactically modified or morphologically augmented derived nouns and stand-alone nouns. Their focus is on the stand-alone sub-type in rural Palestinian Arabic. Their observations, at least semantically, seem valid for Arabic as a whole. Using the semantic features of phasality and boundedness, they characterise the semantic function of the stand-alone construction as "to lay focus on a semantic feature of the verbal event and exhaust its semantic potential, thus indicating that the event is carried out to its utmost effectiveness" (Shachmon and Marmorstein 2018, 59). They state that, pragmatically, speakers resort to this construction "in order to display emotionality and involvement," at least in narrative discourse. This semantic characterisation fits our data as well, as most stand-alone nouns indicate "that the event is carried out to its utmost effectiveness."

(448) *ḥakam* *manṭigat* *il-balga* *hōna* *ḥakam-ha* *ḥukum*
rule.PFV.3MS region DEF-Balga here rule.PFV.3MS-3FS rule
'He ruled the Balga area here, he ruled it firmly'

(449) *bōxḏu* *šwayye* *b-ṃayy* *sāxne* *bufurkū-ha*

take.IPFV.3MP few with-water hot rub.IPFV.3MP-3FS

hēk *bumursū-ha* *marīs*

so soak.IPFV.3MP-3FS soaking

'They take some in hot water, they rub like this, and soak it properly'

(450) *ana* *haḏ̣āk* *il-ḥīn* *mā* *laḥḥagət* *ʔumma*

1SG DEM DEF-time NEG know.PFV.1SG but

basmaʕ *siməʕ*

hear.IPFV.1SG hearing

'I was not around at that time (but) I do hear about it'

Form II verbs usually select a masdar in taCCīC / tiCCāy(e). One instance of tCiCCiC, formally similar to the masdar of form V verbs, was recorded in (451). Interestingly, the selection of this pattern for form II verbs is also reported by Shachmon and Marmorstein (2018) in rural Palestinian, in which it is a common alternative.

(451) *dāru* *warā-hum* *tā* *gaṭṭaʕū-hum* *tgiṭṭiʕ*

turn.PFV.3MP-3MP behind-3MP until cut.PFV.3MP-3MP cutting

'They circled (them from) behind until they cut them into pieces'

Although the most common type found in the corpus is the standalone one, instances of syntactically modified nouns and nouns augmented with the singulative morpheme *-a* were also recorded. In (452), the speaker uses the verbal noun *simʕ* 'hearing' augmented with the singulative morpheme *-a* to indicate that the event occurred once.

(452) *smiʕət* *simʕ-a* *bī-ha*
hear.PFV.1SG hearing-SING in-3FS
'I only heard about it once (on the grapevine, did not witness it)'

In (453), the speaker uses the derived noun *ʕirəf* 'knowing' and modifies it with the adjective *ṭayyib* 'good'. It seems, however, that the pattern exhibited in (453) belongs to an archaic register, because it is found only in the speech of the broadest speakers and is possibily lexically restricted.

(453) *laḥḥagt-o* *ana,* *baʕərf-o* *ʕirəf* *ṭayyib*
follow.PFV.1SG-3MS 1SG know.IPFV.1SG-3MS knowing good
'I was already there when he was around, I know him well'

Another possibility is for the derived noun to be the head of a genitive construction, as shown in (454).

(454) *tbāṭaḥu* *mbāṭaḥat* *ḥamīr*
wrestle.PFV.3MP wrestling donkeys
'They wrestled like donkeys'

The tokens in our data do not seem to imply any emotional involvement on the part of the speaker. The pragmatics of the construction as described by Shachmon and Marmorstein (2018) cannot be confirmed for our sub-set of data. This is probably due to the fact that they were mostly found in descriptive genres which involved little or no emotional modality. In a recent study, the cognate object construction has also been described as a focus marking strategy (Dìez 2019).

4.5. Pragmatically Marked Structures

4.5.1. Negation[4]

Compared to the standard variety, spoken Arabic has substantially reshuffled negation markers. The dialects under discussion here are no exception to this. Broadly speaking, the language uses different markers for the negation of verbal predication and non-verbal predication. Non-verbal predication makes use of the negator *miš* (or variants thereof), or much more marginally a negative copula. Verbal predication employs the preposed marker *mā* and a postposed *-š*, the distribution of which is detailed below. Existential and possessive predicates are negated like verbal predicates.

4.5.1.1. *mā…*, *mā… -š*, *a-… -š*, *…-š*

There is a wealth of literature on negation in both standard and dialectal Arabic, a review of which is beyond the scope of this chapter (Brustad 2000, 277–315; Lucas 2010). The main issue is the conditions for the use of the post-posed element *-š*. In addition to this, southern Levantine dialects also permit a conditioned elision of the first negator *mā*, leaving *-š* alone to mark negation. The dialect discussed here has a fourth possibility, which is the reduction of *mā* to *a-*. This is a well-known case of instantiation of Jespersen's cycle:

[4] For a general overview of the negation strategies in the dialect of Salt, see Palva (2003).

Stage 1	*mā bašrab*	'I don't drink'
Stage 2	*mā bašrab-əš*	
Stage 3	*a-bašrab-əš*	
Stage 4	*bašrab-əš*	

Jespersen's cycle is conceived of as a diachronic process to explain the renewal of negation markers. We are not dealing with diachrony per se, because all the stages are attested in synchrony, and there is no evidence at all that stage 4 is the final stage. The sequence reflects an order of appearance, rather than an order of disappearance. The main question is what the formal and semantic constraints on the distribution of each marker are. The categories relevant to our discussion are perfective, imperfective, bare imperfective, existential/possessive/pseudo-verb predicates and to a lesser extent the active participle, combined with the four formal possibilities *mā…*, *mā... -š*, *a-… -š*, *…-š*.

- Perfective

In the perfective, only two combinations are attested: *mā…* (455) and *mā… -š* (456). Omission of *mā* is not attested.

(455) *ana mā laḥḥagt šāriʕ iš-šwām*
1SG NEG come_across.PFV.1SG street DEF-Syrians
'I haven't seen the street of the Syrians'

(456) *mā maddēt-š īd-i ʕalē-ha*
NEG extend.PFV.1SG-NEG hand-1SG on-3FS
'I did not touch her'

- *b*-Imperfective

Four possibilities are attested for the *b*-imperfective:

(457) *iḥna mā mniḥči bi l-kāf*

1PL NEG speak.IPFV.1PL with DEF-kāf

'We don't speak with the (sound) *kāf* (i.e., we affricate /k/)'

(458) *il-muxtār mā biswā-š*

DEF-chief NEG be_worth.IPFV.3MS-NEG

'The (village) chief is hopeless'

(459) *a-bansā-š faḏl-o hāḏa z-zalame*

NEG-forget.IPFV.1SG-NEG kindness-3MS DEM DEF-man

'I can't forget the kindness of this man (towards me)'

(460) *badrī-š ʕal(a) ēš bithāwašu*

know.IPFV.1SG-NEG on what quarrel.IPFV.3MP

'I don't know what they are quarrelling about'

- Bare imperfective

Except in the second person, the bare imperfective only allows *mā*… and *mā*… *-š*.

(461) *aṭlub əl-girš, mā anūl-o*

ask.SBJV.1SG DEF-piaster NEG get.SBJV.1SG-3MS

lā ʔil-i wala la wlād-i

neither for-1SG nor for children-1SG

'I would ask for some money, and I wouldn't get any, neither for me nor for my children'

(462) *mā yrūḥ-əš ʕa l-mistašfa ġēr*

NEG go.SBJV.3MS-NEG to DEF-hospital other

illi mā wara wara

REL NEG behind behind

'Nobody would go to the hospital except those who are very ill (whose cases are hopeless)'

The negative imperative that involves the second person of the bare imperfective is different, because the marker *lā* is also used. The number of possibilities is higher: *mā tiǧi, mā tiǧī-š, tiǧī-š, lā tiǧi* 'don't come'. Also possible are *a-tiǧī-š* and *lā tiǧī-š*, but these were obtained only through elicitation.

- Pseudo-verbs

Two categories ought to be distinguished: *badd-* 'want', existential *bī* ~ *fī* and possessive *maʕ-* 'with' on the one hand, and possessive *ʕind-* and *ʔil-* on the other. The first group allows all four markings:

mā badd-i ~ *mā badd-ī-š* ~ *a-badd-ī-š* ~ *badd-ī-š* 'I don't want'
mā bī ~ *mā bī-š* ~ *a-bī-š* ~ *bī-š* 'there is not'
mā maʕ-o ~ *mā maʕ-hū-š* ~ *a-maʕ-hū-š* ~ *maʕ-hū-š* 'he doesn't have'

With *ʕind-* and *ʔil-*, only *mā*... and *mā*... *-š* are permitted. The omission of *mā* is not grammatical.

mā ʕind-o ~ *mā ʕind-hū-š* 'he doesn't have'
mā ʔil-o ~ *mā l-o* ~ *mā l-hū-š* 'he doesn't have'

The preposition *ʕala* 'on' may also function as a predicative base and be negated with *mā*... *-š*, as shown in (463). The omission of *mā* is not grammatical.

(463) *nuškur* *aḷḷa* *mā* *ʕalē-kī-š* *xōf*
thank.SBJV.1PL God NEG on-2MS-NEG fear
'Thank God you have nothing to fear'

- Active participle

Active participles are normally negated with *miš*, but one instance of *mā*... and one instance of *mā*... *-š* were recorded. The counter-assumptive use of *(mā)… -š* instead of *miš* is not obvious from the context.

(464) *mā ṭāliʕ-ilhū-š iši*
NEG exit.AP.MS-DAT.3MS-NEG thing
'He has not got anything'

(465) *wal̤l̤a ssāʕ yimma mā ṭāfī-ni ġēr ʕīd*
by_God now mother NEG put_out.AP.MS other ʕīd
'No one except ʕīd has me so sad'

Table 224 summarises the possibilities that are attested and the number of tokens for each combination.

Table 224: Distribution of *mā…*, *mā... -š*, *a-… -š*, *…-š*

Perfective	*mā…*	120	57%
	mā… -š	88	43%
b-imperfective	*mā…*	110	48%
	mā… -š	33	15%
	a-… -š	15	7%
	…-š	69	30%
Bare imperfective (except second person)	*mā…*	17	25%
	mā… -š	52	75%
Negative imperative	*mā…*	1	11%
	mā… -š	1	11%
	…-š	4	44%
	lā…	3	34%
Pseudo-verbs (*badd-, bī ~ fī, maʕ-*)	*mā…*	63	36%
	mā… -š	44	25%
	a-… -š	23	13%
	…-š	47	26%
Pseudo-verbs (*il-, ʕind-*)	*mā…*	5	23%
	mā… -š	17	77%

The following observations can be made:

a) Postposed *-š* is permitted in all environments.
b) In the perfective, *mā* is compulsory. Used alone, it occurs more frequently in the data than *mā... -š*.
c) The same goes for the *b*- imperfective, where *mā...* occurs most frequently. However, the frequency of the occurrence of all three forms with *-š* combined is slightly higher than bare *mā*- (52% vs 48%, respectively).
d) The pseudo-verbs *badd*- and *maʕ* and the existential *bī* ~ *fī* clearly follow the same pattern as the *b*-imperfective, both in terms of the negators they permit, and the relative frequencies. This is further evidence of the phonological basis of *mā* dropping (see below).
e) In the bare imperfective, there is a clear preference for *mā... -š*.
f) The negation of the second person in the bare imperfective, that is, the negative imperative, should be treated separately, because the negator *lā* is added. The paucity of tokens does not allow for any conclusive statements.
g) The possessive predicates *ʕind*- and *il*- clearly follow a similar pattern to the bare imperfective, in terms of both the negators used and the numbers, which is also further evidence for the phonological basis of *mā* dropping.
h) The structure *a-... -š* is by far the least frequent and should be considered a variant of *-š*, because they surface in the same environment, namely, labial obstruents (Hoyt 2007).

These figures do not lend support to the claim that *mā…* is the unmarked negation strategy. The relative number of tokens of *mā…* and *(mā)… -š* is either close to even (perfective, labial pseudo-verbs and *b*-imperfective), or clearly in favour of *(mā)… -š* (bare imperfective and non-labial pseudo-verbs). Moreover, the main restriction on *-š* is the presence of an assertivity marker such as *wa̤l̤la* (or a variant thereof), which is extremely frequent across the corpus with at least 400 tokens. A significant number of instances of *mā…* co-occur with an assertivity marker. Compare in this regard (466) and (467). In (466), adding *-š* is ungrammatical and, in (467), adding *wa̤l̤la* is ungrammatical. Consequently, if one compares *mā…* and *(mā)… -š* excluding *wa̤l̤la* clauses, the balance is clearly in favour of *(mā)… -š*.

(466) *wa̤l̤la mā badri*

by_God NEG know.IPFV.1SG

(467) *a-badrī-š ʕād*

NEG-know.IPFV.1SG-NEG DM

'I don't know'

Although there are signs that *(mā)… -š* is becoming the unmarked strategy, there is a consistent pattern in the data as far as the distribution of *mā…* and *(mā)… -š* is concerned. When speakers use one negation strategy and then repeat the negation, whether it is the same speaker or the interlocutor who repeats it, they often do so using the other strategy, as illustrated in (468) and (469).

(468) *mā ǧābat-š - lā lā lā mā ǧābat*

NEG bring.PFV.3FS-NEG - no no no NEG bring.PFV.3FS

'She didn't have kids. No, she didn't'

(469) *mā bagdar aṭilʕ-o, lawinno*
NEG can.IPFV.1SG take_out.SBJV-3MS even_if
b-arḍ-i bagdar-š aṭilʕ-o
in-land-1SG can.IPFV.1SG-NEG take_out.SBJV-3MS-NEG
'I can't kick him out, even if he is on my land, I can't kick him out'

Finally, as far as the phonological motivation for the deletion of *mā* is concerned, Hoyt (2007) noted regarding Palestinian Arabic that "Omission of *mā-* is possible only with stems beginning with labial obstruents [b] or [f], and only in the presence of *-š*," which, in his view, suggests that homorganicity is the trigger for the reduction to *a-* and subsequent total deletion of *mā*. This, as noted by Lucas (2010), does not explain the dropping of *mā* in negative imperatives or, conversely, the fact that *mā* cannot be dropped before perfective verbs beginning with a labial consonant: ***bal-laš-əš* (begin.PFV.3MS-NEG; intended: 'he did not begin'). However, as pointed out by Al-Qassas (2012), the negative imperative cases can be brought into line with the homorganicity approach if the deleted negative operator is not *mā*, but *lā*, which is the preferred preverbal negator in these constructions and is homorganic with the apical prefix *t-* of the subjunctive verb: *lā txāf* 'don't be afraid' (NEG fear.SBJV.2MS). Moreover, Alrashadan (2015) suggests further that the impossibility of *mā* deletion with labial-initial perfective verbs can be accounted for, without recourse to a condition based on tense or mood, by a morphological requirement that the homorganic consonant must be the initial segment of a 'functional element', i.e., a prefix (*b-* or *t-*) or a 'pseudo-verb' such as *bi* or *fi*. Our data confirm Hoyt's (2007) observations that *mā* deletion and *mā* reduction to *a-* have the same distribution, because they can only occur before labial obstruents (*b*-imperfective, existential *bī* ~ *fī*, *badd-*, *maʕ-*), and are also consistent with the refinements outlined above.

4.5.1.2. Formal Constraints on *-š*

As already noted, under certain conditions, the negator *-š* cannot co-occur with *mā*, leaving *mā* the only permitted negator:

(a) with oath and oath-like phrases of the type *wa̤l̤la* 'by God, I swear'

(470) *bi-llāh il-karīm mā maʕ-i ʕašar əgrūš*
with-God DEF-generous NEG with-1SG ten piasters
'I swear I didn't have ten piasters (in my pocket)'

(b) with the morpheme *ʕumər* 'never' (although see examples in §4.5.1.10.3)

(471) *ʕumər-na mā sawwēnā*
never-1SG NEG do.IPFV.1PL.OBJ.3MS
'We never did it'

Some speakers disfavour the use of *-š* in cases of polarity focus, but corpus data suggest that both *mā* and *-š* are possible. The context of (472) is a dialogue in which speaker 1 expresses reluctance about spreading oil or ointment on the skin before sleeping, fearing that it could stain either her sleepwear or the bed sheets. Speaker 2 (472) contradicts this assertion once with *-š* and then with *mā* (the phonetic correlates are discussed below).

(472) *lā… bitwassx-əš* *mā bitwassix* *hāy…*
no stain.IPFV.3FS-NEG NEG stain.IPFV.3FS DEM
mā bitwassix
NEG stain.IPFV.3FS
'No! It doesn't stain, this doesn't, it doesn't!'

While both negators can be used in polarity focus, they cannot co-occur, because this yields conflicting stress assignment rules: *mā* drags primary stress to the left while *-š* drags primary stress to the right (see below).

4.5.1.3. The Phonological and Morphosyntactic Status of the Negators *mā*, *a-* and *-š*

The morpheme *mā* is best interpreted as an independent phonological word, mostly because, as noted above, it carries stress and full length when used as the sole negator: *mā bidd-i* [ˈma: bɪddɪ] 'I don't want' (Figure 4).

(473) *mā bidd-i*
NEG want-1SG
'I don't want'

Figure 4: Prosody of *mā bidd-i* 'I don't want' (pitch in blue and intensity in green)

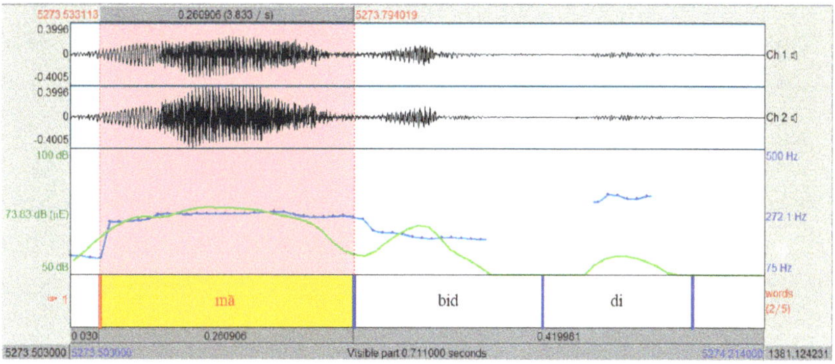

When *mā* and *-š* co-occur, *mā* is de-stressed and *-š* creates a new phonological word, dragging stress to the right and lengthening the contact vowel. Although *mā* is de-stressed, it is still perceiveably long (except in allegro speech), unlike in other Levantine varieties, in which de-stressing causes shortening of long vowels. Accordingly, *mā* seems to undergo a drift toward boundedness, whereas *-š* is clearly bound (although not fully affixal; see the discussion below). This is exemplified in (474) and Figure 5: *mā ʕind-hū-š* 'it doesn't have' [ma: ʕɪnˈtu:ʃ].

(474) *hāḏa mā ʕind-hū-š laban*
DEM NEG at-3MS-NEG yoghurt
'This (person) doesn't have yoghurt'

Figure 5: Prosody of *mā ʕind-hū-š* 'he doesn't have' (pitch in blue and intensity in green)

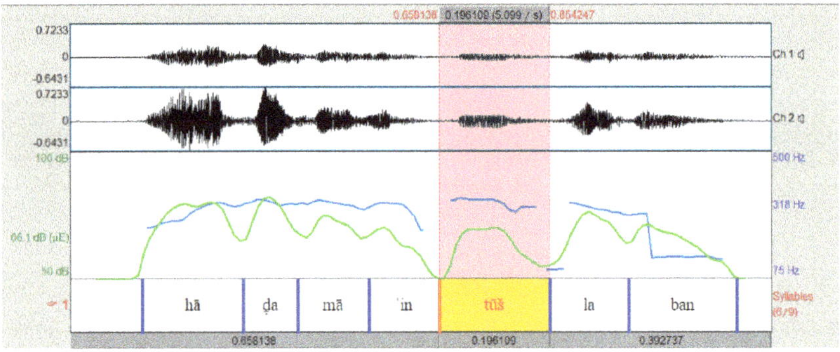

The reduced form *a-* of *mā* only occurs with *-š*. As shown in (475) and Figure 6, *a-* is not prominent pitch- and intensity-wise. Although it may still retain perceivable length, it is clearly a bound form: [a(ˑ)bɪˈhɪmmɪʃ]. It is not possible to settle precisely where it stands on the word–clitic–affix scale but, because it retains length and because material that attaches to the left usually tends to exhibit clitic-like behaviour, it seems more consistent to classify *a-* as a non-affixal bound form.

(475) *ygūlin* *a-bihimm-əš*

say.SBJV.3FP NEG-be_important.IPFV.3MS-NEG

'They used to say (that) it doesn't matter'

Figure 6: Prosody of *ygūlin a-bihimm-əš* 'it doesn't matter' (pitch in blue and intensity in green)

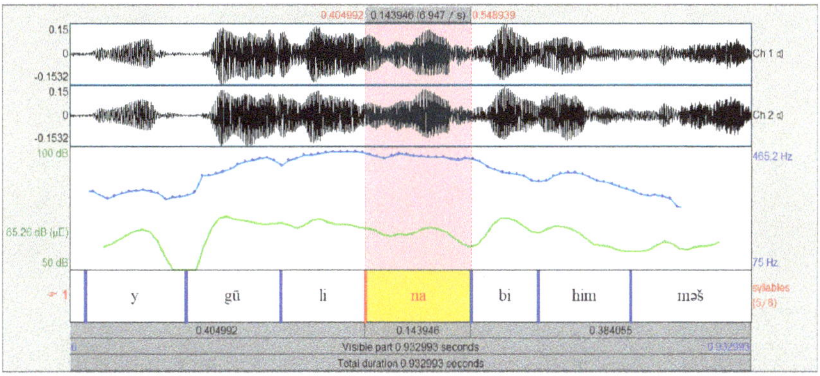

The prosodic characteristics of *mā* and *-š* are further exemplified in Figure 7 [ˈmaː bɪtˌwassɪx] and Figure 8 [bɪtˈwassxɪʃ]. In the case of *mā bitwassix*, the negator bears primary stress, both pitch-wise and intenstity-wise. The verb is partially de-stressed but a secondary stress is still perceivable in lieu of the primary stress in positive polarity: *mā* + *bitwássix* → *mā́ bitwàssix* [ˈmaː bɪtˌwassɪx].

(476) *mā* *bitwassix*

NEG stain.IPFV.3FS

'It doesn't stain'

Figure 7: Prosody of *mā bitwassix* 'it doesn't stain' (pitch in blue and intensity in green)

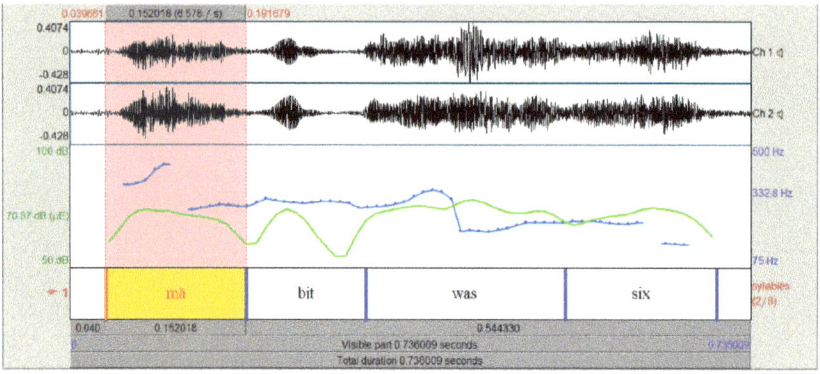

An interesting prosodic characteristic of *-š* is illustrated in (477) and Figure 8. The positive form is *bitwassix* 'it stains' (stain.IPFV.3FS). If *-š* were fully affixal, the expected development would be the following: **bitwássix* + *-š* → **bitwassíx-š* (stress shift) → *bitwassíx-əš* (anaptyctic insertion), and this is indeed what happens in other dialects such as Ammani and urban Palestinian. The traditional form *bitwássx-əš* is the result of another path: **bitwássix* + *-š* → **bitwássx-š* (no stress shift but vowel deletion) → *bitwássx-əš* (anaptyctic insertion). This does not, however, happen in aC# contexts: *tmaddanat* 'she became urbanite' (become_urbanite.PFV.3FS). The negated form surfaces as follows: *mā tmaddanát-əš* 'she did not become urbanite' [ma(:) tmadda'natɪʃ]. The path that led to this surface form is similar to the Ammani/Palestinian one highlighted above: *mā* + *tmáddanat* + *š* → *mā tmaddanát-š* (stress shift) → *mā tmaddanát-əš* (anaptyctic insertion). What this means is that *-š* tends to be clitic-like after iC# and affixal after aC#.

(477) *lā bitwassx-əš*

no stain.IPFV.3FS-NEG

'No, it doesn't stain'

Figure 8: Prosody of *bitwassx-əš* 'it doesn't stain' (pitch in blue and intensity in green)

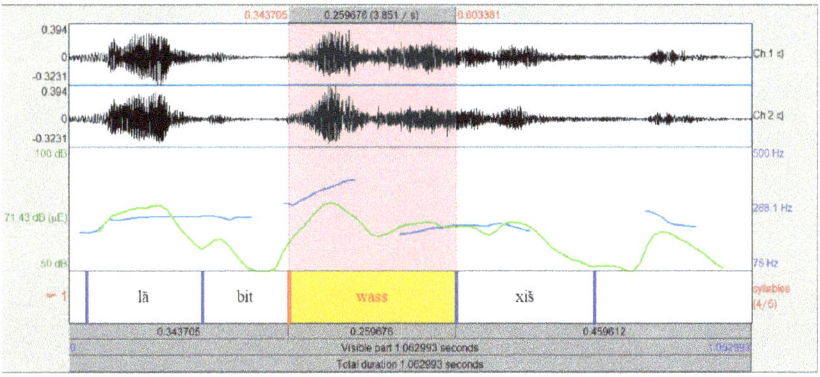

Table 225 summarises the different boundedness statuses of the negators *mā*, *a-* and *-š*. The negator *mā* tends to behave like a free morpheme when it is used as the sole negator, but its boundedness increases when it is used with *-š*. The reduced form *a-* can only be interpreted as a bound form, but, because it retains some length and attaches to the left, it seems best considered an in-between unit. Finally, *-š* has mostly affixal properties, but behaves in certain contexts as a clitic.

Table 225: The status of *mā a- and -š*

	Free		Bound		
			Clitic		Affix
mā		X			
a-			X		
-š				X	

4.5.1.4. Negative Copula

Many dialects of Arabic innovated a negative copula that arose from the grammaticalisation of the negator *mā* and independent or bound pronouns. Although historically an innovation, its frequency of use in sedentary Jordanian is extremely low and it is only attested in the speech of the broadest speakers, to the point that it did not make it into the speech of younger generations or the dialect of Amman (which only has *miš* or variants thereof). Two series are attested, one with *mā* + pronoun and one with *mā* + pronoun + *-š* (Table 226).

Table 226: The negative copula

	mā…		*mā… -š*	
	Singular	Plural	Singular	Plural
1	*māni* ~ *māna*	*maḥna*	*manī-š*	*maḥnā-š*
2M	*mant(e)*	*mantu*	*mant-əš*	*mantū-š*
2F	*manti*	*mantin*	*mantī-š*	*mantinn-əš*
3M	*māhu*	*māhu*	*mahū-š*	*mahumm-əš*
3F	*māhi*	*māhin*	*mahī-š*	*mahinn-əš*

Formally, bound pronouns are selected for the 1SG (*-ni*), 3MP (*-hum*) and 3FS (*-hin*), although 1SG *māni* ~ *manī-š* may be reminiscent of the 1SG pronoun *ani*, commonly found in northern Jordan but extremely marginal in central Jordan, which exhibits *ana*. The forms *māna* and *māni* are attested in the corpus (478), but not *manā-š*, only *manī-š*, which may suggest an asymmetry in the paradigms. The 1SG copula can be reduced to *min* or simply /n/ in *min dāri* ~ *ndāri* 'I don't know' (< *māni dāri*). For the other persons, the free pronouns are selected.

(478) *waḷḷa māna dāri lēš*

by_God COP.NEG.1SG know.AP.MS why

'I really don't know why'

waḷḷa māni xābir

by_God COP.NEG.1SG know.AP.MS

'I really don't know'

Brustad (2000, 297) suggests that, in dialectal Arabic, the main trigger for the use of the negative copula instead of the uninflected negator is "to negate a presupposition on the part of the interlocutor." It parallels the use of *miš* and *mū* as counter-assumptive negators. This interpretation partially fits our data. Consider the following passage (479). The speaker qualifies the social and economic situation of his interlocutor with the term *midin* 'urbanite' and states that, contrarily to his interlocutor, he himself belongs to a social stratum that cannot afford basic commodities such as a mat or a bed. The use of the negative copula *maḥna* 'we are not' negates the assumption of the interlocutor that they too have easy access to these commodities.

(479) *intu midin kṯīr ʕalē-na waḷḷa maḥna mlāgīn*

2MP urbanite much on-1PL by_God COP.NEG.1PL find.AP.MP

ǧambiyye nnām ʕalē-ha frāš nugʕud

mat sleep.SBJV.1PL on-3FS bed sit.SBJV.1PL

ʕalē waḷḷa maḥna mlāgīn əfrāš

on.3MS by_God COP.NEG.1PL find.AP.MP bed

'My friend, you are much more urbanised than us, I swear we can't even find a mat to sleep on, a bed to sit, we can't even find a bed!'

In other cases, the counter-assumptive use of the copula cannot be inferred from the context, as shown by the following passage in which there is no apparent assumption on the part of the interlocutor. There are very few semantic restrictions on the use of the post-posed negator *-š*. The main one is that it cannot co-occur with the assertion marker *wa̤l̤la* 'by God' or any of its variants. The use of *miš* is therefore inhibited by the presence of *wa̤l̤la*, which in turn imposes the use of the negative copula, at least in the speech of those speakers whose grammar still has it.

(480) *wa̤l̤la yā ʕamm-i māhum əmgaṣṣrīn law ʕind-ak*
by_God VOC uncle-1SG COP.NEG.3MP mistake.AP.MP if at-2MS
ruzgut id-dinya u ʕind-ak akl id-dinya u mā
provision DEF-world and at-2MS food DEF-world and NEG
bitnām-əš mirtāḥ wa̤l̤lāhi mant əbxēr
sleep.IPFV.2MP-NEG relax by_God COP.NEG.2MS well
'They (the rulers of Jordan) did well by us. I'm telling you, you could have wealth, enough food and all of that, but you would not be well unless you have peace of mind.'

4.5.1.5. *miš*

The negator *miš* has much currency across the Levant. It is by far the most common one in central and northern Jordan. The realisation *muš* is also sporadically attested (ten tokens). The reflex *mū* is also used, but is extremely marginal (only four tokens across the corpus). *miš* is used to negate nouns, adjectives, participles, prepositional phrases and their respective pro-forms used as predicates.

(481) *miš gādir aḥči*
NEG can.AP.MS speak.SBJV.1SG
'I can't speak'

(482) *ǧīl awwal miš zayy ǧīl il-yōm*
generation before NEG like generation DEF-day
'Yesterday's generation is not like today's generation'

The morpheme *miš* can surface before verbal predicates, but in this case it has scope over the whole clause, not only the predicate, and is used to negate an assumption that the speaker judges inferable from the context or the co-text. Interestingly, all the examples of *mū* fall within this category, as illustrated in (485), which may suggest a partial complementary distribution between *miš* and *mū*.

(483) *ana bōkil yā xāḷa miš mā bōkl-əš*
1SG eat.IPFV.1SG VOC aunty NEG NEG eat.IPFV.1SG-NEG
'Not that I don't eat, aunty, I do eat (fruits)'

(484) *ha-z-zalame tarak ha-l-mara miš tarak-ha*
DEM-DEF-man leave.PFV.3MS DEM-DEF-woman NEG leave.PFV.3MS-3FS
il-mara badd-(h)a trawwiḥ ʕala ahəl-ha
DEF-woman want-3FS go.SBJV.3FS to family-3FS
'The man left the woman, well it's not that he left her, the woman wanted to go back to her family'

(485) *mū xalīl kān ybīʕ banāt-o bi l-kīlo*
NEG Khalil be.PFV.3MS sell.SBJV.3MS daughter-3MS in DEF-kilo
'Wasn't Khalil selling his daughters in huge quantities (i.e., marrying them off one after the other)?'

4.5.1.6. Auxiliaries

In auxiliary constructions involving *kān*, *ḍall* and *baga*, negation can mark either the auxiliary, as in (486), or the auxiliated predicate, as in (487) and (488).

(486) *mā kāṇ-əš bī-ha nās əkṯīr*
NEG be.PFV.3MS-NEG in-3FS people many
'There weren't many people in it'

(487) *kān mā bī-hā-š madāris banāt*
be.PFV.3MS NEG in-3FS-NEG schools girls
'There were no schools for girls in it'

(488) *ḍallu mā ykallilū-hā-š*[5]
stay.PFV.3PM NEG crown.SBJV.3MP-3FS-NEG
'They used not to marry her (to close cousins)'

4.5.1.7. *lā*

As shown above, the negator *lā* is also used in the negative imperative. The negative imperative is simply the bare imperfective in the second person negated with *(mā)... (-š)* or *(lā)... (-š)*. It is also used in optative clauses:

(489) *aḷḷa lā yuğubr-ič yā mēmt-i*
God NEG repair-2FS VOC mother-1SG
'May God not heal you mother!'

---

[5] *kallal–ykallil* is a specifically Christian term that refers to getting married in church. The term *ykallil* is derived from *klīl*, which is the crown placed on the heads of the bride and groom in the church ceremony.

4.5.1.8. *balāš*

The morpheme *balāš* arose from the lexicalisation of *bala* 'without' and *ši* 'thing'. It became a noun whose meaning is close to 'nothing', because it is most commonly found as the object of a preposition, such as *b-balāš* 'for nothing, gratis', *aḥsan min balāš* 'better than nothing'. The morpheme further grammaticalised into a negation marker which can precede another nominal or a verb in the bare imperfective, as shown in (490).

(490) *sakkr-o* *balāš* *yḏall* *šaġġāl*
close.AP.MS-3MS nothing remain.SBJV.3MS working
'Switch it off, no need for it to keep working'

4.5.1.9. *lā... walā...* 'neither... nor...'

Arabic uses the morphemes *lā... walā* in contrastive negation coordinations. There is no restriction on the nature of the coordinated constituents, whether phrasal as in (491) or clausal as in (492). The first element can be realised as *wala*, as in (493). When two non-clausal constituents are coordinated, the main predicate is negated and the morpheme *lā* can be omitted, as in (494).

(491) *mā ʕind-čī-š lā hadrāt walā fatlāt*
NEG at-2FS-NEG neither excessive_speech nor turning
'Neither do you speak nonsense nor are you sneaky'

(492) *lā bigra walā buktub*
neither read.IPFV.3MS nor write.IPFV.3MS
'He can't read or write'

(493) *walā ʕalē-ha laban walā ʕalē-hā zibde*

nor on-3FS yoghurt nor on-3FS butter

'There is neither yoghurt nor butter on it'

(494) *a-btiʕirf-əš tuṭbux walā tunfux*

NEG-know.IPFV.2MS-NEG cook.SBJV.2MS neither inflate.SBJV.2MS

'You can neither cook nor inflate (i.e., you won't be able to cook at all)'

The morpheme *walā* is also used as a categorical negation marker. It can have scope both over clausal (495) and non-clausal constituents (496). This construction presumably arose from the grammaticalisation of the ellipsis of the first element.

(495) *walā gādir atṣawwar-hum*

no can.AP.MS imagine.SBJV.1SG-3MP

'I can't even bear them'

(496) *walā guṭʕa b-ḥačy-ak*

no cut in-speech-2MS

'I don't mean to interrupt you'

4.5.1.10. Negation of Indefinites

4.5.1.10.1. 'Nothing'

The negation of non-human indefinites is done with a negated predicate and the morpheme *iši*, irrespective of the syntactic function in which it appears. Note that there is no restriction on the negation marker *-š*, which can co-occur with an indefinite.

(497) *mā ḏall-əš iši barra*

NEG stay.PFV.3MS-NEG thing outside

'Nothing remained outside'

(498) *mā badd-i min ruzugt iši*
NEG want-1SG from wealth thing
'I don't want any (of his) wealth'

4.5.1.10.2. 'Nobody'

The negation of human indefinites employs three morphemes: *ḥada, nās* and *wāḥad.* The morphemes *ḥada* and *nās* refer to non-specific indefinites. The distribution of *ḥada* in the data suggests that speakers favour *ḥada* in subject position and *nās* in other syntactic positions. In subject position, *ḥada* combines with *mā,* with which it exhibits various degrees of coalescence: *mā ḥadd, mā ḥada, maḥada.* Another variant is *maḥadāš,* but it was recorded only once in Northern Jordan (501).

(499) *mā ḥadd yigdar ygarrib ʕalē-hum*
NEG someone can.SBJV.3MS approach.SBJV.3MS on-3MP
'Nobody could approach them'

(500) *il-yōm maḥada bismaʕ la harǧ wāḥad*
DEF-day nobody hear.IPFV.3MS to speech one
'These days nobody listens to what someone has to say'

(501) *maḥadāš biʕrif ġēr ana*
nobody know.IPFV.3MS except 1SG
'No one knows except me'

The morpheme *ḥada* was recorded alone (not in *maḥada*) in spontaneous speech only once, as the one-argument of an existential clause. The same speaker repeated the same sentence but this time using *nās* in the same position (502).

(502) *a-bī-š* *ḥada* *bsakkir* *ʕalē-na*

a-bī-š *nās* *bsakkir* *ʕalē-na*

NEG-EXIST-NEG anyone close.IPFV.3MS on-1PL

‘No one is blocking the view in front of us’

The morpheme *nās* has no restrictions and can be used in all syntactic positions. In subject position, it also combines with *mā*, but unlike *maḥada*, they remain two separate phonological words, as in (503).

(503) *il-ḥāle* *lli* *ḏugət-ha* *mā* *nās*

DEF-situation REL taste.PFV.1SG NEG anyone

ḏāg-ha *bi* *d-dinya*

taste.PFV.3MS-3FS in DEF-world

‘Nobody in this world went through the things I went through’

Example (504) illustrates the use of *nās* in object position. When examples with *ḥada* in object position are elicited, speakers judge them grammatical. The fact that this option was not recorded in spontaneous speech suggests that the native morpheme for non-specific human indefinites is *nās* and that *ḥada* is a new-comer. It was first integrated in subject positions in *maḥada*, and is making its way to other syntactic positions.

(504) *bilāgī-š* *nās* *yiḥči* *maʕ-o*

find.IPFV.3MS-NEG anyone speak.SBJV.3MS with-3MS

‘He can’t find anyone to talk to’

The morpheme *wāḥad* can also be used in negative polarity, but it refers to a specific indefinite. In subject position, it also combines with *mā* without phonological integration, as in (505).

(505) *mā wāḥad ʕalē w ana mawǧūd*

NEG one on.3MS and 1SG present

'None (of you) shall pick on him while I'm here'

4.5.1.10.3. 'Never'

Speakers of Arabic encode the negation of the temporal indefinite with the morpheme *ʕumr* 'life'. Two constructions are attested: *ʕumər mā* and *mā ʕumər*. If the subject is an indefinite NP, *ʕumər mā* is selected (506). If the subject is definite, both orders are possible, but the subject is coreferenced by a bound pronoun that attaches to *ʕumr*, as in (507) and (508).

(506) *ʕumər mā mara ḥačat maʕ mara*

life NEG woman speak.PFV.3FS with woman

'No woman ever quarrelled with another woman'

(507) *lə-fḥēṣ ʕumər-ha mā ġilṭat maʕ wāḥad*

DEF-Fḥēṣ life-3FS NEG be_mistaken.PFV.3FS with someone

'Fḥēṣ never did anything wrong to anyone'

(508) *mā ʕumr-ū-š yaʕgūb axaḏ arāḏ̣ī-na*

NEG life-3MS-NEG Yaʕgūb take.PFV.3MS lands-1PL

'Yaʕgūb (Jacob) never took our lands'

Pronominal subjects permit both orders. The postposed negator *-š* is not permitted with *ʕumər mā* (509), only with *mā ʕumər* (510).

(509) *ʕumər-ha mā ndāsat*

life-3FS NEG be_stepped.PFV.3FS

'It was never stepped on'

(510) *mā ʕumər-hā-š ağat*

NEG life-3FS-NEG come.PFV.3FS

'She never came'

4.5.1.11. Exceptive Constructions

Semantically, exceptive constructions are defined as the expression of a quantificational relation between a set X and a set Y in which the property assigned to X is denied to Y (Galal and Kahane 2018). The following conditions have to be fulfilled:

- X and Y have inverse predicative polarities
- Y set is within X set
- Both sets have to be delimited
- X is universally quantified
- X must substantially outnumber Y

In the dialects discussed here, the most common exceptive markers are *ġēr* and *illa*. Their different natures are reflected in their different morpho-syntactic behaviour.

The morpheme *ġēr* is a nominal whose lexical meaning is 'other'.

(511) *brāhīm mā ʕind-hū-š ġēr walad u bint*

Ibrahim NEG at-3MS-NEG except boy and girl

'Ibrahim only has a boy and a girl'

It can be followed by a bound pronoun, as in (512) and (514), or a free pronoun, as in (513) and (515). The free pronoun construction is pragmatically marked and is selected when the excepted entity is focused. Focus marking is flagged by means of rising pitch on the pronoun. Interestingly, the syntactic role of the excepted referent plays no role at all, because both constructions are permitted with objects, as in (512) and (513), and subjects, as in (514) and (515).

(512)	*mā*	*ǧāb-əš*	*ġēr-ha*
	NEG	bring.PFV.3MS-NEG	except-3FS

‘She was his only daughter (he had no other offspring)’

(513)	*mā*	*ǧāb-əš*	*ġēr*	*hī*
	NEG	bring.PFV.3MS-NEG	except	3FS

‘She was his only daughter (he had no other offspring)’

(514)	*maḥada*	*yǧīb-li*	*kāst*	*il-gahwa*	*ġēr-o*
	nobody	bring.SBJV.3MS-DAT.1SG	glass	DEF-coffee	except-3SG

‘No one except him would bring me a cup of coffee’

(515)	*maḥada*	*yǧīb-li*	*kāst*	*il-gahwa*	*ġēr*	*hū*
	nobody	bring.SBJV.3MS-DAT.1SG	glass	DEF-coffee	except	3SG

‘No one except him would bring me a cup of coffee’

If the excepted constituent is pronominal, the marker *illa* can only be followed by a free pronoun, whether a subject (516) or an object (517).

(516)	*mā*	*ʔil-ha*	*ʔilla*	*hummu*
	NEG	for-3FS	except	3PL

‘She only has them’

(517)	*mā*	*xallaf-əš*	*illa*	*hū*
	NEG	procreate.PFV.3SG	except	3MS

‘He was his only son’

The morpheme *minʕada* was also recorded once (518), which is reminiscent of the preposition *min* and the exceptive marker *ʕada*, as found elsewhere in Arabic. The morpheme *siwa* was also recorded once, but in an incomplete utterance. Unlike in other varieties, like Maghrebi Arabic, exceptive morphemes do not restrict the occurrence of the negative marker *-š*.

(518) *wlād-i* *kull-hum* *bi* *s-salṭ* *minʕada* *bičr-i*
children-1SG all-3MP in DEF-Salt except elder-1SG
'All my children are in Salt except my eldest'

4.5.2. Focalisation and Topicalisation

We follow Krifka (2008, 247), who provides the following definition for focus: "Focus indicates the presence of alternatives that are relevant for the interpretation of linguistic expressions." Krifka (2008, 265) also gives the following working definition for the notion of topic: "The topic constituent identifies the entity or set of entities under which the information expressed in the comment constituent should be stored in the C(ommon) G(round) content." We explore here the formal means of marking a term as occupying the discursive roles of topic and focus respectively. These can be prosodic, or morphosyntactic. It should be kept in mind that the study of information structure in spoken Arabic is still in its infancy (although see the articles in Owens and Elgibali 2010) and the strategies discussed below are not claimed to be exhaustive.

(a) Topicalisation
  a. Left-dislocation
  b. Right-dislocation
  c. Y-movement

(b) Focalisation
  a. Pitch-raising and fronting
  b. Clefting
  c. The proclitic *ma*

4.5.2.1. Left-dislocation

Left-dislocation is the most common topicalisation strategy. All syntactic roles are eligible for left-dislocation. A resumptive pronoun occupies the position of the dislocated term. In (519), both the first-person subject and the locative adjunct are left-dislocated. The locative adjunct *manṭiga* 'area' is cross-referenced on the preposition *fī* 'in' with the 3FS bound pronoun *-ha*. The first-person subject is already indexed on the verb *tbahdalt*, so no resumptive pronoun is available in this case.

(519) *ana ha-l-manṭiga hāḏi lli tbahdalt*
1SG DEM-DEF-area DEM REL be_scolded.PFV.1SG
fī-ha mā raḥ aḏ̣all sākin fī-ha
in-3FS NEG FUT stay.SBJV.1SG dwell.AP.MS in-3FS
'I, in this place where I was scolded, I won't stay (I won't stay in a place where I was humiliated)'

Example (520) illustrates left-dislocation of the object *il-arbʕīn lēra* 'the forty dinars', and the 3FP resumptive pronoun *-hin* that suffixes to the verb. Only entities that are part of the common ground are eligibile for topicalisation. These are typically proper nouns and definite NPs. Consequently, left-dislocated constituents are either proper nouns or definite NPs. In terms of prosody, the left-dislocated term has a separate intonational contour.

(520) *il-yōm il-arbʕīn lēra btistaḥi*

DEF-day DEF-forty dinar be_ashamed.IPFV.2MS

tiʕṭī-hin la bint-ak

give.SBJV.2MS-3FP to girl-2MS

'Nowadays you would be ashamed to give forty dinars to your daughter (because money has decreased in value due to inflation)'

Contrastive topicalisation through left-dislocation also often occurs with adversative conjunctions such as *bass* 'but' (§4.6.5.2.1) and *amma* 'whereas' (§4.6.5.2.2), which are followed by the focused constituent, as in (521), where the adverb *awwal* 'before' occurs right after *amman* and is topicalised.

(521) *il-yōm hōšātt-(h)um ʕan ṭarīg iz-zaʕrane*

DEF-day quarrels-3MP from way DEF-thuggery

amman awwal miš ʕan ṭarīg iz-zaʕrane

whereas before NEG from way DEF-thuggery

'These days, the way they quarrel is pure thuggery, whereas back in the day, it wasn't'

4.5.2.2. Right-dislocation

Right-dislocation is also a common feature of the present dialect. Like left-dislocation, it involves a resumptive pronoun. Prosodically, right-dislocated constituents are de-accented, unlike left-dislocated constituents, which can be prosodically prominent. These facts are in line with what has been observed cross-linguistically (Lambrecht 2001). Lambrecht (2001, 1072) also notes that, although dislocation in general is a topic-marking device, left-dislocation flags a topic announcement and right-dislocation flags a topic continuation. In all the examples below, the dislocated constituent is already topical. In (522), the conversation was about Muslim-Christian relations, so the topic 'Christians' is already established. In (523), the discussion is about an individual named Ǧamāl who is a candidate in a local election, and in (524), the informant talks about her first boy (*il-walad* 'the boy' is indexed on *bī* 'in him').

(522) *barḏo minrūḥ ənʕazzī-hum il-masīḥiyye*
also go.IPFV.1PL offer_condolences.SBJV.1PL DEF-Christians
'Also, we (Muslims) offer condolences to them, the Christians (when they have a bereavement)'

(523) *waḷḷa ġēr aṣawwit-lo la ǧamāl*
by_God HORT vote.SBJV.1SG-DAT.3MS to Ǧamāl
'I will definitely vote for him, Ǧamāl (the candidate)'

(524) *mā kunt əmfakkir bī l-walad*
NEG be.PFV.1SG think.AP.MS in.3MS DEF-boy
'I didn't use to pay attention to him, the boy (her son)'

There is an interesting formal difference between left- and right-dislocation with dative objects, as shown in (523), where the dislocated constituent is marked with the preposition *la*. Left-dislocation would have yielded (525). The right-dislocated construction bears resemblance to the differential object marking with *la* in Northern Levantine dialects and a diachronic link is not excluded.

(525) *waḷḷa ǧamāl ġēr aṣawwit-lo*
by_God Ǧamāl HORT vote.SBJV.1SG-DAT.3MS
'I will vote for Ǧamāl'

4.5.2.3. Y-movement

The term Y-movement here is taken from Givòn (2001, 262). Very common in English (e.g., 'That I don't like'), it is characterised as a contrastive topicalisation strategy. Formally, it refers to the fronting of a constituent without a resumptive pronoun. Our data only provides tokens in negative polarity and with indefinite objects, as exemplified below. Semantically, it could be glossed 'as far as X is concerned…'. It differs prosodically from the pitch-raising and fronting strategy (§4.5.2.4) because no rising pitch is assigned to the fronted constituent.

(526) *ʕaša, badd-nā-š*

dinner want-1PL-NEG

'Dinner, we don't want'

(527) *mallīm, mā axaḏ*

money_unit NEG take.PFV.3MS

'A dime, he didn't take'

(528) *ḥaki zyāde mā badd-na nismaʕ*

talk excessive NEG want-1PL hear.SBJV.1PL

'More talk (like that), we don't want to hear'

4.5.2.4. Pitch-raising and Fronting

As in other languages, the dialect discussed here combines one prosodic strategy and one syntactic strategy to flag that a constituent is focused: rising pitch and intensity combined with fronting. In (529), one speaker asks another speaker whether they used to get their water using animals to carry it from the spring. The second speaker replies in (530) that women would carry it on their head. The focus on *in-niswān* (DEF-women) and *ʕa rūs-hin* (on head-3FP) is signalled by means of a rising pitch, followed by a lowering pitch on *yṭīḥin* 'they go down' and *yğībin* 'they bring', as shown in Figure 9. Both constituents are fronted. The subject *in-niswān* 'women' occurs preverbally and not postverbally because it is focused, although the preverbal position is normally available to subjects.

(529) *intu mnēn tišrabu kuntu?*
2MP whence drink.SBJV.2MP be.PFV.2MP
twarrdu ʕala d-dawāb?
get_water.SBJV.2MP on DEF-animals
'Where did you get your water from? Did you carry the water on animals?'

(530) *lā waḷḷa [n-niswān]$_{\text{FOC}}$ yṭīḥin,*
no by_God DEF-women descend.SBJV.3FP
[ʕa rūs-hin]$_{\text{FOC}}$ yğībin
on head-3FS bring.SBJV.3FP
'No, women used to go down (to the spring), they used to bring (water) on their heads'

Figure 9: Rising pitch (blue) and intenstity (green) on focused constituents

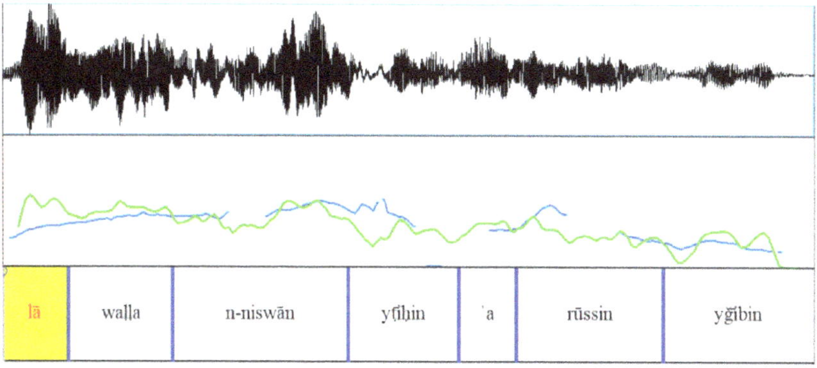

4.5.2.5. Clefting

Cleft constructions are a topicalisation strategy. Payne (1997, 278–79) formalises cleft constructions in the following way: NP_i (COP) $[...NP_1...]_{Srel}$, that is a noun phrase (NP_i) and a relative clause whose relativised nominal is coreferential with NP_i. Such constructions are also attested in the dialects described here, only with a slight difference: the use of a pronoun to avoid a headless relative clause. The clefted term is clause-initial, followed by a coreferential pronoun and a relative clause, yielding a non-verbal predicate, as shown in (531) and (532). The construction described here is not very common in the corpus.

(531) [*is-sukkar*]$_{SUBJ}$ [*hū lli mišġil bāl-i*]$_{PRED}$
DEF-sugar 3SG REL occupy.AP.MS mind-1SG
'(Blood) sugar (level) is what worries me'

(532) [*lə-bhārāt*]$_{SUBJ}$ [*hinne lli bifassdin il-akəl*]$_{PRED}$
DEF-spices 3FP REL corrupt.IPFV.3FP DEF-food
'Spices are what spoil food'

4.5.2.6. The Proclitic *ma*

Although the morpheme *ma* is found in many dialects of Arabic, both western and eastern, many descriptions do not even mention it. It is, however, mentioned in Ritt-Benmimoun (2014) for Southern Tunisia, Woidich (2006) for Cairo, Roset (2018) for Darfour and Herin (2010) for Salt. Manfredi (2008) provides an in-depth analysis of *ma* in Kordofan, where he defines *ma* as a counter-assertive focus marker. In Kordofanian Arabic, it exhibits very few restrictions as far as its host is concerned. The prosodic characteristics of *ma* seem to be shared by all dialects of Arabic in that it remains unstressed and does not affect stress assignment on the host, unlike the negation marker *mā*, which attracts stress. This is exemplified in (533), whose prosody is shown in Figure 10. The proclitic *ma* is clearly less prominent in terms of duration, pitch (blue) and intensity (green) than the negator *mā*.

(533) *ma hummu mā l-(h)um mixtār hōna*
TOP 3MP NEG for-3MP chief here
'(As you know), they don't have a chief here'

Figure 10: The prosody of the proclitic *ma* vs the negator *mā*

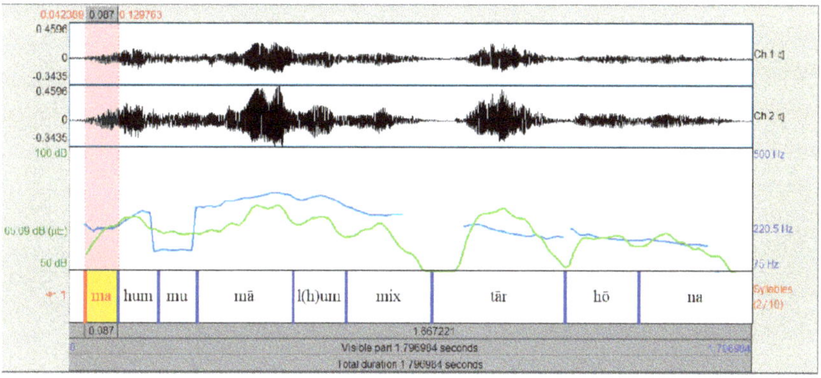

In the dialects considered here, the marker *ma* only selects verbs and free pronouns as hosts. Cliticisation on verbs mostly occurs with the verb *gāl–ygūl* 'say' (534), although sporadically on other verbs too (535), making free pronouns the most common host. When *ma* cliticises to free pronouns, vowel-initial pronouns undergo apheresis, as shown in Table 227.

Table 227: *ma* + free pronouns

	Singular	Plural
1	*ma-na*	*ma-ḥna*
2M	*ma-nt* ~ *ma-nte*	*ma-ntu*
2F	*ma-nti*	*ma-ntin*
3M	*ma-hū* ~ *ma-huwwa*	*ma-hummu*
3F	*ma-hī* ~ *ma-hiyye*	*ma-hinne*

(534)

il-mirbaʕāniyye	*ma*	*bagul-lak*	*bikūn*
DEF-mirbaʕāniyye	TOP	say.IPFV.1SG-DAT.2MS	be.IPFV.3MS

bī-ha	*bard*	*u*	*ṣagʕa*	*kṯīr*
in-3FS	cold	and	ice	much

'The *mirbaʕāniyye*, I'm telling you, it's when it's freezing cold'[6]

(535) Speaker 1:

gult-ilha	*ma-banēt-lič*	*ʕamāra*
say.PFV.1SG-DAT.3FS	TOP-build.PFV.1SG-DAT.2FS	block

'I told her "(as you know), I did build a (whole) block for you"'

Speaker 2:

ma-banēt-ilha	*ʕamāra*
TOP-build.PFV.2SG-3FS	block

'You did build a (whole) block for her'

The discourse function of *ma* is to signal that the speaker considers that the information conveyed should already be known to the hearer, either because it has been previously mentioned or

[6] The term *mirbaʕāniyye* is derived from *arb ʕīn* 'forty' and refers to the coldest period during the winter season, which is roughly 21 December–30 January.

because it is part of the common ground. In the conversation reported below (536), speaker 1 asks about the health of a woman called ʕawāṭif. Speaker 2 replies saying that she is fine, after which speaker 1 recalls that her health condition has improved. Speaker 2 then adds that it is not unexpected that she is feeling better, because, as speaker 1 may have heard, she had an operation.

(536) Speaker 1:

ʕawāṭif mnīḥa ṣiḥḥitt-(h)a?
ʕawāṭif good health-3FS
'Is ʕawāṭif's health ok?'

Speaker 2:

ḥamdilla xāla mnīḥa
praise_God aunt good
'She is fine, auntie'

Speaker 1:

baṭṭalat tōǧiʕ-ha miʕditt-(h)a
stop.PFV.3FS hurt.SBJV.3FS-3FS stomach-3FS
'She stopped having stomach ache'

Speaker 2:

ma-hī ʕimlat ʕamaliyye
TOP-3FS do.PFV.3FS operation
'Well (as you may have heard) she had an operation'

In example (537), the conversation is about ʕōde Abu Tāyih, an important figure in Jordanian history who rebelled against the Ottomans. Speaker 1 says that he was from Maan, a city in southern Jordan, and belonged to the Ḥwēṭāt tribe, an important confederation of tribes in Southern Jordan. Speaker 2 asks whether he was imprisoned, to which speaker 1 answers that he was imprisoned in the local Ottoman jail in Salt. Speaker 3, wanting to emphasise that ʕōde Abu Tāyih was an important man, says he was a sheikh from the Bani Ṣaxr tribe, another important Bedouin tribe, contradicting speaker 1. Speaker 1 corrects him, saying that he was from Maan, and that Maan is mostly inhabited by members of the Ḥwēṭāt tribe. The use of *ma* in the last utterance signals to speaker 3 that the correct assertion is part of the co-text (it has been previously mentioned), and also the context, because speaker 3 is expected to be aware that Maan is mostly inhabited by members of the Ḥwēṭāt tribe.

(537) Speaker 1:

ʕōde abu tāyih hāḏa ḥwēṭi min mʕān ʕurbān mʕān
NAME DEM ḥwēṭi from Maan Bedouins Maan
'ʕŌde Abu Tāyih was from the Ḥwēṭāt tribe from the Bedouins of the city of Maan'

Speaker 2:

tara nḥabas willa…
DM imprison.PFV.3MS or
'Was he imprisoned or (was he not)?'

Speaker 1:

hōn bi s-siǧən bass mā laḥḥagnā-ha ḥna
here in DEF-prison but NEG know.PFV.1PL-3FS 1PL
'Here, in the prison, but we didn't witness it'

Speaker 3:

ʕōde abu tāyih hāḏa šēx min mašāyix bani ṣaxər

NAME DEM sheikh from sheikhs Ṣaxr tribe

'ʕōde Abu Tāyih was a important man from the Bani Ṣaxr tribe'

Speaker 1:

lā lə-mʕāniyye lə-ḥwēṭāt ā

no DEF-Ma'anis DEF-Ḥwēṭis yes

ma-hī mʕān kull-ha ḥwēṭāt

TOP-3FS Ma'an all-3FS Ḥwēṭis

'No, (he was from) the Maanis, Ḥwēṭāt Tribe. (You should know that) all the inhabitants of Maan are Ḥwēṭis'

As noted above, the morpheme *ma* can only attach to verbs and free pronouns, so when it has scope over a NP, it attaches to a free pronoun coreferential with said NP, as in (537) in *ma-hī mʕān*, where 3FP *hī* coreferences the proper noun *mʕān* 'Ma'an' (names of cities are feminine). Consequently, a hypothetical sequence such as ***ma-mʕān* is not attested in our dataset. Other examples of *ma* attaching to free pronouns are found below in (538) and (539).

(538) *ma-na kunt aštġil bi l-furən*

TOP-1SG be.PFV.1SG work.SBJV.1SG in DEF-oven

w ana zġīr u ʕāriff-(h)in

and 1SG young and know.AP.MS-3FP

'As for me, I used to work in a bakery when I was young, and I know them (the bakeries)'

(539) *iǧ-ǧēš rahal min iḏ-ḏiffe ma-hummu*

DEF-army leave.PFV.3MS from DEF-bank TOP-3MP

ġaǧǧū-hum

expel.PFV.3MP-3MP

'The army left the West Bank, well, (as you know), they (the Israelis) pushed them out'

The morpheme *ma* can also have scope over clausal constituents, in which case the 3MS free pronoun *hū* seems to be selected by default, as in (540), where *ma-hū* has scope over the clause *staḥallū-ha lə-fḥēṣiyye.*

(540) *ṣāfūṭ ma-hū staḥallū-ha lə-fḥēṣiyye*

Ṣāfūṭ TOP-3MS control.PFV.3MP-3FS DEF-Fḥēṣis

'Ṣāfūṭ, (as you know), The Fḥēṣis took control of it'

Although *ma* is mostly used as a topicaliser, one instance of *ma* used as a focaliser was recorded, in (541), where *ma-hī* coreferences *umm-ha* 'his mother', which is seemingly focused, as suggested by what looks like a pseudo-cleft structure. Another possibility is that *ma-hī* has scope over the entire clause, and the feminine agreement is triggered by the adjacency with *umm* 'mother'.

(541) *lā btiʕrif ma-hī umm-ha lli sāyga*

no know.IPFV.2MS FOC-3FS mother-3FS REL drive.AP.FS

'No, you know, it was her mother who was driving'

The stance here is that *ma* is primarily a topic marker because it mostly precedes left-dislocated nominals. However, since topic and focus are often the two parts of an utterance, flagging a term as a topic is also a way of marking the rest of the utterance as focus. Accordingly, it could also be maintained that *ma* is a strategy for highlighting the focus of an utterance, albeit indirectly.

4.5.3. Non-declarative Sentence Types

4.5.3.1. Exclamatives

The interrogatives *(š)šū* 'what' and *gaddēš* 'how much' can be used to introduce exclamative clauses, as in (542) and (543).

(542) *lakn əššū bačat ʕalē*
 but what cry.PFV.3FS on.3MS
 'How intensely she grieved his death!'

(543) *gaddēš maddēna ḥayāt əb-ha-ǧ-ǧadʕa*
 how_much spend.PFV.1PL life in-DEM-DEF-Ǧadʕa
 'What an eventful life we lived in Ǧadʕa (neighbourhood in Salt)!'

Another construction, commonly found cross-dialectally, involves the morpheme *mā* followed by the elative derivation aCCaC of adjectives (§3.3.1.11). In (544), *aṯgal* derives from the adjective *ṯgīl* 'heavy'. The idiom *ṯgīl id-damm*, literally 'heavy-blooded', is normally used to refer to an annoying person. It remains unclear what the real nature of *mā* is in this construction. It could be a reflex of interrogative *mā*, pronominal *mā*, or the negator *mā*.

(544) *mā (a)ṯgal damm-ak*
 EXCLAM heavier blood-2MS
 'How dreary you are!'

The vocative morpheme *yā* followed by *mā* and a clause can also be used as an exclamative device.

(545) *yā mā mārig ʕa d-dinya*

VOC EXCLAM pass.AP.MS on DEF-world

'How many things have unfolded in this world!'

(546) *yā mā ʕabbēna*

VOC EXCLAM fill.PFV.1PL

'How many times have we packed (vegetables)!'

4.5.3.2. Interrogatives

4.5.3.2.1. Polar Questions

The varieties of Arabic discussed here do not mark polar questions morphosyntactically and rely on intonation. As in many languages, polar questions are marked with a rising contour on the last segment of the utterance, as shown in (547) and Figure 11, where intonation is raised on *mangala* 'mancala game'.

(547) *abu ʕimād gal-lik bukra hū*

Name say.PFV.3MS-DAT.2FS tomorrow 3SG

nāzil yilʕabu mangala

descend.AP.MS play.SBJV.3MP mancala

'Did Abu ʕimād tell you he was going (downtown) tomorrow to play mancala?'

Figure 11: Intonation contour in polar questions

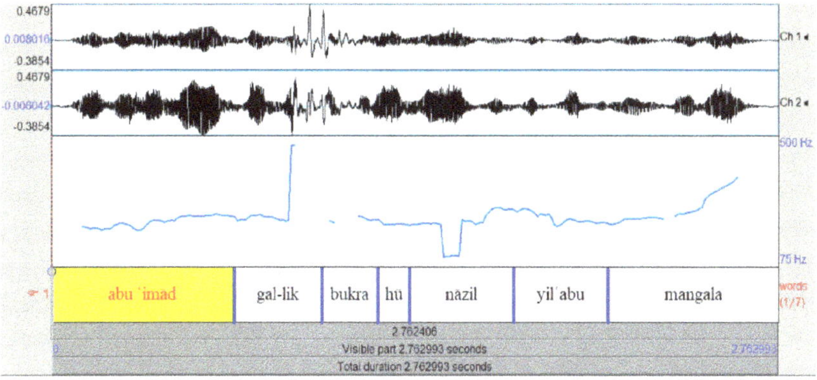

One strategy involves the noun *(i)ši* 'thing' placed clause-finally. This construction seems to originate from the reduction of the phrase *aw (i)ši* 'or something', as shown in (548). This strategy is not fully grammaticalised in Jordanian Arabic, unlike many Lebanese and Syrian varieties which make use of clause-final *ši* as a polar question marker.

(548) *maʕ-hin sayyāra aw ši*
with-3FP car or thing
~
maʕ-hin sayyāra iši
with-3FP car thing
'Do they have a car or anything?'

Tag question markers are clause-final, as exemplified in (549), where the tag marker is *hā*. The intonation contour is also rising on the tag marker (Figure 12).

(549) *inte (a)xatt ragm-(h)a (a)bu ʕimād hā?*
2SG take.PFV.2MS number-3FS name TAG
'Abu ʕimād, you took her number didn't you?'

Figure 12: Rising contour in tag questions

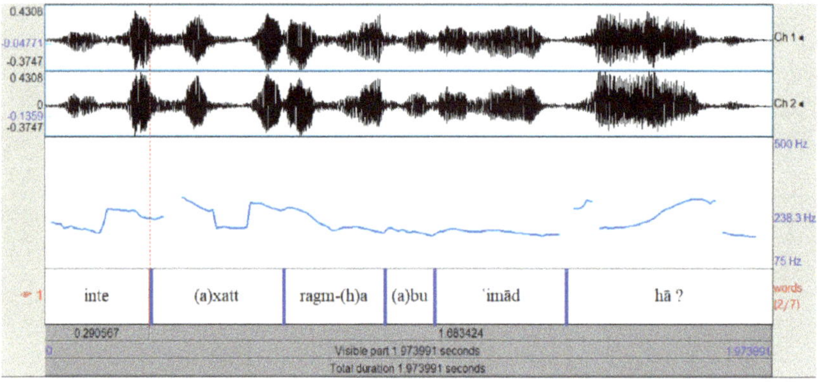

4.5.3.2.2. Content Questions

As in most dialects of Arabic, interrogatives in content questions occur clause-initially, as in (550), where the interrogative *šlōn* 'how' is clause-initial.

(550) *šlōn ṣiḥḥt-ak inšaḷḷa b-xēr*
how health-2MS hopefully in-good
'How is your health? Hopefully good'

If the interrogative is in a non-subject position, a common strategy is to put the interrogative in subject position and use a headless relative clause as non-verbal predicate.

(551) [*manu*]SUB [*lli badd-ič tōxḏī*]PRED
who.M REL want-2FS take.SBJV.2FS.OBJ.3MS
'Who is he whom you want to take (i.e., who do you want to marry)?'

Although the phenomenon is very marginally attested, it seems that the relativiser *illi* may drop, as suggested both by corpus data (552) and elicited examples (553).

(552) *šū* *badd-ak* *iyyā* *issāʕ*
what want-2MS OBJ.3MS now
'What is it that you want now?'

(553) a. *mīn* *ištarēt* *bēt-o*
who buy.PFV.1SG house-3MS
b. *mīn* *illi* *štarēt* *bēt-o*
who REL buy.PFV.1SG house-3MS
c. *bēt* *mīn* *ištarēt*
house who buy.PFV.1SG
'Whose house did you buy?'

If the interrogative is the object of a preposition, the prepositional phrase remains clause-initial.

(554) *ʕal(a)* *ēš* *inḥakam*
on what be_judged.PFV.3MS
'What was he sentenced for?'

As far as word order in interrogative clauses is concerned, our data only exhibit VS:

(555) *šū* *bagat* *in-nās* *tōkil*
what be.PFV.3FS DEF-people eat.SBJV.3FS
'What did people use to eat?'

(556) *wēn* *rāḥu* *z-zġār*
where go.PFV.3MP DEF-small.PL
'Where did the kids go?'

In situ syntax occurs when the speaker knows the answer to the question but has trouble retrieving it, as in (557), where the speaker asks who bought a certain piece of land. The *in situ* placement of the interrogative signals that the speaker knows the answer but is requesting help from the hearer to retrieve it. This non-canonical order is also used when the speaker wants to ask for confirmation of previously given information (echo-questions).

(557) *hāy xad̠att-(h)a manī*
DEM take.PFV.3FS-3FS who.F
'This (land), who took it?'

In situ placement is also used as a discursive device when the speaker wants to introduce a focused constituent, as in (558), where the speaker wants to express that old houses were also built using mud and uses *in situ* syntax to introduce the focused constituent *ṭīn* 'mud'. The same thing occurs in (559), where the speaker introduces a new participant under focus *ʕamm-ha* 'her paternal uncle'.

(558) *hāḏa biʕmalū min ʔēš? min iṭ-ṭīn barḏo*
DEM do.IPFV.3MP from what from DEF-mud too
'What is this it made of? (It is made) of mud too'

(559) *u axaḏ il-arḏ min man? min ʕamm-ha*
and take.PFV.3MS DEF-land from who? from Paternal_uncle-3FS
'And who did he take the land from? From her paternal uncle'

4.5.3.3. Imperatives

In positive polarity, the most straightforward way of expressing imperatives is to use the imperative form of the verb, as in (560), where *uṭubxin* is the second-person feminine plural inflection of the imperative of the verb *ṭabax–yuṭbux* 'cook'.

(560) *iḥna* *minṭīḥ* *tiḥət* *w* *intin*
1PL descend.IPFV.1PL under and 2FP
uṭubxin *ir-ruzz* *fōg*
cook.IMP.FP DEF-rice up
'We go downstairs and you, cook the rice upstairs'

There are of course various ways of softening imperatives by adding phrases such as *baḻḻa* 'by God' and *aḻḻa yisiʕd-ak* 'may God make you happy', sometimes combined with the bare imperfective form of the verb (which expresses subjunctive mood), as in (561).[7]

(561) *tfarǧī* *baḻḻa*
show.SBJV.2MS.OBJ.3MS by_God
'Would you please show him'

The unreal condition conjunction *law* (§4.6.4.11.2) also has a pragmatic function of softening a request:

(562) *law* *ətǧībi* *ha-l-ġaṭa* *maʕlešš*
if bring.SBJV.2FS DEM-DEF-cover you_mind
'Would you mind bringing the cover?'

In negative polarity, the bare imperfective is used, negated with a negator (*lā, (m)ā… -š*; cf. §4.5.1.1)

---

[7] Jordanian Arabic for the most part employs imperfective morphology to express politeness, rather than phrases such as *min faḍlak* 'please', e.g., *(b)taʕṭī-ni l-miləḥ* 'would you pass the salt please'. This strategy is replaced in Ammani by straightforward imperative forms followed by politeness phrases or even English *please*.

(563) *lā tizraʕī-hin bi l-arḏ̣ ḥuṭṭī-hin əb-tanaka*

NEG plant.SBJV.2FS-3FP in DEF-soil put.IMP.FS-3FP in-tin_pot

'Don't plant them in the soil, put them in a tin pot'

4.6. Complex Predicates and Complex Clauses

4.6.1. A Serial Construction

Serial constructions are usually not discussed in the case of Arabic (but see Altakhaineh and Zibin 2018; Versteegh 2011). Creissels (2006b, 280, our translation) defines serial constructions as "complex predicates whose elements lack any overt mark of integration. Either the two verbs are inflected as two independent items or one of them occurs in the bare form and they are not linked by any connecting element."[8] This definition is also echoed in Haspelmath (2016, 296), who states that "a serial verb construction is a monoclausal construction consisting of multiple independent verbs with no element linking them and with no predicate-argument relation between the verbs." According to these definitions, one construction in Jordanian Arabic would qualify as verb serialisation. As far as it is attested in our data, it involves a verb of motion and a verb of action in the imperative (564) or in the perfective (565). Serialisation occurs because the verbs lack any overt mark of integration and because the imperative

[8] « ...des prédicats complexes dont aucun des deux éléments ne présente de marque explicite d'intégration : ou bien les deux verbes sont fléchis comme deux formes verbales indépendantes, ou bien l'un des deux est systématiquement à la forme nue et aucun élément de relation ne les relie. »

and the perfective are not integrative forms of the verb (only the subjunctive is).

(564) *rūḥ* *išrī-lak* *ṣafaṭ* *duxxān*
go.IMP.MS buy.IMP.MS-DAT.2MS pack smoke
'Go get yourself a pack of cigarettes'

(565) *ṭāḥu* *rabaṭu* *xēl-hum* *ʕa* *ha-l-bēdar*
descend.PFV.3MP tie.PFV.3MP horses-3MP to DEM-DEF-granary
'They went down to tie their horses to the granary'

This also extends to the (re)iterative construction with the auxiliary *radd* ~ *riǧiʕ* (566) and the verb *gām* used as sequentialiser (567).

(566) *raddēt* *ruḥət* *ʕa* *l-miḥkama*
return.PFV.1SG go.PFV.1SG to DEF-court
'I went back to court'

(567) *gāmu* *axaḏu* *l-ʕarūs-ēn*
stand.PFV.3MP take.PFV.3MP DEF-bride-DU
'Then they took the two brides'

In the imperfective, the construction does not qualify as verb serialisation, because the second verb is in the subjunctive, which is an integrative form of the verb, as in (568), where the verb *ywaddi* is in the subjunctive.

(568) *ṭāḥ* *ywaddi* *naglit* *gaməḥ*
descend.PFV.3MS carry.SBJV.3MS load wheat
u *ma* *ǧā-š*
and NEG come.PFV.3MS-NEG
'He went to deliver a load of wheat and hasn't come back (yet)'

4.6.2. Complementation

Argumental clausal constituents, whether subject or object, are introduced by the complementiser *inn-*, which inflects as follows. The 3MS form *inno* underwent lexicalisation and became the default uninflected allomorph.

Table 228: Inflections of *inn-*

	Singular	Plural
1	*inn-i*	*in-na*
2M	*inn-ak*	*inn-ku*
2F	*inn-ič*	*inn-čin*
3M	*inn-o*	*inn-hum*
3F	*inn-ha*	*inn-hin*

In subject position, the linear order is PREDICATE SUBJECT, as in (569) and (570). Innovative Levantine dialects permit the use of the relativiser *illi* to introduce clausal constituents in subject position with adjectival predicates. In the current state of the dialect, a sentence such as *mlīḥ illi ṭalaʕt* is not judged ungrammatical but does not occur in the speech of the broadest speakers, which suggests that the traditional dialect only had *inno* in that position.

(569) [*b-munā-y*]$_{PRED}$ [*inn-ak ətrūḥ ətǧīb-hum*]$_{SUBJ}$
in-wish-1SG COMP-2MS go.SBJV.2MS bring.SBJV.2MS-3MP
'My hope is that you would go and bring them'

(570) [*mlīḥ*]$_{PRED}$ [*inno ṭalaʕt*]$_{SUBJ}$
good COMP exit.PFV.2MS
'It's good that you left'

In object position, the clause follows the predicate:

(571) *a̤l̤la biʕrif*$_{\text{PRED}}$ [*inn-ha bint ḥalāl*]$_{\text{OBJ}}$
God know.IPFV.3MS COMP-3FS girl licit
'God knows that she is a good person'

(572) *wa̤l̤la*$_{\text{PRED}}$ [*inno l-ganābil yṭīḥin ʕalē-na*
by_God COMP DEF-grenades descend.SBJV.3FP on-1PL
min lə-xyām]$_{\text{OBJ}}$
from DEF-tents
'I swear the bombs were falling on us while we were in the tents'

Contrary to what happens in the standard variety, adpositional marking is inhibited with verbs whose objects are coded like obliques, as evidenced in (573), where the preposition *bi*, which marks the object of *fakkar* 'think' if it is a NP, does not surface with clausal constituents (** *bi-ʔinno*).

(573) *mfakkir*$_{\text{PRED}}$ [*inno badd-o yiktil-ni hnāk*]$_{\text{OBJ}}$
think.AP.MS COMP want-3MS beat.SBJV.3MS-1SG there
'I thought he wanted to beat me up on the spot!'

The complementiser *inno* is also used when a clausal constituent is used as the modifier in a genitive construction (574):

(574) *ṭallag-ha b-ḥuǧǧit*$_{\text{HEAD}}$ [*inno mā*
divorce.PFV.3MS-3FS in-pretext COMP NEG
badd-ha tuskun əb-qarye]$_{\text{MOD}}$
want-3FS dwell.SBJV.3FS in-village
'He divorced her on the pretext that she didn't want to live in a village'

Although it is not ungrammatical, clausal objects of predicates of volition and related meanings are normally not introduced by the complementiser *inno* (*badd-i inno* 'I want that…'), even when the subjects in the main clause and the complement clause are different. The presence of *inno* is more linked to careful speech planning to avoid ambiguity.

For the sake of comprehensiveness, it should be added that one instance was recorded of the morpheme *tā*, normally used to introduce purpose clauses, as a complementiser, as shown in (575), where it introduces the clausal subject of a non-verbal predicate.

(575) *nādir tā tlāgi wāḥad*
rare COMP find.SBJV.2MS someone
lābis ḥaṭṭa zayy hēk
wear.AP.MS garment like so
'It is very rare to find someone wearing such a (traditional) head garment (called ḥāṭṭa)'

With certain verbs of perception and cognition, such as *fakkar* 'he thought' and *šāf* 'he saw', the subject of the complement clause can be indexed as the object of the verb of the main clause, as in (576) and (577). With the pseudo-verb *badd-* 'want', the subject of the complement clause is referenced on the object carrier *iyyā-*, because it lacks the morphological slot of pronominal objects available on plain verbs, as shown in (578).

(576) *fakkarnā-k ǧāy tisʔal-na*
think.PFV.1PL-2MS come.AP.MS ask.SBJV.2MS-1PL
kēf awḍāʕ-ku
how situations-2MP
'We thought you came to ask us how we were'

(577) *šift-ak gadd id-dār*

see.PFV.1SG-2MS size DEF-house

'I saw you as big as the house'

(578) *kānat il-ḥukūma mā badd-ha yyā yiḥkum*

be.PFV.3MS DEF-government NEG want-3FS OBJ.3MS rule.SBJV.3MS

'The government didn't want him to rule'

4.6.3. Indirect Questions

Indirect polar questions are normally introduced by the conditional morpheme *iḏa* 'if' (579), although *čān* was also recorded once (580):

(579) *mā baʕrif iḏa našart-o*

NEG know.IPFV.1SG if publish.PFV.1SG-3MS

'I don't know if I published it'

(580) *badrī-š čān hū aw wlād-o*

know.IPFV.1SG-NEG if 3MS or children-3MS

ṣār maḥ-ḥum

become.PFV.3MS with-3MP

'I don't know whether (the accident) happened to him or to his children'

Indirect content questions are introduced by interrogative proforms, as in (581) and (582).

(581) *ndāri čēf ǧāb-ha*

I.ignore how bring.PFV.3FS

'I don't know how he got hold of her'

(582) *abṣar* *manu* *māt* *il-yōm*
I_wonder who.M die.PFV.3MS DEF-day
'I wonder who died today'

4.6.4. Adjunctive Subordination

Arabic has a rich set of conjunctions for introducing adjunctive clauses. Some are bare nominals or prepositions such as *yōm* 'day, when' or *min* 'from, as soon as', but most often, they combine a nominal or prepositional element and the complementiser *inno* or the morpheme *mā*, which in the present dialects functions as a negator, a complementiser or a marker of exclamation. The semantic taxonomy used in the sections below is adapted from Thompson, Longacre and Hwang (2007).

4.6.4.1. Temporal/Locational

4.6.4.1.1. *lamma* 'when'

The morpheme *lamma* is attested in all eastern varieties of Arabic. The variant *lamman* has also been recorded.

(583) *waḷḷa* *lamma* *bišidd* *īd-i* *buʕṣur-ha*
by_God when grab.IPFV.3MS hand-1SG squeeze.IPFV.3MS-3FS
'When he grabs my hand, he squeezes it'

4.6.4.1.2. *yōm* 'when'

The noun *yōm* 'day' has grammaticalised into a temporal conjunction 'when'. This is often seen as a feature that made its way into sedentary Jordanian through contact with Bedouin dialects, in which this item is well documented. Many variants were recorded: *yōmin*, *yōminno*, *lōmin*, *lōminno* and also *yāminno*.

(584) *yōminno simiʕ il-harǧ minn-o*
when hear.PFV.3MS DEF-talk from-3MS
gal-lo gūm
say.PFV.3MS-DAT.3MS get_up.IMP.MS
'When he heard the story from him, he told him: get up!'

4.6.4.1.3. *min* 'since'

Originally an ablative preposition, *min* subsequently grammaticalised into a conjunction 'since'.

(585) *min tarak abū-y mātat ḥēl*
since leave.PFV.3MS father-1SG die.PFV.3FS strength
il-arḍ kull-ha
DEF-land all-3FS
'Since my father left, the land lost all its strength'

4.6.4.1.4. *baʕəd-mā* ~ *ʕugub-mā* 'after'

Commonly found in other dialects, the conjunction *baʕəd-mā* combines the preposition *baʕəd* 'after' and *mā*. The variant *ʕugub-mā* is most likely borrowed from neighbouring Bedouin varieties. In this case too, the preposition *ʕugub* 'after' combines with *mā*. Regressive assimilation between /b/ and /m/ frequently occurs, yielding [ʕugumma].

(586) *ʕugum-mā ṣalla gafaz u*
after pray.PFV.3MS jump.PFV.3MS and
ḍall ṭāliʕ bī-ha
stay.PFV.3MS leave.AP.MS with-3FS
'After he prayed, he jumped (from the window) and kept riding (the horse)'

The verb in the complement clause may be in the perfective or the bare imperfective, which correlate respectively with realis and irrealis mood. In the perfective, the event is located in the past and is considered to have occured, whereas the bare imperfective indicates a possible state of affairs without any specific temporal anchoring:

(587)	*baʕəd-mā*	*yiṭilʕū*	*min*	*in-nār*
	after	take_out.SBJV.3MP.OBJ.3MS	from	DEF-fire
	ybarrdū			
	cool.SBJV.3MP.OBJ.3MS			

‘After they take (the pottery) out of the fire, they cool it’

4.6.4.1.5. *gabəl-mā* ‘before’

The conjunction *gabəl-mā* combines the preposition *gabəl* ‘before’ and the subordinator *mā*. Unlike with *baʕəd-mā* ~ *ʕugub-mā*, the verb in the embedded clause is always in the bare imperfective, even if the time of reference is located prior to the time of utterance.

(588)	*gabəl-mā*	*tṣīr*	*marat-i*	*aṭīḥ*
	before	become.SBJV.3FS	wife-1SG	descend.SBJV.1SG
	ʕalē-hum	*ʕa*	*ṣāfūṭ*	
	to-3MP	to	Ṣafūṭ	

‘Before she became my wife I used to go to them in Ṣāfūṭ (to spend time in the dīwān)’

The use of *gabəl* without the subordinator *mā* is also marginally attested:

(589) *xan-ni* *ahaddb-o* *gabl* *ətrūḥi*

let.IMP.MS-1SG trim.SBJV.1SG before go.SBJV.2FS

'Let me sew a frill before you go'

4.6.4.1.6. *ʕa bēn-mā* 'while'

This conjunction combines the prepositions *ʕa* 'on' and *bēn* 'between' and *mā.*

(590) *marrāt* *nitʔaxxar* *ʕa-bēn-mā* *nžīb* *il-ḥaṭab*

times be_late.SBJV.1PL while bring.SBJV.1PL DEF-firewood

'Sometimes we would be late while we fetched firewood'

4.6.4.1.7. *awwal-mā* 'as soon as, when first'

This conjunction combines the ordinal *awwal* 'first' and the subordinator *mā.*

(591) *awwal-mā* *badu* *n-nās* *yusuknu* *fī-ha*

first start.PFV.3MP DEF-people dwell.SBJV.3MP in-3FS

kānat *kull-ha* *ġābāt* *w* *ašǧār*

be.PFV.3FS all-3FS woods and trees

'When people first came to live in it (the town of Fḥēṣ), it was all woods and trees'

4.6.4.1.8. *kull-mā* 'every time'

This conjunction combines the quantifier *kull* 'all, each' and the subordinator *mā*. It means 'every time' (592).

(592) *kull-mā* *yšūf* *ṭifəl* *yibči* *ḥafənt* *ədmūʕ*

every_time see.SBJV.3MS child cry.SBJV.3MS handful tears

'Every time he saw a child, he would shed a handful of tears'

It can also be used in the structure *kull-mā... kull-mā...* in the sense of 'the more... the more...', as shown in (593). Normally there is strict adjacency between *kull* and *mā*, but the speaker in (593) stopped midway through the conjunction and inserted the subject between the two morphemes, which suggests that *mā* is not strictly bound to its host, although it may well be a performance error.

(593) *kull-mā*	*miši*	*ššwayy*	*kull*	*il-ʕiǧəl*	*mā*	*kibir*
the_more	walk.PFV.3MS	few	all	DEF-calf	SUB	grow.PFV.3MS

'The more he walked, the bigger the calf would grow'

4.6.4.1.9. *sāʕit-mā* 'the hour when'

This conjunction combines the construct form of *sāʕa* 'hour' and the subordinator *mā*.

(594) *sāʕit-mā*	*aǧa*	*gaḏ̣ab*	*il-kāse*
when	come.PFV.3MS	grab.PFV.3MS	DEF-glass

'When he came, he grabbed the glass'

4.6.4.1.10. *nhār-mā* 'the day when'

This conjunction combines *nhār* 'day(time)' and *mā*. Only one instance is attested, in an incomplete utterance:

(595) *nhār-mā*	*ṭāḥu*	*ʕa*	*l-bayyāra*
when	descend.PFV.3MP	to	DEF-citrus_trees

'The day they went down to the citrus grove'

4.6.4.1.11. *sant-mā* 'the year when'

This conjunction combines the construct form of *sane* 'year' and *mā*.

(596) *sant-mā ḍarab ʕabdirraḥīm*
when hit.PFV.3MS AbdelRaheem'
'The year he hit AbdelRaheem'

4.6.4.1.12. *maḥall-mā* 'the place where'

This conjunction combines *maḥall* 'place' and *mā*. Equally possible are *makān-mā* and *miṭraḥ-mā*.

(597) *maḥall-mā bidd-ak ətwaggif*
where want-2MS stop.SBJV.2MS
'The place where you want to stop'

4.6.4.2. Manner

4.6.4.2.1. *kaʔinno* 'as if'

This conjunction combines the preposition *ka* 'like' and the subordinator *inno*. It may be reduced to *kinno* or *kanno*. The morpheme *ka* is used in these varieties as a functive preposition 'in the quality of' (§3.9.1.21).

(598) *kaʔinn-ič abṣar ǧārrīt-ni ʕa wiǧh-i*
as_if-2FS I_wonder drag.AP.FS-1SG on face-1SG
'I don't know, it's as if I was dragged there'

4.6.4.2.2. *gadd-mā* 'as much as'

This conjunction combines the noun *gadd* 'size, quantity' and *mā*.

(599) *gadd-mā ʕind-ak rǧāl btigdar*

as_much_as at-2MS men can.IPFV.2MS

tōxuḏ naṣīb-ak min iṯ-ṯānyīn

take.SBJV.2MS share-2MS from DEF-others

'The more men you have, the more you can claim your due from others (i.e., the more power you have, the more rights you can claim)'

4.6.4.2.3. *miṯəl-mā* ~ *zayy-mā* 'like, as'

In the same way as the prepositions *miṯəl* and *zayy* 'as, like' are synonymous, the conjunctions *miṯəl-mā* and *zayy-mā* are fully interchangeable.

(600) *il-lahǧe ḍallat miṯəl-mā hī*

DEF-dialect stay.PFV.3FS as 3FS

'The dialect stayed as it is'

(601) *zayy-mā badd-ak yā daktōr*

as want-2MS VOC doctor

'As you want, doctor!'

4.6.4.3. Causal

4.6.4.3.1. *liʔanno* 'because'

This conjunction combines the preposition *li* 'for' and the subordinator *inno*. Another variant is *lanno*.

(602) *il-balad kull-ha ṣāḥat ʕalē lanno waḥdāne*

DEF-town all-3FS cry.PFV.3FS on.3MS because alone

'The whole town cried (when his son died) because he was the only child'

4.6.4.3.2. *mā dām* ~ *mā zāl* 'given that'

These two conjunctions are equivalent. They arose from the grammaticalisation of the negator *mā* and the verbs *dām* 'last' and *zāl* 'cease'. They do not inflect as verbs any more and can be augmented by bound pronouns coreferencing the subject. The variant *mā dām* is much more common than *mā zāl.* Our data even attest the variant *mā zūn,* from the imperfective stem of *zūl* and the shift of /l/ to /n/.

(603) *mā dām inte ʕind-ak binət w ana ʕind-i binət*

given 2MS at-2MS girl and 1SG at-1SG girl

xalli l-banāt yisharin maʕ baʕəḍ

let.IMP.MS DEF-girls stay_up_at_night.SBJV.3FP with RECP

'Since you have a daughter, and I have a daughter, let them spend the evening together'

(604) *mā zūn-o ḥsēn mabsūṭ*

given_that-3MS Hussein happy

'As long as Hussein is in good health'

4.6.4.4. Result and Purpose

Result and purpose conjunctions are followed by the subjunctive for uncompleted events and by the perfective for completed events.

4.6.4.4.1. *ḥatta* 'until'

The morpheme *ḥatta* has many functions: preposition, scalar additive focus particle, and conjunction. It can surface in collocation with the preposition *la* 'to'.

(605)

biḍall-hum	*yḥarrku*	*fī-ha*	*ḥatta*
stay.IPFV.3SG-3PL	move.SBJV.3PL	in-3FS	until
ṣṣīr	*maḥrūga*		
become.SBJV.3FS	burnt		

'They keep stirring it until it (the coffee beans) is roasted dark'

(606)

btisilgi	*d-dağāğ*	*la*	*ḥatta*	*yistwi*
boil.IPFV.2FS	DEF-chicken	to	until	be_ripe.SBJV.3MS

'You boil the chicken until it's cooked'

4.6.4.4.2. *tā* 'until, in order to'

The conjunction *tā* is also well attested in the area, in varieties of Arabic and in several other languages in the region (e.g., Persian, Kurdish, Aramaic, etc.).

(607)

ḏ̣all	*yrakkiḏ̣*	*yrakkiḏ̣*	*tā*	*sağğal-ha*
stay.PFV.3MS	run.SBJV.3MS	run.SBJV.3MS	until	register.PFV.3MS-3FS

'He kept running and running, until he registered it (a piece of land)'

(608)

biṭḥuṭṭ	*ʕalē-hin*	*šwayyit*	*ṃayye*	*tā*	*yitfakfakin*
put.IPFV.2MS	on-3FP	few	water	until	be_detached.SBJV.3FP

'You pour some water on them until they separate from each other'

4.6.4.4.3. *la-mā* ~ *ta-mā* 'until'

The preposition *la* 'to' and the conjunction *ta* can be augmented with the subordinator *mā*.

(609)

minṭarrg-o	*čfūf*	*la-mā*	*ygūl*	*bass*
knock.IPFV.1PL-3MS	palms	until	say.SBJV.3MS	enough

'We slap him repeatedly until he says enough'

(610)

rāḥat	*ta-mā*	*tirǧaʕ*
go.PFV.3FS	until	return.SBJV.3FS

'It's gone (an idea). (Wait) until it comes back'

The forms *la-mā* and *ta-mā* can be further augmented with the complementiser *inno*, which causes the /ā/ of *mā* to drop: *laminno* (< *la-mā inno*) and *taminno* (< *ta-mā inno*), to which bound pronouns coreferencing the subject of the subordinate can suffix. Reduced forms *lamin* and *tāmn* were also recorded.

(611)

biširrū	*ʕala*	*ṭbāg*	*laminn-o*	*yabas*
spread.IPFV.3MP	on	straw_trays	until-3MS	get_dry.SBJV.3MS

'They spread it (the tomato) on straw trays until it gets dry'

(612)

baġayyib	*taminn-hin*	*yusuktin*	*ʕann-i*
fall_unconscious.IPFV.1SG	until-3FP	hush.SBJV.3FP	from-1SG

'I fall unconscious so that they give me a break'

(613)

ḍall	*waṣfi*	*warā*	*warā*	*tāmn*	*aṭlaʕ-o*
stay	Waṣfi	behind.3MS	behind.3MS	until	take_out.PFV.3MS-3MS

'Waṣfi (t-Tall) pursued the matter until he got him out (of jail)'

4.6.4.4.4. *mšān* 'in order to'

The conjunction *mšān* grammaticalised from the ablative preposition *min* 'from' and the nominal *šān* (< Standard Arabic *šaʔn* 'matter, status'). Other variants are *mišān* and *miššān*, but the full form *min šān* was never recorded. The morpheme *ʕašān* (< *ʕala šān*), which in other varieties may be used as a benefactive preposition 'for', a purpose conjunction 'in order to' and a causal conjunction 'because', is mostly employed as a preposition in the dialects investigated here.

(614) *xallaṣu* *l-gamḥāt* *yinuglū-hin* *mšān*
finish.PFV.3MP DEF-wheat transport.SBJV.3MP-3FP to
yxazznū-hin
store.SBJV.3MP-3FP
'(when) they finished (harvesting) the wheat, they used to transport it in order to store it'

4.6.4.5. Substitutive *badāl-mā* 'instead'

This conjunction combines the conjunction *badāl* 'instead' and the subordinator *mā*. The verb in the subordinate clause is in the subjunctive or the perfective.

(615) *badāl-mā* *ḥaṭṭ-ha* *b-ism* *iṯnēn*
instead put.PFV.3MS-3FS in-name two
ḥaṭṭ-ha *b-ism-o* *hū*
put.PFV.3MS-3FS in-name-3MS 3MS
'Instead of registering (the land) in two names, he registered it in his name'

(616) *badāl-mā yimšin ha-s-salṭiyyāt*

instead walk.SBJV.3FP DEM-DEF-Salti_women

əb-xulgān kān hū yǧīb it-tūbēt

with-traditional_dresses be.PFV.3MS 3MS bring.PFV.3MS DEF-fabric

'Instead of the traditional dresses (made from cheap fabric) that Salti women used to wear, he made available to them Tobit fabric (a better quality fabric)'

4.6.4.6. Additive *xlāf* 'besides'

The morpheme *xlāf* was recorded three times as a preposition (§3.9.1.22) and once as a conjunction (617). It belongs to the old dialect and is probably not making it into the speech of the younger generation.

(617) *xlāf yiǧī-na min barra šurṭa ṯānye*

besides come.SBJV.3MS-1PL from outside police other

'Besides, more policemen came to us from other places'

4.6.4.7. Concessive *maʕinno* 'although'

This conjunction combines the preposition *maʕ* 'with' and the subordinator *inno*.

(618) *kān ʕind-o ġāz maʕinno bēt šaʕər*

be.PFV.3MS at-3MS gas_burner although house hair

'He had a gas burner, although he lived in a tent'

4.6.4.8. Indefinite Concessive

Indefinite concessive clauses are introduced by conjunctions that combine an interrogative and the subordinator *mā*: *mah-mā* ~ *šū-*

mā 'whatever', *mīn-mā* 'whoever', *wēn-mā* 'wherever' and *mēta-mā* 'whenever'.

4.6.4.8.1. *mahmā* ~ *šū-mā* 'whatever'

This conjunction combines the interrogative *šū* 'what' and the subordinator *mā*. As for *mahmā*, it combines the interrogative *mā* 'what', not found in this dialect, and the homophonous subordinator *mā*.

(619) *mahmā nsāwa bas?al-š*

whatever be_done.PFV.3MS ask.IPFV.1SG-NEG

'Whatever is done (to me), I don't ask (anything)'

(620) *šū-mā kān milikk-(h)um mā ḥabbēt-o*

whatever be.PFV.3MS property-3MP NEG like.PFV.1SG-3MS

'Whatever property they possessed, I didn't like it'

4.6.4.8.2. *mīn-mā* 'whoever'

This conjunction combines the interrogative *mīn* 'who' and the subordinator *mā*.

(621) *mīn-mā kān*

whoever be.PFV.3MS

'Whoever it is'

4.6.4.8.3. *wēn-mā* 'wherever'

This conjunction combines the interrogative *wēn* 'where' and the subordinator *mā*.

(622) *wēn-mā* *gaḏ̣abū* *ḏabaḥū*
wherever catch.PFV.3MP.OBJ.3MS slaughter.PFV.3MP.3MS
ysammu *l-ʔarḍ̣* *b-ism-o*
name.SBJV.3MP DEF-land in-name-3MS
'Wherever they caught him and killed him, they would name the place after his name'

4.6.4.8.4. *mēta-mā* ~ *ēmta-mā* 'whenever'

For 'when', the traditional dialect only has *(a)mēt* and *wēnta*. The form *ēmta*, commonly found elsewhere in the Levant, including Amman, is unattested in our corpus, except when augmented with the subordinator *mā* to form the conjunction *ēmta-mā* (***wēnta-mā* is also unattested). The form *mēta-mā* seems to be the proper traditional reflex.[9]

(623) *mēta-mā* *fakku* *wlād* *il-maʕārif*
whenever detach.PFV.3MP children DEF-state_schools
'When(ever) the pupils get out of school'

4.6.4.9. Circumstantial *bidūn-mā* 'without'

This conjunction combines the preposition *dūn* ~ *min dūn* ~ *bidūn* 'without' and the subordinator *mā*. The conjunction *bala-mā* does not surface in our data but was equally accepted in elicitation.

[9] In (623), *il-maʕārif* refers to state schools. They used to be called this because the ministry of education was officially titled *wazārt il-maʕārif* 'ministry of knowledge'; it is currently called *wizārat at-tarbiye w at-taʕlīm* 'ministry of education'.

(624) *awwal kān yuxṭub-ha*

before be.PFV.3MS get_engaged.SBJV.3MS-3FS

bidūn-mā yšūf-ha

without see.SBJV.3MS-3FS

'Before, he (the man) would get engaged to her (the woman) without seeing her'

4.6.4.10. Complex Conjunctions

4.6.4.10.1. (*min*) *xōf-mā* 'fearing that'

This complex conjunction combines the preposition *min* 'from' (optionally), the noun *xōf* 'fear' and the subordinator *mā*.

(625) *ḥuṭṭ maʕ-ak bi s-sayyāra ḥabbit*

put.IMP.MS WITH-2MS in DEF-car piece

əmlabbas xōf-mā yinzil maʕ-ak

candy fear descend.SBJV.3MS with-2MS

'Take a piece of candy in the car with you in case your (blood sugar) drops'

4.6.4.10.2. *min gillit-mā* 'for want of'

This complex conjunction combines the preposition *min* 'from', the construct form of *gille* 'little' and the subordinator *mā*.

(626) *waḷḷa baṭīḥ mā balāgi ṯnēn*

by_God descend.IPFV.1MS NEG find.IPFV.1MS two

aḥči maʕā-hum min-gillit-mā (a)ʕriff-(h)um

speak.SBJV.1SG with-3MP for_want_of know.SBJV.1SG-3MP

'(When) I go downtown, I can't even find two (persons) with whom to speak, for want of enough local people in town these days'

4.6.4.11. Conditionals

According to Thompson, Longacre and Hwang (2007, 256), the semantic space of condition is divided into real and unreal. Real conditionals further divide into present, generic and past. Unreal conditionals divide into imaginative and predictive. Imaginative unreal conditionals include hypothetical and counterfactual conditions. The examples below are taken from Thompson, Longacre and Hwang (2007, 255–56).

(a) Real
   a. Present 'If it's raining out there, my car is getting wet'
   b. Generic 'If you step on the brake, the car slows down'
   c. Past 'If you were at the party, then you must know about Sue and Fred'

(b) Unreal
   a. Imaginative
      i. Hypothetical 'If I saw David, I'd speak Barai with him'
      ii. Counterfactual 'If you had been at the concert, you would have seen Ravi Shankar'
   b. Predictive 'If he gets the job, we'll all celebrate'

The dialects investigated here employ four conjunctions to introduce conditional clauses: *iḏa*, *law*, *in* and *čān*. The conjunctions *iḏa* and *law* are by far the most frequent, whereas the distribution of *in* and *čān* is much more limited and seems to belong to an archaic register attested only in the speech of the broadest speakers. The main distinction is therefore between *iḏa*, which encodes realis conditions, and *law*, which encodes irrealis conditions. Consider the following contrast:

(627) *inti iḏa badd-ik ašya min in-nōʕ hāḏ*

2FS if want-2FS things from DEF-type DEM

ətsağğlī-ha rūḥi ʕa dār anṭōn

record.SBJV.2FS-3FS go.IMP.FS to house Anton

'If you want to record things like that, go to Anton's house'

(628) *bagdar-š bagul-lik law bidd-i*

be_able.IPFV.1SG-NEG say.IPFV.1SG-DAT.2FS if want-1SG

ōkil yaʕni mustaḥīl

eat.SBJV.1SG I_mean impossible

'I can't, I'm telling you, (even) if I wanted to eat, I wouldn't be able, (it's) impossible'

4.6.4.11.1. *iḏa*

The conjunction *iḏa* is used to express real conditions. As with *law*, an augmented form with the complementiser *inn-* has also been reported, in the shape of *iḏa-nno*, but no instances were recorded. Formally, the predicate in the protasis can be in the perfective, as in (629) and (630), the *b*-imperfective, as in (631) and (632), or a non-verbal predicate, as in (633) and (634).

- Perfective

(629) *iḏa l-kalb fāt id-dār il-malāyka*

if DEF-dog enter.PFV.3MS DEF-house DEF-angels

mā bitfūt

NEG enter.IPFV.3FS

'If a dog gets into the house, the angels won't enter'

(630) *iḏa mā žibna ḥaṭab mā nitdaffā-š*

if NEG bring.PFV.1PL wood NEG get_warm.SBJV.1PL-NEG

'If we didn't bring firewood, we wouldn't get warm'

- *b*-imperfective

(631) *iḏa baṣīr raʔīs ḥukūma, b-šarṭ*

if become.IPFV.1SG president government with-condition

wāḥad, ʔinn-i ʔabayyiḍ is-sğūn

one comp-1SG whiten.SBJV.1SG DEF-prisons

'If I become prime minister, (I will accept) on one condition, that I free all prisoners'

(632) *iḏa mā btungul iš-šiʕər kull-o waḷḷa*

if NEG copy.IPFV.2MS DEF-poetry all-3MS by_God

la arassb-ak

ASSER fail.SBJV.1SG-2MS

'If you don't copy the whole poem, I swear I'll give you a fail!'

- Non-verbal

(633) *iḏa xāl-o karīm biṭlaʕ karīm*

if uncle-3MS generous exit.IPFV.3MS generous

'If the maternal uncle is generous, (the boy) turns out generous'

(634) *šū hāhēti aʕṭi waḥade min-hin*

what chant.PFV.2FS give.IMP.FS one.F from-3FP

iḏa miḏḏakre

if recall.AP.FS

'What did you chant, give us one of the chants if you (can) remember (any)'

As stated by Brustad (2000, 266), the use of the perfective refers to a punctual action, whereas the imperfective is normally selected to denote a continuous or stative event, as suggested in (629), where the event is considered to be punctual. Brustad (2000, 266) further notes that the perfective is selected when the speakers consider the event to be more hypothetical, as suggested in (630), although a punctual aspect could also be the trigger for the perfective. The match is not perfect between the semantic space of real conditions and the semantics of *iḏa*. In (629), the condition can be interpreted as a habitual/generic. The condition in (630) refers to a past situation. A non-verbal predicate in the protasis can either refer to a habitual/generic condition, as in (633), or a present condition, as in (634). When the verb in the protasis is in the *b*-imperfective, as in (631) and (632), the condition is predictive. Predictive conditions are technically unreal, but are often coded as real conditions cross-linguistically (Thompson, Longacre and Hwang 2007, 258). Predictive conditionals can also be coded with the conjunction *law* and the *b*-imperfective (§4.6.4.11.2). The difference lies in the degree of likelihood of the condition: *iḏa* refers to a more likely condition to occur than *law*.

The bare imperfective does surface in the protasis, but it seems more the result of ellipsis of a modal predicate or auxiliary which requires an integrative form of the verb, as in (635), where the *b*-less verb *yīǧi* is arguably the result of ellipsis of the auxiliary *kān*.

(635) *iḏa wāḥad yīǧi ʕa l-balad lāzim*
if someone come.SBJV.3MS to DEF-land must
yīǧi yiḏḏayyaf ʕind in-nās
come.SBJV.3MS be_hosted.SBJV.3MS at DEF-people
'If someone came to this land, he had to be hosted at the local people's homes'

The fact that *iḏa* denotes realis mode is further confirmed by its use in what look like 'when' clauses, as in (636), where the speaker refers to the unforgettable sight of an old woman who used to sit in a small entrance to her house that had been turned into a shop.

(636) *ʔumm-o fātḥa tukkāne bi d-dār*
mother-3MS open.AP.MS shop in DEF-house
iḏa gaʕdat bi ǧ-ǧūra hāy btinsā-hā-š
if sit.PFV.3FS in DEF-hole DEM forget.IPFV.2MS-3FS-NEG
'His mother had opened a shop in her house. When she sat in the little enclosure (service counter), you wouldn't forget her'

4.6.4.11.2. *law* ~ *lawinn-*

The conjunction *law* is often augmented with the complementiser *inn-*, yielding *lawinn-*, to which bound pronouns attach:

Table 229: Inflections of *lawinn-*

	Singular	Plural
1	*lawinn-i*	*lawin-na*
2M	*lawinn-ak*	*lawinn-ku*
2F	*lawinn-ič*	*lawinn-čin*
3M	*lawinn-o*	*lawinn-hum*
3F	*lawinn-ha*	*lawinn-hin*

Formally, the verb of a *law* protasis can be in the perfective, the bare imperfective or the *b*-imperfective. The conjunction *law* closely matches the divisions of the semantic space mentioned above. When the verb of protasis introduced by *law* is in the perfective, it is counterfactual. If the verb is in the bare imperfective, it refers to a hypothetical condition, and if the verb is in the *b*-imperfective, it denotes a predictive unreal condition. The predicate of the apodosis can be in the perfective, in the bare imperfective, in the *b*-imperfective or a non-verbal predicate. The tense selected in the apodosis reflects the aspectuo-temporal relation that the event of the protasis has towards the event of the apodosis. The use of the perfective indicates a punctual completed event, had the condition been fulfilled, as in (637). Conversely, the use of the imperfective indicates an ongoing event (638).

- Perfective—perfective (counterfactual, punctual)

(637)	*law*	*ḍallu*	*ḏabaḥū-hum*
	if	stay.PFV.3MP	slaughter.PFV.3MP-3MP

'If they had stayed, they would have massacred them'

- Perfective—*b*-imperfective (counterfactual, progressive)

(638)	*lawinno*	*ǧāb*	*šihāde*	*minlāgī*
	if	bring.PFV.3MS	degree	find.IPFV.1PL
	b-ġanāni	*u*	*zaġārīt*	
	with-songs	and	ululations	

'If he had brought back a degree, we would have been welcoming him with songs and ululations (at the airport)'

The use of the bare imperfective in the protasis indicates a hypothetical event unrealised at the time of utterance. The use of the perfective in the apodosis indicates a completed event in relation to the event of the protasis (639). This example also features the use of *čān* as a conjunction to introduce the apodosis. A verb in the imperfective indicates either ongoingness or futurity in relation to the event of the protasis, as in (640).

- Bare imperfective—perfective (hypothetical, punctual)

(639) *law yirǧaʕ ʕa ha-l-balad čān wala*
If return.SBJV.3MS to DEM-DEF-country then NEG
rāḥ wala dilim la l-ġarīb
go.PFV.3MS NEG dunum to DEF-stranger
'If he came back to this land, no dunum would be sold to strangers'

- Bare imperfective—*b*-imperfective (hypothetical, futurity)

(640) *law tʕiddī-hum kull-hum maʕ*
if count.SBJV.2FS-3MP all-3MP with
baʕəḏ̣-hum mā bwaffū-š miyye
RECP-3MP NEG complete.IPFV.3MP-NEG hundred
'If you counted them all, they wouldn't reach one hundred'

The use of the *b*-imperfective in the protasis indicates a non-factual predictive condition. The use of the bare imperfective in the apodosis is only attested with the asseverative marker *la*, which strengthens the intentional value of the verb (641). If the verb of the apodosis is in the *b*-imperfective, the aspectuo-temporal relation to the event expressed in the protasis is one of either ongoingness or futurity, as in (642). The predicate of the apodosis can be non-verbal. In that case, it refers to a generic present in relation to the event of the protasis (643).

- *b*-imperfective—bare imperfective (predictive, intentional)

(641) *law badri inn-i mā badd-ī-š arǧaʕ*
if know.IPFV.1SG COMP-1SG NEG want-1SG return.SBJV.1SG
ʕa balad-i inn-i l(a) awaṣṣil arḏ̣-ku
to country-1SG COMP-1SG ASSER reach.SBJV.1SG land-2MP
min hōn la masǧid il-ḥusēn
from here to mosque DEF-Hussein
'If I knew that I wasn't returning to my country, I would extend your land to the Hussein mosque'

- *b*-imperfective—*b*-imperfective (predictive, futurity)

(642) *law bitḥuṭṭ māl-ak kull-o mā*
if put.IPFV.2MS money-2MS all-3MS NEG
baʕṭī-k iyyā-ha
give.IPFV.1SG-2MS OBJ-3FS
'(Even) if you put down all your money, I wouldn't give her (my daughter) to you'

- *b*-imperfective—non-verbal predicate (predictive, generic present)

(643) *law mnōkl ətrāb hōna niʕmit xēr*
if eat.IPFV.1PL soil here blessing good
'(Even) if we were to eat soil here, it would still be a blessing (compared to what people in other countries have to put up with)'

- Non-verbal predicate—*b*-imperfective (predictive, ongoingness)

(644) *law ʕalē-na iḥna u ʕa niswān-na Wardiyye*

if	on-1PL	1PL	and	on	women-1PL	Wardiyye

mā bitʕīš

NEG live.IPFV.3FS

'If we and our women had to take care of Wardiyye, she wouldn't be alive'

4.6.4.11.3. Concessive Conditionals

Concessive conditionals are coded like unreal conditions with the morpheme *law* ~ *lawinn-*, as exemplified in (645) and (646).

(645) *walla mā baxtār ʕalē ǧīrān lawinn-o axu*

by_God	NEG	chose.IPFV.1MS	on.3MS	neighbours	if-3MS	brother

'I wouldn't choose a neighbour other than him, even if it (the hypothetical neighbour) were (my) brother'

(646) *law d̲ābiḥ ʕašar əzlām mā bitfūtu*

if	slaughter.AP.MS	ten	men	NEG	enter.IPFV.2MP

'Even if he had killed ten men, you wouldn't be allowed to enter the house'

4.6.4.11.4. *lōla*

The morpheme *lōla* arose from the lexicalisation of *law* and the negation marker *lā*. The monophthongisation of /aw/ into /ō/ shows that the sequence is a single phonological word, because monophthongisation does not occur across word boundaries: *walaw lā tazāl* 'even though it is still…'. *lōla* should be considered a variant of *law* used when the protasis is a non-verbal predicate in negative polarity. If the subject is pronominal, it is indexed on *lōla* by way of bound pronouns, as in (647) and (648). Note also that the apodosis is introduced by *kān* (the de-affricated variant of *čān*) in (647) and the asseverative marker *la* in (648).

(647)	*intu*	*lōlā-ku*	*kān*	*iḥna*	*mā*	*kān*	*ʕin-na*	*ḥayā*
	2MP	if.NEG-2MP	then	1PL	NEG	be.PFV.3MS	at-1PL	life

'If you hadn't been there, we wouldn't have had a life'

(648)	*lōlā-k*	*yā*	*ṣubḥi*	*la*	*biʕna*
	if.NEG-2MP	VOC	Ṣubḥi	then	sell.PFV.1PL
	lli	*fōgī-na*	*w*	*illi*	*tahṭī-na*
	REL	above-1PL	and	REL	under-1PL

'Ṣubḥi, if you hadn't been around, we would have sold everything (i.e., we would have been penniless)'

4.6.4.11.5. *in*

The conjunction *in* belongs to an archaic register and surfaces in the speech of broad speakers. Phonetically, the conjunction can be realised [ʔin], [in], [an] and even [n]. There seems to be a large overlap between *in* and *iḏa* in terms of functions in that they can both encode real conditions and predictive conditions. The only clear difference is formal: *in* always selects the perfective. Examples (649) and (650) denote real present conditions.

(649)	*n*	*ṣār*	*mušāġabāt*	*minrūḥ-əš*	*ʕa*	*z-zētūnāt*
	if	become.PFV.3MS	agitations	go.IPFV.1PL-NEG	to	DEF-olives

'In case of disturbances, we don't go to the olive groves'

(650) *il-wāḥad in ṭāḥ ʕa s-sūg*

DEF-one if descend.PFV.3MS to DEF-market

a-blāgī-š nās yiḥči maʕ-o

NEG-find.IPFV.3MS-NEG people speak.SBJV.3MS with-3MS

'When we go down to the market, we can't find anyone to speak with'

Examples (651) and (652) entail a predictive reading, but the event of the apodosis is conceived of as happening within the time-frame set by the protasis.

(651) *an rağaʕt issāʕ bağīb la*

if come_back.PFV.1SG now bring.IPFV.1SG to

ḥāl-i iš-šibha w ana barī(ʔ)

REFL-1SG DEF-suspicion and 1SG innocent

'If I go back now, I'll bring suspicions on myself although I'm innocent'

(652) *ʔin ʔana mā satart ibn*

if 1SG NEG protect.PFV.1SG son

axū-y manu badd-o yusutr-o

brother-1SG who want-3MS protect.SBJV.3MS-3MS

'If I don't marry off my nephew, who will (i.e., nobody will)?'

Example (653) denotes a past situation, but the events coded in the apodosis are conceived of as happening within the time frame set by the predicate in the protasis and as an immediate consequence thereof, which makes it equivalent to (651) and (652).

(653) *in* *lāgu* *nās…* *yṭuxxū-hum*

if find.PFV.3MP people shoot.SBJV.3MP-3MP

'If they found people (thieves), they would shoot them'

4.6.4.11.6. *čān*

The conjunction *čān* was in all likelihood borrowed from neighbouring Bedouin varieties. Although etymologically linked to the verb *kān* 'he was', this morpheme has a long history of grammaticalisation both into a conditional marker and into a conjunction used to introduce the apodosis in many Arabic dialects. Although they have the same lexical origin, the syntactic contexts they arose from are different. The conditional marker most likely arose from the apheresis of lexicalised formations involving the conjunction *in* (or *iḏa* or *law*) and *kān*: *inkān* > *nkān* > *kān* > *čān*. The morpheme *čān* used as an apodosis marker arose from the grammaticalisation of the auxiliary *kān* + perfective used in counter-factual conditionals. Very few tokens were recorded, which suggests either that *čān* is a recessive variant of *in*, or that it never had much currency in the dialect in the first place. When used as a conditional marker, similarly to *iḏann-* and *lawinn-*, it can be augmented with the complementiser *inn-* to give the form *čānn-*, to which subject-referencing bound pronouns attach, as shown in (655). The verb of the protasis is in the perfective, unless the predicate is non-verbal, as in (654). Semantically, *čān* is used in real present conditions. It appears, therefore, that both the syntax and the semantics of *in* and *čān* are partly similar, which, in addition to their common etymology, suggest that they are variants of a single morpheme. Although our corpus lacks firm evidence, it is possible that *in* and *čān* are in partial complementary distribution, with *čān* being always selected with nonverbal predicates and alternating freely with *in* with verbal (perfective) predicates.

(654) *čān bī-ha ši ġalaṭ yā xayy timḥā-ha*
if in-3FS thing wrong VOC brother erase.SBJV.2MS-3FS
'If there is anything wrong (in the recording) would you erase it?'

(655) *čānn-o mā fāt-əš hāḏa ǧamal-ku*
if-3MS NEG enter.PFV.3MS-NEG DEM camel-2MP
'If the camel doesn't enter (the house), (then) it is yours'

4.6.4.11.7. Negative Conditionals

One way of coding negative conditionals in the present dialect is by means of the exceptive morpheme *illa*:

(656) *mā bixallū-k tsūg sayyāra urduniyye illa*
NEG let.IPFV.3PL-2MS drive.SBJV.2SG car Jordanian except
ykūn maʕ-ak ruxṣa urduniyye
be.SBJV.3MS with-2MS licence Jordanian
'They won't let you drive a Jordanian car (with a Jordanian number plate) unless you have a Jordanian licence'

(657) *hassa mā btigdar titǧawwaz*
now NEG can.IPFV.2MS marry.SBJV.2MS
illa tōxuḏ ḥilliyye
except take.SBJV.2MS permission
'Now you can't get married (to your cousin) unless you are granted permission'

4.6.4.11.8. Summary of Conditionals

Table 230 sums up the different values of the conjunctions *iḏa*, *in/čān* and *law*. It shows that, while *law* is only used for unreal conditions, overlap occurs for unreal predictive conditions. In that case, *law* encodes conditions that speakers do not judge possible or likely to be fulfilled, as opposed to *iḏa* and *in/čān*, which encode conditions likely to be fulfilled.

Table 230: Summary of conditional markers

		iḏa	*in/čān*	*law*
Real	Present	x	x	-
	Generic	x	x	-
	Past	x	?	-
Unreal	Predictive	x	x	x
	Hypothetical	-	-	x
	Counterfactual	-	-	x

4.6.5. Coordination

In Arabic, coordination between constituents is done by means of a coordinator in constituent-initial position (prepositive). Some coordinators can be used for both clausal and non-clausal constituents, while other conjunctions can only coordinate clausal constituents. Asyndetic coordination is of course possible, but the language makes use mostly of syndetic constructions. These are mostly monosyndetic, although two bisyndetic constructions are also in usage: *yā… yā…* and variants thereof 'either… or…' and *lā… walā* 'neither… nor…' (§4.5.1.9). Using Haspelmath's (2007) typology, Arabic exhibits A co-B for monosyndetic constructions and co-A co-B for bisyndetic constructions (where 'co' stands for coordinator).

4.6.5.1. Clausal and Non-clausal

4.6.5.1.1. Conjunctive *w* 'and'

- Clausal

(658)	*kul*	*faggūs*	*w*	*uskut*
	eat.IMP.MS	cucamelon	and	shut_up.IMP.MS

'Eat a cucamelon and shut up'

- Non-clausal

(659)	*yōm*	*thāwašu*	*wlād-ič*	*hummu*	*w*	*ahəl*	*māḫiṣ*
	when	quarrel.PFV.3MP	children-2FS	3MP	and	people	Māḫiṣ

'When your children quarrelled with the people of Māḫiṣ'

4.6.5.1.2. Disjunctive

aw 'or'

There are two disjunctive coordinators: *aw* and *willa* ~ *walla*. The former is used in declarative sentences, and the latter is favoured in interrogative sentences (§4.6.5.1.2).

- Clausal

(660)	*kunt*	*bidd-i*	*atǧawwaz*	*maṯalan*
	be.PFV.1SG	want-1SG	marry.SBJV.1SG	example
	aw	*badd-i*	*azīd*	*rātb-i*
	or	want-1SG	increase.SBJV.1SG	salary-1SG

'I wanted to get married for example, or increase my salary'

- Non-clausal

(661) *mā baʕrif iš-šaxəṣ hū ʕīd aw ġēr-o*
NEG know.IPFV.1SG DEF-person 3MS ʕīd or other-3MS
'I don't know if that person is ʕīd or someone else'

willa ~ *walla* 'or'

As noted above, the coordinator *walla* ~ *willa* is favoured in interrogative sentences, as in (662) and (663), although some speakers extend its use to declarative sentences as well, as illustrated in (664).

- Clausal

(662) *id-dār il-gadīme baʕəd-ha il-ku willa bitʕtū-ha*
DEF-house DEF-old still-3FS to-2MP or sell.PFV.2MP-3FS
'Is the old house still yours or did you sell it?'

- Non-clausal

(663) *badd-o yīǧi l-yōm walla bukra*
want-3MS come.SBJV.3MS DEF-day or tomorrow
'Does he want to come today or tomorrow?'

(664) *mā badri ʕād hū ṣ-ṣaḥīḥ willa lā*
NEG know.IPFV.1SG DM 3MS DEF-correct or no
'I don't know if this is correct or not'

yā… yā… 'either… or…'

The bisyndetic coordinator *yā… yā…* is commonly found in many Levantine dialects. Other variants are *yā… aw…*, *imma… aw…*, *yā ʔimma… aw…*, *yā… yā ʔimma…*.

- Clausal

(665) *yā* *nġuzz* *yā* *nʕaššib* *zarəʕ*
either plant.SBJV.1PL or weed.SBJV.1PL sowing
'We used to either plant, or weed the fields'

- Non-clausal

(666) *gabəl* *lə-fḥēṣ* *yā* *dār* *yā* *dār-ēn*
before DEF-Fḥēṣ either house or house-DU
'Earlier, Fḥēṣ had just one or two houses'

4.6.5.2. Clausal

4.6.5.2.1. *bass and lākin* ~ *lakn* 'but'

Jordanian Arabic has two adversative coordinators, *bass* and *lākin*, which are to a large extent interchangeable. General adversative coordinators are expected to express both 'denial of expectation' and 'semantic opposition', which are defining features of concessivity and contrastivity, respectively (Malchukov 2004). The most common of these coordinators is *bass*. Found in eastern varieties of Arabic, it is polyfunctional, because it is also a restrictive focus-sensitive particle 'only' and a temporal conjunction 'as soon as'. The adversative coordinator *lākin*, found in most varieties of Arabic, can also be realised *lakn* in the dialect described here. In contrast to what is observed in Standard Arabic, it cannot be augmented with bound pronouns.

(667) *wa̤l̤la l-yōm bisawwu hōšāt akṯar min ʔawwal*
by_God DEF-day do.IPFV.3MP quarrels more from before
bass ʔawwal in-nās ʕārfe baʕəḏ̣-ha l-baʕəḏ̣
but before DEF-people know.AP.FS RECP-3FS DEF-RECP
'Now they quarrel more than before, but before people knew each other'

(668) *šaġġāl bass ʕa l-fāḏ̣i*
active but on DEF-empty
'(I) work, but (I work) in vain'

(669) *twaffa ʔil-o šahər lakn əššū bačat ʕalē*
die.PFV.3MS for-3MS month but what cry.PFV.3FS on.3MS
'He died a month ago, but she cried so much (because of his death)'

(670) *wa̤l̤la ḥāfiḏ̣ lākin yamm birūḥin ʕan bāl-i*
by_God preserve.AP.MS but surely go.IPFV.3FP from mind-1SG
'I have learnt them, but they do disappear from my memory'

4.6.5.2.2. *amma* 'whereas'

The coordinator *amma* has many different realisations: *amma* ~ *amman* ~ *umma* ~ *umman*. Compared to *lākin* and *bass*, which are used as general adversative coordinators, *amma* is corrective. In (671), the adverb of time *hassaʕ* 'now' in the first clause is corrected by *umma* followed by *awwal* 'before' in the second clause. Additionally, the morpheme *amma* is not neutral in terms of information structure, because, very much like left-dislocation, it flags a topic shift.

(671) *hassaʕ muntāz a-bī-hū-š bala umma*
now excellent NEG-in-3MS-NEG problem but
awwal ġād ʕaglīt-o
before there mind-3MS
'Now he is ok, but back in the day, he was out of his mind'

4.6.5.2.3. *fa* 'so'

The conjunction *fa* is most likely a borrowing from the standard variety, because it surfaces mostly in the speech of those who have enjoyed a certain level of schooling. It is used mostly after a pause in narration as a resuming device:

(672) *kull iṭ-ṭurug kānat turābiyye aywa*
all DEF-paths be.PFV.3FS dirt yes
fa l-maṯal ʕind-hum inno l-ʕamm
so DEF-proverb at-3MP COMP DEF-uncle
binazzil il-ʕarūs ʕan il-faras
take_down.IPFV.3MS DEF-bride from DEF-horse
'All the roads were dirt (roads)… so the custom was for the paternal uncle to take the bride down from the horse (i.e., prevent her from marrying outsiders)'

4.6.6. Cosubordination: *ḥāl* Clauses

Cosubordination is a term that has been put forward to account for structures that exhibit properties of both coordination and subordination (Van Valin and LaPolla 1997). A case in point is what have been called in the Arabic grammatical tradition *ḥāl* clauses (*ǧumlat al-ḥāl*), which express simultaneity between two events, both of which are coded in clauses that appear in a paratactic relation. The cosubordinated clause is introduced by the conjunctive coordinator *w* 'and'. To put it differently, *ḥāl* clauses are a case of syntactic coordination and semantic subordination. Two orders are attested cross-dialectally for the cosubordinated clause: [*w* SUBJECT PREDICATE] and [SUBJECT *w* PREDICATE]. In the present dialect, both orders are found, as shown in (673), where the speaker started with one order, then paused, and resumed using the second order. The most frequent order in the corpus is [*w* SUBJECT PREDICATE], as in (674), although the [SUBJECT *w* PREDICATE] order does have some currency (675). The subject can be a pronoun or a full NP, as in (676).

(673) *w* *ana* *zġīre…* *ana* *w* *zġīre*
and 1SG small.F… 1SG and small.F
ḏ̣allēt *asraḥ* *ġanam*
stay.PFV.1SG tend.SBJV.1SG sheep
'When I was young, I used to tend sheep'

(674) *aḏ̣ʕanat* *bi* *ṭ-ṭarīg* *u* *hummu* *ṭālʕīn*
give_birth.PFV.3FS in DEF-path and 3MP exit.AP.MP
'She gave birth on the way as they were leaving'

(675) *waḷḷa* *šāb* *hū* *w* *ʕumr-o* *xaməsṭaʕšar* *sane*
by_God turn_grey.PFV.3MS 3MS and age-3MS fifteen year
'His hair turned grey when he was fifteen'

(676) *w* *axū-y* *bi* *ǧ-ǧāmʕa* *bagēt* *laḥāl-i*
and brother-1SG in DEF-university be.PFV.1SG alone-1SG
maʕ *abū-y* *ništaġil* *bi* *l-karəm*
with father-1SG work.SBJV.1PL in DEF-vineyard
'When my brother was in university, I was with my father working in the vineyard'

5. TEXTS

The texts are samples from our data. They depict three narratives: a folktale and two personal stories. Below, we provide some further details about the narrators and further clarifications.

The first text, *il-ʔamīr il-Mihdāwi* 'Prince Mihdāwi', was extracted from a recording carried out in 2012 with a speaker in his 80s from the town of Fḥēs, which is located almost halfway between Amman and Salt. He was recorded for two hours in his home in the presence of members of his family. He narrates a story, famous among locals, of a battle that purportedly took place during the first half of the seventeenth century between clans from Fḥēs and their allies the ʕAdwān tribe on one side, and Prince Ǧūda al-Mihdāwi, the ruler of the region at the time, and his cavalrymen on the other. The story, which has become a folktale, was recounted on numerous occasions during our research in Fḥēṣ and Salt. Often the details varied from speaker-to-speaker, but the gist and moral of the story are uniform, namely the courage of the local tribes in standing up to a powerful, ruthless ruler, and the alliances that local tribes have kept with one another, regardless of religious affiliation. The Fḥēṣ tribes are Christian while the ʕAdwān are Muslim.

The second text, *il-bagara* 'the cow', was recorded in 2006 with a male speaker in his 70s from the city of Salt. The context of this recording is a customary social gathering of local men, which continues to be practised in the community of Salt. Men, usually of the same generation, gather in traditional cafes or the central square for a game of mancala and a chat. In this narrative,

 https://doi.org/10.11647/OBP.0410.05

the speaker recounts a bitter-sweet incident dated to the 1950s, which had him end up in prison and paying bail money simply as a result of being in the wrong place at the wrong time while searching for his lost cow. The narrative contains several interesting footnotes that document a period when progressive political movements, such as the Ba'ath party, which is mentioned at the beginning of the narrative, were oppressed by the state. The narrator's stance in favour of such ideologies and in condemnation of the heavy-handedness of the police force is implied throughout.

The third text, *riḥlit ṣēd* 'a hunting trip', was recorded in 2006 with a male speaker in his 70s from Salt. The setting is the same as that for the second text. In this narrative, the speaker recounts a hunting trip undertaken by a group of local friends (whom he names) from Salt to the warm valley of the Ghor (the Jordan Valley) below the city. He speaks of the hunters' success, which was so great that they could barely lift their kill. However, the trip was spoilt by one of the men catching a cold and falling ill as the weather turned cold and snowy while they were ascending back to Salt. The character whose story is reported by the narrator walked back alone to Salt to fetch food supplies and a warm coat for the sick friend, which he loaded onto a mule's back. Following a rub of his chest with ghee and grape molasses, and a meal of bread and halva, the sick hunter recovered, and went home, carrying his share of the hunt.

In the three narratives, we find a tendency to digress from the main plot by including details that are irrelevant to it. Another tendency is to drop names of several local people. For example, in narrative 1, the speaker, towards the end, drops the name of Riyāḍ il-Miflih̭, a notable local man, deceased in 2000, who owned the petrol station near the site where the prince was killed (even though he had already identified the site as in Siru, a well-known hill nearby). In narrative 2, the speaker names several of the men who were jailed with him. He also names the owner of the house beside which the cow was spotted. In narrative 3, the speaker names the owners of the only public transport cars that were available at the time. In the recordings, it is noticeable that when such digressions happen the audience tend to respond with short, affirmative comments. Digressions and mentioning names of local people seem to be stylistic devices that serve to establish a rapport with the audience and keep them listening, as well as to give further credibility to the speakers' narrations and knowledge of the local community.

5.1. Text 1: *il-ʔamīr il-mihdāwi* 'Prince Il-Mihdāwi'

il-ʔamīr il-mihdāwi kān hū ʔamīr ʕala ha-lə-blād kull-ha gabəl il-malik ʕabdaḷḷa u gabəl kull in-nās, kān bī ʔamīr, il-ʔamīr ağa marra ʕala lə-fḥēṣ, hāḏa l-ḥaki gabəl arbaʕ mīt sane mīn illi kān hōn, kān fī d-dayyāt, ṯalāṯ arbaʕ zlām, w iz-zyēdāt ṯalāṯ arbaʕ zlām, is-

Prince il-Mihdāwi was the ruler of the whole of this land. This was well before King Abdullah (I) and all those people. He once came to Fḥēṣ. This was four hundred years ago. There were present three or four men of the Dayyāt (clan), three or four men of the Zyādāt (clan), three or four men of the Salmān (clan). In those days *salmān ṯalāṯ arbaʕ zlām, yaʕni b-muġur ʕāyšīn farašū-lo b-gāʕ šaǧara, la l-ʔamīr, šāf bint, il-bint bint xūri, a-bī-š aǧmal min-ha winno bugūl ḥaḏḏrū-li l-bint hāy hāḏi ʔil-i badd-i atǧawwaz-ha l-amīr il-mihdāwi, gālū-lo ʔamr-ak y(ā) amīr, lə-fḥēṣiyye, ṣḥāb humm(u) w l-ʕadwān, u xuwwa bēn-hum, min awwal, rāḥu waddu wāḥad min iz-zyēdāt ism-o ʕfēn, gālū-lo, urkuḏ nādi, nādi l-ʕadwān, l-ʕadwān kān ġāǧǧ-hum min hōn, l-amīr il-mihdāwi wēn, ʕala ṭayybit il-ʕarānke, ʕa ṭ-ṭayybe tabʕat-na, ā fa rāḥ yirkuḏ, kān yusbug ič-čalb ʕala (a)dē, hāḏa ʕfēn gālu ʕann-o inno busbug ič-čalb ʕala (a)dē u riǧlē, rāḥ b-surʕa, gāl la l-ʕadwān hēk hēk w in-nhār lə-flāni, ġadā ʕin-na l-mihdāwi u badd-o yiǧi yōxuḏ bint il-xūri, gālū-*

people lived in caves. They laid a mattress for the prince under a tree. He saw a young woman. She was the daughter of a priest. She was the prettiest woman ever seen. (Upon seeing her) the prince said, "Get this young woman ready for me; she's the one I want to marry." "Your wish is our command," they replied. The Fḥēṣ clans and the ʕAdwān tribe had had a friendship (brotherhood) pact for a long time, and so they sent a man of the Zyādāt whose name was ʕfēn. They said to him, "Run and call upon the ʕAdwān for help." The ʕAdwān had previously expelled prince Mihdāwi from here to Tayybit il-ʕarānke (village), our Tayybe. So ʕfēn ran quickly to call for help. He was known to be able to run faster than a dog. He told the ʕAdwān the story and that the prince would be having lunch in Fḥēṣ on such and such a day and that he would be taking the priest's daughter on that day. The ʕAdwān asked "Are you our allies?" and we replied, "We *lo intu wāgfīn maʕ-na gallilhum, kull-na wāgfīn maʕ-ku m(a) ġēr ilḥagū-na, haḏōl kṯār, il-mihdāwi, winno ǧāyib maʕā arbʕīn xayyāl, l-mihdāwi, w ağu rabaṭu xēl-hum gāmu lə-fḥēṣiyye ʕala bṭānāt il-xēl u fakkū-ha, fakku bṭānāt il-xēl mšān il-wāḥad lamma badd-o yirkab ʕala l-faras, tiglib bī, fa ağu w аğa l-mihdāwi wēn l-ʕadwān, il-ʕadwān wara ǧ-ǧabal, аğa ʕfēn yurkuḍ, gal-lo l-mihdāwi wēn ḅāgi, ruḥət ǧibt il-ʕadwān? gaddēš hummu, gal-lo l-ʕadwān, ndāri yā sīdi, a-badrī-š gaddēš, gal-lo yaʕni ṯalāṯīn arbʕīn farak ḥabbit frīke ḥaṭṭ bī-ha arbʕīn ḥabbe b-īd-o gal-lo šāyif haḏōl ʕadwān-ak, laham-hum, gal-lo ṭayyib lahamt-hum lahamt-hum aṭlaʕū-lo ṭ-*

are your allies so come and help us as the Mihdāwi men are plenty." On the day, the Mihdāwi arrived with forty horsemen. After they dismounted and tied their horses, the Fhēs men loosened their horses' saddles so that they would fall off when they tried to mount their horses. The prince arrived. The ʕAdwān were hiding behind the mountain. The prince spotted ʕfēn running back, so he said to him, "Did you go to fetch the ʕAdwān? How many of them came to help you?" ʕfēn replied, "I don't know." The Prince said, "Are they thirty, forty?" And he grabbed forty grains of frīke (smoked wheat). Pointing to the grains, he said to ʕfēn, "These are your ʕAdwān allies," and he devoured the grains. ʕfēn replied, "Ok fine, you devoured them." They served him the food, seven, eight or ten platefuls of Mansaf (the traditional Jordanian dish) without salt.[1] As soon as he

[1] In the local customs, serving unsalted food signals animosity, and is a code for rejection of this person's request.

ṭabīx sabʕa ṯaman ʕašar manāsif bidūn miləḥ min awwal-mā madd īd-o u ḏ̣āg iṭ-ṭabīx winno bugūl bugtu yā fḥēṣiyye gallū-lo l-bōg ağa min tiḥt šārb-ak ağa wāḥad min is-salmān, gāl b-rās-o winno la miṯl əhnāk gaṭaʕ rās il-mihdāwi gāmu haḏolāk badd-hum yirkabu ʕa xēl-hum w yhāwšu, illi yirkab, yisguṭ, ağu l-ʕadwān, ṭāyrīn bi ḏ̣hūr xēl-hum barḏ̣o, maʕā-na w aḏbaḥ walā tiḏbaḥ, illi liḥgū b-ğabal abu l-ḥasan, wāḥad ismo abu l-ḥasan, sammu abu l-ḥasan b-ism-o, is-sgēriyye, sammū-ha b-isəm wāḥad ism-o ṣagir, arḏ̣-na hāy ṭalʕit raḥīl, sammū-ha b-isəm rḥayyil, wēn-mā gaḏabū ḏabaḥū ysammu l-ʔarḏ̣ b-ism-o kān b is-siru, ʕand kāziyyit riyāḏ̣ il-mifliḥ. nḏabaḥ il-mihdāwi, u ha-l-marra lə-fḥēṣiyye, lə-fḥēṣiyye biğū-š ʕašara

tasted the unsalted food, addressing Fḥēṣ people, he said "You have betrayed us." They replied, "Betrayal came from you first." Then a man from the Salmān (clan) beheaded and killed the Mihdāwi. His men rushed to mount their horses in order to fight us but every one of them fell off as he tried to mount his horse. The ʕAdwān then rushed in, also on their horsebacks to fight on our side. Together we slaughtered the Mihdāwi men. One of them was pursued to a hill, which was later named after him, the mount of Abu l-Ḥasan; named after someone called Abu l-Ḥasan (his name); Ṣgēriyye (place name) was named after someone called Ṣagir. This plot of land of ours, Ṭalʕit Raḥīl, was named after a man called Rḥayyil. Wherever they grabbed and killed a man they called the place after him. It was in the Siru (area nearby), by Riyāḏ̣ il-Mifliḥ's petrol station that the Mihdāwi was killed. The Fḥēṣ men who fought and won were no more *xamsṭaʕaš w il-ʕadwān arbʕīn, ḍallu yikḥatu ǧamāʕt il-mihdāwi, u kull xēl-o u kull zlām-o la-mā waṣṣalū-hum l-əʕrāg.*

than ten or fifteen, the ʕAdwān men were forty. Together they kept pushing the Mihdāwi men and their horses all the way to l-əʕrāg (place name).

5.2. Text 2: *il-bagara* 'the cow'

bi l-xamsīnāt, baʕd il-xamsīnāt bi šwayye, il-maššīni kān yʕallig ʕa ḥizb il-baʕəṯ, slēmān, ḍarabu nās ḥǧār, ḍarabū ḥǧār a-badrī-š, il-muhimm ḥaṭṭū-lo ḥirāsa, ḥaṭṭū-lo ḥirāsa, li-ʔaǧl ən-naṣīb il-ḥaǧǧe kānat ǧāybe naḏīr u ġāyle bi l-walad əṯ-ṯāni, mā bī-š ḥalīb nīdo wala bī iši, illi hū haḏāk il-yōm, gālu walḷa mā lak ġēr tištri miʕza, mā lkī-š ḥīle bi l-miʕza, ištrī-lak bagar, štarēt bagara b-wāḥad u ṯalāṯīn dīnār ʕan wāḥad u ṯalāṯīn ʔalf hassaʕ, biġallbin, ḥaṭṭētt-(h)a b-ha-d-dār, gaʕdat sane santēn

During the 1950s, or shortly after, Slēmān Maššīni mocked the Ba'ath Party. Someone threw stones at him; I don't know who, but some people threw stones at him. The point is guards were appointed to protect him. By coincidence, my wife had recently given birth to Naḏīr and was pregnant with the second son. In those days, there was no Nido,[2] there was nothing in those days. People said, the best thing is for you to buy a cow; you cannot cope with goats so buy yourself a cow. So, I paid thirty-one dinars for a cow, which is equivalent to thirty-one thousand in today's money, a heavy burden. I brought the cow home. For one or

[2] 'Nido' is the name of a brand of powdered milk, which is commonly used to refer to any brand of powdered milk.

ʕindi illi hī sane aḷḷa aʕlam bī-ha, tịsrah w ətrawwiḥ laḥāl-ha tīǧi ʕa š-šafa hōn tiṣraḥ trawwi(ḥ) ʕind ibən-ha, lēle mā rawwaḥat-š, ġrabat əd-dinya mā rawwaḥat-š ruḥt adawwir ʕalē-ha mā lagētt-(h)ā-š, bi-l-lēl, əṣ-ṣubəḥ ma ʕrift-š anām hadạ̄k il-lēle, gult ma nimt-əš hadạ̄k il-lēle, ṭūl il-lēl w ana gāʕid, rāḥat il-bagara, əṣ-ṣubəḥ ağīt sāri adawwir winn il-ḥaraka ġēr šikəl, yōmin ṭabbēt gaṭaʕət dār il-ḥalīg ġād, dār ğabir, winn-ha ḥamra ṣāfi, is-sayyārāt sayyārāt w il-ḥirāsāt w il-xēl w il-… dawriyye, gult an rağaʕt issāʕ bağīb laḥāli iš-šibəh w ana barī, ḍallēt mʕaddi il-muhimm gaḍabū-ni, wēn rāyiḥ gult(h)um waḷḷa mḍayyiʕ bagara, kēd kēd, bigul-li ḍ-ḍābiṭ, sāʔil, il-miġərbiyyāt, sāʔil ʕaskari ʕan-ha, gāl-li lā mā šiftt-

two years, the cow would wander out to graze and come home all by itself. It would come here to the plain (part of the land) and then return to its calf. One night the cow did not come back home. The sun set but it still did not come back. I went out to look for it, but I did not find it at night. I did not sleep at all that night. All night I was awake thinking the cow has gone. In the morning, I got up early to look again. Outside, I noticed an unusual commotion. When I walked past il-Ḥalīg's house over there, Jabir's house, there was a real kerfuffle; cars and guards, horses and police patrol all over the place. I thought to myself, if I go back now it'll look suspicious although I am innocent, so I walked on. To cut a long story short, they stopped me. "Where are you going?" they asked. "I have lost a cow," I replied. I told them the whole story. The evening before I had asked a soldier about the cow, and he had told me he hadn't seen it. On the day they *(h)ā-š, iṣ-ṣubəḥ winn bī ʕišrīn ʕaskari ʕind midrast iṯ-ṯānawiyye, wēn rāyiḥ taʕāl ǧāy taʕāl, u ǧīt, gult waḷḷa yā sīdi mḏ̣ayyiʕ bagara u rāyḥ adawwir ʕalē-ha, winno bgūl ǧāy tičšif il-mawgaʕ, ana badrī-š šū s-sīre waḷḷa mā baʕlam əššū bī, gult waḷḷa yā sīdi mā…w il-ʕaskari tara maʕā…winno bgūl yā walad mā lagētt-(h)a…gult-lo waḷḷa mā lagētt-(h)a, gāl-li ḏ̣-ḏ̣ābiṭ šū, šū yā ʕaskari, gal-lo sīdi kān əs-sāʕa sitte ydawwir ʕalē-ha winno bgul-li rūḥ a-badd-kī-š bagar, rūḥ, rūḥ, a-badd-kī-š bagar, ruḥət rağaʕət winn sayyārāt ha-ğ-ğēb…winno bgūl yaḷḷa xuḏ-o waddī ʕa s-siğən, bagūl la l-ʕaskari ya xayy-i šū s-sīre intu māl-ku ʕalē-na, šu s-sīre, gāl əs-sīre ban nisxaṭ ha-l-balad, ṭayyib tisxaṭu ha-l-balad min dūn ḏanb, gāl əssāʕ*

stopped me, there were twenty soldiers near the secondary school. They shouted to me, "Where are you going? Come here!" I came. I said, "Sir, I have lost a cow and I'm on my way to look for it." He replied, "Are you here to check out the site?" I swear to God I had no clue what the story was or what was going on. The soldier whom I had asked about the cow the previous evening was present; so, he asked me, "Hey you, did you not find it?" I replied that I did not find the cow. The officer then said to the soldier, "What's going on, soldier?" The soldier said "Sir, he was looking for his cow at six o'clock yesterday evening." The officer then said to me, "Go away, you don't want cows, no cows here for you, go away!" I moved on but then there was this Jeep car and the officer said, "Take him, take him to prison!" I said to the soldier, "What's the matter, why are you doing this to us?" He replied, "The matter is we want to wreck this town." "You *biššūf əḏ-ḏanb, šū mfakkir ana, mfakkir inno badd-o yiktil-ni hnāk, giddām-ak tšūf il-, lamma ṭallēt winn ha-l-faras maktūle, w iḥna mārgīn, gut-lo hāḏ ḏanb əs-salṭiyye, gult la ḥawla wala, ṯalat tiyyām w ana bi s-siğən, u arbaʕa u ʕišrīn wāḥad, nḥabasna, ṯalat tiyyām w ana maḥbūs, ana u ğamāʕt-i, ha-n-nās, ən-nhār ər-rābiʕ ṭayyaḥū-na la l-ḥākim il-ʕaskari, illi badd-(h)um iyyā ʕaggabū w ət-tāli gallū-lo rawwiḥ, kafālt-i min əṭ-ṭawābiʕ arbʕīn girš, əz-zalame badd-o ğimʕa tā yğīb-hin, gālu rūḥ ğīb kafīl, walḻa (a)ğa aḻḻa yirḥam ğamīl lə-bšayyir gāʕid, gult yā bū hāni badd-(h)um kafīl gāl ana bakfal-ak, gāl rūḥ ğīb arbaʕīn girš ṭawābiʕ, əz-zalame yōmēn a-bğīb-hinn-əš, ruḥt ğibt arbʕīn girš ṭawābiʕ lā b-baṭn-i wala b-ḍahr-i, wala*

want to wreck the town for committing no offence?" I asked. He replied, "You'll soon see what the offence is." I thought he meant he was going to kill me. When I peeped, I saw a slaughtered horse (that belonged to the cavalry). He said, "This is the offence committed by Salt people." I replied, "There's no power but from God" (supplication). Three days I was in prison, and twenty-four men were imprisoned with me, all because of the murdered horse. On the fourth day, we were summoned before a military judge. They kept some of us in jail, and released the rest. My bail was forty piasters' worth of stamps, which is a whole week's wage. They said, "Go fetch a guarantor, someone to pay your bail." I found Ğamīl lə-Bšayyir, peace be upon his soul; I said to him, "Abu Hāni, they need a sponsor." He said, "I'll sponsor you; go fetch stamps to the value of forty piasters." It would take a man two days and we would still not manage this amount. I went and *msawwi ši…n irǧaʕu ʕa s-siǧən, baḏkur munīr ər-rašīd, u wāḥad ḏ̣ābiṭ ism-o ʕabd ər-razzāg əš-šarīf, dār-hum əbgāʕ ha-d-daraǧāt, rǧaʕū-hum miš dāri manū baʕəd, ṯalat tiyyām lā na msawwi ši wala ši, w il-bagara rawwaḥat laḥāl-ha… ṯāni yōm yōmin laddu min ʕind id-dār, willa hī ʕind dār aḥmad lə-ʕbēd əbtisraḥ, gālu harwi ha-l-bagara rūḥu ǧībū-ha*

fetched the stamps. I'd done nothing. Of those who were kept in prison, I remember Munīr ir-Rašīd and an officer called ʕAbd ir-Razzāg iš-Šarīf, whose house was at the bottom of these steps. I can't remember who else was returned to prison. Three days I was in the nick. I did nothing to deserve it, and the cow came home by itself! One or two days after it was lost, it was spotted wandering around Aḥmad lə-ʕbēd's house. They went and fetched it.

5.3. Text 3: *riḥlit ṣēd* 'a hunting trip'

gāl maṛṛa ṭiḥna nṣīd ana u salāme n-nwērān
ʕa l-ḥumra t-tiḥta
gāl gaʕadna biǧi yōmēn ṯalāṯ
badd-(h)um ysanndu min il-ḥumra
hummu bʕād ʕan il-ḥumra ḥādir
yaʕni bitgdar ətgūl il-ḥumra
ḥadd il-ġōr is-sahəl min il-waʕər
u ʕilm-ak min əhnāk min is-salṭ la hnāk bitʕaǧǧiz kṯire
ṣaddig

He said, "Once upon a time I and Salāme n-Nwērān went hunting in il-Ḥumra t-Tiḥta (locality in the vicinity of Salt). We stayed two or three days." They wanted to descend from il-Ḥumra… they were still some distance away. Il-Ḥumra is down below; it is the border between the plain Ghor (the Jordan

illi bimši ʕa-ğrē ṭūn-nhār yaʕni la s-sāʕa waḥade la s-sāʕa ṯintēn ta yaṣal-ha maši
gāl waḷḷa
ənbāt əb-ʕurug nugʕud ʕala ha-l-ṃayye ta yīğí l-ḥağal u yīğí bʕīd ʕann-ak nyāṣ u yīğí ġuzlān
gāl tā nuḏrub-hin
gāl ʕabbēna ḏhūr-na yā ḷḷa nigdar nimši
ṣādu ʕabbu gadd-mā badd-hum
gāl yā ḷḷa nigdar nimši
gāl yōmin ṭabbēna
miṯəl mā tgūl yamm ʔumm yanbūte tala čifər hūda… min ʔumm yanbūte ğāyīn
gāl winn id-dinya ṯalğ
gāl salām in-nwērān nkaraz
nkaraz min il-bard u š-štā w il-hāḏa
gāl bī mġāra hnāk ḥaṭṭēt-o bī-ha
gāl w asḥab ḥāli
w āğí mʕaddi gāl ana aṭlag minno bi-l-maši
xafīf
gāl waḷḷa w āğí mrawwi(ḥ) ʕa s-salṭ
gāl u aʕabbi xubz u ḥalāwa

Valley) and the rugged terrain. And as you know, it is a difficult trip from Salt to there. Believe me, it takes all day. Anyone who takes the trip on foot won't arrive until one or two in the afternoon. He said, "So, we stay overnight in… we sit by the water waiting for the arrival of partridge, porcupine, gazelles, so we hunt them. I tell you, we were so loaded we could barely walk." They hunted plenty. "When we got near ʔUmm Yanbūte towards Čifər Hūda, it started to snow. Salāme in-Nwērān caught a cold because of the cold weather and rain. There was a cave there and I put him in it while I walked on. I'm faster than him in walking; I'm lighter. Upon arriving in Salt, I got supplies of bread and halva, fetched the mule." There were no cars then. Back then, there were only

u ōxuḏ ǧallak aḷḷa ha-l-baġəl
bī-š sayyārāt gabəl
yaʕni ʕa xaṭṭ il-ġōr ma tlāgī-š ġēr
sayyārtēn la l-ḥadāyde
wāḥad ismo raǧa
aywa gāl waḷḷa w arūḥ u ʕabbi
ʕbāb xubəz gāl mayytīn min iǧ-ǧūʕ
ḥalāwa u xubəz, ḥalāwa ʔawwal
aḥsan akle
waḷḷa gāl w āǧi rāyi(ḥ) ʕalē gāl w
w āǧi w āxuḏ-lo maʕā-y farwa
gāl w aḥuṭṭ-ha ʕa ḏ̣ahr-o
arakkb-o ʕala ǧallak aḷḷa ʕala ha-l-baġəl w intu b-karāma
gāl w asḥab ḥāli w arawwiḥ gālu
winno makrūz
m-il-bard
gāl waḷḷa w aǧīb-lo
gal w nkabbir ha-n-nār
w aǧīb samən u dibəs, dibs il-ʕinəb
gāl w ənḥuṭṭ-lo ... dibs u samən
gāl w ṣiḥi nǧīb-lo ha-l-ʕaša u nʕaššī-h
gāl yōminno ṭāb yōm ṭalaʕ ən-nhār gut-lo yaḷḷa zimm ḥuṣṣt-ak w aḷḷa ysahhil ʕalēk
gāl waḷḷa makrūz
bard bard u ṯalǧ

two cars on this road, which belonged to two men of the Ḥadāyde (clan), one was Abu ʕīd and the other Slēmān ir-Raǧa.

He said, “I went ahead and fetched stacks of bread, we were starving, halva and bread.” Halva in those days was considered the finest of food. He said, “I went back to him. I also brought him a ‘farwa’ (heavy coat, made from sheep skin), which I put on his back. I then put him on the back of the mule and headed back to Salt.” He caught a cold. He said, “We lit fire, and I fetched ghee and molasses, grape molasses, we rubbed his chest and brought him dinner. He recovered. When the day broke, I said to him, ‘Carry your share (of the hunt) and God be with you.’ He caught a cold; it was cold and snowing.”

REFERENCES

Abdel-Jawad, Hassan. 1981. 'Lexical and Phonological Variation in Spoken Arabic of Amman'. PhD dissertation, University of Pennsylvania.

Abu Ain, Noora Qassim Mohammad. 2016. 'A Sociolinguistic Study in Saḥam, Northern Jordan'. PhD thesis, University of Essex. http://repository.essex.ac.uk/19387/, accessed 5 November 2024.

Abū Ǧābir, Fārūq. 1992. اللهجة السلطية في النكات الأردنية. Amman: Farḥān Abū Ǧābir.

Al-Hawamdeh, Areej M. M. 2016. 'A Sociolinguistic Investigation of Two Hōrāni Features in Sūf, Jordan'. PhD thesis, University of Essex. http://repository.essex.ac.uk/17607/, accessed 5 November 2024.

Al-Jallad, Ahmad. 2015. *An Outline of the Grammar of the Safaitic Inscriptions*. Studies in Semitic Languages and Linguistics 80. Leiden: Brill.

Al-Khatib, Mahmoud. 1988. 'Sociolinguistic Change in an Expanding Urban Context'. PhD thesis, University of Durham.

Alqassas, Ahmad. 2012. 'The Morpho-Syntax and Pragmatics of Levantine Arabic Negation: A Synchronic and Diachronic Analysis'. PhD dissertation, Indiana University.

Alrashdan, Imran. 2015. 'Clause Structure of North Jordanian Arabic with Special Reference to Negation: A Minimalist Approach'. PhD thesis, University of Essex.

Al-Shawashreh, Ekab, Marwan Jarrah, and Malek J. Zuraikat. 2021. 'The Functions of the Verb "to Say" in the Jordanian

Arabic Dialect of Irbid'. *Poznan Studies in Contemporary Linguistics* 57 (2): 221–48. https://doi.org/10.1515/psicl-2021-0010.

Altakhaineh, Abdel Rahman Mitib, and Aseel Zibin. 2018. 'Verb + Verb Compound and Serial Verb Construction in Jordanian Arabic (JA) and English'. *Lingua* 201 (January): 45–56. https://doi.org/10.1016/j.lingua.2017.08.010.

Al-Tamimi, Feda'. 2001. 'Phonetic and Phonological Variation in the Speech of Rural Migrants in a Jordanian City'. PhD thesis, University of Leeds. https://etheses.whiterose.ac.uk/6750/, accessed 5 November 2024.

Al-Wer, Enam. 1991. 'Phonological Variation in the Speech of Women in Three Urban Areas in Jordan'. PhD thesis, University of Essex.

———. 1999. 'Why Do Different Variables Behave Differently? Data from Arabic'. In *Language and Society in the Middle East and North Africa: Studies in Variation and Identity*, edited by Yasir Suleiman, 38–58. Richmond: Curzon Press.

———. 2002. 'Jordanian and Palestinian Dialects in Contact: Vowel Raising in Amman'. In *Language Change: The Interplay of Internal, External, and Extra-Linguistic Factors*, edited by Edith Esch and Mari Jones, 63–80. Contributions to the Sociology of Language 86. Berlin: Mouton de Gruyter.

———. 2003. 'Variability Reproduced: A Variationist View of the [d]/[ḍ] Opposition in Modern Arabic Dialects'. In *Approaches to Arabic Dialects*, edited by Martine Haak, Rudolf de Jong, and Kees Versteegh, 21–31. Leiden: Brill. https://doi.org/10.1163/9789047402480_006.

———. 2007. 'The Formation of the Dialect of Amman: From Chaos to Order'. In *Arabic in the City: Issues in Dialect Contact and Language Variation*, edited by Catherine Miller, Enam Al-Wer, Dominique Caube, and Janet C. E. Watson, 55–76. Abingdon: Routledge. http://www.routledge.com/books/details/9780415773119/.

———. 2011. 'Jordanian Arabic (Amman)'. In *Encyclopedia of Arabic Language and Linguistics Online*, edited by Lutz Edzard and Rudolf Erik de Jong. Leiden: Brill. https://doi.org/10.1163/1570-6699_eall_EALL_COM_vol2_0065.

———. 2014. 'Yod-Dropping in *b-imperfect* Verb Forms in Amman'. In *Perspectives on Arabic Linguistics XXVI: Papers from the Annual Symposium on Arabic Linguistics, New York, 2012*, edited by Reem Khamis-Dakwar and Karen Froud, 2: 29–44. Amsterdam: John Benjamins. https://doi.org/10.1075/sal.2.03wer.

———. 2020. 'New-Dialect Formation: The Amman Dialect'. In *Arabic and Contact-Induced Change*, edited by Christopher Lucas and Stefano Manfredi, 551–66. Berlin: Language Science Press. https://doi.org/10.5281/ZENODO.3744549.

Al-Wer, Enam, and Bruno Herin. 2011. 'The Lifecycle of Qaf in Jordan'. *Langage et société* 138 (4): 59–76.

Al-Wer, Enam, Uri Horesh, Bruno Herin, and Maria Fanis. 2015. 'How Arabic Regional Features Become Sectarian Features: Jordan as a Case Study'. *Zeitschrift für Arabische Linguistik* 62: 68–87.

Bani-Yasin, Raslan, and Jonathan Owens. 1984. 'The Bduul Dialect of Jordan'. *Anthling Anthropological Linguistics* 26 (2): 202–32.

———. 1987. 'The Phonology of a Northern Jordanian Arabic Dialect'. *Zeitdeutmorggese Zeitschrift der Deutschen Morgenländischen Gesellschaft* 137 (2): 297–331.

Behnstedt, Peter. 1997. *Sprachatlas von Syrien*. Wiesbaden: Harrassowitz.

Bellem, Alex. 2008. 'Towards a Comparative Typology of Emphatics: Across Semitic and into Arabic Dialect Phonology'. PhD thesis, School of Oriental and African Studies (University of London).

Bergsträsser, Gotthelf. 1915. *Sprachatlas von Syrien und Palästina: 42 Tafeln nebst 1 Übersichtskarte und erläuterndem Text von dr. G. Bergsträsser*. Leipzig: J. C. Hinrichs.

Bettega, Simone. 2019. 'Rethinking Agreement in Spoken Arabic: The Question of Gender'. *Annali Sezione Orientale* 79 (1–2): 126–56. https://doi.org/10.1163/24685631-12340074.

Blanc, Haim. 1970. 'Dual and Pseudo-Dual in the Arabic Dialects'. *Language* 46 (1): 42–57.

Bourdieu, Pierre. 1977. *Outline of a Theory of Practice*. Translated by Richard Nice. Cambridge: Cambridge University Press. https://doi.org/10.1017/CBO9780511812507.

Brustad, Kristen. 2000. *The Syntax of Spoken Arabic: A Comparative Study of Moroccan, Egyptian, Syrian, and Kuwaiti Dialects*. Washington, D.C.: Georgetown University Press.

Burckhardt, Jean Lewis. 1822. *Travels in Syria and the Holy Land*. London: John Murray.

Cantineau, Jean. 1940. *Les parlers arabes du Ḥōrān: Atlas*. Paris: Klincksieck.

———. 1946. *Les parlers arabes du Ḥōrān: Notions générales, grammaire*. Paris: Klincksieck.

Cleveland, Ray L. 1963. 'A Classification for the Arabic Dialects of Jordan'. *Bulletin of the American Schools of Oriental Research* 171: 56–63.

Comrie, Bernard. 1976. *Aspect: An Introduction to the Study of Verbal Aspect and Related Problems*. Cambridge Textbooks in Linguistics 2. Cambridge: Cambridge University Press.

Comrie, Bernard, and Tania Kuteva. 2013. 'Relativization on Subjects'. In *The World Atlas of Language Structures Online*, edited by Matthew S. Dryer and Martin Haspelmath. Leipzig: Max Planck Institute for Evolutionary Anthropology. https://wals.info/chapter/122, accessed 5 November 2024.

Cowell, Mark W. 1964. *A Reference Grammar of Syrian Arabic*. Washington, D.C.: Georgetown University Press.

Creissels, Denis. 1988. 'Quelques propositions pour une clarification de la notion d'adverbe'. *Cahiers d'études hispaniques médiévales* 7 (1): 207–16. https://doi.org/10.3406/cehm.1988.2123.

———. 2006a. *Syntaxe générale, une introduction typologique*. Vol. 1, *Catégories et constructions*. Paris: Hermès Science.

———. 2006b. *Syntaxe générale, une introduction typologique*. Vol. 2, *La phrase*. Paris: Hermès Science.

Creissels, Denis, and Jeff Good. 2018. 'Current Issues in African Morphosyntax'. In *The Languages and Linguistics of Africa*, edited by Tom Güldemann, 709–881. Berlin: De Gruyter. https://doi.org/10.1515/9783110421668-007.

Croft, William. 2001. *Radical Construction Grammar*. Oxford: Oxford University Press. https://doi.org/10.1093/acprof:oso/9780198299554.001.0001.

———. 2002. *Typology and Universals*. 2nd ed. Cambridge: Cambridge University Press. https://doi.org/10.1017/CBO9780511840579.

Dahlgren, Sven-Olof. 1998. *Word Order in Arabic*. Orientalia Gothoburgensia 12. Gothenburg: Acta Universitatis Gothoburgensis.

de Jong, Rudolf. 2000. *A Grammar of the Bedouin Dialects of the Northern Sinai Littoral: Bridging the Linguistic Gap between the Eastern and Western Arab World*. Handbuch der Orientalistik, Erste Abteilung: Der Nahe und Mittlere Osten 52. Leiden: Brill.

———. 2003. 'Characteristics of Bedouin Dialects in Southern Sinai: Preliminary Observations'. In *Approaches to Arabic Dialects*, edited by Martine Haak, Rudolf de Jong, and Kees Versteegh, 151–76. Leiden: Brill. https://doi.org/10.1163/9789047402480_013.

———. 2011. *A Grammar of the Bedouin Dialects of Central and Southern Sinai*. Leiden: Brill.

Diessel, Holger. 1999. *Demonstratives: Form, Function and Grammaticalization*. Typological Studies in Language 42. Amsterdam: John Benjamins.

Dìez, Ana Iriarte. 2019. 'The Communicative Grammatical Function of Cognate Infinitives in Lebanese Arabic'. Beirut: American University of Beirut.

Dryer, Matthew S., and Martin Haspelmath, eds. 2013. *The World Atlas of Language Structures Online*. Leipzig: Max Planck Institute for Evolutionary Anthropology. https://wals.info/, accessed 5 November 2024.

Eckert, Penelope. 1989. 'The Whole Woman: Sex and Gender Differences in Variation'. *Language Variation and Change* 1 (3): 245–67. https://doi.org/10.1017/S095439450000017X.

———. 2000. *Linguistic Variation as Social Practice: The Linguistic Construction of Identity in Belten High*. Language in Society 27. Malden, Mass.: Blackwell Publishers.

François, Alexandre, and Maïa Ponçonnet. 2013. 'Descriptive Linguistics'. In *Theory in Social and Cultural Anthropology: An Encyclopedia*, edited by R. Jon McGee and Richard Warms, 1: 184–87. Thousand Oaks, Calif.: SAGE Publications. https://doi.org/10.4135/9781452276311.n61.

Galal, Mohamed, and Sylvain Kahane. 2018. 'Les constructions exceptives vues comme des listes paradigmatiques: À propos de la syntaxe de *sauf, excepté, hormis*… en français'. In *6ᵉ Congrès Mondial de Linguistique Française*, edited by F. Neveu, B. Harmegnies, L. Hriba, and S. Prévost, SHS Web of Conferences 46: 14005. https://doi.org/10.1051/shsconf/20184614005.

Germanos, Marie-Aimée. 2008. 'Quelques emplois de baˀa en arabe dialectal libanais'. In *Between the Atlantic and Indian*

Oceans: Studies on Contemporary Arabic Dialects—Proceedings of the 7th AIDA Conference, Held in Vienna from 5–9 September 2006, edited by Stephan Prochazka and Veronika Ritt-Benmimoun, 207–16. Vienna: LIT Verlag.

Givón, Talmy. 2001. *Syntax: An Introduction.* Vol. 2. Rev. ed. Amsterdam: John Benjamins.

Hallonsten Halling, Pernilla. 2017. 'Prototypical Adverbs: From Comparative Concept to Typological Prototype'. *Acta Linguistica Hafniensia* 49 (1): 37–52. https://doi.org/10.1080/03740463.2017.1292801.

Haspelmath, Martin. 2007. 'Coordination'. In *Language Typology and Syntactic Description*, edited by Timothy Shopen, 2nd ed., 2: 1–51. Cambridge: Cambridge University Press. https://doi.org/10.1017/CBO9780511619434.001.

———. 2010a. 'Comparative Concepts and Descriptive Categories in Crosslinguistic Studies'. *Language* 86 (3): 663–87. https://doi.org/10.1353/lan.2010.0021.

———. 2010b. 'Framework-Free Grammatical Theory'. In *The Oxford Handbook of Linguistic Analysis*, edited by Bernd Heine and Heiko Narrog, 341–65. Oxford: Oxford University Press. https://doi.org/10.5281/zenodo.814947.

———. 2013. 'Ditransitive Constructions: The Verb "Give"'. In *The World Atlas of Language Structures Online*, edited by Matthew S. Dryer and Martin Haspelmath. Leipzig: Max Planck Institute for Evolutionary Anthropology. https://wals.info/chapter/105, accessed 5 November 2024.

———. 2016. 'The Serial Verb Construction: Comparative Concept and Cross-Linguistic Generalizations'. *Language and*

Linguistics 17 (3): 291–319. https://doi.org/10.1177/2397002215626895.

Hellmuth, Sam. 2013. *Phonology*. Edited by Jonathan Owens. Vol. 1. Oxford University Press. https://doi.org/10.1093/oxfordhb/9780199764136.013.0003.

Herin, Bruno. 2010. 'Le parler arabe de Salt (Jordanie): Phonologie, morphologie et éléments de syntaxe'. Doctoral thesis, Université Libre de Bruxelles.

———. 2013. 'Do Jordanians Really Speak like Palestinians?'. *Journal of Arabic and Islamic Studies* 13: 99–114. https://doi.org/10.5617/jais.4629.

———. 2019. 'Traditional Dialects'. In *The Routledge Handbook of Arabic Sociolinguistics*, edited by Enam Al-Wer and Uri Horesh, 93–105. New York: Routledge. https://doi.org/10.4324/9781315722450-7.

Herin, Bruno, and Enam Al-Wer. 2013. 'From Phonological Variation to Grammatical Change: Depalatalisation of /č/ in Salti'. In *Ingham of Arabia*, edited by Clive Holes and Rudolf de Jong, 55–73. Leiden: Brill. https://doi.org/10.1163/9789004256194_004.

Hoyt, Frederick. 2007. 'An Arabic Wackernagel Clitic? The Morphosyntax of Negation in Palestinian Arabic'. In *Perspectives on Arabic Linguistics*, edited by Mustafa A. Mughazy, 105–31. Current Issues in Linguistic Theory 290. Amsterdam: John Benjamins. https://doi.org/10.1075/cilt.290.10hoy.

Huehnergard, John. 2008. 'Afro-Asiatic'. In *The Ancient Languages of Syria-Palestine and Arabia*, edited by Roger D. Woodard,

225–46. Cambridge: Cambridge University Press. https://doi.org/10.1017/CBO9780511486890.012.

Huneety, Anas, and Bassil Mashaqba. 2016. 'Emphatic Segments and Emphasis Spread in Rural Jordanian Arabic'. *Mediterranean Journal of Social Sciences* 7 (5): 294–98. https://doi.org/10.5901/mjss.2016.v7n5p294.

Ingham, Bruce. 1994. *Najdi Arabic: Central Arabian*. Amsterdam: John Benjamins.

Keenan, Edward L., and Bernard Comrie. 1977. 'Noun Phrase Accessibility and Universal Grammar'. *Linguistic Inquiry* 8 (1): 63–99.

Krifka, Manfred. 2008. 'Basic Notions of Information Structure'. *Acta Linguistica Hungarica* 55 (3–4): 243–76. https://doi.org/10.1556/ALing.55.2008.3-4.2.

Lambrecht, Knud. 2001. 'Dislocation'. In *Language Typology and Language Universals*, edited by Martin Haspelmath, Ekkehard König, Wulf Oesterreicher, and Wolfgang Raible, 1050–78. Berlin: Walter de Gruyter. https://doi.org/10.1515/9783110171549.2.10.1050.

Larcher, Pierre. 1999. 'Syntaxe et sémantique des formes verbales dérivées de l'arabe classique: Vues "nouvelles" et questions en suspens'. *Quaderni di Studi Arabi* 17: 3–27.

Lentin, Jérôme. 2011. 'Damascus Arabic'. In *Encyclopedia of Arabic Language and Linguistics Online*, edited by Lutz Edzard and Rudolf Erik de Jong. Leiden: Brill. https://doi.org/10.1163/1570-6699_eall_EALL_COM_0077.

Littman, Eno. 1905. *Modern Arabic Tales*. Leiden: Brill.

Lucas, Christopher. 2010. 'Negative -*š* in Palestinian (and Cairene) Arabic: Present and Possible Past'. *Brill's Annual of Afroasiatic Languages and Linguistics* 2 (1): 165–201. https://doi.org/10.1163/187666310X12688137960623.

Malchukov, Andrej L. 2004. 'Towards a Semantic Typology of Adversative and Contrast Marking'. *Journal of Semantics* 21 (2): 177–98. https://doi.org/10.1093/jos/21.2.177.

Manfredi, Stefano. 2008. 'Counter-Assertive Focus in Kordofanian Baggara Arabic'. *Studi Magrebini* 6: 183–94.

———. 2014. 'Demonstratives in a Bedouin Arabic Dialect of Western Sudan'. *Folia Orientalia* 54: 27–50.

Milroy, Lesley. 1987. *Language and Social Networks*. 2nd ed. Language in Society 2. Oxford: Wiley-Blackwell.

Mion, Giuliano. 2012. *L'arabo parlato ad Amman*. Rome: Edizioni Q.

Owens, Jonathan, and Raslan Bani-Yasin. 1987. 'The Lexical Basis of Variation in Jordanian Arabic'. *Linguistics* 25 (4): 705–38.

Owens, Jonathan, Robin Dodsworth, and Trent Rockwood. 2009. 'Subject–Verb Order in Spoken Arabic: Morpholexical and Event-Based Factors'. *Language Variation and Change* 21 (1): 39–67. https://doi.org/10.1017/S0954394509000027.

Owens, Jonathan, and Alaa Elgibali, eds. 2010. *Information Structure in Spoken Arabic*. Routledge Arabic Linguistics Series. London: Routledge.

Palva, Heikki. 1969a. 'Balgāwi Arabic: 1. Texts from Mādabā'. *Studia Orientalia* 40 (1): 13 pages.

———. 1969b. 'Balgāwi Arabic: 2. Texts in the Dialect of the *Yigūl*-Group'. *Studia Orientalia* 40 (2): 15 pages.

———. 1970. 'Balgāwi Arabic: 3. Texts from Ṣāfūṭ'. *Studia Orientalia* 43 (1): 26 pages.

———. 1976. *Studies in the Arabic Dialect of the Semi-Nomadic al Ağārme Tribe (al-Balqā' District, Jordan)*. Gothenburg: Acta Universitatis Gothoburgensia. http://catalog.hathitrust.org/api/volumes/oclc/3335194.html, accessed 6 November 2024.

———. 1978. *Narratives and Poems from Ḥesbān: Arabic Texts Recorded among the Semi-nomadic al-'Ağārima tribe (al-Balqā' district, Jordan)*. Gothenburg: Acta Universitatis Gothoburgensis.

———. 1980. 'Characteristics of the Arabic Dialect of the Bani Ṣaxar Tribe'. *Orientalia Suecana* 29: 112–38.

———. 1984a. 'A General Classification for the Arabic Dialects Spoken in Palestine and Transjordan'. *Studia Orientalia* 55 (18): 357–76.

———. 1984b. 'Characteristics of the Dialect of the Ḥwēṭāt Tribe'. *Orientalia Suecana* 33–35: 295–312.

———. 1989. 'Linguistic Sketch of the Arabic Dialect of El-Karak'. In *Studia Linguistica et Orientalia Memoriae Haim Blanc Dedicata*, edited by Paul Wexler, Alexander Borg, and Sasson Somekh, 225–51. Wiesbaden: Harrassowitz.

———. 1992a. *Artistic Colloquial Arabic: Traditional Narratives and Poems from al-Balqā' (Jordan)—Transcription, Translation, Linguistic and Metrical Analysis*. Studia Orientalia 69. Helsinki: Finnish Oriental Society.

———. 1992b. 'Typological Problems in the Classification of Jordanian Dialects: Bedouin or Sedentary?' In *The Middle East Viewed from the North: Papers from the First Nordic Conference of Middle Eastern Studies, Uppsala, 26–27 January 1989*, edited by Bo Utas and Viktor Knut, 53–62. Bergen: Nordic Society for Middle Eastern Studies.

———. 1994. 'Bedouin and Sedentary Elements in the Dialect of Es-Salṭ: Diachronic Notes on the Sociolinguistic Development'. In *Actes Des Premières Journées Internationales de Dialectologie Arabe de Paris*, edited by Dominique Caubet and Martine Vanhove, 459–69. Paris: INALCO.

———. 2003. 'Negations in the Dialect of Es-Salṭ, Jordan'. In *Approaches to Arabic Dialects*, edited by Martine Haak, Rudolf de Jong, and Kees Versteegh, 221–36. Leiden: Brill. https://doi.org/10.1163/9789047402480_016.

———. 2004. 'Remarks on the Arabic Dialect of the Ḥwēṭāt Tribe'. *Jerusalem Studies in Arabic and Islam* 29: 195–209.

———. 2007. 'Arabic Texts in the Dialect of Es-Salṭ, Jordan'. *Acta Orientalia* 68: 161–205.

———. 2008. 'Sedentary and Bedouin Dialects in Contact: Remarks on Karaki and Salṭi (Jordan)'. *Journal of Arabic and Islamic Studies* 8: 53–70. https://doi.org/10.5617/jais.4589.

Payne, Thomas E. 1997. *Describing Morphosyntax: A Guide for Field Linguists*. Cambridge: Cambridge University Press. https://doi.org/10.1017/CBO9780511805066.

Procházka, Stephan. 2003. 'Unmarked Feminine Nouns in Modern Arabic Dialects'. In *Approaches to Arabic Dialects*, edited by Martine Haak, Rudolf de Jong, and Kees Versteegh, 237–

62. Leiden: Brill. https://doi.org/10.1163/9789047402480_017.

Procházka-Eisl, Gisela. 2018. 'A Suffix on the Move: Forms and Functions of the Turkish Suffix /-Ci/ in Arabic Dialects'. *Mediterranean Language Review* 25: 21–52. https://doi.org/10.13173/medilangrevi.25.2018.0021.

Ritt-Benmimoun, Veronika. 2014. *Grammatik des arabischen Beduinendialekts der Region Douz (Südtunesien)*. Semitica viva 53. Wiesbaden: Harrassowitz.

Roset, Caroline Jeanne. 2018. *A Grammar of Darfur Arabic*. Utrecht: LOT, Netherlands Graduate School.

Shachmon, Ori, and Michal Marmorstein. 2018. '*badhačak dahič* "I'll Smash You Altogether!": The Unmodified Cognate Complement in Rural Palestinian Arabic'. *Zeitschrift für Arabische Linguistik* 68: 31–62. https://doi.org/10.13173/zeitarabling.68.0031.

Shlonsky, Ur. 1997. *Clause Structure and Word Order in Hebrew and Arabic: An Essay in Comparative Semitic Syntax*. Oxford Studies in Comparative Syntax. New York: Oxford University Press.

Shopen, Timothy. 2007. *Language Typology and Syntactic Description*. 2nd ed. 3 vols. Cambridge: Cambridge University Press.

Souag, Lameen. 2017. 'Clitic Doubling and Language Contact in Arabic'. *Zeitschrift für Arabische Linguistik* 66: 45–70. https://doi.org/10.13173/zeitarabling.66.0045.

Sowayan, Saad A. 1995. 'Taww in Najdi Arabic'. *Studia Orientalia Electronica* 75: 251–56.

Stassen, Leon. 2013a. 'Comparative Constructions'. In *The World Atlas of Language Structures Online*, edited by Matthew S. Dryer and Martin Haspelmath. Leipzig: Max Planck Institute for Evolutionary Anthropology. https://wals.info/chapter/121, accessed 6 November 2024.

———. 2013b. 'Predicative Possession'. In *The World Atlas of Language Structures Online*, edited by Matthew S. Dryer and Martin Haspelmath. Leipzig: Max Planck Institute for Evolutionary Anthropology. https://wals.info/chapter/117, accessed 6 November 2024.

Thompson, Sandra A., Robert E. Longacre, and Shin Ja J. Hwang. 2007. 'Adverbial Clauses'. In *Language Typology and Syntactic Description*, edited by Timothy Shopen, 2nd ed., 2: 237–300. Cambridge: Cambridge University Press. https://doi.org/10.1017/CBO9780511619434.005.

Treis, Yvonne. 2018. 'Comparative Constructions: An Introduction'. *Linguistic Discovery* 16 (1): i–xxvi. https://doi.org/10.1349/PS1.1537-0852.A.492.

Trudgill, P. 1996. 'Two Hundred Years of Dedialectalisation: The East Anglian Short Vowel System'. In *Samspel och Variation: Språkliga Studier Tillägnade Bengt Nordberg aå 60-Aårsdagen*, edited by M. Thelander, 471–78. Uppsala: Uppsala Universitet.

van der Wal, Jenneke. 2016. 'Diagnosing Focus'. *Studies in Language* 40 (2): 259–301. https://doi.org/10.1075/sl.40.2.01van.

Van Valin, Robert D., and Randy J. LaPolla. 1997. *Syntax: Structure, Meaning and Function*. Cambridge: Cambridge University Press. https://doi.org/10.1017/CBO9781139166799.

Versteegh, Kees. 2011. 'Serial Verbs'. In *Encyclopedia of Arabic Language and Linguistics Online*, edited by Lutz Edzard and Rudolf Erik de Jong. Leiden: Brill. https://doi.org/10.1163/1570-6699_eall_EALL_COM_0305.

Watson, Janet C. E. 2011. 'Word Stress in Arabic'. In *The Blackwell Companion to Phonology*, edited by Marc van Oostendorp, Colin J. Ewen, Elizabeth Hume, and Keren Rice, 1–29. Oxford: John Wiley & Sons, Ltd. https://doi.org/10.1002/9781444335262.wbctp0124.

Woidich, Manfred. 2006. *Das Kairenisch-Arabische: Eine Grammatik*. Porta Linguarum Orientalium, n.s., 22. Wiesbaden: Harrassowitz.

INDEX OF AUTHORS

Abdel-Jawad, Hassan, 5
Abu Ain, Noora Qassim Mohammad, 5, 29
Abū Ǧābir, Fārūq, 221
Al-Hawamdeh, Areej M. M, 5, 8–9
Al-Jallad, Ahmad, 2
Al-Khatib, Mahmoud, 5
Al-Shawashreh, Ekab, 245
Al-Tamimi, Feda', 5
Al-Wer, Enam, 5–6, 8, 11, 13, 15, 19, 75, 225, 242, 334
Altakhaineh, Abdel Rahman Mitib, 418
Bani-Yasin, Raslan, 4–5, 42
Behnstedt, Peter, 261, 263
Bellem, Alex, 24
Bergsträsser, Gotthelf, 4
Bettega, Simone, 341
Blanc, Haim, 292
Bourdieu, Pierre, 14 n. 3
Brustad, Kristen, 280, 292–93, 299, 304, 335, 352, 372, 387, 442
Burckhardt, Jean Lewis, 7
Cantineau, Jean, 4, 23, 25–26, 104, 124, 221–22, 261–62
Cleveland, Ray L., 5, 261–62
Comrie, Bernard, 93, 278, 284, 304
Cowell, Mark W., 292
Creissels, Denis, 3, 213, 258, 284, 418
Croft, William, 3, 212
Dahlgren, Sven-Olof, 352
de Jong, Rudolf, 31, 42, 229, 310
Diessel, Holger, 180
Dìez, Ana Iriarte, 371
Dryer, Matthew S., 3
Eckert, Penelope, 14 n. 3
Elgibali, Alaa, 398
François, Alexandre, 2
Galal, Mohamed, 396
Germanos, Marie-Aimée, 241
Givón, Talmy, 402
Good, Jeff, 258
Hallonsten Halling, Pernilla, 212
Haspelmath, Martin, 2–3, 212, 355, 418, 452
Hellmuth, Sam, 25–26
Herin, Bruno, 1, 5, 7–8, 12–13, 334, 404
Horesh, Uri, 263
Hoyt, Frederick, 377, 379
Huehnergard, John, 258
Huneety, Anas, 25
Hwang, Shin Ja J., 424, 439, 442
Ingham, Bruce, 168
Jarrah, Marwan, 245

Keenan, Edward L., 278
Krifka, Manfred, 398
Kuteva, Tania, 278, 284
Lambrecht, Knud, 400
LaPolla, Randy J., 457
Larcher, Pierre, 119
Lentin, Jérôme, 263
Littman, Eno, 263
Longacre, Robert E., 424, 439, 442
Lucas, Christopher, 372, 379
Malchukov, Andrej L., 455
Manfredi, Stefano, 180, 404
Marmorstein, Michal, 369–71
Mashaqba, Bassil, 25
Milroy, Lesley, 7
Mion, Giuliano, 5
Owens, Jonathan, 5, 42, 352, 354, 398
Palva, Heikki, 4–6, 24, 166, 221, 224, 263, 372 n. 4
Payne, Thomas E., 404
Ponçonnet, Maïa, 2
Procházka, Stephan, 74
Procházka-Eisl, Gisela, 88
Ritt-Benmimoun, Veronika, 404
Roset, Caroline Jeanne, 404
Shachmon, Ori, 369–71
Shlonsky, Ur, 352
Shopen, Timothy, 3
Souag, Lameen, 271
Sowayan, Saad A., 219
Stassen, Leon, 295, 348
Kahane, Sylvain, 396
Thompson, Sandra A., 424, 439, 442
Treis, Yvonne, 295
Trudgill, P., 13 n. 2
van der Wal, Jenneke, 247
Van Valin, Robert D., 457
Versteegh, Kees, 418
Watson, Janet C. E., 35
Woidich, Manfred, 248, 306, 404
Zibin, Aseel, 418
Zuraikat, Malek J., 245

GENERAL INDEX

ʕAbābīd, ʕAbbādi (tribe), 73, 177
ʕAdwān (tribe), 8, 12, 194, 249, 319, 330, 461, 464–67
adnominal, *see under* demonstrative
affix, 45–48, 272, 364, 382, 385
affrication, 17, 20–24, 178, 188–89, 256, 309, 330, 374, 448
ʕAǧārma (tribe), 4, 12
Ajloun, 5–6, 8
Akkadian, 258
ʔĀl ʕĪsa (tribe), 12
allomorphy, 22, 34, 78–80, 89, 92, 166–68, 171, 180, 188, 194, 218–19, 243, 246, 258, 260, 268, 275–77, 281–82, 284, 420
allophone, 20, 25, 27, 75, 77
Amman, 1, 5, 10, 12–14, 20, 78, 167, 191, 193, 217, 220, 223, 225, 260–61, 299, 306, 310, 315, 325–26, 334, 340, 344, 365, 384, 386, 400, 417 n. 7, 437, 456, 461
anaptyctic, 56, 384
apheresis, 405, 450
apical, 20, 24, 379
apocopated, 36, 47, 166, 179–80, 189, 192, 217, 228, 260
apodosis, 329, 444–45, 448–50
apophonic, 98, 136, 364
apposition, 254–55, 269, 283, 285–86, 290
approximant, 17, 166
Aqaba, 11–12, 26, 55, 344
Aramaic, 272, 432
Aranki, 264, 267
article, 36, 41, 47–48, 175, 189, 192, 227, 254–55, 258, 267, 270, 277, 281, 284, 294
aspect, 93, 298, 300–301, 303–6, 309–15, 317–19, 321, 323–25, 330, 442, 444–45
asseverative, 329, 445, 448
assimilation, 27, 41–43, 119, 144, 185, 206, 425
asyndetic, 178
auxiliary, 241, 298, 301, 306–7, 309–13, 315–19, 321, 323–25, 335–36, 349, 390, 419, 442, 450
b-imperfective, 40, 99–102, 104–6, 108–9, 111, 113, 115, 117–18, 120–21, 125–27, 129–32, 134–35, 137–38, 140–41, 143, 145–46, 148–49, 151–54, 156, 158–59, 161, 303, 309, 315–16, 321, 373, 376–78, 380, 440–42, 444–47

backgrounding, 354
Balga, 8, 10, 75, 88, 296, 342, 369
Bani Ḥasan (tribe), 12
Bani Ṣaxr (tribe), 12, 408–9
Bdūl (tribe), 5, 12
Bedouin, 4, 7–8, 12, 19–24, 70, 81, 122, 168, 194, 198, 220–21, 229–31, 261, 297, 306, 330, 335–36, 344, 408, 424–25, 450
beneficiary, 360–61
Cairo, 404
causative, 18, 116, 122–24, 127–28, 359–60
cessative, 323–24, 350
Christian, 6, 14–15, 81, 92, 116, 177, 202, 246, 346, 390 n. 5, 401, 461
Circassians, 70
cleft, 399, 404, 410
clitic, 36, 45–48, 85, 95, 170, 271–72, 382–85, 405
Člūb (clan), 22
coalescence, 46, 48, 184, 256, 269, 327, 393
collective, 70–71, 81, 86, 178, 257–58, 334–35, 337, 341
comitative, 191, 194, 347, 351
comparative, 17, 295
complementation, 420
complementiser, 235, 243, 327, 329, 420–22, 424, 433, 440, 443, 450
compound, 224, 259
concessive, 435, 447
conditionals, 439, 442, 447, 450–52
conjunction, 185, 197, 239–40, 301, 309, 330, 400, 417, 424–40, 442–45, 448, 450, 452–53, 455, 457–58
construct (state), 78–80, 89, 180, 203, 209, 224, 228, 254–55, 257–58, 267–70, 272, 274, 276, 296, 428–29, 438
copula, 314, 342, 372, 386–88
coronal, 25, 75, 77, 166
cosubordination, 457
counterfactual, 439, 444
Dabābse (clan), 6, 73
Damascus, 10, 49, 263
dative, 43, 45–46, 80, 94, 165, 169–72, 360–61, 401
deaffrication, 20, 24, 188
declarative, 234, 411, 453–54
decrease, 14
dedialectalisation, 13
degemination, 88
demonstrative, 36, 45, 47, 74, 179–81, 189, 192, 217, 228, 253–55, 263, 268, 285–89, 294, 337
    adnominal, 179, 285
deontic, 307–8, 349
determiner, 188–89, 253–55, 275

devoicing, 21, 43
diminutive, 63, 65–66, 82, 214, 274
ditransitive, 172, 355, 357–59
durative, 304, 311–12, 314
Egypt, 11, 73, 306
elative, 18, 91, 295–97, 411
ellipsis, 178, 225–26, 257, 259, 301, 327, 392, 442
epenthesis, 33–35, 38–39, 100, 149
equative, 297
exceptive, 274, 327–28, 396–98, 451
exclamative, 238, 411–12
existential, 247, 332, 343–44, 348, 372–73, 375, 377, 380, 393
Fḥēṣ, 6–8, 33, 81, 83, 165, 185, 199, 215, 220, 262, 266, 269–71, 291, 305, 337, 343, 395, 427, 455, 461, 463–66
focus, 4, 9, 47, 185, 214, 218, 243, 247–50, 256, 267, 293, 342, 369, 371, 380–81, 396, 398–400, 402–4, 410–11, 416, 432, 455
fractions, 211
fronting, 342, 399, 402
functive, 202, 429
futurity, 306–7, 309, 445–46
garawi, 13
gemination, 17, 43, 78, 85, 142, 146, 167–68, 181, 183, 192–93, 197
gender, 10, 13–14, 74, 84, 93–96, 101, 105, 107, 165–67, 175, 180–81, 183–84, 207–8, 260–64, 266, 290, 298, 310, 315, 319, 332–33, 335, 337, 340–41, 349, 361
genitive, 79, 83–84, 180, 184, 193, 212, 220, 224, 228, 254–55, 257, 259, 262–63, 266–72, 276, 282, 348, 371, 421
gerunds, 212
Ghouta, 10
Ghor, 462, 471
grammaticalisation, 46, 169, 174, 200, 250, 254, 272, 274, 290, 301, 310, 316, 320, 324, 327, 330, 349, 386, 392, 431, 450
guttural, 25, 29–30, 75, 78
habitual, 300, 303, 309, 312–14, 330, 442
hapax, 215, 233, 248, 308
harmony (vowel), 34, 77, 256
Ḥōrān, 10, 23, 75, 221–22, 262
Ḥōrāni, 8–11, 20, 25, 35, 88, 104, 124, 143, 165–66, 168, 196, 222, 260–62
hortative, 274, 327
Ḥuwwāra, 9

Ḥwēṭāt (tribe), 4, 11–12, 82, 408–9
imperative, 93, 96, 100–103, 107, 109, 111, 114–15, 117–22, 126–27, 129–30, 132–35, 137–40, 142, 144–48, 150–52, 154–55, 157–61, 298, 312–14, 322, 328, 375–77, 379, 390, 416–18
imperfective, 12, 38–40, 43, 93–95, 98–106, 108–13, 115, 117–18, 120–21, 125–27, 129–32, 134–35, 137–38, 140–41, 143–46, 148–49, 151–54, 156, 158–59, 161, 163, 201, 232, 241, 298–301, 303, 308–16, 318–19, 321–23, 328–30, 360, 373–78, 380, 390–91, 417, 419, 426, 431, 440–42, 444–47
inalienable, 346
inanimate, 266, 286, 307, 316, 334, 337
inceptive, 299, 304
inchoative, 317, 350
indefinite, 173–76, 178, 188, 215, 224, 270, 273, 275, 280, 296, 332–33, 335–36, 348, 352–53, 392–95, 402, 435
individuation, 174, 280, 335–36, 338
infixation, 136, 362
interdentals, 17, 19
interjection, 4, 216, 234–35, 237–38
interrogative, 40, 174, 176, 182–85, 187–89, 194, 235, 256, 271, 275, 300, 411–12, 414–16, 423, 435–36, 453–54
intransitive, 348, 351, 354–55, 363–65, 368
Irbid, 5, 10, 13, 221, 245
irrealis, 426, 439
iterative, 300, 303, 309–10, 312–14, 317, 321, 330, 419
Jaffa, 263
Jerash, 8, 199, 230
Jerusalem, 262–63
Jespersen's cycle, 372–73
jussive, 322
Kerak, 5–6, 11, 13, 79, 166, 191 n. 9
labial, 34, 40–41, 77–78, 377–80
Lebanon, 71, 237, 293, 413
Levant, 1, 6, 9–12, 20, 23, 28, 32, 34, 38, 74–75, 78, 83, 88, 100, 113, 115, 122, 169, 171, 178, 183–87, 189, 191, 194–95, 197, 199, 203, 207, 211, 214, 216–17, 219–21, 223–24, 229–31, 237, 241, 249, 260, 271, 286, 293, 299, 306, 308, 315, 321, 323–26, 344, 346, 349, 355, 372, 382, 388, 401, 420, 437, 454

levelling, 167
lexicalisation, 83, 217, 224, 227–28, 231–32, 235, 241, 323, 391, 420, 447
locative, 47, 187, 191, 194, 348, 399
Maan, 407–9
madani, 13
Mafrag, 67, 249
Maltese, 240
Masāʕīd (tribe), 12
masdar, 70, 161–64, 318, 368, 370
Mesopotamian, 271, 355
monotransitive, 172, 341, 350–51, 355, 358
monovalent, 123, 354, 359, 364
Muʔābi, 11, 191 n. 9
Nablus, 73, 262
negation, 4, 9–10, 36, 94, 167–68, 170, 174, 324, 349, 372–73, 377–78, 390–93, 395, 405, 447
non-specific, 177, 393–94
non-verbal, 180, 218, 278, 281, 285, 341, 343, 351, 372, 404, 414, 422, 440–42, 444, 446–47, 450–51
numeral, 45, 84–85, 88–89, 173, 188, 207–10, 255, 257, 280, 290–91, 294
obstruents, 377, 379–80
optative, 301–2, 326–27, 390
Ottomans, 19, 87, 190, 407–8
Palestine, 8, 13, 20, 23, 26, 75, 80, 88, 178, 181, 237, 262–63, 313, 315, 324, 369–70, 379, 384
partitive, 192, 257
passivisation, 357, 362–64
pause, 11, 39, 201, 215, 236, 457
perfective, 36, 43, 93, 95–96, 98–99, 101, 103, 107–8, 110, 112–14, 116–21, 125–26, 128–35, 137–39, 141–47, 149–54, 156–60, 163, 232, 298–99, 301, 311–13, 318, 321, 323–24, 329–30, 373, 376–79, 418–19, 426, 431, 434, 440, 442, 444–45, 448, 450–51
pharyngeals, 24, 29
pluperfect, 310
presentative, 19, 180–81
prosody, 381–85, 399, 405
prospective, 301, 306
protasis, 440, 442, 444–47, 449–50
quantifier, 4, 175–76, 188, 250, 257, 273, 427
realis, 426, 439, 443
reciprocal, 42, 133, 273, 365–66
reflexive, 131, 136, 142, 160, 360–61, 365
relativisation, 278, 282, 345, 368

reportative, 245
resultative, 304
resumptive, 236, 278, 399–400, 402
resyllabification, 142
Salt, 1, 4–10, 12–13, 18, 20–21, 26–28, 51, 78–79, 81, 165, 179, 182, 185, 190, 218, 220–22, 237, 242, 258–60, 262–64, 270, 283, 287, 290, 312, 314, 335, 340, 372 n. 4, 398, 404, 408, 411, 461–62, 470–73
Salti, 81, 222, 258–59, 435
sandhi, 38, 43
sedentary, 1, 4, 19–20, 23–24, 29–30, 100, 207, 211, 215, 221, 223, 229, 231, 243, 248, 260, 271–72, 286, 293, 313, 321, 330, 352, 386, 424
sequentialiser, 319, 321, 419
serialisation, 418–19
Shawbak, 11
singulative, 50, 71, 81–82, 85–86, 293, 370
Sirḥān (tribe), 12
Skāfiyye, 204, 258
specificity, 174, 280
stress, 9, 19, 34–39, 45–47, 167–68, 170, 174, 255, 381–84, 405
subjunctive, 96, 299, 379, 417, 419, 431, 434
subordination, 424, 457–58
substratal, 272
superessive, 195, 351, 355
superlative, 296–97
suppletive, 103, 115, 174, 210
syllable, 33, 35–39, 45–47, 78, 88, 99–100, 104–6, 168, 170, 174, 232
Syria, 4, 10, 49, 237, 373, 413
Systemzwang, 30
topicalisation, 398–400, 402, 404
Transjordan, 20
trochaic, 168
Tunisia, 296, 404
Turkish, 19, 82
velarisation, 24–28, 30–31, 34
vernacular, 6, 49, 148, 150, 226, 234, 277, 294 n. 2
Zawāyda (tribe), 12

About the Team

Alessandra Tosi and Geoffrey Khan were the managing editors for this book and provided quality control.

Anne Burberry performed the copyediting of the book in Word. The fonts used in this volume are Charis SIL and Scheherazade New.

Annie Hine created all of the editions—paperback, hardback, and PDF. Conversion was performed with open source software freely available on our GitHub page at https://github.com/OpenBookPublishers.

Jeevanjot Kaur Nagpal designed the cover of this book. The cover was produced in InDesign using Fontin and Calibri fonts.

www.ingramcontent.com/pod-product-compliance
Lightning Source LLC
Chambersburg PA
CBHW040319300426
44111CB00023B/2952
9781805113348